FRANCO AND HITLER

FRANCO AND HITLER
SPAIN, GERMANY, AND
WORLD WAR II

Stanley G. Payne

Yale University Press   New Haven & London

To the memory of Javier Tusell (1945–2005)

Library
University of Texas
at San Antonio

Yale University Press wishes to thank Stanley Goldstein for first suggesting that the Press publish a book on Franco and Hitler.

Copyright © 2008 by Stanley G. Payne.

Designed by James J. Johnson and set in New Aster and The Sans types by Keystone Typesetting, Inc., Orwigsburg, Pa.
Printed in the United States of America.

Library of Congress Cataloging-in-Publication Data

Payne, Stanley G.
Franco and Hitler : Spain, Germany, and World War II / Stanley G. Payne.
p. cm.
Includes bibliographical references and index.
ISBN 978-0-300-12282-4 (cloth : alk. paper)
1. World War, 1939–1945—Diplomatic history. 2. World War, 1939–1945—Spain.
3. Spain—Politics and government—1939–1975. 4. Spain—Foreign relations—Germany.
5. Germany—Foreign relations—Spain. I. Title. II. Title: Spain, Germany, and
World War II.
D754.S6P39 2008
940.53'46—dc22   2007033570

A catalogue record for this book is available from the British Library.

The paper in this book meets the guidelines for permanence and durability of the Committee on Production Guidelines for Book Longevity of the Council on Library Resources.

10 9 8 7 6 5 4 3 2 1

Contents

Part III.   The Struggle to Escape the "Axis Stigma"

Preface

The policy of the Franco regime during World War II, and particularly its relationship with Nazi Germany, is arguably the most controversial aspect of the regime's long history. Though key Spanish documents are unavailable, much research has been conducted in this area, and its conclusions are clear. Despite the extensive bibliography, however, there is no study that deals synthetically with the full range of relations between the Spanish and German regimes. The present work is an effort to fill that gap.

It is dedicated to the memory of Javier Tusell, the past generation's leading historian of twentieth-century Spanish politics, whose premature death deprived the country of one of its greatest scholars and public analysts. Tusell was the author of the principal history of Spanish diplomacy during World War II, and my debt to his work will become clear in the pages that follow.

In addition, this study builds on the previous research of many scholars who have worked in this area, such as Haim Avni, Alfred Bosch, Wayne Bowen, Charles Burdick, Carlos Caballero, Carlos Collado Seidel, James Cortada, Rafael García Pérez, Genoveva García Queipo de Llano, Norman Goda, Rafael Ibáñez Hernández, Gerald Kleinfeld, Christian Leitz, José María Manrique García, Antonio Marquina Barrio, Pablo Martín Aceña, Manfred Merkes, Lucas Molina Franco, Enrique Moradiellos, Víctor Morales Lezcano, Xavier Moreno Juliá, Gustau Nerín, Gloria Inés Ospina, Jesús Palacios, Rosa Pardo Sanz, Paul Preston, Manuel Ros Agudo, Fernando Rosas, Bernd Rother, Klaus-Jorg Rühl, Denis Smyth, Lewis Tambs, António José Telo, Joan María Thomàs, José Varela Ortega, César Vidal, Angel Viñas, Robert Whealey, and others. I am indebted also to Félix Morales and the Fundación Nacional Francisco Franco for the opportunity to do research in the Franco archive.

The manuscript has been read by a stellar array of critics—Juan Linz, John Lukacs, and Michael Seidman—who have improved it and saved it from a number of errors. My thanks to all of them.

Madison, Wisconsin
1 February 2007

PART I
From Civil War to World War

CHAPTER 1

The Spanish Civil War
Origins of the Franco Regime

Spain's convulsions during the 1930s, which swiftly carried the country from democracy to revolution to civil war, made it a center of the world's attention. In 1931, it had been the only European country to introduce a new democratic regime during the Depression decade, a time when half the states of Europe turned to one or another form of authoritarianism. A foreign visitor observing the popular jubilation in April 1931 would have found it hard to believe that the new regime would break down into the most bitter civil war within scarcely more than five years.

In retrospect, the democratic breakthrough had been made possible by the accelerated economic growth and modernization Spain experienced between World War I and 1930, during some of these years one of the highest growth rates in the world. Such social, economic, and cultural transformation within a brief period was unprecedented in the long history of Spain, as for the first time the agricultural proportion of the active population dipped under 50 percent. This accelerated growth did not, however, succeed in turning Spain into a developed modern society, but advanced it only to the middle of the road—the most dangerous place. By 1931 it had triggered a revolution of rising expectations. The widespread confidence that rapid social and economic improvement would continue indefinitely was unrealistic in the midst of the Great Depression, and its political consequences would be explosive.

Democracy may produce as many new problems as it solves, and by

1934 it became clear that the new regime had opened the way to a revolutionary process unparalleled elsewhere. A classic theory posits that revolutionary growth is the product not of extreme oppression but of relatively rapid improvement in conditions in countries where notable internal problems are followed by a downturn or significant new frustrations, which stimulate a revolutionary response.[1] Spain was unique in harboring the world's only mass anarcho-syndicalist movement, a large Socialist party which turned increasingly to what it called *bolchevización* (Bolshevization), a small Communist party (PCE) operated by the Comintern, a tiny opposed "Leninist" communist party (BOC-POUM), and a variety of radical separatist movements. Three revolutionary insurrections by the anarchosyndicalists between January 1932 and December 1933 were punctuated by an abortive rightist military revolt in 1932. A major Socialist revolutionary insurrection in October 1934 ignited increasingly intense left–right polarization. Having failed at insurrection, the left returned to electoral tactics, and the new Popular Front alliance won a narrow but decisive victory in the elections of February 1936.

During the next five months there developed what Gabriel Jackson and some other historians have called a "pre-revolutionary situation," a breakdown of order and constitutional government without precedent in a European country in peacetime. The Spanish crisis featured widespread strikes, some of them in support of impossible demands; considerable destruction and burning of churches and other property; extensive illegal seizure of farmland, legitimized ex post facto by an intimidated government; the takeover of church and other property; the arbitrary closure of Catholic schools; the politicization of the courts; and progressive distortion of the electoral process and falsification of results. Members of Popular Front parties engaged in criminal behavior with relative impunity, and the smaller rightist organizations were progressively declared illegal. Political violence spread, and the government sometimes appointed Socialist and Communist militants as auxiliary police. The kidnapping and murder of the government's most outspoken opponent in parliament by one of these mixed detachments served as the final catalyst for a widespread military revolt, supported by rightist volunteers, on 18 July 1936.[2]

The Spanish Civil War

The civil war that ensued became probably the most mythic event of the twentieth century, most frequently, if inaccurately, described as a contest between democracy and fascism. More than a little fascism was involved, but there was no real democracy on either side. The rebellion was designed as an exclusively military affair to remove the left from power and convert the existing regime into a very right-wing republic, in which democracy would be severely curtailed. The military, however, were almost as divided as the rest of Spanish society. Instead of being able to carry out a coup d'état, they ended up in control of little more than half of the country's army, a third of the air force, and a third of the navy, and in possession of scarcely as much as a third of Spain. These were conditions for full-scale civil war, and yet the rebels at first held such limited strength that they might soon have been defeated had they not been able to obtain limited military support from Italy and Germany.

The minority left Republican government resorted to arming the leftist worker organizations, which they called "arming the people." The revolutionary militias created by these organizations proved ineffective militarily but they produced an explosive popular revolution with few precedents in world history. Thus it is somewhat surprising that the Spanish revolution of 1936–39 is sometimes all but ignored in the comparative history of twentieth-century revolutions, for three reasons: (a) the Spanish revolution was soon completely defeated, and history prefers winners; (b) both Republicans and the Comintern denied the reality of revolution in order to avoid alienating opinion in the capitalist Western democracies;[3] and (c) nearly all the major left-collectivist revolutions of the century were largely one-party Communist revolutions, whereas the Spanish revolution was semi-pluralist, the largest revolutionary movements being anarcho-syndicalist and Socialist, not Communist.

Conversely, the extreme revolutionary left championed their cause as the most direct and spontaneous worker revolution yet seen, distinctly more so than that of Russia in 1917, which was soon dominated by a single party, was supported by a much smaller proportion of workers, and mobilized proportionately much less of the rural population in new revolutionary institutions. To the Marxist sector of the extreme revolutionary left, it was the most Marxist revolution, more broadly borne by genuine workers, and all the extreme revolutionary left hailed their revolution as the beginning of a new era in world history.

The problem was that while the one-party regime in Russia had eventually proved quite effective in waging a fierce civil war, what one historian calls the "revolutionary Republican confederation" in Spain[4] proved too disorganized to be effective. Therefore on 5 September 1936 the first all–

Popular Front government, representing all the revolutionary groups except the anarcho-syndicalists, took office under the Socialist leader Francisco Largo Caballero. Its task was to restore an effective government and to organize a new disciplined "*ejército popular*" (people's army) to wage the civil war.

The new government hoped for support from democratic Britain and France, but much foreign opinion was alienated by the widespread destruction and the revolutionary terror, which killed approximately 55,000 people (most of them between July and December 1936), one of the great slaughters of the century—though equaled or exceeded by that carried out by its rightist opponents—which was extensively covered in the foreign press.

The British government, dominated by Conservatives, quickly adopted a hands-off policy, which it maintained throughout the conflict. The situation of its ally in Paris was different, for a Popular Front coalition, more moderate than that of Spain, had recently taken office in France. There, however, conservative opinion was soon intensely mobilized and polarized by the Spanish conflict. Léon Blum, the French Socialist prime minister, wished to support the Spanish left, at least with military equipment, but was vetoed by his British associates and even his own government coalition, as well as by all the conservative parties.

The initial shipment of French military equipment was therefore soon canceled, and the French government instead began to promote agreement among all the European powers on nonintervention in the Spanish war. The nonintervention policy was intended to discourage German and Italian support for the Spanish rebels, and thus permit the left to win the military struggle. In September an official nonintervention committee began to meet in London, as it would continue to do throughout the war, with all three of the major dictatorships—Germany, Italy, and the Soviet Union —participating, while proceeding almost unhindered in their own military intervention. The British government professed indifference to the outcome of the struggle, so long as Spain remained independent and the war did not expand into a general European conflict. The goals of British policy were thus largely achieved by the time the war ended in 1939.

The real French policy was considerably different, consisting of what Blum later described as "relaxed nonintervention," meaning extensive forms of assistance to the Republic short of direct sales of military equipment. This policy took the form of providing extensive financial and commercial facilities, serving as a conduit for the volunteers of the International Brigades and of large-scale transshipment of Soviet and other military matériel and for other secondary forms of aid. At least twice the French government and general staff considered the possibility of limited direct military intervention, but on each occasion decided against it.[5]

The only major power to intervene actively on the Republican side was the Soviet Union, whose leaders hesitated for two months before doing so. Though the Soviet Union was the only country to maintain its own political party in Spain, Comintern policy had been to "work the system," using the complete leftist domination of institutions to institute a "new type" of all-leftist republic from which all conservative forces would be eliminated through nominally legal means. The Comintern had even sought to moderate the extreme revolutionary left, for a civil war would introduce incalculable new elements into the equation. Once the Civil War broke out, however, Stalin came under considerable pressure from Communist opinion abroad and also within the Soviet Union to support the only active worker revolution in the world.

The intervention policy that Stalin finally decided upon in mid-September 1936 was predicated on several factors. One was the willingness of the Republican government to use the sizable Spanish gold reserve—as a result of Spain's recent prosperity, the fourth or fifth largest in the world—to pay for Soviet arms, thus enabling the Communist regime to turn a commercial profit from a nominally revolutionary intervention. Victory in Spain would then give the Soviet Union a major voice in southwestern Europe for the first time. The last important factor was maintenance of the Comintern and Soviet propaganda, denying the reality of revolution and even of Soviet intervention while espousing the banner of "democratic antifascism." Thus intervention might enable the revolutionaries to win the war under increasing Communist tutelage, while France and Britain would not be inhibited from embracing collective security with Moscow. It was a complex policy, contradictory to outsiders, and ultimately it failed in every dimension.

Sizable amounts of Soviet matériel, including the latest-model planes and tanks, accompanied by hundreds of Soviet military advisers and specialized personnel, turned the tide in the Civil War by November 1936, making possible a successful defense of Madrid and turning the conflict into a longer war of attrition. The Comintern assisted by mobilizing the soon-famous International Brigades, a grand total of approximately 42,000 foreign volunteers, most of them Communists. Mussolini and Hitler countered Stalin's escalation with an even greater escalation of their own, which ensured that the fighting would continue with no resolution in sight.

The Civil War catapulted the Spanish Communist Party from a small, marginal organization into a major force. The Soviets' assistance and their emphasis on military organization and rebuilding the state permitted them to play an increasingly hegemonic role in the Republican government and military in the second half of the Civil War. They insisted on a channeling of the revolution, reducing some of its more extreme features to privilege state and military power, with the goal of achieving the "new type" of "people's republic" they had introduced in Mongolia in 1924. The collectivist revolution should be trimmed in favor of a Soviet-style New Economic Policy, as introduced by Lenin in 1921, which eschewed collectivization in favor of state nationalization of the industrial "commanding heights," for the time being leaving most property in private hands.[6]

A striking feature of the Civil War was that both sides proclaimed it to be a struggle for national independence. The insurgents developed a discourse insisting that the revolt had preempted an armed takeover by the Communists (though in fact the Communists envisioned such a thing only in the more distant future, as their policy made clear). To Franco and his followers, the Civil War had been instigated by the Soviet Union, now said to be trying to take direct control of Spain. Conversely, the Republicans held that the Civil War had been started by a Nazi-Fascist conspiracy to seize Spain, using the military insurgents as puppets. Both sides thus claimed to be waging a war of national liberation.[7]

The last twenty-one months were the period of Communist (and Soviet) hegemony, which grew somewhat stronger during 1938. Within the Republican zone, the Communists declared the revolutionary wartime Republic to be a *república popular,* according to the Soviet and Comintern formula. Subsequently both the *Nacionales* on the one hand and the extreme revolutionary left on the other would agree on only one thing: that the wartime Republic had become the first Soviet-type "people's republic" of the sort imposed in Eastern Europe after 1945.

They were exaggerating. The wartime Republic was indeed a people's republic of a sort, an exclusivist revolutionary regime of the left with all centrist and conservative elements eliminated, but it was a semi-pluralist, not a Soviet-type, people's republic. Relative Communist hegemony in Spain was not the same thing as total Soviet domination in Eastern Europe. In Spain the Soviets could not completely control the government, or impose their full economic program or control all aspects of the military and the police. Communist hegemony was relative, never absolute. As war weariness grew, impatience mounted against the attempt to keep the war going until a general European war broke out, when the Nacionales hoped to benefit from French intervention. The feeling grew that Soviet policy was simply to fight to the last Spaniard, and by early 1939 the Communists were in fact becoming politically isolated. In March 1939 a military revolt backed by all the other leftist forces seized control of Madrid and deposed the existing Republican government, which had to flee the country. The regime surrendered at the end of the month.

Origins of the Franco Regime

Both sides were radicalized during the first weeks of the Spanish conflict. Full-scale revolution broke out in the Republican zone, but the rebels could not impose their initial plan to set up a military government to "rectify" the Republic in the direction of a more rightist, authoritarian system because of the partial failure of the revolt. The rebel commanders set up a Junta of National Defense (echoing language common since the French Revolution) in Burgos on 23 July 1936 as a sort of government by military committee. As the struggle became an intense civil war of the most violent and atrocious kind and the rebel forces attempted a decisive drive on Madrid, the junta selected a commander in chief. There was only one real candidate: Major General (General de División) Francisco Franco Bahamonde, the most prominent figure in the Spanish army.

It cannot be said that Franco enjoyed any great personal popularity among his colleagues, but he held the respect of nearly all of them and was widely recognized as the most imposing commander. Manuel Azaña, wartime president of the Republic, generally scorned all Spanish generals, but five years earlier, as minister of war, he had astutely judged that, of them all, Franco was "the only really dangerous one."[8] Franco was not the most highly intelligent or the most technically proficient or the most personally likeable or the most rightist politically, but he was generally perceived as the most capable overall military commander and the most astute politically and professionally—the one who best combined qualities of self-control, intelligence, political adroitness, military experience and ability, personal courage, and, above all, the singular quality of command.[9]

Franco was not a nineteenth-century Spanish political general, for he had avoided direct involvement in politics for most of his career. He had won his reputation through unusual courage and successful combat leadership in the bloody campaigns in Morocco between 1913 and 1926, where many of his fellow officers had been killed. Promoted to brigadier at the age of 33 in 1926, he had become the youngest new peacetime general in any European army. Right-wing, Catholic, and monarchist in his personal beliefs, like all the rest of Spain's military commanders he had done nothing to contest the collapse of the monarchy and the advent of the democratic Republic, which until 1936 he had loyally served, being named chief of the general staff in May 1935. Deposed after the left returned to power, Franco was in contact with the military conspiracy from the beginning but showed little eagerness to commit himself fully. As late as 12 July he urged that the revolt be postponed to see if the situation would not improve, but finally reversed himself within twenty-four hours, fully and firmly committing himself to the revolt after the kidnapping and assassination of the monarchist leader Calvo Sotelo. By that time the cautious Franco had concluded that the situation had deteriorated so far that it was more dangerous not to rebel than to rebel.

He commanded the veteran combat elites in the Moroccan protectorate, the only combat-worthy elements in the Spanish army. There is no indication that he failed to share the initial political scheme behind the revolt. His initial proclamation invoked the Republican constitution, which, he said, "ignored by everyone, is suffering total eclipse," promising "fraternity, liberty, and equality." Even his first subsequent announcement as chief of state promised that "Spain will be a non-confessional state,"[10] although this formulation was quickly rendered more ambiguous after the Church protested. During the interim as head of what was designated the Army of Africa, charged with the main drive on Madrid, he assured the correspondent of Lisbon's *O Século* that "the new regime will be republican," that "the movement is exclusively military," and that "I am in favor of short dictatorships," so that the new military government would last only long enough to complete its most basic tasks.[11]

Franco's leadership was crucial in the first weeks of the revolt. He commanded the only experienced military force that might be capable of winning the war, and was also responsible for the new contacts that won the support of Hitler and Mussolini. Thus, as his forces began what the rebels hoped would be the crucial drive on Madrid, his was the only name raised at a meeting of the junta near Salamanca on 21 September to choose a commander in chief. The issue was pressed primarily by several monarchist commanders, who believed that Franco was the general most likely to restore the monarchy, and by a number of personal supporters who considered his leadership indispensable to victory.

By that time Franco's own political ideas had become increasingly radical. As a possible regime model, at one point he had publicly alluded to the Estado Novo (New State) in neighboring Portugal, a semi-corporative rightist and authoritarian republic that combined the institutions of a nominally elected assembly with a corporative economic chamber, but after becoming chief of state he found such an alternative too liberal. It is doubtful that he ever read the early nineteenth-century reactionary theorist Joseph de Maistre, but he seemed to quickly absorb the functional equivalent of Maistre's maxim that "the counterrevolution is not the opposite of a revolution, but is an opposing revolution."[12] Something more original, radical, and authoritarian was needed.

Franco ruled Spain so long and his regime went through so many phases and changes that it has sometimes been alleged that he had few political convictions, but changed tack according to circumstances. In fact, from the 1920s to the end of his life Franco held firmly to certain basic convictions that underwent little change. He believed in Spanish nationalism and unity, directed by an authoritarian political system. He was also an observant Catholic of a very traditional kind and sought to restore as much as possible of traditional Catholic culture. He was strongly imperialist in foreign policy, believing in the importance of retaining what little remained of the Spanish Empire, and of adding to it as circumstances permitted. In domestic affairs, he wished to maintain a relatively traditional social structure, though he recognized the need to expand the middle classes and achieve a more technically proficient society, its stresses to be meliorated by modern economic development. In economics Franco strongly favored a nationalist and corporative regime, designed to foster industry and technology even while maintaining a largely traditional cultural and social system.

At one time these goals might have been met under a monarchist regime or a rightist, corporative republic, but under the desperate conditions of a revolutionary civil war Franco soon came to the conclusion, strongly pressed and encouraged by the Italians, that something like the Italian Fascist model was needed. By the winter of 1937, if not before, he had decided that only a radical new system could save what was left of the old order while building a strong new Spain. Franco had imbibed an earlier discourse about the need for an "iron surgeon," and had been well impressed by the dictatorship of Miguel Primo de Rivera (1923–30), but was equally concerned about what he understood to have been Primo de Rivera's mistake—maintaining an "empty dictatorship" without a clear goal and a fully articulated new system.

His principal lieutenant in the new political enterprise was his brother-in-law Ramón Serrano Suñer, a sometime leader of the main Catholic party, CEDA. Serrano had been a close friend of José Antonio Primo de Rivera, eldest son of the former dictator and himself the founder of the fascist party Falange Española (Spanish Phalanx). Imprisoned in the Madrid of the Red Terror, which killed two of his brothers, Serrano had been heard to denounce Franco and the military vigorously for having been so slow to act against the left. Serrano managed to escape from the Republican zone in February and immediately established himself at the headquarters of his brother-in-law, where the two quickly came to a meeting of political minds. Franco and Serrano soon agreed on the need to create a completely new political system structured on the basis of a single national party, a *partido único*.

The dominant motif would be nationalism, which had been weaker in Spain than in almost any other European country, due to the weakness of the state, the strength of the Church, the slow pace of social and cultural change during the nineteenth century, and the absence of international rivalry, war, or menace. All the rightist groups, however, had espoused a greater or lesser degree of nationalism in reaction to the Republic, and from the start of the conflict the insurgents invoked above all else Spanish patriotism against "international" revolution. At the beginning of the conflict, which foreign observers referred to as a matter of Whites against revolutionary Reds, in the terminology of civil war Russia, the rebels were routinely called fascists by their enemies but soon presented themselves as Nacionales, or Nationalists. "Nacionales" would remain their preferred designation throughout the war, and the term would be used in Spanish historiography for many years after.

In April 1937, Franco suddenly merged the Falangists, now grown very numerous, with the traditionalist Carlists and other rightist groups to form his new state party, Falange Española Tradicionalista (FET). The Twenty-six Points of the Falange, based to some extent on Italian Fascism, were adopted as the official program of the state party, and by extension of the new state itself. Among other things, they theoretically committed Franco's nascent regime to carry out a "national syndicalist revolution," the Falangist term for approximating something like Italian Fascist corporatism in a more radical form. Yet, although Franco was committed to the transformation of the Spanish economy through authoritarian and corporatist policies, he and his closest collaborators, not the original Falangists, would determine the exact form the regime would take.

In announcing the new state party Franco declared that it was much more a beginning than an end, that its program was not fixed but would be subject to whatever addition or amendment the future might require. This was a prescient forecast of the pragmatic tacking that he would display during the next four decades. The various rightist parties prudently dissolved themselves. All their members, together with all other Spanish patriots of whatever background (left, right, or center), were encouraged to join the new party.[13]

The ideological fascism of the original Falange had always been modified by a certain emphasis on cultural and religious traditionalism, involving unresolved contradictions. From its outset the party had been officially Catholic, even if slightly anticlerical, and hallowed the traditional, ultra-Catholic cultural heritage of Spain's Golden Age. This heritage had given the Falange more of a rightist cast than was common among revolutionary fascist movements, and the overlay with the extreme right would become even more pronounced within the FET. This rightward tilt owed little to the Carlists, who would soon withdraw more and more from the new party, leaving it largely in the hands of veteran Falangists (the *camisas viejas*, or old shirts). It had much more to do with the culture and policy of Franco's regime itself.

The insurgent military leaders had initially upheld the Republic's separation of church and state, but the violent revolution that they indirectly helped to touch off in the Republican zone produced the most extensive and violent persecution of Catholicism in Western history, in some ways even more intense than that of the French Revolution. It was particularly virulent during the opening months of the Civil War, during which nearly 7,000 clergy and many thousands of lay Catholics were slaughtered. To an even greater degree than anticipated, Catholics rallied to the Nationalists en masse, left as they were with scant alternative. Within two months, the bishop of Salamanca, Enrique Pla y Deniel, declared that the movement was not a mere revolt or civil war but a "sacred crusade." The military leaders soon responded in kind, and before long their whole cause became closely identified with Catholicism. Franco's troops were soon participating en masse in open-air *misas de campaña* (field masses). *La Cruzada* would eventually became an official synonym for the entire war effort. Catholicism, not fascism, became the main emotional, psychological, and even to some extent ideological support of the Nacionales, contributing greatly to their morale and fighting spirit. Moreover, the temper of the Civil War was not at all that of a twentieth-century liberal or modernist religiosity but that of a neotraditionalist Catholicism. On occasion the Nationalist zone, or at least parts of it, seemed to be swept by a neotraditionalist revivalism that affected all culture and mores—even if its effects were often more apparent than real. An equivalent neotraditionalist revivalism had never taken place so officially or extensively in any other Catholic country in modern times, or for that matter in any Christian country during the preceding century. La Cruzada would eventually become the nearest Christian equivalent to Islamist neotraditionalist revivalism in the Middle East and elsewhere.[14]

Franco's leadership during the Civil War was successful in all four key dimensions of military affairs, international diplomacy, domestic politics, and economic support, though the latter was left in the hands of a small coterie of experts. His great political achievement was simply to maintain unity among the various rightist and even center-right political forces supporting the Nacionales, and to succeed in largely banning domestic political activity for the duration of the conflict. Thus he guaranteed that his own war effort would not be weakened by anything equivalent to the sometimes severe internal discord in the Republican zone. Within the party there was considerable resentment over the high-handed manner in which Franco had seized control, but very little overt dissidence. More than 200 members were arrested in April and May for what were deemed obstructionist activities, but that was the extent of the retaliation.

Political activity was essentially restricted to the FET, which had become an arm of the new state. It did not lead and administer the state, as did the Communist Party in the Soviet Union, but rather served more nearly as its instrument, as in Fascist Italy. Its initial role was simply to support the war effort wholeheartedly and to generate the new system's propaganda, even as it became by far the largest organization in Spanish history, with 932,000 members. Its Sección Femenina soon numbered 580,000 women, also a Spanish record, and engaged in extensive social and medical services. The limitations of this seemingly impressive mobilization are nonetheless revealed by the statistics of the party's youth groups, which would at no time organize more than 18 percent of boys and 9 percent of girls between 7 and 18 years of age, compared with 65 percent and 44 percent, respectively, in Fascist Italy.[15]

The Falangists were also assigned to develop a system of national trade unions for workers, but comparatively little was accomplished while the war lasted. In 1938 a Fuero de Trabajo or Labor Charter was developed, based on an uneasy mixture of the Italian Fascist Carta del Lavoro and

Catholic social norms, to provide guidelines for labor. The Fuero declared the Spanish state a "totalitarian instrument in the service of the integrity of the Fatherland," proclaiming eventual formation of a "single and vertical" union to bring all "branches of production hierarchically beneath the direction of the state." This language was in fact more rigid than that of the original Italian charter.[16]

The New State

Franco self-legitimized his rule in juridical terms through a law of government promulgated on 30 January 1938. It declared that "the Chief of State possesses supreme power to dictate juridical norms of a general nature," and also stipulated that the office of president of the government (prime minister) was "united with that of Chief of State." Thus Franco endowed himself with the power to govern personally and directly. Initial administration by a Junta Técnica then gave way on the following day to Franco's first regular cabinet, comprising the heads of the government ministries. Of the eleven posts, three went to veteran generals, two to monarchists, one to a Carlist, two to relatively apolitical technical experts, and only three to Falangists. Among the latter, however, was Serrano Suñer, who became minister of the interior and general supervisor of press and propaganda as national delegate of press and propaganda of the FET, while only one of the Falangists was a camisa vieja. Serrano moved quickly to introduce a strict new press and censorship law on 22 April 1938, with a rigid system of control and prior censorship. Propaganda and censorship were at this point the most significant official responsibilities of the state party.[17]

This first regular government revealed Franco's adroit manipulation of what would later be termed the diverse political "families" that supported his regime. Though he and his spokesmen regularly used the term "totalitarian" during the new system's early years, he also affirmed that totalitarianism was no modern invention but something characteristic of the first Spanish united monarchy in the fifteenth century. By "totalitarian" he simply meant a unified and authoritarian government. (One leading political commentator among the Nacionales pointed out that only the Soviet regime, which owned its own economy and controlled every single institution, could be considered fully totalitarian in a literal sense.) Franco was well aware that he led a broad rightist coalition, and thus was careful to provide varying representation to monarchists, Carlists, army officers, and former militants of the Catholic CEDA, as well as Falangists. To this list might be added smaller subfamilies such as representatives of the Basque and Catalan bourgeoisie, particularly in the early years of the regime.

The new state's economic administration was quite successful so long as the Civil War lasted. It emphasized maximal stimulation of the existing economic structure under stringent state regulation, at least in key sectors, maintaining full employment, a high level of food production, and the restoration of production in industrial zones as they were incrementally conquered. There was an abundance of food, particularly noteworthy compared with the increasing shortages of the opposing zone; an adequate supply of other resources; sound government credit, despite the complete absence of gold reserves; and a relatively stable currency. The economic administration of the Nacionales seemed especially successful in contrast to the growing disarray of the Republican zone.[18]

Franco was called the Caudillo, the nearest Spanish equivalent to Führer or Duce, and a mounting cult of political personality was developed. Eventually the chant of "Franco, Franco, Franco" was adapted from "Duce, Duce, Duce," and the second half of the conflict produced a political style increasingly fascist,[19] with emphasis on the Caudillo's personal charisma, though it was a charisma of accomplishment rather than of personality. The term "fascist" had been spontaneously adopted in some parts of the Nationalist zone early in the Civil War, though Franco had formally denied in interviews with foreign journalists that the Falange should be considered fascist, admitting only that some of its individual members were. What was undeniable was a growing expression of the fascist style in politics and an increasing political "vertigo of fascism," even though the regime was eclectic in its personnel and origins, and culturally and spiritually depended as much or more on Catholicism. Its foreign policy was oriented toward the Axis powers, which had helped it to victory, but it had gained the complacency of the British government and of much political opinion in France, which accepted it as an independent counterrevolutionary Spanish regime, whose policies would remain Spanish and independent.

Though his troops flagged somewhat during 1938 due to heavy combat and attrition, Franco succeeded in retaining an effective supply line to Italy and Germany and in maintaining a superior army. He sustained the initiative militarily, was occasionally checked but never suffered more than a temporary local defeat, won major triumph after major triumph, and was able to announce complete and unconditional victory on 1 April 1939.

He now had greater power than any previous ruler of Spain. Moreover, if at most half the population had supported the war effort of the Nacionales, in

1939 much of the other half was disposed at least passively to accept Franco's rule, given the mass hunger, weariness, and disillusionment of the Republicans. Spain's most eminent intellectual of the second half of the century, Julián Marías, was a young Republican in 1939 and later described the feelings of most of his fellow Republicans in the following terms:

> In the Republican zone deep disillusionment added to the fatigue. People felt tricked, deceived, manipulated, and exploited by their most representative leaders. . . . The defeated knew they had been defeated, and the majority of them accepted this with character, dignity and resignation; many thought—or confusingly felt—they had deserved defeat, though this did not mean that the other side had deserved victory.[20]

Such a disposition on the part of many former Republicans might have given Franco a remarkable opportunity to forge a positive new national consensus, but such was not his intention.

Liquidation of the Civil War's legacy meant a harsh and rigorous policy of repression to punish large numbers of the vanquished. Many among the latter had committed crimes of violence against civilians, for the approximately 120,000 military fatalities suffered in combat by both sides combined (exclusive of the many casualties among foreign participants) was roughly equaled by the number of people liquidated by the repression in both zones. The Republicans executed approximately 55,000 people and the Nationalists rather more than that.[21] Thus there were very many perpetrators to prosecute, but only ex-Republicans were prosecuted, and indeed most targets of the repression were condemned for political activities, not for crimes of violence.

The period of harshest repression was the years 1939–41, when the most serious cases were prosecuted, in every instance by military tribunals under the terms of martial law, which was not lifted until 1948. More than 75 percent of all postwar executions took place during these two years. Altogether, at least 50,000 death sentences were passed, but as early as March 1937 Franco seems to have adopted a rule of thumb whereby about half of such sentences were commuted, so that the total number of postwar executions seems to have been around 28,000–30,000.[22] In this regard the beginning of the Franco regime was, paradoxically, similar to that of the Communist regimes in Russia and Yugoslavia, rather than to the first and milder phases of Fascist rule in Italy and the Nazi regime in Germany. Franco and his military colleagues had followed the more typically communist route of coup d'état, massive military action, civil war, and bloodthirsty repression. Conversely, Spanish communism had followed the fascist tactic of coming to power through political alliance, though the revolutionary Republic in Spain had been much more repressive than the first phases of Fascist and Nazi rule.

Historians have spoken of the "cumulative radicalization" of the Armenian genocide and the Holocaust, which became increasingly lethal as time went on. The opposite was true in Spain, where both sides in the Civil War had moved to dampen the massacres of the early months, and in less than a year after the war ended, Franco moved in the same direction. On 24 January 1940 he instituted new centralized military juridical commissions to supervise and review all sentences, with the power either to confirm or to reduce them but never to extend them. The first limited amnesties for prisoners with lesser sentences were announced in the autumn of 1939, followed by a lengthy sequence of such measures starting in June 1940. The prison population, which stood at 270,519 at the close of 1939, thus declined to 54,072 five years later, and thenceforth continued to shrink steadily.[23]

The policy of repression was very broad, much more extensive than the juridical prosecution of individuals, for it involved rigorous censorship and a purge of educational and other state personnel.[24] The entire decade of the 1940s was a time of strict repression in Spain.

In the aftermath of the Civil War Franco and most of his subordinates were firmly convinced that the new European order was moving firmly toward national "organic" authoritarian regimes. He continued to run his government very much as though it were an army, ruling by *leyes de prerrogativa*, personal decrees issued by the head of state. A Law of the Head of State, published on 9 August 1939, expanded the powers originally defined by the decree of 29 January 1938. It declared that "the powers of government are permanently entrusted" to Franco, who was categorically relieved of the need to submit new legislation or decrees to his cabinet when "urgent problems require it."[25] Revised statutes of the FET, issued a few days later, further extended his control of the party. The new Spanish state was not genuinely as totalitarian as it claimed, because it permitted a limited semi-pluralism, but in formal juridical terms it was the most thoroughgoing personal dictatorship in Europe.

Franco completely reorganized his cabinet on 8 August 1939, on the eve of war in Europe. The only important minister to be retained was Serrano Suñer. Five posts were given to Falangists, three more than in the preceding government, reflecting an effort to approximate, at least symbolically, the new fascist era that seemed to be dawning. Yet three of the Falangists were in fact army men. Whereas the military had held four of twelve ministries in the preceding government, they held five in the new cabinet. Thus, though some at first dubbed this a Falangist government, it was obviously no such thing, but the next phase in what would soon be seen as Franco's regular balancing act between the various political families supporting his regime.

The major source of power was still the military, even though the officers held no corporate autonomy of their own. Franco astutely gave many new commands and state posts to the younger commanders who had risen with him in the Civil War, rather than to the older, more moderate or conservative generals who had placed him in power. For the first time in Spanish history, he appointed a minister for each of the three branches of the armed forces, selected for loyalty and denied any independent authority. He relied on military men more than any others, and during the entire first phase of his regime down to the end of World War II in 1945, military personnel would hold 45.9 percent of the ministerial appointments and 36.8 percent of all the top government positions, concentrated primarily in the armed forces ministries, the Ministry of the Interior, which dealt with police and security, and, until mid-1944, the Ministry of Foreign Affairs. Falangists, by comparison, would hold 37.9 percent of the ministerial appointments and only 30.3 percent of all top administrative positions, concentrated in party administration, labor, and agriculture.[26]

The military saw themselves as the true elite of the new system. At the time of the official "victory visit" to Italy, the regime's closest ally, in May 1939, a representative of the military had told Count Galeazzo Ciano, Mussolini's foreign minister and son-in-law, that the main difference between Spain and Italy was that the role played by the Fascist Party in Italy was held by the military in Spain. Most Spanish military men viewed Falangists as mimetic opportunists who sought to arrogate for themselves a corrupt and artificial political monopoly based on foreign styles. During the next few years, their hostility toward Falangists would continue to grow.[27]

Despite their complete victory over the left, the disparate forces supporting Franco would not be as united in time of peace as in time of war. With the crisis over, political rivalries would reappear, exacerbated by severe shortages of resources, the corruption that became increasingly evident under the new authoritarian system, and the strain of the broader war in Europe. There would be more tension within Franco's regime during the first years after the Civil War than at any other time in its long history.

CHAPTER **2**

Hitler's Strategy in the Civil War

The political doctrines of Adolf Hitler depended on a peculiar racial theory in which Spain played no role. The Iberian peninsula was scarcely mentioned in *Mein Kampf*, while in his unpublished second book, written in 1928, Hitler's only additional comment was that Spain, like Hungary, had traditionally been rather hostile to France, and might be rallied in opposition to the French. His ideas about Spanish history and culture have been recorded only in the transcripts of his *Table Talk*, in which he observed that the only superior racial element in the Spanish people, the Visigoths, had been heavily diluted by inferior elements. His knowledge of Spanish history was extremely vague and, like most northern Europeans, he largely accepted the Black Legend concerning Spain as a backward and reactionary society dominated by benighted clerics and made up largely of lazy peasants. Hitler knew nothing of Spanish culture and perhaps was unaware that Spain's Golden Age had ever existed, but he particularly detested the Spanish Catholic Church.

Conversely, Hitler considered Islam, with its simple theology and ethos of holy war, the best of the major religions. He believed that the highest culture ever seen in Spain was that of the Muslims, since it was so refreshingly non-Christian, and later lamented that the Muslim expansion had been checked in France. Hitler conjectured that if the Germans had been converted to Islam, rather than to decadent love-oriented Christianity, they might already have conquered the world in the Middle Ages.[1]

If Spain held no prestige in Hitler's eyes, Germans had for some time had high prestige in Spain. There had never been any significant friction between the two countries, in contrast to Spain's relations with France, Britain, and the United States. The German colony in Spain was fairly large, about 15,000 (roughly similar to that of France), and the Germans had a reputation for honesty, efficiency, scientific achievement, and respectful treatment of the Spanish. Though Germany's culture had not been as influential as that of France, German intellectuality and philosophy were greatly respected by the Spanish elite, and German Idealism had exerted significant influence on recent education.[2]

Spain and Spanish Morocco had been the targets of German revolutionary strategy during World War I, as German agents sought to foment a native rebellion in French Morocco while helping to touch off labor unrest in Barcelona. The German navy also made limited use of Spanish ports to send supply ships to submarines, but these activities had been discreet and small-scale, and did not provoke major friction. Subsequently, German industry provided facilities for manufacture of sizable amounts of poison gas used by the Spanish army in 1922–25 to repress the native insurgency in Morocco.[3] Later efforts to negotiate German participation in Spanish naval development yielded few results, however, though German interests played a large part in the founding of Iberia Airlines in 1927.

Spanish diplomacy under the Republic tended to be oriented toward France, as in general had been Spanish military theory and planning, such as it was, but relations with Germany, a major trading partner, remained good. Germany had no direct involvement in Spanish politics, and the Nazis spent only a modest amount on propaganda in Spain.[4] Spain was not even mentioned in the plans drawn up for the military development of the German economy, though Spanish mineral imports played some small role in that development. Direct German investment in Spain was modest. Attempts to increase arms purchases in Germany in 1935 largely failed, though a few arms were imported, and the Republic's Ministry of War negotiated two small contracts with the Krupp companies in April 1936 to purchase artillery. Later, after the conflict began, the Republican government made further attempts to buy arms from German firms.[5]

The Italian Fascist regime was much more interested in Spain, which was of some importance in Mussolini's Mediterranean-centered foreign policy. Though the effort to build a close relationship with the dictatorship of Miguel Primo de Rivera had achieved little[6] and mutual commerce was limited, Italy invested more than Germany in cultural activity within

Spain.[7] After the center and moderate right won the Spanish elections of 1933, monarchists despaired of the domestic politics in Spain and turned to Mussolini for assistance. An agreement signed on 31 March 1934 pledged the Italian government to provide arms, financing, and military training facilities for a monarchist effort to overthrow the Republic. Some money changed hands and a few volunteers were trained in Libya, but the Spanish monarchists proved so weak that the understanding soon became a dead letter. As part of its comparatively short-lived "Universal Fascism" promotion of fraternal parties abroad, the Italian government provided a modest subsidy to the Falange for about eight months in 1935–36, but soon ended it.[8] Mussolini had come to the conclusion that the attempt to promote the radical right in Spain was a waste of effort and money, a conclusion no doubt fully justified so long as the constitutional system endured. Neither Germany nor Italy went so far as the Soviet Union, which for more than fifteen years had maintained its own political party in Spain.

During the military conspiracy of 1936, agents made attempts to buy arms on the commercial market in Germany and to garner new support in Rome, which rejected them. After the military rebellion began with such uncertain success, the insurgent commanders began to look for foreign assistance within a matter of days. General Emilio Mola, the commander in the north and the organizer of the revolt, was in desperate need of ammunition as well as arms, while Franco especially sought airplanes to help break the Republican blockade of his forces in Morocco. Emissaries were dispatched by both generals and arrived first in Rome. Franco's representatives to Germany, taken to see Hitler at the Bayreuth opera festival after the performance ended on the night of 25 July, met with more immediate success.

The proposal to assist a military rebellion in Spain came as a surprise to Hitler, who had been paying little attention to events there. His fanatical ideology was fixed on the twin poles of race and space. Spaniards were at the very best marginal to his concept of the Aryan race, while his spatial goals were fixed on lebensraum in Eastern Europe. The Mediterranean was an area in which Hitler showed little interest. He preferred to leave that to Mussolini, whom he considered a significant potential ally. Relations were improving after a bout of nasty polemics on the part of Fascist Party journalists in 1934, and by 1935–36 Mussolini was shifting to the German side.[9]

During the weeks following the Popular Front electoral victory in February, the embassies of Germany, Italy, and Portugal in Madrid had been the targets of numerous threats and hostile demonstrations. On 2 April the ambassadors of Argentina, Britain, Germany, the Netherlands, and Switzerland had met to discuss the issue of granting asylum should violent revolution break out.[10] By mid-April the German ambassador had been transferred to the embassy in Paris and, in view of the climate in Madrid, Berlin was in no hurry to appoint a replacement. The embassy had been left in the hands of the chargé, who informed Berlin of all the political rumors flying in the Spanish capital but had no access to privileged information.

None of the German intelligence agencies had direct prior knowledge of the revolt, even though agents of Mola, as well as certain other rightist conspirators, had made low-level contacts with German arms dealers and with Nazi Party and state officials. None of these minor contacts had been extended to the higher levels of German government.[11]

The military revolt was presented to Hitler as a revolt by patriotic Spaniards, friendly to Germany and to National Socialism, to prevent the imminent establishment of a pro-Soviet Communist regime in Madrid. After three hours of deliberation, he made a quick decision, as was not unusual for him, agreeing to provide limited military assistance. The first Junkers-52 transport plane arrived in Tetuán on 27 July, followed during the next two weeks by nineteen more, as well as six fighter planes and small quantities of arms. Hermann Göring, commander of the newly created Luftwaffe, set up a Sonderstab W (Special Staff Wilberg) to coordinate this aid.

What were Hitler's motives in beginning very limited intervention? Nazi propaganda had already charged the Soviet Union with having provoked the conflict in Spain. Anticommunism had always been fundamental to Hitler's ideology and to his rise to power. By the summer of 1936, as Germany entered the major phase of rearmament and was on the verge of restoring compulsory military service—measures that could only alarm its neighbors—Hitler was beginning to use anticommunist propaganda more actively than ever, employing it as a major device to allay concerns abroad about Germany's intensifying military policy. The formation of an international anti-Comintern pact was his major ploy in establishing a new relationship with Japan, his proposed new ally in the Far East, and some historians have seen anticommunism as the main motive for intervention in Spain.

The fundamental concern, however, seems to have been simply geostrategic, in which anticommunism obviously played a role. A victorious

Popular Front regime in Madrid, strongly antifascist and increasingly oriented to the Soviet Union, would be a natural ally of France, which had signed a defensive pact with the Soviet Union in 1935 (later ratified but never fully implemented). According to the information Hitler had at that time, the Paris government was acting on such a premise to send military assistance to Madrid. Hence Hitler's primary concern on 26 July 1936 was to prevent the establishment of a leftist Hispano-French alliance against Germany in southwestern Europe, which would also be to some extent oriented toward the Soviet Union, and would also form a strategic bridge to northwest Africa. If the limited intervention were successful, a new right-wing military regime in Madrid would neatly reverse the looming danger, establishing a friend of Germany on the other side of France and to some degree further constraining that country.[12]

Meanwhile, other representatives were sent to Rome separately by Mola and by Franco, but Mussolini at first was less decisive. He had dealt with potential Spanish rightist rebels before, and they had proved totally ineffective. A request prior to the insurrection had been ignored. Nonetheless, the Mussolini of July 1936 found that his situation had changed considerably since the year before. In the interim he had taken advantage of the incipient destabilization of the European balance of power to initiate the aggressive phase of his own foreign policy, launching the invasion of Ethiopia. Germany had been the only foreign power to support Italian policy in Ethiopia, where the Duce had declared victory by May, just two months before the conflict began in Spain. Mussolini's policy was now becoming increasingly assertive and adventuresome.[13]

Though his son-in-law and foreign minister, Count Galeazzo Ciano, proved immediately receptive, Mussolini did not completely make up his mind to send warplanes and other supplies to Franco until 27 July. He was initially unaware of Hitler's separate but parallel decision, but had been assured that the revolt was a major effort with a genuine chance for success, and also learned that France was not going to intervene, making this initially minor enterprise less risky for Italy. On 30 July, three days after the first German planes were sent, Mussolini dispatched twelve Savoia-Marchetti S-81 medium bombers to Spanish Morocco. Three lacked adequate fuel and had to crash-land in adjacent French territory, providing international notice of the beginning of Italian intervention. The government in Rome quickly announced that these were private exports, while German officials also denied that their government was intervening in Spain.[14]

During August the French initiative for international agreement on nonintervention went forward, with Hitler, Mussolini, and Stalin all nominally concurring. The major powers sought further to restrict the scope of the war by seconding Germany's refusal to recognize the official status of belligerency for either side in Spain. Berlin had announced this policy to prevent the Republican fleet from blockading ports through which Germany was sending military supplies.

German aid to the Nationalists increased during August, and on the 28th of that month Hitler authorized the small number of German military in Spain to engage directly in combat operations, if necessary. Approximately one month later, German assistance was expanded under Operation Otto, and then, in quick response to the Soviet intervention, before the close of October the decision was taken to dispatch a small German air corps, the Condor Legion, comprising 92 planes and 3,900 men, which began to arrive on 6 November. In return, Franco had to agree to certain conditions: that all German forces and their attendant services would be grouped in a special autonomous corps, under German command; that Franco would guarantee the security of their bases; and that henceforth he would conduct the war in a "more active and rational" manner, with priority given to the neutralization, destruction, or seizure of the Mediterranean ports through which Soviet assistance was transmitted. At this point, the amount of Germany's assistance temporarily outstripped that of Italy.

The context of the Spanish war stimulated German foreign policy, leading to two important new agreements on 23–24 October 1936. The Anti-Comintern Pact was signed between Germany and Japan, providing Hitler with a major associate in the Far East. In Spain, Hitler and Mussolini found themselves intervening on the same side, accelerating the rapprochement begun during the Ethiopian war. On the 24th, Hitler and Mussolini reached the agreement that the latter would say formed the "Rome-Berlin Axis." This was neither a treaty nor a pact, but an agreement for mutual consultation and preferential relations, though Mussolini at first announced that it was not exclusive. Mutual intervention in the Spanish war did not bring about this special relationship, long desired by Hitler, but helped to expedite it. This was the beginning of the "brutal friendship"[15] between the two dictators that would eventually lead to a military alliance in 1939 and finally to the downfall of the Fascist regime.

It had taken Mussolini nearly four years to sign his first important agreement with Hitler, for his attitude toward the Führer was marked by a combination of fear and envy. He took the point that Hitler's advent to power would initiate a destabilization of European affairs that would help to open a window of opportunity for Italy's imperial expansion, and also that they had common adversaries in the three major imperial powers—Britain, France, and the Soviet Union. But Italy and Germany had been enemies in World War I and, despite Hitler's enticing remarks in *Mein Kampf* and elsewhere, Mussolini and other Fascists knew that Italians had a subordinate place in the Nazi racial hierarchy. Thus Mussolini had permitted the Fascist press polemic against Nazism in 1934, even possibly participating in it under a pseudonym, and Italy had been the only power to make a strong military gesture on behalf of Austria's independence at the time of the failed Nazi putsch in Vienna in July 1934. The Ethiopian war had marked the beginning of the change in Italian policy, not merely in large-scale military aggression but also in Mussolini's inclination to place that policy on a course increasingly parallel with that of Germany.

On 18 November both Hitler and Mussolini recognized the insurgent command as the legitimate government of Spain and provided Franco with much-needed diplomatic support at the very moment that his efforts to seize Madrid were being stymied. Within the next month Franco also signed a secret agreement promising that in the event that Italy became involved in war with another power or powers, the Spanish regime would pursue a policy of neutrality favorable to Italy, providing economic and logistical support. By December Mussolini was in fact planning to go much further than Hitler, beginning the shipment of what would soon become an Italian infantry corps of 49,000 volunteers (soon downsized by one-third), aerial units twice as large as the Condor Legion, and a significant artillery force. Mussolini's commitment was distinctly larger than that of either Hitler or Stalin, because he perceived the outcome of the Spanish war as crucial to his regime, a key to achieving dominance in the Mediterranean. Though Italian diplomats also intermittently encouraged the Spanish regime to become increasingly fascist politically,[16] Italy's principal focus would always remain on military affairs and it did not interfere significantly in the domestic politics of the Nationalist zone.

By contrast, Hitler vetoed German political interference, stressing that Germany must concentrate instead on obtaining economic concessions to fuel vital mineral imports. The German Foreign Ministry recorded his position as holding that "the political system which might obtain in Spain at the end of the war—whether a military dictatorship, an authoritarian regime, or a monarchy of either liberal or conservative tendency—was a matter of indifference to him."[17] The only thing that mattered was that such a regime be supportive of German policy. Hitler continued to send military equipment and supplies but refused to increase his commitment further, letting Mussolini lead the new escalation.

Though Germany desired Franco's victory, German policy would best be served by the continuation of the Spanish conflict in order to distract Europe's attention from Germany's rearmament and initial expansion. Hitler's policy at the close of 1936 was later paraphrased by a leading German official as follows:

> If the attention of the European powers could further be directed to Spain, this would entail considerable advantages for German policy in Europe. . . . Germany's interests, which alone should be considered, were therefore not so deeply involved in an early conclusion of the Spanish Civil War as to risk a limitation of its own rearmament. On the contrary, German policy would be advanced if the Spanish question continued for a time to occupy Europe's attention and therefore divert it from Germany.[18]

This would remain Hitler's policy for nearly two years, through the greater part of the Spanish war, until the autumn of 1938. Any expanded assistance to Franco would come from Mussolini, not from Hitler. On 5 November 1937, Hitler reiterated this policy to his subordinates: continuation of the Spanish conflict was still Germany's main interest. It would distract attention from Hitler's next moves against Austria and Czechoslovakia, while keeping Mussolini heavily embroiled and at odds with France and Britain. Mussolini was by no means entirely happy with this policy, for it left Italy to carry the brunt of the effort while, as the Duce conceded, worsening his relations with Paris and London even as it left Hitler's hands free. Nonetheless, Mussolini continued to move nearer Germany, signing the Anti-Comintern Pact in November 1937, and at that time also withdrawing Italy from the League of Nations.

Hitler's policy turned even more cynical in 1938. Since the first weeks of the Spanish war, he had appreciated its divisive effects on France. So long as it continued, it would weaken France internally and make any united response to German initiatives that much more difficult. Since France was more conflicted over Spain than was any other country, at times Hitler even harbored hope that civil war would spread to France itself. Even if it did not, it would continue to cause France problems.

After Franco's successful offensive in Aragon in April 1938, which cut the remaining Republican zone in half, Hitler shocked Colonel Erwin Jaenecke, chief of staff of Sonderstab W, by telling him that he did not wish to see Franco conquer Catalonia immediately, as at that moment Franco might potentially have done rather easily. At least for the time being, Hitler preferred what he called a "Red Catalonia." Catalonia would thus remain a bone of contention between Franco and the French government, eliminating any danger of a rapprochement between the two. The status quo would cut off Catalonia from the rest of the Spanish economy, making it easier for Germany to drain off raw materials, while it would continue to keep Mussolini fixated on Spain in opposition to France. Hitler instructed Jaenecke to advise Franco to avoid Catalonia and strike to the south instead.[19] This advice, together with intelligence concerning French military discussions about intervening in Catalonia or the Balearic Islands, was one factor behind Franco's otherwise militarily somewhat dubious decision to renounce a swift and decisive triumph in Catalonia, concentrating instead on a slow, difficult advance through the hills and down the narrow coastal road toward Valencia—a move that bewildered Franco's chief subordinates.

During most of the war German military commanders complained about the slow pace and unimaginativeness of Franco's military operations, which occasionally caused morale problems in the Condor Legion. Ambassador Wilhelm von Faupel opined of Franco that "his personal military experience and knowledge are insufficient for the conduct of operations of the present dimensions," while General Hugo Sperrle, commander of the Condor Legion, judged that "Franco is not an adequate leader for such major tasks. By German standards he lacks military experience. He was made a very young general after the Riff war and never commanded larger units, so that he is only prepared to be a battalion leader."[20] Whenever these concerns were brought to Hitler's attention, he brushed them aside, for Franco's seemingly dilatory tactics suited the Führer very well.

The only potential involvement in Spanish domestic politics took place early in 1937. Ambassador von Faupel had received instructions to offer advice about Spanish domestic affairs only on invitation, but he tended to exceed his guidelines. Faupel arranged for some fifty German military advisers, most of them reserve officers, to be sent to supervise the new Falangist training schools for junior combat officers. He also urged Falangist leaders to play a more active political role, but such opportunities came to an end when Franco seized control of the party in April 1937. The Falangist officer schools, together with their German advisers, were then incorporated into the unified training facilities of the Nationalist army, and before long Faupel was replaced as ambassador.

In 1938 Hitler approved the suggestion of his foreign minister, Joachim von Ribbentrop, that a special treaty of friendship with Franco would be a useful means of tying him to Germany's side. Franco avoided any such step, however, for he was painfully aware of the need to avoid doing anything that might provoke confrontation with Britain and France so long as the Civil War lasted. Not until the end of the conflict was he willing to go beyond a secret protocol, signed in March 1937, that merely promised benevolent neutrality in any broader European war, similar to the earlier secret agreement with Italy.

The principal friction between Nazi Germany and the Franco regime during the Civil War lay in economic relations. There Berlin, unlike Rome, was determined to exact maximal advantage, particularly in the control and importing of Spanish minerals. Germany's economic relations with Spain were administered by two trading corporations, HISMA (Hispano-Marroquí de Transportes, S.L.), only nominally a private corporation (half of its capital was eventually provided by the Spanish state), which channeled the arms shipments, and a German state import corporation, ROWAK (Rohstoff-Waren-Handelsgesellschaft, A.G.), in charge of imports from Spain. Franco would have preferred more direct bilateral clearing arrangements but signed two trade protocols in 1937. These agreements provided that the Spanish state would pay 4 percent annual interest on the arms debt (though there was provision for renegotiation), would provide minerals and other raw materials regularly (partly as debt repayment), and would permit German capital to be invested in new mining companies in Spain, subject to Spanish law. At the same time, Franco sought to maintain normal economic relations with Britain, and the British government reciprocated, nearly 75 percent of British imports to Spain in 1937 going to the Nationalist zone, considered by the British a more reliable trading partner than the revolutionary Republic. Before the Civil War, commerce with France had been twice as large as that with Germany, but under German pressure exports to France from the Nationalist zone declined greatly.

The German regime especially sought pyrites, very important to arms production, and iron ore. Export of pyrites to Germany doubled in 1937 and also increased to Britain, while shipments to France dwindled to the vanishing point. Similarly, exports of iron ore to Germany steadily increased, while those to Britain sharply decreased in 1938. By then the German share of total Spanish exports (both zones combined) had risen from less than 11 percent in 1936 to nearly 41 percent, and the percentage from the Nationalist zone was of course much greater yet.

The Hitler regime sought direct ownership and control of key new

Spanish mining companies in order to dominate production of strategic minerals. Within little more than year, ROWAK created eleven companies in Spain, some in mining and others in agriculture and other raw materials. This activity roused the apprehension of Franco's strongly nationalist new regime, which did not want to see foreigners, German or otherwise, dominating key sectors of Spanish production. Hence a decree issued by Franco on 12 October 1937 declared null and void all purchases of mining rights in Spain since the beginning of the Civil War. This diktat respected previously established foreign investments (primarily British and French) but nullified seventy-three purchases of mining rights recently completed by ROWAK.

The German goal was creation of a huge holding corporation for mining rights, MONTANA, whose development was placed in jeopardy by this new ruling. After much haggling and negotiation, Franco signed a decree at the beginning of June 1938 that permitted Germans to own up to 40 percent of the capital in new mining companies. The Germans hoped to get around the restriction by buying additional shares through Spanish proxies.

It quickly developed that such arrangements were not acceptable to Hitler, however, and for the first time relations between the two dictatorships began to deteriorate in the summer of 1938, exacerbated by the official position of neutrality taken by Franco at the time of the Sudeten crisis in September. By that point the extreme attrition exacted by the battle of the Ebro had sharply diminished Franco's stocks of key German arms and supplies, and Hitler proved unwilling to replenish them without economic concessions.

The military situation finally forced Franco's hand, and in November 1938 he grudgingly agreed to German control of shares in four of the five main MONTANA companies, in which they would hold between 60 and 75 percent of the equity. This agreement brought resumption of German military supplies for the war's final campaign.[21]

By that time Hitler was moving directly into the most aggressive phase of his foreign policy and the Spanish war no longer served as a useful distraction. For the first time since the early months of the conflict, he desired a quick victory by Franco. The new arms shipments helped to prime Franco's forces for the successful invasion of Catalonia—French intervention no longer a threat—and the war soon entered its final phase.

Though Hitler exacted much stronger terms than Mussolini, Franco's economic relations with Germany were generally effective from the viewpoint of his regime. He was forced to make concessions but avoided any general German economic domination, and succeeded in maintaining significant military support throughout the war. Though Hitler's financial terms were less generous than Mussolini's, only about 18 percent of the German military assistance was repaid through debt service and designated raw materials down to the end of the Civil War.

At no time did Spain play a major direct role in Hitler's policy, which consigned the entire Mediterranean primarily to the Italian sphere of influence. Hitler had attained his two main goals—a longer Spanish conflict that distracted and divided his adversaries while Franco moved inexorably toward triumph, and a friendly antileftist regime in Spain, oriented toward the Axis powers, even if not exclusively so, which guaranteed major shipments of key raw materials to Germany. Equally or more important, from his point of view, the Spanish war had provided him with a major collateral dividend as well—a much closer association with Italy, which as a result was now increasingly at odds with France and Britain.

In the final days of the Civil War, Franco became the fourth signatory of the Anti-Comintern Pact (with Germany, Italy, and Japan). On 31 March 1939 a treaty of friendship was signed between Germany and Spain, providing for benevolent neutrality in the event that either was involved in war with a third power and "relations of comradeship and the exchange of practical military experiences between the respective armed forces."[22] Both of these agreements were kept completely secret, to avoid any complications for the new Spanish regime, but the friendship treaty accurately predicted Franco's policy for the greater part of World War II. Yet the latent differences between the German and Spanish regimes were revealed by the fate of a special cultural agreement negotiated with Germany at the same time. It was never ratified, mainly because of opposition by the leaders of the Spanish Church, who feared inundation with pagan Nazi racist propaganda. Berlin was disappointed, but the issue was secondary at a time when the most pressing German interests in Spain were economic. Hitler had achieved his principal goals.

CHAPTER 3

Military and International Significance of the Civil War

Foreign military intervention played a major role in the Civil War, that of the Axis powers being more extensive than the Soviet intervention. It began earlier and in toto provided both more weapons and more men. A grand total of at least 16,500 German military personnel served in Spain (though never that many at one time), about 75,000 Italian military personnel (though as many as 50,000 for only two months, and usually not more than 35,000), and possibly as many as 10,000 Portuguese volunteers, contrasted with approximately 42,000 volunteers in the International Brigades and a total of between 2,000 and 3,000 Soviet military personnel.

The Italian and German intervention was also militarily more effective, though not in every respect. The Condor Legion included one German panzer battalion, named for its commander as Panzer-gruppe Thoma (also called Panzer-gruppe Drohne). At its height in March 1938 this battalion amounted to 6,200 men organized in four units of very light German Mark I (Pkw-I) tanks (sixteen per company) and two more potent companies manning larger captured Soviet tanks (twenty-two tanks each), plus twenty companies of light antitank guns (ten guns each). Altogether about three hundred German antitank guns were sent to Spain. They played an important role, though when possible Franco's forces preferred to use more powerful captured Soviet antitank guns. The very light German and Italian tankettes were almost complete failures, thoroughly outclassed by the larger Soviet tanks.

The 140 German 77-mm artillery sent to Spain played a more modest role than the more numerous and sometimes larger Italian cannon. Three batteries of more powerful German artillery arrived only in the very last phase. Conversely, the 79 88-mm antiaircraft guns provided by the Germans were the best on either side, marking the baptism of fire of a remarkable weapon that would become perhaps the best-known artillery piece of World War II. The other 218 German anti-aircraft guns were much lighter and rather similar to those sent to the Republic by the Soviets. Altogether, however, the German anti-aircraft guns were important in helping to frustrate Republican bombing operations.[1]

In small numbers, German and Italian units provided important assistance to Franco's initial drive on Madrid and then, in larger numbers, established an effective counterbalance to the Soviet intervention. Italian and German planes and pilots enabled Franco to establish superiority in the air from about the middle of 1937, even though at that time they were still slightly outnumbered. Together with their artillery counterparts, they made possible the world's first effective use of World War II–style combined arms in most of Franco's major operations from April 1937 on. Even the infantry of the Italian Corpo di Truppe Volontarie (CTV) had a better record than it has been given credit for (and, contrary to the standard notion, most of the men were volunteers).[2] Altogether, continued supply of matériel enabled Franco to arm an ever-expanding number of troops during the final two years of the war, even though Axis weapons were insufficient for his entire army, a significant minority of which was equipped with captured Republican weapons and miscellaneous other equipment. The latter fact underscores the reality that there was comparatively little difference in the overall volume of arms received by the two sides, but employment by Franco's forces was more effective. One of several reasons for the Nationalists' superiority was that more German officers than Soviet officers on the other side assisted in the training of junior officers (alféreces provisionales) and NCOs, the instructors of what was called the Gruppe Imker helping to achieve a higher level of combat readiness.

The quantitative commitment was particularly noteworthy in the Italian case. Apparently more than two-thirds of all Italian air force pilots served in comparatively rapid rotation in Spain, where they made up the largest sector of Franco's air force, at least prior to the final phases of the war. The Italian navy also played an important role. Its ships provided assistance in the Strait of Gibraltar and later helped screen Mallorca from further Republican assault. They also helped to protect ships bound for the Nationalist zone, assisted in training part of Franco's naval personnel, and, together with the German navy, provided naval intelligence.

Italian ships, primarily submarines, intermittently engaged in combat operations. Several submarines operated against Republican shipping at the end of 1936, and a larger number during August and September 1937. Mussolini sold to Franco two new submarines, four old destroyers, and four torpedo boats, and leased four more Legionnaire submarines for Spanish service for five months beginning in September 1937. The Italian submarines did not sink many ships but they were instrumental in closing the Mediterranean shipping lanes from the Soviet Union, while Italian and German planes based on Mallorca proved more effective in sinking Republican ships.[3]

It is not possible to give precise statistics on the absolute number of weapons sent, but the approximate volume is fairly clear. Italy dispatched more than 700 warplanes, nearly 2,000 pieces of artillery, and 8,750 machine guns and submachine guns. Germany sent slightly fewer warplanes and much less artillery. The Soviet Union dispatched about 800 warplanes, to which might be added some 250 fighter planes manufactured on Soviet designs in the Republican zone, as well as 332 late-model tanks. When airplanes from other sources are included, the disparity may not have been very great, particularly since the Republicans began the fighting with twice as many.[4]

The heaviest losses among the intervening powers were logically suffered by the Italians, with about 4,300 fatalities. Approximately 300 Germans and about 200 Soviet military personnel were killed.

The ultimate outlay of the Republicans for foreign military supplies must have been more than $800 million at then-current prices, all paid for immediately with large amounts of gold and other valuables (Spain having had the fourth or fifth largest gold reserve in the world in 1936). In addition, during the final year of the war, the Soviet Union extended a total of $230 million in loans for war goods, though nearly half of the weapons purchased with these loans never reached Spain. By comparison, the cost of the German equipment and related expenditures for the Nationalists amounted to somewhat more than $215 million and an even larger amount of Italian arms and other assistance to more than $355 million—nearly all this provided by Italy and Germany through generous terms of credit.

Whereas the Republicans had paid the Soviet Union and other suppliers for nearly all the goods and services immediately, Mussolini reduced the large debt owed to Italy by 33 percent after the war ended, and the German debt was lowered by a lesser amount. As will be seen in later chapters, most of Spain's debt to Germany was retired through exports during World War II. Beginning in 1942, Franco slowly and systematically repaid the remaining Italian debt in increasingly inflated lire until it was fully retired twenty-five years later. Other terms of credit were also extended to Franco by foreign suppliers, most notably American oil companies. Altogether, when we include approximately $76 million of matériel and supplies from other countries, Franco received nearly $650 million of goods and services from foreign sources, primarily on credit, much less than the Republican government with its much greater resources paid out directly, and through that credit received in toto a somewhat larger volume of military supplies and support and, in the final analysis, more comprehensive and decisive assistance.

Military "Lessons" and Their Significance in Military History

When the greater European war began only five months later, defeated Republicans started to describe the Spanish conflict as the "first battle" or "opening round" of what would eventually be called World War II. It would later be claimed that the Spanish war had also been a sort of military proving ground for weapons and tactics. There is some truth to that contention, though it is exaggerated. The Spanish Civil War was for the most part a low-intensity conflict punctuated by occasional high-intensity battles. To a large extent, it was fought with weapons that were already becoming obsolescent (in some cases, obsolete) and, in that sense, sometimes resembled World War I more than World War II.

It was also the case, however, that some of the latest and most advanced weaponry appeared in Spain, a process begun by the Soviet shipment of late-model tanks and planes in October 1936. The Germans, some of whose arms at first were outclassed by Soviet weapons, responded with more advanced models of planes, but, though their 88-mm anti-aircraft gun was outstanding, aside from this weapon they never caught up with the Soviets in quality of armor or antitank guns.

Testing of new weapons and tactics was not the primary reason for involvement of any of the three major intervening powers, whose concerns were predominantly political and geostrategic. None of the professional military commands was initially enthusiastic about such a complex and risky new initiative, but once the intervention was under way, all three took advantage of it to evaluate weapons and tactics. The only major new tactic essayed in Spain was the coordinated employment of infantry, motorized troops, artillery, armor, and air-to-ground support. Such tactics had been partially foreshadowed in World War I, but in different ways they were becoming standard doctrine in both the German and Soviet forces.[5] These concepts were inevitably applied in a somewhat hit-or-miss fashion by the respective Spanish commands, though in general much more effectively by Franco's forces.

Air-to-ground support was the chief new feature, but means were simply inadequate to attempt the full World War II pattern of combined arms.[6] The claim that the Germans tested later blitzkrieg tactics is a total exaggeration. The German military had not developed that idea even in 1939, and the German tanks in Spain were small and inadequate. Much of the Spanish war was fought in mountainous terrain, a far cry from the environment in which most of World War II was fought in Europe.

Tank operations were poorly developed in Spain. The Soviets were rarely able to employ their superiority in tanks to very good effect, with the result that some Red Army commanders began to question their own doctrines, which prior to 1937 had developed mobile warfare concepts more elaborately than anything found in Germany. The very small German and Italian tanks sent to Spain could be used in only limited ways; by the last part of the war, Franco's best armor were the eighty or so Soviet tanks captured from the Republicans and organized into two tank units of the Nacionales.

Another military myth is that because of the heavy bombing of the Basque town of Guernica in April 1937, as well as a number of other cities, Spain became a testing ground for strategic bombing. Through the experience of the Condor Legion, the Germans did learn to improve their bombing techniques, but no serious strategic bombing took place in Spain. There were many bombing raids on cities, but all were small in scale and none were systematically continued. Nothing remotely approached the scale of World War II–style strategic bombing. Many of these raids were terrifying for those who had to suffer them, but in the Spanish war a large air raid was one in which a hundred or so people were killed. There was not the slightest comparison with the hecatombs of World War II.

The German Luftwaffe had made no very serious preparations for strategic bombing, designing its planes for tactical bombing in combined arms operations and air-to-ground support. This would be one of the main reasons why it lost the Battle of Britain in 1940. The first German bombers in Spain were not even true bombers, but very slow Junkers-52 transport planes that could be outfitted with bombs. The two towns proportionately most damaged by bombing—Durango and Guernica—were targeted not for strategic bombing (in that case the target would have been the major city in the region, Bilbao, which in fact suffered little damage) but because they formed the immediate rear guard of the Basque battlefront, Guernica being only about 15 kilometers distant.

Of all the European powers, the Soviet Union showed the greatest theoretical interest in the Spanish war, displayed not in the number of Soviet military personnel, which were considerably fewer than those of Italy and Germany, but in the extent of military analysis. The Germans were appropriately skeptical and selective in respect to the lessons they chose to draw; the Soviet approach was broader and also more credulous. Mary Habeck, the leading Western specialist in this area, has written that "Soviet officers . . . unlike their German counterparts, believed that the conflict presented a valid picture of a future great war." The Soviet "command staff became convinced that the conflict was a reliable model of modern war and treated each new experience of combat as a valuable lesson of how the Soviet army should fight in the future."[7] Soviet study of operations in Spain was massive, covering virtually every aspect of weaponry and organization.[8]

But the question has been raised as to whether the Red Army analysts learned valid lessons or managed to deceive themselves, and here the situation is complex. The main error, partly derived from the relative failure of Soviet armor in Spain, was to abandon the relatively sophisticated Soviet doctrine of massed armor and "deep operations," somewhat similar to the slowly emerging doctrine of the Wehrmacht. Though the decision was not solely the result of the Spanish experience, in November and December 1939 the Red Army tank corps were broken up.

Conversely, the Red Army was able to make improvements in a variety of technical areas, from military administration and engineering to certain weapons systems. As a result, the advanced B-5 tank, introduced in Spain, was developed within four years into the subsequently famous T-34, ton for ton the best tank of World War II. By 1937–38 Soviet aircraft, which at first ruled the skies over Madrid, were becoming somewhat obsolescent in comparison with the newest German models, stimulating development of the newer aircraft that began to be produced in 1942–43. Improvements were also made in artillery and infantry weapons and in other kinds of equipment.

If the Red Army sometimes drew inaccurate lessons, it was not alone. For French analysts, the Spanish war tended to reconfirm the importance of the defensive and of antitank weapons.[9] For the Italian military, the success of their small units most of the time, together with Franco's victory, merely reconfirmed their own otherwise generally inadequate priorities and policies. Italy, in fact, paid the heaviest price of all the intervening powers. It lacked the industrial capacity of either Germany or the Soviet Union, so that the nearly 800 planes and 7,500 motor vehicles of all kinds shipped to Spain constituted a sizable percentage of its military arsenal. Nearly all the surviving machines were left in Spain, and their loss had not been fully made good by the time Italy entered the European war in 1940. Moreover, Italian military planners failed to pay close attention to the experience of the Spanish conflict. The fact that the Fiat CR 32 was the only fighter plane able to fight more or less successfully from the beginning to the end of the conflict blinded them to the fact that this durable but increasingly obsolescent biplane, as well as the Savoia-Marchetti medium bomber, was falling behind the competition and not being adequately replaced. The glaring deficiencies of the Italian tankettes, a yet more obvious weakness, drew little attention. Other failings in the training of infantry officers and troops were similarly passed over, as was the weak performance of Italian submarines. More than a few of the deficiencies that would be revealed in World War II first showed up in Spain, yet they drew little response.

The only military command that drew the correct lessons, so to speak, was that of Germany, which concluded that the Spanish conflict was a special kind of war from which it would be a mistake to draw any major new conclusions. The Germans did learn to improve important new aerial techniques, especially air-to-ground support, including improved communications and cooperation, mobile air action in support of a moving offensive, intensive aerial bombardment to supplement artillery, night operations, radio use, sustained consecutive attacks to open a breach or take out a strong position, first use of napalm bombs, carpet bombing, and new use of anti-aircraft guns, as well as improved employment of artillery to support advancing infantry.[10] German fighter pilots developed the "finger four" formation, which became standard in World War II. All these were important lessons, but the Germans did not plan the development of the Wehrmacht around the Spanish experience. They failed to draw proper conclusions about the need to improve antitank weapons, the slack in Spain sometimes having been taken up by the 88-mm anti-aircraft gun.

Nor can it be said that the clear evidence of superior Soviet tank designs spurred the Germans into rapid or decisive improvement of their own models. Just as foreign political observers tended to construct their interpretations of the Spanish conflict according to their own preferences, prejudices, and domestic politics, so the military insights varied extensively from country to country.

International Significance

Both sides of the Civil War developed a strongly patriotic discourse that defined their struggle as a battle for independence against a foreign invader. The Republicans termed their battle a resistance to international fascism; the Nationalists called theirs a war of liberation against communism and the Soviet Union. They also labeled their struggle a crusade for the reaffirmation of the nation and of Christian civilization. International calculations became especially important in the conduct of the war during 1938, as the situation in Europe grew increasingly tense. In the spring of that year Franco took increasing care to avoid any provocation of France, while Juan Negrín, the Republican leader, became convinced that the international dimension was the key to victory. Certain that a major war would soon break out, the *negrinista* slogan "Resistir es vencer" (To resist is to win) was predicated on continuing the struggle in Spain until it could become part of a larger conflict in which British and French intervention might enable the Republic to achieve victory. Soviet expectations were eventually based on somewhat similar calculations.

After the European war began, many Republicans held that it constituted an internationalization of the issues that Spain had faced. Franco and his subordinates took an extremely opportunistic approach to this interpretation. During the Spanish war itself and in the opening phases of World War II, they publicly denied any connection, only to claim a common identity of both wars as soon as the Germans seemed about to win. Later, after the strategic complexion of the European war changed, they once more denied any connection between the two conflicts. Some scholarly studies, such as Patricia van der Esch's *Prelude to War: The International Repercussions of the Spanish Civil War* (1951), have echoed the Republican interpretation.

Others have disagreed. Pierre Renouvin, the distinguished French diplomatic historian, judged the consequences of the Spanish war merely "modest," concluding that "it would be an exaggeration to see in this war a prelude to a European war."[11] In his controversial *Origins of the Second World War* (1961), A. J. P. Taylor calculated that the Spanish conflict had no "significant effect" on the great powers. P. M. H. Bell, author of *The Origins of the Second World War in Europe* (1986), concluded that the Spanish war was simply "much ado about nothing" as far as broader events were concerned.[12]

In one obvious sense, Bell's conclusion must be correct. The Spanish war was a clear-cut contest between left and right, with the fascist totalitarian powers supporting a semi-fascist right and the Soviet totalitarian power supporting the revolutionary left. World War II, on the other hand, began in Europe only when a pan-totalitarian entente was formed by the Nazi-Soviet Pact with the aim of allowing the Soviet Union to seize a sizable swathe of Eastern Europe while Germany was left free to conquer as much of the rest of the continent as it could. This was a complete reversal of the terms of the Spanish war.

The formula might be inverted, with the conclusion that the Spanish revolution and civil war constituted the last of the revolutionary crises of the early twentieth century, most of which had occurred in the aftermath of World War I.[13] Just as the military characteristics and weaponry of the Spanish war sometimes resembled those of World War I almost as much as those of World War II, the Spanish situation had more characteristics of a post–World War I revolutionary crisis than of a domestic crisis of the era of World War II. Among these characteristics were (1) the revolutionary breakdown of institutions, as distinct from the coups d'état, legalitarian impositions of authoritarianism, and direct military invasions more typical of the World War II era; (2) the development of a full-scale revolutionary–counterrevolutionary civil war, a relatively broad phenomenon after World War I, but elsewhere unheard of during the 1930s and appearing only in the Balkans during and after World War II; (3) development of a post–World War I–type Red Army in the form of the Republican Ejército Popular; (4) an extreme exacerbation of nationalism in the Nationalist Zone, Catalonia, and the Basque Country, more typical of World War I than of World War II; (5) frequent use of World War I–style military matériel and concepts; and (6) the fact that it was not the product of any plan by the major powers (contrary to the conspiracy theories of both sides in Spain), and thus more similar to post–World War I crises than to those of World War II. Similarly, the extreme revolutionary left both inside and outside Spain hailed the revolution as the last and one of the greatest of the revolutionary upsurges of the post–World War I era.

Whereas World War II began in Europe as a kind of alliance of the two major opposing powers that had intervened in Spain, in December 1941 a sort of international popular front was created, primarily through the recklessness of Germany and Japan. The resulting alliance, however, was politically much broader than that of the Popular Front in Spain, since it included very conservative major sectors of capitalist society in the United States, Great Britain, and other countries. Did not the Spanish war foreshadow this development? Not really, for the wartime Spanish Republic represented only the forces of the left, whereas the alliance of 1941–45 included the equivalent of many of the sectors on Franco's side during the Spanish war (among which the Britain of Winston Churchill had initially been included). If Hitler had had to fight only the forces of the left, he would have won his war decisively. Neither the European war of 1939 to 1941 nor the truly world war of 1941–45 merely replicated the Spanish conflict.

Even though the Spanish war was no mere prelude to or opening round of World War II in Europe, it contributed significantly to the terms in which the European war developed. Without directly linking the Spanish war and World War II, historians often advance the argument that the Spanish war contributed greatly to the perceptions and psychology that precipitated the greater conflict. Thus it has not infrequently been contended that the behavior of Britain and France vis-à-vis the Spanish war stimulated the false perception by Hitler and Mussolini that the Western democracies lacked the will to fight, and therefore would not respond to much broader aggression. In this interpretation the Spanish war would not be any special prelude but simply the longest and most indirect in a series of crises in which the fascist powers acted aggressively and the democracies passively: Ethiopia (1935), the Rhineland (1936), Spain (1936–39), Austria (1938), the Sudetenland (1938). In this sequence, the Munich decision over the Sudetenland was much more important and more influential than the Spanish war.

Hitler's policy of using and prolonging the Spanish conflict as a grand international distraction to deflect attention from his own rearmament and expansion was generally successful. On the one hand, he used the complications arising from the Spanish war as an excuse to avoid any broader understanding with Britain and France. On the other, he calculated successfully that continuation of this war would continue to divide France internally and distract it from focusing firmly on Germany during the period (1936 to 1938) when German rearmament had still not proceeded far enough to achieve military parity.

The Spanish war also provided immediate incentive for the beginning of the Italo-German entente that Hitler had always sought. Mussolini became totally committed to the Spanish struggle, depriving Italy of freedom of maneuver and thereby tying it increasingly to a Germany that became the dominant partner and exercised all the major new initiatives, progressively burning Italy's bridges to Britain and France. It was the Italian realignment that made it possible for Hitler to incorporate Austria as early as March 1938, while also making it more feasible for Hitler to move rapidly against Czechoslovakia.

From this perspective it was not that Britain and France ignored the Spanish war but indeed sometimes dedicated more attention to it than to Austria and Czechoslovakia. Willard Frank has observed, "Even in 1938, the year of Munich, British MPs asked almost half again as many parliamentary questions about Spain and the Mediterranean as about Germany and central Europe. . . . The French Chamber of Deputies had to suspend its deliberations twice in one day for fear of a free-for-all fight over the Spanish questions."[14] The Spanish issue significantly divided France internally, complicating and disorienting broader policy. One result was to encourage France to defer more and more to British decision-making, so that British initiatives became dominant in the alliance of the two democracies.

The Italian and German intervention in Spain stimulated a Soviet counterintervention that Stalin would not expand sufficiently to ensure Republican victory, for fear of the international consequences. Nonetheless, for Germany the Soviet intervention had the benefit of intensifying the democracies' suspicion of and alienation from the revolutionary Soviet Union. It only confirmed the conviction of the French General Staff that the goal of Soviet policy was to provoke war among the Western powers. The more Moscow intervened in Spain and the more aggressive the Soviet role in the Non-Intervention Committee, the less likely any rapprochement between Paris and Moscow against Berlin. Soviet policy proved largely counterproductive, except for the gains in espionage made by the NKVD. The Soviet Union was more isolated in April 1939, when the Spanish war ended, than it had been in July 1936. Hitler largely outsmarted Stalin, as he would do again during 1939–41.

The European war in no way depended on the Spanish conflict and would doubtless have broken out even if there had been no war in Spain, but the ramifications of Spain's war helped to determine the pace and timing of broader European affairs. Without the complications arising from Spain, the Western democracies might have taken a stronger stand against Hitler, and conceivably Mussolini might have delayed or even avoided an entente with him. Similarly, without these complications and distractions, Hitler might not have been able to move as rapidly as he did in 1938. Thus the Spanish war helped to condition European affairs, even though it did not determine any other outcomes elsewhere.[15]

CHAPTER 4

A Tilted Neutrality
1939–1940

In the aftermath of the Civil War, Spanish policy was clearly oriented toward Italy and Germany, the two powers that had made Franco's victory possible. They set the prime examples of the new national authoritarian state on which the Spanish regime was modeled, however loosely, and constituted a diplomatic and military alignment whose strength was steadily increasing. Moreover, they were bent on the disruption of the status quo and the creation of a new order both in Europe and in its colonies, though Nazi Germany and Fascist Italy differed considerably in their views of the exact form that this new order would take.

All these features of the Axis states were attractive to Franco and to most of the leaders and activists of the new Spanish regime. The Axis powers were leaders and guarantors, so to speak, of Franco's political model, while their growing strength seemed to offer prestige and opportunities. It was not clear what form their further disruption of the status quo would take, but that too was potentially attractive. Though the energies of the regime had hitherto been absorbed by civil war, Franco had made it clear from the beginning that the goal of the Movimiento Nacional was not merely to win the struggle but afterward to build a strong and prosperous Spain that would reaffirm both its traditional culture and a new nationalism and imperialism, enabling it to recover at least part of the status it had lost in modern times. Foreign policy aims had inevitably been muted during the Civil War, but there had been increasing assertions of leadership in the Spanish-speaking world[1] and an occasional suggestion about regaining Gibraltar as well as influence and territory in Africa. Such ambitions, however, would come to the fore only after the fall of France. The signing of the Anti-Comintern Pact and a friendship treaty with Germany in the closing days of the Civil War were veiled in secrecy, for the economic prostration of Spain and its reconstruction required correct relations with France and Britain, at least for the time being, but Madrid's general alignment was clear. On 8 May 1939, in line with the other signatories of the Anti-Comintern Pact, Spain officially withdrew from the League of Nations.

Spain's withdrawal did not mean that it was a satellite of either Axis power, for Franco was a nationalist whose policy would be based on his judgment of the best interests of Spain.[2] The country identified itself much more closely with Rome than with Berlin, for Spain and Italy were the two large European countries that most resembled each other, and Mussolini had been more generous than Hitler. His regime was the nearest thing that the new Spanish system had for a model, and Serrano Suñer's "victory visit" to Rome in May 1939 was intended to reflect this special relationship.[3] Count Galeazzo Ciano, Mussolini's son-in-law and foreign minister —the second most important figure of the Fascist regime—then returned the visit by coming to Spain the following month. Franco told him that Spain must concentrate on reconstruction and avoid foreign ambitions for the time being, and that it would not be ready to face any further war for five years, a remarkably optimistic assessment. The Caudillo in turn was slated for his first official trip abroad with a visit to Rome in the fall, but it was canceled due to outbreak of the European war.

The visit to Berlin was more muted, consisting of a military and Falangist delegation headed by General Antonio Aranda that accompanied the return of the Condor Legion. The corpulent, bespectacled Aranda was one of Franco's most astute and politically ambitious generals, and also anti-Falangist. In Berlin, in fact, he stressed the importance of good relations with Britain and tended to downplay the role of the FET.[4]

With the Civil War over, Spain once more receded from Hitler's attention. At the beginning of March, Hitler had sent Franco a letter with regard to the secret friendship treaty, explaining that Spain's benevolent neutrality in the coming crisis and possible war would be the policy of greatest benefit to Germany, since it would produce the greatest uncertainty and deterrent effect on Britain and France.[5]

The only branch of the German armed forces that had shown any strategic interest in Spain was the navy, concerned about the country's geographic and logistical possibilities. Spanish leaders had made clear their own ambition to develop a sizable new navy after the Civil War ended, and a number of German naval and industrial representatives had examined possibilities within Spain during 1938, but Hitler showed little interest and the conclusion, as ever, was that Italy should take the lead. The large German fleet that was sent to Spanish waters in mid-April 1939 seems to have been intended as a sort of naval demonstration to impress foreign opinion.[6]

War debts to Italy and Germany were potentially a heavy obligation. Italy was owed more than 7 billion lire, which Mussolini generously reduced to 5 billion (around $250 million), partly with the hope of facilitating Italy's economic penetration of Spain. After long and hard bargaining, a twenty-five-year table of payments was eventually established to begin in mid-1942.[7] Hitler's government was considerably less generous, having absorbed nearly 41 percent of Spanish exports in 1938. A German trade delegation arrived in Madrid in June 1939 to press further demands, having set up a new holding company, SOFINDUS (Sociedad Financiera e Industrial, S.A.), under ROWAK to administer German investments in Spain. Pressure was considerable, one Spanish report prepared for Franco complaining that "the Germans consider Spain a colony of theirs."[8]

The Spanish response was contradictory. On the one hand, Spain was heavily tilted toward the Axis; on the other, with the end of the Civil War and of arms shipments, economic relations were becoming a one-way street headed toward Germany. The result was that Spanish authorities proved stubborn, signing only limited new agreements that avoided further major German investment.[9] At the same time, there persisted the naive tendency to regard Germany as a benevolent power that could be of major technological, industrial, and military assistance. Meanwhile, London sought to limit German influence by dangling the possibility of a badly needed loan. It was becoming clear that the reconstruction of Spain depended on not inconsiderable foreign cooperation, little of which seemed to be forthcoming from Berlin, but how the new regime would respond to the alternatives was far from clear.

As tensions heightened in Europe during the summer of 1939, Franco used the term *hábil prudencia* (adroit prudence) to describe Spain's foreign policy at a July meeting of the FET's National Council. The regime was meanwhile trying to build closer relations with Latin American states, the Philippines, and even the Arab world in an attempt to reestablish a presence abroad. The foreign minister in the new government that Franco appointed in August 1939 was Colonel Juan Beigbeder y Atienza, one of the more enigmatic figures of those years. Four years older than Franco, Beigbeder was descended from an Alsatian immigrant. An engineers officer who had been considered an intellectual, he had served as military attaché in Paris and Berlin from 1926 to 1935. Highly critical of the bureaucratic routine characteristic of the Spanish army, he was a devotee of Morocco, where he had learned Arabic and later served with distinction as high commissioner from 1937 to 1939.

Though he deemed the French model of colonial rule a more sophisticated one to follow, for geopolitical reasons Beigbeder was now Germanophile and had helped to provide Franco with decisive Nazi contacts at the start of the Civil War. Obsequious with the Caudillo, he had also joined the FET and had helped to build it up in Morocco, so that theoretically he fitted into both major power constellations of the new government. Like Franco, he attached great importance to an imperial future in Africa.[10] Just as Italy had spent enormous amounts of money in Ethiopia during 1936–40, so the new Spanish government spent disproportionate sums in Morocco during 1939–40, when funds were badly needed for reconstruction at home.

With German relations friendly but somewhat distant and those with London correct but cold, the two most salient features of Spanish foreign relations in mid-1939 were the close and friendly contacts with Rome and the relative hostility of relations with Paris. Though the first French ambassador to the new regime was the highly conservative Marshal Henri-Philippe Pétain, very favorably disposed toward Franco, the Spanish authorities viewed France as always favoring the Republicans. Paris had returned the remaining gold of the Bank of Spain that it held as surety, but Franco and his associates believed that it was providing Republican political leaders special opportunities to conspire while not returning other assets,[11] and the French in turn found the Franco regime hostile and uncooperative. Consequently tensions were high along the borders of the two zones in Morocco in mid-1939, and the Spanish regime built modest fortifications along the Pyrenees, while strengthening its forces in the protectorate. The French did the same, diverting forces to the Pyrenees (though not nearly as many as it assigned to the Italian frontier) and maintaining a strong military presence in Morocco.

Meanwhile Ambassador Eberhard von Stohrer repeated the advice Hitler had given Franco earlier that, although Germany expected no more than benevolent neutrality in the deepening European crisis, it was important that Spain not tip its hand in advance. It was of the "maximum importance" to Germany that London and Paris be completely uncertain as to Spanish policy, which might be a further factor in helping Hitler win the completely free hand that he sought to liquidate Poland. Though Mussolini had signed a full military alliance, the Pact of Steel, with Germany in May, neither Rome nor Madrid was kept informed of Hitler's planning in the countdown to war during August. Spain had already pledged its benevolent neutrality, and Beigbeder informed Stohrer that "Spain wanted to help Germany as much as it could."[12]

Sectors of the French right looked to Franco as a possible mediator, a suggestion that the latter took up with Mussolini. The Duce had been nominally responsible for organizing the Munich conference and replied that he would try to undertake such a task himself, not wishing to yield the role to Franco, but when, on 30 August (less than forty-eight hours before the German attack), the French foreign minister suggested to the Spanish ambassador in Paris that Franco attempt mediation, Mussolini vetoed the enterprise as coming too late.[13]

In the meantime, Hitler's signing of the Nazi-Soviet Pact came as a shock to Madrid, which looked on the Soviet Union as its archenemy. The chief Falangist organ, *Arriba* was at a loss to justify the "tremendous surprise" it professed. There was some dismay in Madrid over the invasion of Poland, whose Catholic national-authoritarian regime had supported Franco in the Civil War[14] and, though more moderate, had more than a little in common with the new Spanish state. Stalin would soon dismiss its fate as the justifiable liquidation of "Polish fascism."[15]

On 3 September, when Britain and France declared war on Germany, Franco publicly called on them to reconsider their action and return to negotiation. He expressed no concern over the fate of Catholic Poland; his effort was simply to localize a conflict that, if extended to Western Europe, might cause grave damage to Spain. Neutrality was announced the next day. Beigbeder informed Stohrer that there could be no further consideration of the stalled cultural agreement between Madrid and Berlin, but the Reich thanked the Spanish government for its effort to discourage the British and French from declaring war. Franco also agreed privately that German submarines could be resupplied from Spanish ports, an indication of the degree of tilt in his neutrality from the very beginning, though he was careful to conceal it. On 6 September he telegraphed his ambassador in Rome to urge Mussolini to work toward Poland's surrender as soon as possible to avert the danger of a Soviet military advance into Europe. Franco also stressed to Stohrer the importance of keeping the Polish state from disappearing altogether, since it could form a barrier to the Soviet Union. When he later publicly condemned the destruction of Catholic Poland, he was more mindful of the Soviet conquest of the eastern half of the country than of the Nazis' aggression.[16] Nonetheless, only the hard-core pro-Nazis among the Falangists were pleased with the outbreak of the European war, which they were confident would vindicate the authoritarian New Order. The regime's leaders viewed it as a dangerous complication for a country still prostrate from the Civil War. The more conservative favored genuine neutrality, while the more fascistic elements espoused the carefully controlled tilt toward Germany.

Franco rejected a French proposal for a nonaggression pact between Paris and Madrid, pointing out that France had not yet ratified a recently negotiated commercial agreement, but continued to offer his services to Berlin for mediation. The most active in this regard was the ambassador in Paris, the slippery and cynical José Félix de Lequerica. Among his proposals was that France end its alliance with Britain, withdraw from the war, and join a new Unión Latina with Spain and Italy. In communications to Beigbeder of 22 September and 3 October, he expanded this notion into a broader entente of European neutrals that could put an end to the war, while apparently leaving Germany in possession of western Poland. Late in October Beigbeder offered his own proposals, which involved a major campaign for diplomatic and cultural support in Latin America, concerted pressure against Gibraltar, and above all the need to tighten relations with Mussolini, which the Spanish foreign minister felt had been weakened during the crisis of the past two months. Franco's planned visit to Rome had been canceled sine die, but Beigbeder stressed the importance of establishing a Rome-Madrid axis so that the two countries could coordinate their policies, especially when peace returned. Franco was more realistic and well knew that under present circumstances Spain could never equal Germany in Mussolini's thinking, writing skeptically on the margin of Beigbeder's letter "axis without strength?"[17]

Mussolini was embarrassed by his inability to honor the Pact of Steel by immediately joining Hitler in the war into which the Führer had plunged Europe, and had declared for Italy the newly defined status of nonbelligerence, technically nonexistent in international law. It meant that Italy was not at present entering the war but was nonetheless oriented in favor of Germany. This status did not prevent the restless and uncertain Duce from considering other options, as he toyed briefly with some variant of the Latin bloc or neutralist bloc idea. Yet the Italian government made no gesture in this regard and refused to second Madrid's urgings for an end to the war as soon as possible, for nonbelligerence meant support of the German war effort.

At the beginning of December Franco and Mussolini could agree, however, on expressing the strongest sympathy for Finland when it was suddenly invaded by the Soviet Union. The Spanish government termed this act "barbarous"—apparently much worse than Germany's invasion of Poland—and subsequently made available to the Finns a small quantity of Spanish arms. Mussolini allowed a few Italian aviators to volunteer for the Finnish air force, withdrew his ambassador from Moscow, and seemed on the verge of breaking relations with the USSR, even though Italy's public pronouncements, out of consideration for Germany, were not as strong as those of Spain. The aggression by Hitler's associate Stalin slightly tarnished German prestige in Madrid, for the Nationalist army had received more volunteers, as a proportion of population, from Finland (where many people saw the Spanish war as an analogue of the Finnish anticommunist civil war of 1917–18) than from any other non-Axis country.[18] At the same time, the lack of effective response by the Western democracies on behalf of little democratic Finland, compared with the bellicosity of their response to the invasion of Poland, would allow Franco to conclude further that the democracies lacked serious principles.

Military Planning

When the Civil War ended, Franco had approximately a million men under arms, including about 850,000 infantry—the largest military force in Spanish history, slightly greater than that of the Republicans at their high point. Given the rapidly deteriorating economic conditions, this number had to be reduced rapidly, to little more than 230,000, plus 20,000 Moroccan troops. Modern weaponry consisted largely of what the Germans and Italians had left behind. Combat potential and firepower were inadequate for hostilities against a major European power or for any period of protracted combat.

Outbreak of general war, followed by Germany's rapid victory over Poland, suddenly altered the military perspective. The war in Western Europe continued, with the possibility of major changes in the international balance of power and the weakening of Britain and France, the two powers that the new regime considered its main antagonists in Western Europe. Franco and his colleagues wanted to be prepared to take advantage of any new developments.

To consider such eventualities, Franco called the first (and secret) meeting of his new Junta de Defensa Nacional, comprising the head of the recently created Alto Estado Mayor (AEM—Supreme General Staff)[19] and the top officials of the three armed forces ministries, which convened on 31 October. The members of the junta agreed to a rapid and massive expansion of military strength to be in a position to close the Strait of Gibraltar and seize the British base there, occupy part or all of French Morocco, and dominate the waters around the Iberian peninsula as well as the shipping routes to southern and southwestern France, although they recognized that this last goal could not be attained without the full assistance of the Italian and German fleets. No timetable for action was drawn up, for that would depend on the marshaling of Spain's strength and even more on the course of the war.[20]

The junta approved a plan drawn up four days earlier that would place the Spanish army on a fully mobilized wartime footing, involving formation of fifty first-line *divisiones de asalto* for offensive warfare, totaling 450,000 men. They were to be supported by fifty second-line divisions with 450,000 more men, followed by yet another fifty third-line and weakly equipped divisions designed only for secondary defensive purposes.[21] How such a massive army was to be paid for was not explained.

Vast expansion of the army was only one part of the new military planning, for those who thought most broadly in strategic terms were the naval commanders. They had already taken the lead in initial proposals of June 1938 and April 1939, which took final form in a gigantic eleven-year naval construction program approved by the government on 8 September 1939. It proposed, startlingly, to build 4 battleships, 2 heavy and 12 light cruisers, and no fewer than 54 destroyers, 36 torpedo boats, 50 submarines, and 100 torpedo launchers within the next decade. Costs for a nearly bankrupt economy were estimated at approximately 5,500 million pesetas (ESP), to be paid at the rate of 500 million per year. It was assumed that this deliriously grandiose program would be carried out with the technological assistance and industrial investment of Italy and Germany, although, as events proved, neither showed much interest in providing support.

The original naval proposal of the preceding year was based on the assumption that Spain would join the "autarchic group," meaning the Axis, but on the basis of full "liberty" and "independence." The hope was that the weight of the new Spanish fleet might, in the right moment, become decisive. The effect would be to "break the equilibrium" between the Axis and its enemies, so that Spain would become "the key to the situation," the "arbiter of the two blocs."[22] Such an independent strategy, even though inclined toward the Axis, was not what Hitler and Mussolini had in mind, and the discovery of the Spanish plan by Italian intelligence helps to explain the lack of support for Spanish naval development.

The proposal presented by the new air force minister, General Juan Yagüe, was equally grand and unrealistic. The Civil War had left the air force 1,400 planes of a bewildering variety in all states of repair, a minimum of 250 of them completely worthless.[23] Yagüe conceived of a greatly expanded and modernized air force that would bear responsibility for "the strategic offensive missions" of Spain and guarantee "domination of the sea." This new utopian air force would take over much of the navy's responsibilities, and rested on the assumption that Spain did not need a large surface fleet (to which Franco's marginal comment was "no") but a great many submarines (to which Franco responded with a question mark) and "many planes" (to which Franco responded "yes").[24]

Though Franco was skeptical about the foregoing strategic assumptions, Yagüe presented a proposal on 3 October to increase the air force by 3,200 planes.[25] This proposal was expanded and approved officially on 21 June 1940, at the time of the fall of France, projecting no fewer than 5,000 planes at a cost of ESP6,000 million.[26] Once more German technical assistance and investment were sought, but an air ministry mission to Berlin in May had gained only the counterproposal that Germany would do little more than possibly provide financial assistance to Spain to try to buy planes from the United States, which might reduce the number that the Americans were shipping to Britain.

Planning had already begun for an assault on Gibraltar, for Franco had appointed in August 1939 a Commission for the Fortification of the Southern Frontier under an artillery general. Its task was to prepare a series of 495 fortified strong points on a 120-kilometer stretch of the Spanish coastline along the Straits and plan for conquest of the British base, though the commission soon concluded that the base was too strongly defended and would have to be reduced through a long-term siege.[27] As will be seen in the next two chapters, Franco would soon reject this conclusion.

Unsurprisingly, none of these grand designs came anywhere near completion. The army was expanded to nearly 450,000 poorly armed troops, but exceeded that number only temporarily during the emergency mobilization decreed at the time of the Allied invasion of French North Africa in November 1942.[28] Financial and industrial support was revisited in July 1940 with proposals for development of an elaborate military-industrial complex far beyond the country's possibilities, while the naval construction project was cut back to a somewhat more realistic nine light cruisers, nine destroyers, nine torpedo boats, and ten submarines, which, given Germany's total disinterest in the project, would hopefully be developed on the basis of new Italian models and Italian assistance.[29] This goal too proved unattainable. During the next five years the shrunken Spanish economy was able to construct only three submarines and six corvettes, while a fourth submarine was purchased from Germany. Two new destroyers were begun but completed only later. Naval personnel grew only slightly during World War II, from about 1,600 officers and 20,000 men in 1940 to more than 2,600 officers and 23,000 men in 1945. The air force added very few new planes and grew only from 3,800 officers and 25,000 men in 1940 to nearly 4,000 officers and almost 31,000 men by 1945.[30]

The bellicosity of Spain's military leaders was strictly a matter of circumstance. As the "phony war" dragged on through the winter of 1940, the costs and complications of these plans became increasingly evident, while resentment over the ambitions and pretensions of the FET in domestic politics continued to increase. As Javier Tusell summarizes it, "The military considered the activity of the Falangists, to the extent that it was 'revolutionary,' as proof that they differed little from the so-called 'Reds,' since they exhibited the same demagogy, tendency to ignore the law, lack of serious preparation and tendency toward abuse which they imputed to their opponents."[31] Worst of all, the Falangists thought they were the dominant elite of the new Spanish system, a position that the military arrogated for themselves, and there was further concern that the Falangists might try to stampede the country into war on Germany's side. In March 1940 the senior generals who made up the Supreme War Council therefore approved a statement prepared by the monarchist general Alfredo Kindelán, who had been head of Franco's air force during the Civil War, which declared it impossible for Spain to enter the war because of its economic deficiencies and lack of matériel. The generals also questioned the role of the FET, flatly insisting that the army was "the only instrument prepared to guide Spanish policy."[32]

Radical Falangists depended more and more on German victories abroad to enhance their position in Spain. At the close of 1939 a small group even began to plan to assassinate Franco and install a more directly fascistic Falangist regime. They found support very limited, however, and in frustration finally turned to Hans Thomsen, *Landesgruppenleiter* for the National Socialist Party among German residents in Spain. The party's foreign division sometimes sought to promote its own brand of radical foreign policy, usually without success,[33] though Nazi leaders in Morocco had been crucial middlemen in helping Franco gain direct access to Hitler in July 1936. The Falangist conspirators would later claim that Thomsen would or could offer support on terms that would have reduced Spain to the status of a satellite, or even a puppet, placing themselves under the direct orders of the Führer, and they were further discouraged by rumors that a clique of rightist dissidents was also intriguing for German assistance.[34]

Franco was more concerned about any sign of dissidence among the military than among Falangists, and his main concern was his old comrade General Juan Yagüe, the ambitious air force minister, who was overly prone to criticize the government. Yagüe's aspirations, both for himself and for his ministry, generated considerable resentment. Some of his military colleagues called him too radical, pro-Falangist and even soft on former Republican air officers, some of whom he wanted to incorporate into the air force. Others said that he was too close to the Germans, but even some top Falangists opposed him, because he acted completely independently of the party hierarchs. The fall of France in June 1940 brought matters to a head, for, while it quickly led Franco to hope to enter the war on his own terms, it also made him more wary of pro-German political intrigue. When the military governor of San Sebastián invited the new German occupation authorities at the Spanish border to a reception at which he shouted "¡Viva Hitler!," Franco quickly replaced him. On 27 June Franco called Yagüe in for a final dressing down, berated him for meddling in politics, and summarily replaced him with a more conservative general.[35] Three months earlier Agustín Muñoz Grandes, the army general who had served briefly as secretary of the FET, had resigned his post in frustration. Thus, even as German influence mounted, the two top "Falangist generals" had disappeared from government.

Economic Problems

The European conflict greatly aggravated already severe economic problems. The Civil War had destroyed approximately 9 percent of the national wealth, particularly ravaging the transport system and livestock, while production had been greatly reduced in the former Republican zone and was not easily restored. Gross domestic product was far below the prewar level. Per capita income, ESP1,033 per year in 1935, was only 729 in 1939. In 1935, 26,064 new motor vehicles had been registered, but there were only 5,784 new registrations in 1939. .

The regime's economic policy was "autarky," or self-sufficiency, paralleling the programs of the major dictatorships in Rome, Berlin, and Moscow, with priority for state-protected, state-stimulated import-substitution industry. The Spanish economy was not as dependent on exports as were some other European countries, but it was completely dependent on certain imports, such as oil, possessed little capital, and would find it very difficult to pull itself up by its bootstraps. By 1930 the percentage of the labor force in agriculture had dropped below 50 percent for the first time in Spanish history, but with a shrunken urban economy, that had changed. Autarky privileged industry, an unrealistic and counterproductive priority given existing conditions, and the European war soon produced crucial shortages. Even the FET's Junta Política recommended greater freedom for importers.[36]

The economy was desperately in need of foreign credits, yet Franco wished, for political and strategic reasons, to rely as much as possible on his Axis friends rather than on the more affluent Western democracies. Under wartime conditions, the former had little to give and their goal was more nearly exploitation than assistance. Franco, who had still not fully grasped this fact, turned down the negotiation of badly needed loans with the Western democracies in the summer of 1939, an absurd posture as far as Spain's economy was concerned, since the democracies were willing to provide assistance in order to foster better strategic relations. After the fighting began, the Anglo-French control of the seas put a different light on things. A new commercial treaty was signed with France in January 1940, followed by one with Britain in March, which granted Spain certain import and financial credits. Britain had been Spain's second largest trading partner before the Civil War, and under the new circumstances there was no genuine alternative to this agreement. It would remain crucial to the functioning of the Spanish economy throughout the war, and even after, and would have a political and strategic influence that was extremely distasteful to the Spanish government but was in the best interest of the people of Spain.[37]

The only possibility of trading with Germany during the first phase of the war lay through camouflaged commerce passing through "nonbelligerent" Italy. Soon after the beginning of 1940 a protocol was signed with

Berlin in which Spain and Germany pledged to maintain the closest trade relations that circumstances permitted, in a "spirit of mutual confidence and sincerity." Yet the Germans showed no interest in any further reduction of the Spanish war debt, in fact tending to increase their own charges, in a manner described by one Spanish official as "ruthless pricing."[38]

Mussolini, as ever, was more generous, but a naval mission to Rome that sought assistance for the proposed massive naval construction program ended in relative failure. Only very limited assistance was available and the Italians sought a commercial monopoly over the supplies involved. Even so, Franco rejected the possibility of a $200 million loan from the United States with which to purchase badly needed railroad equipment.

As the war spread into Scandinavia in April 1940, the Spanish government, in accord with its understanding with Germany, spurned a request from France that it pledge continued neutrality in the event of Italy's entrance into the war. Yet it wished to enjoy the same guarantee in reverse, and on 26 April Beigbeder asked for British and French recognition of the territorial integrity of a neutral Spain and its possessions in the event that war spread, a recognition duly granted.

Resupply of German Submarines, 1939–1942

The activity through which the Spanish government most directly, though covertly, expressed the pro-German tilt in its "benevolent neutrality" during the first phase of the war was the resupply of German submarines off three Spanish ports: Cadiz, Vigo, and Las Palmas de Gran Canaria. There had been a precedent of sorts during World War I, technically a violation of Spanish neutrality at that time, and German naval planners had begun to prepare for similar arrangements in a future war even during the 1920s, proceeding further during the Civil War. Franco had indicated willingness, and as the European war approached, the Germans had moved to put this plan into action on 30 August 1939. They were taken aback to receive a letter from Franco on 4 September canceling such arrangements on the grounds that they were too risky for Spain. Yet within four days he reversed himself and preparations moved ahead rapidly.

A total of fifty-four German merchant ships were interned in Spanish ports during the first days of the war and several of them would play key roles in resupplying submarines. The most notorious businessman in Spain, the Mallorcan wheeler-dealer Juan March, involved himself directly in these operations and in the further use of the German ships, of which he hoped to gain control as the main shareholder in Trasmediterránea, Spain's leading shipping company. In this game he played a double or even a triple role, dealing variously with the governments of Spain, Germany, and Britain, and eventually made arrangements to gain control of most of the German ships, while promising contradictory favors to all sides, even though he could not fully consummate the deal.

The resupply operations made use of interned German tanker and supply ships, with materials supplied by Spain (and transferred stocks of German torpedoes), beginning in the waters outside Cadiz on a dark night in January 1940. British intelligence, however, quickly obtained a somewhat garbled version of what was going on, and in the face of stiff British and French protests, Franco temporarily canceled further activity.

Resupplying resumed on 18 June 1940 in the dramatically altered circumstances of the fall of France and continued for the next eighteen months, until one of the resupplied submarines, *U-434*, was captured by the Royal Navy on 18 December 1941. Upon interrogation, crew members divulged information, and this time the British ambassador launched a much stiffer protest, threatening to cut off vital imports of oil and other materials. Denials were hardly effective, so the Spanish government had to suspend all operations. It informed Berlin that it hoped to be able to resume this activity in the future, when conditions became more favorable. Assistance was later provided in El Ferrol to a German submarine in May 1942 and again the following September, when the vessels suffered mechanical breakdowns, but resupply operations had come to an end. In the entire operation, at least twenty German U-boats had been serviced, some more than once.[39]

In addition, several of the nominally interned German vessels were permitted to engage in resupply operations for other kinds of German vessels on the high seas during 1942 and 1943, one of them being specially refitted in Spanish shipyards for this purpose. Other German initiatives included the purchase of a number of large Spanish fishing boats and small merchant ships to be used directly by German agents for supply purposes in the Mediterranean and Atlantic, activities that extended even into 1945. By permitting such actions and providing clandestine facilities, the Spanish government sought to make its neutrality as benevolent as possible for Germany.

PART II
"Nonbelligerence"

CHAPTER 5

Franco's Temptation
May–September 1940

Mussolini was always embarrassed by his inability to honor the Pact of Steel with Germany, and he made preparations to change his policy in the spring of 1940, even though elements of ambivalence remained. In March Hitler revealed to him part of the German planning for spring offensives in the west, and by 10 April, the second day of the German invasion of Denmark and Norway, Mussolini apparently took a preliminary decision. He hoped to carry Franco at least part of the way with him, because the place of Spain as a Mediterranean power was important to the "parallel war" that Mussolini wanted to wage in southern Europe. For five years he had been preparing Italy for war, to the extent that Italian industry and military technology permitted, and he had always insisted that war was the ultimate test of a people. Mussolini concluded that to wait on the sidelines much longer would make a travesty of Fascism.[1] On 10 April he dispatched a letter to Franco announcing his intentions, declaring that the war would conclude only after considerably more hard fighting and that Germany's defeat would bring the destruction of the Fascist regime, even if Italy did not enter the war. Thus he could not permit a war of economic attrition in which the Allies would "strangle" Germany. At this juncture he asked only for Spain's "support" (*simpatía*).[2]

Franco's position was also beginning to change slightly. Though his reply was considerably delayed, he showed clear sympathy for Mussolini's attitude, but warned of the danger of a war of attrition like World War I.

Franco stressed the importance of intervening with "a short campaign that achieves clear success," and once more asked for Italian arms. Soon afterward, the German ambassador reported that for the first time both Beigbeder and Serrano Suñer had begun to speak of the inevitability of Spain's entry into the war.[3]

Though Franco had earlier declared the neutral status of the Low Countries inviolable, he uttered no condemnation of the German invasion that began on 10 May, but increasing expressions of admiration and satisfaction. The shrewd and observant Portuguese ambassador, Pedro Teotónio Pereira, reported to his leader, António Salazar, on the 27th:

> Beyond doubt Spain continues to hate the Allies. There are few who rise above this resentment. German victories are received with joy. . . . Sadly things are working out in such a way that it is not easy to convince them that Germany will not win the war. . . . When one talks with the most reasonable people about the advantages of neutrality, they always mutter: "Yes, in fact we cannot make war, we are ill prepared." This means they do not judge the war to be infamous, but judge themselves in a bad position to take part. If Your Excellency were to ask me how many sense the dangers of German hegemony, I would have to answer they are rarer than a four-leaf clover. In such regard, the instinct for survival, Catholic faith, or Latin spirit is drowned by hatred for France and England.[4]

As the battle of France began, the Spanish ambassador in Paris, José Félix de Lequerica, became an important middleman. He had come to espouse a Nazi-style interpretation of international affairs that was more extreme than the norm among Spanish officials, agreeing with Hitler that "Jewish ferment" was to blame for a war that constituted a "crusade against the fascisms." He had developed excellent contacts with the French right, and the new French government sought to send a special envoy to Rome and Madrid to treat "Mediterranean problems," the French foreign minister even hinting that Britain might return Gibraltar to Spain to ensure the latter's neutrality.[5]

Franco, however, refused to receive a French representative, while the controlled Spanish press mounted a strong campaign in favor of Germany and against the Allies, speaking of "Spanish claims" and the importance of regaining Gibraltar. The press campaign was accompanied by a flurry of special pamphlets and demonstrations outside the French and British embassies and various consular offices. Many observers abroad nonetheless perceived Franco as a rightist who was too conservative to fit the fascist scheme, and a rumor passed into the foreign press that Hitler had assured Mussolini that he would soon see to it that Franco was replaced in Madrid by a real fascist.[6]

"Warrior and worker Italy," as the Mussolini regime headlined it, officially entered the war against France on 10 June, though its forces could make no headway against very strong French border defenses. Mussolini had dispatched a personal letter to Franco the day before, announcing Italy's imminent entry into the war. It asked for "solidarity of a moral and economic nature" and promised that in the ultimate division of the spoils Gibraltar would be returned to Spain. Franco replied immediately that Spain would now assume the status of nonbelligerence occupied by Italy for nine months, pledging to Mussolini "moral solidarity" and economic and other assistance "to the extent of our strength."[7] For his part, Serrano fired off a missive to Italy's foreign minister, a personal friend, promising that the Spanish leaders were "in absolute agreement" that Italian forces could make use of Spanish territory "not only once," as had just been requested in another letter, "but as many times as you wish," declaring that he himself hoped "to participate in the struggle as a soldier." Both Franco and Serrano made it clear that Gibraltar was merely one of a number of territorial claims that Spain would make.[8]

Nonbelligerence, officially declared by the Spanish government on 12 June, was in fact not a status recognized by international law, but a position invented and declared by Mussolini in September 1939 to express Italy's firm support for Germany even though it was not yet prepared to enter the war. It had been suggested to Serrano by Ciano as a temporary alternative for Spain and he had urged it on Franco, who quickly agreed.[9] Nonbelligerence was not in any way a form of neutrality, but rather a repudiation of neutrality in favor of a special status of pre-belligerency. (Years later, even after Franco finally announced in a speech on 1 October 1943 that Spain was returning to neutrality, there was never an official declaration repudiating nonbelligerence.)[10]

José María Doussinague, the foreign ministry official in charge of planning, soon prepared for Beigbeder a report stressing that "Italy's precedent makes clear that a declaration of nonbelligerence is a status preparatory to entering the conflict, which must inspire sharp fear in those countries that may feel threatened by our forces." This declaration would enable Spain to "ask boldly" for much more than it would otherwise have been able to obtain.[11]

Lequerica Mediates the Franco-German Armistice

The Spanish embassy was the most important one in France that represented a government not in the war but with very close relations with
Germany. On 18 June the French government therefore asked that Lequerica begin immediately to negotiate an armistice. He was already a
source of information for the Germans, since many of his reports, as well
as other information received by the Spanish government, were regularly
passed on to Berlin. During the next week Lequerica proved both zealous
and effective in pursuit of mediation, while also passing on to Hitler information as to how best to prevent the French government from fleeing
abroad in the interim. The ultimate terms of armistice amounted to German military occupation of the north and west of France, nearly 60 percent of the metropole, leaving a nominally independent regime under the
elderly Marshal Henri-Philippe Pétain in the south, its government cen-
tered in the resort town of Vichy. At that point the Popular Front parliament abruptly switched its front and voted full powers to the marshal, who
instituted an authoritarian regime more similar to that of Salazar in Portugal than to that of Franco in Spain. Hitler had sought a quick, semi-lenient
armistice to eliminate France from the war as rapidly as possible so as to
be free to concentrate on a quick decision with Great Britain as well. Thus
the new government of a rump France was allowed to retain its overseas
empire (subject to unspecified disarmament), Hitler's other great concern
being neutralization of the large French fleet. He first preferred that it be
interned in Spain, but the French authorities wangled a deal whereby a
portion would be disarmed in southern France but the main part would
still be stationed in northwest Africa. During the next four years, Lequerica
would spend as much or more time in Nazi-controlled Paris as in Vichy.
His relations with the Germans were probably the closest of those of any
ambassador to occupied France, soon earning him in Paris the sobriquet
of the "minister of the Gestapo."

An Empire in Morocco?

During the phase of German expansion and victory, most of Hitler's allies
and associates dreamed of developing parallel empires of their own. Mussolini's concept of his *guerra parallela* to achieve a new Italian empire in the
Mediterranean, Africa, and the Middle East was only the most ambitious
of these projects. Stalin busily pursued large-scale expansion in Eastern

Europe under the umbrella of Hitler's war, while Hitler himself made possible the creation of a new Greater Hungary, and Romania would soon plan to expand to the north and east at the expense of the Soviet Union. Vichy France could not expand its empire, but it emphasized the importance of its huge overseas domains to compensate for its reduced sovereignty in the metropole. Hence it was not surprising that equivalent ambitions emerged in Madrid.

The discourse of empire had developed in the Spanish regime during 1938–40 in a somewhat diffuse way, without any official declaration. The Falangist program declared that "we have a will to empire," but the Falangists had generally defined their empire as one of the spirit, a cultural and spiritual leadership of the entire Hispanic world, not a military conquest of colonies.[12] The Franco regime appropriated the imperial shield of the Holy Roman emperor Charles V and the motto *Plus ultra*, but had never officially formulated any territorial demands. Spanish nationalists had, of course, long sought the return of Gibraltar, while Franco, Beigbeder, and other military commanders with experience in Morocco had begun to think about expanding Spain's dominion there and perhaps in other parts of northwest Africa as well. This dream was not part of the Falangist program or of the ideology of the Spanish right in general (which for the most part had not in modern times been notably imperialistic), but stemmed especially from the *africanista* officers who now dominated the military (beginning with Franco and Beigbeder), combined with the Civil War victory and the power base of a thoroughly authoritarian state seemingly well placed to take advantage of a dynamic new situation. The slogan it officially adopted, *Por el imperio hacia Dios* (Through empire toward God), combined the doctrinal polarities of the regime.

Because Morocco was so close to Spain, so allegedly intertwined with Spanish history and the only part of the world where Spaniards then living had any colonial experience, the theme of Morocco became obsessive. It also reflected a peculiar kind of Spanish Islamophilia on the part of the military, who held that Spain had a special relationship with the Muslim world and would tutor Morocco into modernity. Sir Samuel Hoare, the experienced British politician and diplomat who had been dispatched to Madrid as the new ambassador to keep Spain out of the war, was astounded to be told by Beigbeder that "we Spaniards are all Moors," and reported that entire discussions with the foreign minister, a former high commissioner obsessed by the topic, were devoted to Morocco's importance to Spain.[13]

Germany had played a special outsider's role in Morocco ever since the famous landing of the gunboat at Agadir in 1905, which had precipitated the first Moroccan crisis and helped to set in motion the chain of circumstances that led to the establishment of the French and Spanish protectorates. During World War I French Morocco had been one of the targets of the German effort to inspire rebellion among the numerous Muslim possessions of the Entente powers. The Spanish zone had served as a kind of entry point for this agitation, made the easier by the pro-German attitudes of the Spanish military in command there. Efforts to inspire rebellion were repeated during the months of Franco-German war in 1939–40, the Spanish zone once more serving as a conduit. Herbert Georg Richter, the German consul in Tetuán, actively channeled money and propaganda to potential rebels in the French zone.

Successive Spanish governments had sought an expanded role for Spain in the international zone of Tangier, as well as adjustment of the southern border with the French zone, ever since France had moved forward to occupy the Beni Zerual district in the military operations of 1925. A minor change had been negotiated before the Civil War but never carried out. In addition, Mussolini had his own ambitions in northwest Africa, and before the German offensive in the west, the French had suggested to the Spanish government that the two powers jointly take charge of the international zone of Tangier to keep Italy out. Beigbeder encouraged Franco to take advantage of the imminent collapse of France to act unilaterally in Tangier, and so informed the French, who agreed to such action on 13 June, provided it be recognized that the Spanish initiative was a temporary wartime initiative.

On 14 June Spanish forces (in fact made up of native Moroccans) marched into the international zone of Tangier, an action cautiously announced as a wartime administrative measure. Since Britain, France, and Italy—three of the zone's participating powers—were at war with each other, Spanish occupation was supposed to guarantee its neutrality, a move also accepted by Britain, which formally reserved its full rights for the future.[14]

Later, after negotiations with Germany had advanced, on 3 November Spanish authorities dissolved the international commission that administered Tangier, as well as the city's legislative assembly. For the remainder of the war it would be governed by a Spanish general and a cadre of Spanish administrators and clerks and for practical purposes coordinated with the Spanish Protectorate.[15] In March 1941 a German consulate general was established in the city; it became a hotbed of espionage and grew increasingly active after the Allied landing in northwest Africa in November 1942.

Beigbeder, the main promoter of expansion in Morocco, had already taken up the concept of a direct invasion of the French Protectorate in military conversations in April, and on 19 June Varela, the army minister, received instructions from Franco, according to which "with the greatest secrecy the possibility of carrying out an offensive in some part of the French protectorate must be studied."[16] This was not to be understood as a declaration of war, but as a response to French defeat in which Spain would need to intervene to maintain order.[17] Sizable military reinforcements were rushed to the Spanish Protectorate, while crowds of *pieds noirs* (as the French called European inhabitants of the African protectorates) of Spanish origin demonstrated in Oran to demand the annexation of northwest Algeria by Spain and Spanish agents strove to foment unrest against French dominion in Morocco. The German consul in Tetuán, capital of the Spanish Protectorate, informed Berlin that the Spanish hoped to occupy the entire French zone, depose the sultan, replace him with the caliph of the Spanish protectorate, and declare Morocco's autonomy under Spanish protection on behalf of an artificially contrived and controlled Moroccan nationalism, a political ploy that had its roots in the Civil War years.

Spain's forces in Morocco were nonetheless far inferior to those of France, and hence in no position to act when French resistance collapsed. Hitler, preoccupied with other matters, allowed the new Vichy regime to maintain virtually its full military establishment in northwest Africa, where its air force even increased as hundreds of French planes fled the metropole during the collapse. Thenceforward, Germany would remain the arbiter of the situation. Hitler indicated that he did not support any change in Morocco at that time, while Lequerica's involvement in completing the armistice made any unilateral Spanish military move even more awkward. The idea of military action was canceled within a matter of days, a relief to Richter, the German consul, who had reported that "one cannot describe the Spanish military organization here in bad enough terms."[18] Expansion with German support would nonetheless remain a major goal for the next two years.[19] The programmatic development of Spanish claims began only at this time and took full published form during 1941–42, as the opportunities were passing; they will be treated in Chapter 7.

Formation of Pétain's Vichy regime in southern France added a new

German satellite government to Western Europe, which sought good relations with a Spanish regime supported by Germany but was equally determined to maintain the overseas empire as the main remaining guarantor of France's greatly shrunken prestige. Cultural relations between Vichy and Madrid were good but political relations were more distant. When the first Vichy ambassador, François Piétri, arrived in Madrid at the close of 1940, he was received coldly and Franco used the occasion to denounce "the grave and notorious injustices" that Spain had received at the hands of France. The Vichy position seems to have been to concede Tangier to Spain but to ask for compensation in the form of Spain's cession of its enclave of Ifni, farther south on the French coast.[20]

Madrid also sought Britain's support, and during 1940–42 London paid a certain vague lip service to Spanish claims on the greater share of Morocco, though without making any specific commitment. As Tusell observes, given the perpetual food deficit in the generally poverty-stricken Spanish zone, it was supplied adequately during the war thanks ultimately to the imports that Britain allowed into the main part of Morocco.[21]

Hoare's Mission to Madrid: Diplomacy and Bribery on a Grand Scale

As France began to collapse, Winston Churchill's government placed considerable emphasis on maintaining Spain's neutrality. Britain's policy of equidistance during the Civil War had been based on the consideration that though neither wartime Spanish regime was very savory, Franco's was fundamentally Catholic and conservative and in the future would serve only Spanish, not German, interests. This was certainly the image that Franco had striven to give London. As a strongly conservative anticommunist (indeed, in 1918–19 one of the first and perhaps the most important of major Western anticommunists), Churchill had at first strongly favored the Nationalists over the revolutionary Republicans. Within six months, however, after the escalation of German military support to Franco and the increased Axis presence in the Nationalist zone, Churchill began to change his position for geostrategic reasons. He once put it that as a Spaniard he would support Franco, but as an Englishman he must support the Republic to counterbalance Germany; yet he remained conflicted, not wishing to see Spain under Soviet hegemony. By February 1937 he was recommending new sources of military equipment to the Republican government, but in April 1937 he said in the House of Commons, "I will not pretend that if I had to choose between Communism and Nazism, I would choose Communism."[22] In his memoirs he declared himself neutral in the Spanish war, not being able to decide which outcome might be worse, and did not oppose the British nonintervention policy.

In 1940 Churchill desperately hoped that his Conservative colleagues' calculations in respect to Franco had been correct, though they now looked less certain. Sir Samuel Hoare, the new ambassador to Madrid, was a diplomat of great experience, a veteran Conservative leader strongly identified with prewar appeasement policy. Since he was part of the "peace party" led by Sir Neville Chamberlain and the British foreign minister, Lord Halifax, which still remained strong in London, Churchill wanted to remove him from England and give him an opportunity to appease Franco while keeping him out of the war. As it turned out, Hoare proved an excellent choice, conservative enough to get along reasonably well with Franco while loyally executing British policy. In the long run, his mission worked out better than might have been expected, yet the situation seemed so threatening when he was initially sent on 29 May that for some time a British airplane was maintained for his personal use at Barajas airport in the event that a sudden Spanish declaration of war might require an abrupt exit. Hoare would ultimately prove adroit in managing the carrot and stick, particularly British naval control of vital Spanish imports, to dissuade Franco from ever taking the final plunge into war.[23]

Hoare's first success was to establish friendly relations with Beigbeder, at that point known as an ardent Germanophile. The Spanish foreign minister was unusual among the military in Franco's government because of his love of the exotic, not merely of Morocco but of northern Europe as well. He and Hoare were soon spending a good deal of time in conversation, something noted with great irritation by the Germans, who also became aware of his long-time liaison with a certain "Miss Fox," a young woman who allegedly worked for British intelligence.[24]

British efforts did not rely merely on firm, careful diplomacy or even the most stringent use of the import card alone, but quickly resorted to one of the oldest of indirect methods: large-scale bribery of Spanish military leaders. This scheme was designed by Alan Hillgarth, naval attaché and representative of British naval intelligence in Madrid from 1939 to 1945. Its machinations were referred to as the "chivalry of St. George," from the image of the legendary patron saint of England slaying the dragon on the old gold guineas that the British had used in earlier times to subsidize military allies on the continent. The scheme was approved at the end of June and relied on the ultrapragmatic (and often duplicitous) multimillionaire Juan March (who was also promising his services to Germany in return for control of the German ships interned in Spain), who laundered the money so as to make it appear that it came from Spanish financial and industrial enterprises. March seems to have carried out his task faithfully, and over the next months a large group of high-ranking generals and other senior military officials would be selected who, in return for pledging to discourage Spain's entry into the war, would receive large payments in pesetas (though the money would in fact be drawn secretly from an account in the Swiss Bank Corporation in New York). The source of funding was apparently disguised as a group of wealthy Spanish bankers and commercial and industrial enterprises that, for a combination of patriotic and business motives, sought to keep Spain out of the war. This ploy made it easier for senior military figures to accept the money with relatively good conscience.

During the course of the war no less than $13 million in bribes was paid, a huge sum for that time. The most favored recipient was Antonio Aranda, whom Franco had come to distrust but who was the Spanish general most active in political conversations, both with his colleagues and later with foreign, principally Allied, representatives. He received the lion's share of the bribes, possibly in the neighborhood of $2 million, arguably the biggest single bribe ever paid to any military figure in world history. Altogether, some thirty military commanders received payments, especially Luis Orgaz Yoldi, captain general of Barcelona in 1939–40 and then high commissioner in Morocco from 1941 to 1945. The names of most of the rest do not appear in surviving documentation, though suspicion has naturally fallen on a sizable number of generals who would in later months (though not in the summer and early autumn of 1940) advise against entry in the war and finally in September 1943 respectfully ask Franco to restore the monarchy.[25]

How much effect did the bribery scheme have? It did not by itself determine the issue of whether or not Spain would enter the war, but it inevitably influenced the situation, as Serrano Suñer would later bitterly comment to the Germans regarding certain Spanish military contacts with Great Britain. Before Mussolini invaded Greece in October 1940, he had been bribing high-ranking Greek generals in the expectation that the money would make them more amenable to an Italian takeover, but when the time came, it seemed to have no effect in weakening Greek resistance. Though the bribery did encourage some of the generals to take a more neutralist position, one effect was to improve greatly their economic situation, and thus in the long term make them less fascist on the one hand but more conservative and *franquista* on the other, more determined to support a Franco regime that would maintain their privileged status, so long as it did not plunge Spain into war.[26]

German Negotiations Begin

As French military resistance collapsed, pro-German hysteria and expansionist sentiment seemed to mushroom among the sectors of society that supported the regime, including more than a few converted Republicans. This enthusiasm was led by Franco himself. As a result of German assistance during the Civil War and the smashing victories of Hitler's armies, he had developed a thoroughly romantic concept of the Führer as an "extraordinary man," as he put it to the Portuguese ambassador.[27] Franco saw Hitler as an instrument of divine destiny, who would somehow right the wrongs of the deserving nations of Europe, of which Spain stood at the forefront. Since in historical hindsight this notion seems ludicrous, it should be remembered that Nazi and Fascist propaganda was very active in fostering the image of the Axis states as new kinds of powers that would break up the dominance of the Western liberal and Soviet empires. Hitler had been redrawing the map of much of central and east-central Europe, while, ever since World War I, German imperialism had made a special appeal to the Islamic world, and both Italy and Germany would be very active in this regard during World War II.[28] Such themes were expounded even more widely and vigorous by the Axis's Asian ally, Japan. The consequence was a thoroughly distorted idea of the Third Reich in Madrid.[29]

Franco prepared a personal letter to Hitler on 3 June, soon after it became clear that France was likely to suffer a disastrous defeat but one week before Mussolini entered the war. He hailed the French campaign as "the greatest battle of history," declaring that "my people feel [this campaign] as their own," since in Spain "your soldiers participated with ours in war against the same enemies, though then they were camouflaged."[30] For the first time, Franco gratuitously identified the Civil War with Hitler's aggression in World War II.

He went on to lament that the effects of the Civil War and revolution had left Spain in a gravely weakened condition, to which was added the need to defend its far-flung archipelagos, which had to be protected from "the eternal enemy of our Fatherland," but "I scarcely need to assure you how great is my desire not to remain apart from your concerns and how

great would be my satisfaction in offering you the services that you consider most important." This initial fishing expedition to align Spain more
fully with the Reich was entrusted to General Juan Vigón, head of the
newly created Alto Estado Mayor (Supreme General Staff), who arrived in
Germany on 11 June but was not received by the Führer at his headquarters in Belgium until the 16th.

Vigón's task was to explain Spain's military problems to Hitler, from
whom he requested new arms shipments to enable the Spanish armed
forces to guard against an Allied landing in Portugal or Morocco, since one
of Franco's fears was that the United States might suddenly intervene to
prevent British and French defeat. Vigón also made reference to the plans
Franco already had under way to seize Gibraltar.

Hitler's response was comparatively laconic, since his attention was
riveted on the French campaign. He praised Spain's occupation of Tangier
two days earlier and told Vigón that he intended to establish direct land
communication with Spain in his peace terms, that he would permit no
landing in Portugal, and that, should there be one in Spanish Morocco, he
would provide assistance, while Spain's seizure of Gibraltar would be the
ideal solution for Germany. Vigón then announced for the first time what
would become the leitmotiv of negotiations with Germany for the next
year: Spain's desire to take control of all Morocco. Hitler was noncommit-
tal, deferring the matter to further negotiations with Mussolini.[31]

Beigbeder followed up with a letter of 19 June sent through the Spanish embassies to both Hitler and Mussolini, which for the first time presented the full Spanish shopping list. The Spanish government wished to
seize Gibraltar, gain all of Morocco, incorporate the Oran district of northwest Algeria, and obtain a very broad territorial extension of the Spanish
Sahara and of Spanish Equatorial Guinea, which would permit access to
black laborers, "whom we lack altogether." In return Spain would prepare
to enter the war on Germany's side, provided that Germany guarantee
sizable military and economic assistance. Germany did not respond for a
full week, and then only to acknowledge tersely that note had been duly
taken. Germany's interest was in new trade discussions that would permit
it to regain its dominant position in Spanish foreign commerce, inter-
rupted by the war.[32] As Norman Goda has put it, "a high-priced alliance
with a destitute country for the capture of a distant British naval base
seemed unnecessary."[33] On 1 July Hitler even told the Italian ambassador
that a more active role by Spain, such as advancing farther in Morocco,
would merely provoke the British to intervene and extend the war, though

at the same time acknowledged that the Spanish could be useful in driving the British from Gibraltar, which he saw as a necessary goal.

By this point the armistice negotiations with France, initiated by Lequerica, were coming to a climax, and Hitler was preoccupied with their final terms and with bringing the war with Britain to a successful conclusion as soon as possible. Since the British had now lost all the equipment of their main field army in the evacuation from Dunkirk and were deserted by their major ally, Hitler considered them already beaten. Thus he made the mistake of not offering direct peace terms to the British, arrogantly waiting for them to come to him. Had he offered the London government generous terms, they might well have been accepted, for Churchill had not yet established such firm leadership as he would later enjoy. In the wake of the French disaster, the British prime minister had to admit to his cabinet that truly generous peace terms might be desirable, but gained agreement for the moment that Britain would fight on to avoid major concessions and await developments. Hitler was correct to the extent that in such circumstances the weaker power usually took the initiative in suing for peace, but his failure to present an attractive offer to London was one of his most signal failures in diplomacy and enabled Churchill to play effectively off this ambiguity. The British foreign office even put out several vague peace feelers on its own, but Hitler's lack of an effective response enabled Churchill to keep his cabinet in line.[34] It was Churchill's achievement that he made it necessary for Hitler to come to him, rather than vice versa, as would have been normal, and he also tried to control British diplomatic contacts as much as possible, so that it would have been necessary for the Führer to make the most direct appeal. Hitler refused to do so, merely calling for peace in abstract terms in a speech of 19 July, without any direct gesture or concrete details.

The matter nonetheless remained uncertain during the first half of the summer, and the Spanish military commanders, reluctant to see Spain involved in war before the fall of France, had generally changed tack and were eager to be on the winning side. Whatever effect the bribery had would not begin to take effect for several months. This very situation, however, exacerbated the political tensions within Spain, for Falangist ambitions rose dramatically. Serrano Suñer was at the center of the Falangist pressure, seeing himself either as new foreign minister or perhaps even prime minister (president of government). Falangist propaganda and behavior became increasingly aggressive and overweening, as Falangists picked physical quarrels with monarchist conservatives to demonstrate their own toughness. These developments were alarming to the military, who saw Serrano rising to ever greater prominence.

During July the Spanish government did all it could to support a maneuver designed by the Germans to lure the former British king, the Duke of Windsor, from Lisbon to Spain. Windsor was known for his Germanophilia and opposition to the Churchill government, so that at this juncture Ribbentrop saw him as a key figure who might be used to negotiate peace. Windsor and his wife had passed through Madrid briefly before spending approximately a month in Lisbon. Since the Germans saw Beigbeder as now falling under the influence of Hoare, they used Serrano Suñer as the key organizer of their plot to lure Windsor back into Spain, where he might be held as a sort of hostage to negotiate peace. Spanish authorities cooperated extensively, but the duke could not be lured back, partly for fear of becoming a hostage, and on 1 August he finally departed Lisbon, however distastefully, to take up the post that Churchill had assigned him as governor of the Bahamas.[35]

Franco seemed certain of his course, declaring in a major speech on 18 July, fourth anniversary of the military revolt, that Spain was building "an empire" and that the Spanish crusade had been "the first battle of the European [new] order." Opportunistic bellicosity had become so great that he even boasted that "Spain has two million warriors ready to fight in defense of our rights."[36] This boast was echoed by his controlled press, and at that point his government severed relations with Chile, led by a Popular Front coalition and the nearest thing to a European-type leftist government in Latin America.

At the same time an effort was made to extend Spanish influence over Portugal, with which a treaty of friendship and nonaggression had been signed at the conclusion of the Civil War. This treaty had been fully acceptable to Portugal's traditional ally, Great Britain, which, after the conclusion of the Spanish conflict, desired of Portugal simply that it remain neutral in the looming European war and do what it could to exercise a moderating effect on Spain.

The neutrality of the Portuguese government, led by António de Oliveira Salazar, prime minister and quasi-dictator, was genuine, perhaps even more so than Britain might have preferred. Portuguese leaders remembered the German scheme to partition the Portuguese empire before World War I and, unlike their Spanish counterparts, had few illusions about their place in a Europe dominated by Hitler. Pedro Teotónio Pereira, the ambassador, was personally and politically close to Salazar, and was appalled by the Naziphilia rampant in Madrid, as he was appalled by the mood of extremism and megalomania generally apparent in Spanish ruling circles.

The initiative was taken not by the foreign minister but by Serrano, another indication of his ambition and power. On 26 June he held a secret meeting with Pereira on the outskirts of Madrid to tell him that Hitler would no longer tolerate the independent existence of an ally of Britain on the continent and that Spain might soon be forced to permit the passage of German troops to invade Portugal, as it had permitted the passage of Napoleon's troops in 1807. On his own initiative, Serrano strongly suggested that Portugal should make a gesture that would enable Spain to protect it, clearly implying a move toward making a satellite of the neighboring country.

Pereira hastily returned to Lisbon, where he found Salazar conscious of facing "consistent and total peril on every side," as Salazar put it. The Portuguese leaders were skilled negotiators, however, and neatly maneuvered their way out of Serrano's trap. In consultation with London, Salazar reached an understanding with the Spanish ambassador, who was none other than Franco's more practical and bon vivant older brother Nicolás. This agreement took the form of an additional protocol to the existing treaty, whereby Lisbon and Madrid pledged to consult each other to safeguard their mutual interests in the face of any threat to their security or independence. The Caudillo accepted this protocol as adequate recognition, to the chagrin of the frustrated Serrano.[37]

Hitler's Emerging Design

Reconstruction of the thinking and planning of Adolf Hitler has been one of the more elaborate games played by historians of twentieth-century Europe. On the one hand there is an enormous amount of data stemming from the government of the Third Reich, but on the other Hitler kept no diary and left almost no personal papers. Thus there are many thousands of documents side by side with massive gaps. Moreover, key aspects of Hitler's thinking have seemed so simplistic that there has been a consistent tendency of the sort pointed out by Karl-Dietrich Bracher, when he warned against the *Unterschätzung* or underestimation of Hitler's ability and calculations.[38]

The fall of France placed Hitler in an unprecedented situation that opened a whole series of new questions, for some of which his own thinking was not adequately prepared. He had not intended to involve Germany in a major war as early as 1939, though he had always believed that France must be neutralized before he could eventually concentrate on his major objective, the Soviet Union. Three lightning campaigns had given him control of most of Central and Western Europe within less than a year, enormously accelerating (though also complicating) his strategic designs, and therefore as early as 31 July he gave orders to begin preliminary planning for a possible major assault on the Soviet Union the following year. Given the prospect of a temporary return to peace and the uncertainty of his most immediate plans, at one point he ordered partial demobilization of the German army to save money.

Hitler faced dilemmas. The first was Britain's refusal to make peace, leaving him still in a war he had never directly desired. Hence the desirability of reaching a quick armistice with France on relatively lenient terms, leaving the Vichy regime in charge of a huge overseas empire, primarily in northwest and west Africa, and a sizable colonial military establishment. Another problem was the concern over the American response to Britain's predicament, not because the United States posed the slightest direct military threat at that moment but because of the potential reach of Roosevelt's increasingly active strategic operations in the Atlantic. This problem in turn opened another that Hitler had not even considered at the time of the armistice, the issue of establishing a strategic position for Germany itself in northwest Africa and the eastern Atlantic.[39] Just how Hitler could deal with all these problems at the same time led to a series of sometimes apparently contradictory observations, decisions, and initiatives between July and October.

Hitler had at least five options: (1) Operation Sea Lion, the invasion of England, a very risky undertaking that could destroy the myth of German invincibility; (2) an aerial assault on England, for which the Luftwaffe was hardly prepared; (3) a strategic siege, for which Hitler didn't have the submarines; (4) a Mediterranean strategy, even though that might not be decisive by itself; (5) a grand strategic alliance against Great Britain, which he began with Japan on 27 September and tried for a while to extend to the Soviet Union.[40] In the background there loomed always the major challenge—the decisive war in the east to destroy the Soviet Union, at that time still a friendly associate power. During July Hitler marked time, temporarily ordering resumption of his ambitious naval construction program (the Z-Plan), as well as renewed priority for developing the long-range Amerikabomber.[41] There was no sign of any particular interest in Spain.[42]

For most of July Hitler continued to believe that Britain would soon be forced to make peace, even while a general aerial assault began to get under way and preparations began for an amphibious invasion. The disarming of the French forces in North Africa was left as an Italian initiative, which, as it turned out, would never be consummated. German contingency planners toyed with operations against Egypt and Syria, as well as the possibility of establishing a forward east Atlantic base in the Azores, though Portugal was neutral. More concretely, Hitler looked toward the expansion of Germany's strategic range by requesting of Vichy the establishment of several German airbases near Casablanca, which was refused. This frustration and his continuing problems led him to begin to consider the Spanish option more seriously, for the first time, at the end of the month. By the time of a major meeting with his military chiefs on 31 July, his thinking began to take clearer form. Britain would have to be knocked out of the war either by invasion or by aerial attack, but a broader goal was to think of beginning the assault on the Soviet Union in the spring of 1941, though this was not yet an absolutely firm plan. In the meantime, Spain must be brought into the war.

Why was Spanish belligerence now seen as desirable? First, it would be another blow to Great Britain, making possible the seizure of Gibraltar and closing of direct British access to the Mediterranean, which might finally tilt the balance toward British capitulation. Beyond that, it would improve Germany's strategic situation in northern and western Africa, the French empire, and, farther yet, the east Atlantic islands. It would round off Hitler's domination of the continent and make it possible for Germany to occupy forward positions militarily that might have the effect of preempting any American grand strategy in support of Britain, always a worry in the back of Hitler's mind, and then even provide the first steps toward a strategic advance that would place Germany in a bolder position later to strike south and west, though this was not an immediate priority. During the course of August, as he turned over strategic ploys in his mind, Hitler developed an increasing interest in the possibility of acquiring bases in some or all of the east Atlantic island groups—the Canaries, the Azores, and Cape Verde.

But if Spain entered the war and Gibraltar fell, how decisive would this be? The closing of the Straits would doom the British base at Malta, a great boon for Axis shipping in the Mediterranean, and would be another political and psychological blow to the Churchill government. It would not, however, immediately affect the British position in the Middle East, which was supplied not by the dangerous Mediterranean route but by convoys that went all the way around Africa. The crucial naval route for Britain was the North Atlantic, and Germany lacked the submarines to close that route. Though beleaguered, the Churchill government seemed to be gaining strength, and Spain's entry into the war would not necessarily have been enough to bring the peace faction to power. Moreover, major continuing assistance would be required to keep Spain in the war. Should the conflict continue very long, Germany would not be able to provide it. The cost of keeping Spain in the war would then become even greater than required for Italy, though at this point, revelation of the degree of Italy's dependence was still a few months way. Hitler was not concentrating his forces but adopting a peripheral strategy that sought to give a tactical or operational answer to a strategic problem. Spanish involvement would pose a whole new set of issues, but would not necessarily respond to Hitler's main concern.[43]

Admiral Wilhelm Canaris, head of the German Abwehr (military intelligence), who had long played a major role in German activities in Spain, was sent to Madrid to discuss with the Spanish authorities the entry of camouflaged German troops to attack Gibraltar,[44] and on 2 August Joachim von Ribbentrop, Hitler's foreign minister, telegraphed Stohrer that the German government wanted to arrange Spain's entry into the war as soon as possible. A small German military mission, already sent to the peninsula, rapidly surveyed the situation and came to pessimistic conclusions: Spanish plans for the assault on Gibraltar were totally inadequate, the Spanish forces were woefully equipped and supplied, and Spanish officers generally were not well trained and prepared to execute offensive plans with dispatch and efficiency. Spanish troops scored well with the Germans only in terms of combative spirit.[45] Conquest of the Rock would have to be carried out by German forces.

The Ministry of Economics in Madrid drew up a list of the economic assistance that Spain would need to enter the war and survive a total British blockade. The volume was enormous: 400,000 tons of gasoline, 500,000 tons of coal and other energy supplies, 200,000 tons of wheat, 100,000 tons of cottons, and large amounts of fertilizer, as well as lesser amounts of a long list of other items.[46]

Berlin made no immediate reply, and on 15 August Franco wrote to Mussolini to ask for his assistance in obtaining the necessary support from Hitler. The tone of this missive was quite different from his more cautious letter of two months earlier. Franco now declared flatly that "ever since the beginning of the present war it has been our intention to make every effort to intervene at the moment when a favorable occasion arises which our means might exploit." Germany's dramatic victory in the west had now made this possible, except for the grave shortages from which Spain suffered. Franco therefore asked for Mussolini's support, so that Spain might occupy its place in the struggle against "our common enemies."[47] Mussolini had ambitions of his own in northwest Africa, but had urged Franco to enter the war and pledged support, though it could be no more than political, not military. He viewed the utility of Spain's entry in much the same terms, observing to King Victor Emanuel that, given its military weakness, Spain's participation would be more significant morally than militarily.[48]

After a quick trip to Berlin, Stohrer returned to Madrid to draw up a sketch of a treaty that could seal the terms of Spain's entry. The resulting protocol, prepared by 27 August, included Spain's takeover of Gibraltar and Tangier, as well as recognition of its claims to all of Morocco and the Oran district, though the latter points would be dependent on final peace terms with France. In equatorial Africa, however, there were no concessions, and the Spanish island of Fernando Poo was to pass to Germany in return for other compensation. In addition, there would be German naval bases in postwar Morocco and a dominant economic position for Germany there, particularly with regard to raw materials. Military and economic aid would be provided subject to further military conversations, the war debt fully settled, mineral concessions given to Germany in Morocco and a new cultural treaty signed to replace the one not completed the year before. These terms, however, were not exactly the ones that Franco had in mind, and would require further negotiation.[49]

After Britain and the United States announced their destroyers-for-bases deal on 3 September, in which the latter gave the British a sizable number of overage destroyers for antisubmarine duty in return for eight naval military bases on British possessions in the western hemisphere, ranging from Newfoundland to the British Guianas, Hitler had to give further attention to the Atlantic. The German naval command, particularly, was concerned about America's naval power and possible entry into the war. This possibility led Hitler to consider further strategic advance into the Spanish and Portuguese Atlantic islands to counter the United States, but also to calculate that the position of Vichy France in northwest Africa might have to be respected for the time being, as the simplest way to guarantee the loyalty and security of the region, though that in turn would mean a check to Spanish aspirations.

Ribbentrop had advanced the strategic design of a bloc or alliance of all European states friendly to Germany that would totally stabilize the situation in Europe and Africa under German hegemony, with Japan an associate. The Ribbentrop plan would accentuate the isolation of Britain, help to deter the United States, and, if the Soviet Union would not participate on German terms, menace the Soviet Union from two fronts. If it did not induce Britain to make peace, it would neutralize Britain strategically and make it difficult for the United States to enter the war, while creating a viable strategic framework within which the Soviet Union could be attacked without the danger of a two-front war.[50]

Intensified negotiations with Japan in efforts to restrain the United States led to the fateful signature of the Tripartite Pact between Germany, Italy, and Japan on 27 September 1940. Unlike the earlier Pact of Steel between Italy and Germany, which Italy had not at first been able to live up to, this was not a complete military alliance but only a defensive pact, pledging all three powers to come to the aid of any of them that should be attacked by another power with which it was not presently at war. This pact was aimed directly at the United States; from Hitler's point of view it would provide assistance for Germany should the United States enter the European war, while encouraging Japan to take whatever action it cared to take in the Pacific. There was of course the danger that Japanese aggression might drag Germany into war against the United States, though the terms did not in fact require Germany to declare war in such a circumstance. Hitler seems to have been most interested in the pact's short-term deterrent effect on the United States, an influence that he exaggerated in a way typical of his uncertain grasp of grand strategy.

Admiral Erich Raeder, the German naval commander, and other top naval officers were alarmed at Hitler's multiple and dilettantish strategic conceptions, and in conferences of 6 and 26 September tried to persuade the Führer to adopt a more coherent southern strategy that would give the Axis total control of the Mediterranean. Only limited forces would have been needed at that time to drive the British out of Egypt and seize the Suez Canal as well as Palestine and Syria. This move would cripple the British strategic position in the Middle East and place the Axis powers in a position to seize gigantic petroleum reserves at a time when much Islamic opinion was favorable to them. Whatever was needed in French North Africa could then be easily occupied, facilitating any action against Gibraltar and placing Germany in a position to establish a base in the Canaries. Turkey and Iran would be brought within the German sphere at the same time that Germany was becoming dominant in the Balkans. The Soviet oil fields in the Caucasus would become vulnerable from the south, so that the strategic situation of the Soviet Union would be seriously compromised. And all this could be done at minimal military cost, with no real risk of failure, as in a more expansive venture farther afield. Germany would achieve an impregnable military situation, and Britain would have little alternative to making peace.[51]

This grand strategy conflicted with Hitler's original sphere-of-influence design, for the main part of the Mediterranean and north Africa had been consigned to Mussolini's initiative. Hitler was willing to commit German forces to North Africa to guarantee rapid seizure of the Suez Canal, but Mussolini was emphatic in pursuing his parallel war independently, with Italian forces alone. Therefore, perhaps even against his better judgment, Hitler continued to respect the Italian sphere and focused on the air war against Britain and the attack on Gibraltar, impatient to draw Spain into his scheme despite the fuzzy strategy involved. Even if Gibraltar were seized, the consequences would not be decisive, so long as Britain itself remained secure and held on to its position in the Middle East. The naval command was interested in a Gibraltar operation only as part of a coherent southern strategy, but Hitler had more narrow goals in mind. He seemed to aim primarily only at securing an eastern Atlantic position based on the Straits, Spain's islands, and its Moroccan bases, still leaving Vichy nominally in control of northwest Africa, even though being progressively disarmed under the armistice terms. The drive toward the Middle East was being left in the increasingly feeble hands of Mussolini.

Serrano Suñer's Mission to Berlin

Though the attitude within the Spanish regime generally was very positive toward entering the war, the most important single promoter of this policy, and of a more fascist orientation generally, was Serrano Suñer, whom the German ambassador would soon be able to describe as the most hated man in Spain. Arrogant and almost incredibly overweening, puffed up with his self-importance, the epitome of a certain kind of fascist style, the *cuñadísimo*,[52] as he was known, aspired to become the master of Spanish politics and government, perhaps like Salazar in Portugal or Mussolini in Italy, neither of whom was chief of state. The press, which Serrano controlled, pompously referred to him as the "minister president," since he was also president of the FET's Junta Política, thus imputing to him a title and status superior to those of other cabinet ministers. Franco for some time trusted him implicitly and relied on his intelligence and political knowledge, though by the spring of 1941 he would begin to gauge more accurately the extent of Serrano's ambition and also his unpopularity.

Though renowned for bouts of ill health, mainly due to a stomach ulcer, during his years in government, Serrano would long outlive his more illustrious brother-in-law, becoming the last surviving major European figure of the World War II era, finally dying at the age of 102 in 2003. After Franco's death he devoted himself extensively to rewriting and fictionalizing his political biography,[53] denigrating the role and skills of his brother-in-law (whose lesser degree of education and sophistication he had always looked down on), even though Franco possessed rather more political instinct and prudence. Serrano generally stressed the agreement between the two of them on major issues, but sometimes could not resist the temptation to present Franco as a sort of simpleton eager to plunge Spain into war against the wiser counsel of his brother-in-law, when the truth was more nearly the reverse.[54]

It had been Serrano's ambition to head a delegation to Berlin ever since July, Beigbeder being viewed with increasing suspicion by the Germans because of his friendly conversations with Hoare. Economic talks between the two governments had begun in mid-August, and the German ambassador assured Ribbentrop that Franco was now ready to commit himself even to a long war, as the Spanish government decreed two-year universal military service on 20 August. Soon after the beginning of September Madrid proposed that Serrano be invited to Berlin for formal discussions, and Hitler agreed. Exclusion of the foreign minister was justified on the grounds that the leadership of the interior minister would excite less hostility on the part of the British, perpetually in control of Spanish imports.

Serrano arrived in the German capital with a large delegation on 16 September, though he had never formally conducted a diplomatic negotiation before, and was whisked off to a three-hour private conversation with Ribbentrop. He emphasized the importance to Spain of Morocco as vital space on its southern frontier (Spain's lebensraum, as he put it) and made the attractive offer of a special system of commerce, which would provide the access to Spanish raw materials that Hitler sought.

Serrano also referred specially to Spain's tutelary role regarding a semi-satellite Portugal, saying that in looking at the map of Europe, one could not avoid the realization that geographically speaking Portugal really had no right to exist. He observed, however, that the recent protocol signed with Lisbon constituted a rapprochement by Portugal with the authoritarian states. If at that time Germany and Spain had made a joint diplomatic effort, Portugal could perhaps have been drawn entirely over to the side of the authoritarian states. He underlined once more how easy it was to influence Portugal by means of joint pressure on the part of Germany and Spain.[55]

Ribbentrop agreed to Spanish territorial demands in principle and then dropped his bombshell. Along with taking over all of central Africa after the war (and presumably excluding Spain from that area), Germany would ask for the cession of one of the Canary islands as a military base, as well as for the establishment of bases at Agadir and Mogador in a subsequently Spanish Morocco. Serrano was apparently stunned and responded that Spain could not cede sovereign national territory. Hitler adopted a softer tone with him in a conversation on the morrow, but repeated that Germany needed one of the Canaries as well as bases in Morocco. The Spanish interior minister did not try to refute the Führer as he had Ribbentrop, but also advanced the need for adjustment of the Pyrenees border that would restore the land taken by France in 1659.

The second interview with Ribbentrop on 17 September went more badly yet. Ribbentrop was now less forthcoming on Spain's economic demands, repeated the request for one of the Canaries, and denied any possibility of expansion for Spain in west-central Africa, all of which Germany would want for itself, apparently including Spain's small existing possessions there. Serrano repeated that Spain could not cede sovereign territory and generously suggested that Hitler grab one of the Madeira islands from Portugal, after all a British ally.[56]

At this point, the conversations having stalled, the German authorities extended Serrano's visit for several more days, enabling him to contact Franco and giving Ribbentrop time for a quick trip to Rome. Mussolini voiced no objection to the cession of Morocco and the Oran district to Spain, but he said he preferred a three-power alliance, that would include Italy, to an exclusive arrangement between Berlin and Madrid.[57]

While Serrano and his entourage were taken on a tour of the recent battlefields, a rapid exchange of letters between Hitler and Franco took place, without resolving the points at issue. Hitler emphasized the need for a series of advanced bases, not merely or primarily to fend off the British but to cope with the increasing strategic scope of a rearming United States. Franco replied that among allies, the military base of one could be used by all, and that in time of war Germany could make use of sovereign Spanish bases, without overly emphasizing his point that such bases would need to remain under Spanish control.

Serrano subsequently published Franco's responses to his personal messages during these negotiations, carefully omitting any of his own, which, as Tusell says, were probably too compromising to correspond to his subsequently sanitized position. Franco still assumed that Spain would enter the war, declaring that "the alliance is not in doubt." As he wrote to Serrano on the 24th, "We must guarantee the future with a pact [*protocolizar el futuro*], and though there is no doubt as to our decision, we have to be very careful about the details of an agreement and the obligations of each side." He repeated to Serrano earlier instructions to emphasize the identity between the Civil War and the European war, the former forming a clear precedent for the latter, something that Serrano then publicly did in an interview with the official Nazi daily, *Die Völkische Beobachter*. He insisted that the Spanish conflict had been a struggle against the capitalism of the great democracies, parallel to the Axis powers' line on their war against the capitalist plutocracies. Franco ingenuously suggested that Ribbentrop might not represent the Führer's true thinking (given Franco's exalted opinion of Hitler), and suggested that Spain might be willing to grant Germany a base at Mogador, as well as temporarily rented facilities at Agadir, but that cession of any of the Canaries was out of the question. Franco also seemed encouraged by Hitler's letter, which was more generous in its suggestion of economic assistance than Ribbentrop and other officials had been. Moreover, he expressed confidence that the German aerial assault on Britain, now completing its second month, would eventually force Britain to make peace on German terms.[58] His official letter of reply to Hitler on the 24th dealt mainly with military issues, though he specifically rejected the proposal of German enclaves in a future Spanish Morocco.[59]

More specifically, the negotiating strategy that Franco outlined to Serrano involved three steps or phases. First would come the signing of an initial political protocol between Madrid and Berlin, specifying common interests and goals. This protocol would be followed by detailed agreements on the nature and amount of German economic and military assistance, followed finally by the signature of a formal military alliance, the immediate prelude to Spain's entry into the war. At this point, both Franco and Hitler seemed confident that somehow all difficulties could be worked out, though for Franco a basic problem was whether he would be entering a long war or a short one.

The final conversation between Ribbentrop and Serrano was scarcely any more satisfactory than the first. The German foreign minister proposed a ten-year tripartite treaty, including Italy, with a secret clause specifying the date of Spain's entry into the war, as well as the cession of Morocco, but insisted on bases for Germany. Serrano again rejected any cession in the Canaries, Morocco, or equatorial Africa, but stressed that in wartime Germany could use all Spanish facilities in Morocco, and suggested broad economic facilities for Germany there. In a farewell conversation, Hitler repeated the need for island bases, while Serrano seems to have made himself ridiculous by suggesting that the Cape Verde islands could be protected by artillery from the mainland (in fact 500 kilometers distant) and again referring limply to the absurdity of an independent Portugal, though disclaiming any wish to seize it. On these inconclusive notes the Berlin conversations ended, with agreement that matters would finally be settled at a personal meeting of Hitler and Franco, which Franco suggested might take place at the Spanish border.[60] The only formal understandings that the Germans gave the Spanish delegation consisted of three protocols on economic relations, but just before departure Serrano presented the text of a political protocol, which might constitute the first formal agreement, stating the terms on which Spain would enter a tripartite pact with Germany and Italy.[61]

Though perhaps not quite so totally ingenuous as before the Berlin discussions, the Spanish leaders showed no diminution in their enthusiasm for the Reich and their expectations about entering the war, still hoping to negotiate the details. The Germans reacted more negatively, having formed what would be their lasting impression of what they called the Jesuitical Serrano. The day after Serrano left, Hitler received Ciano and complained that his experience with the Spanish had been that they always asked for more and more, in return for which they pledged their friendship. He complained that they tried to make him feel like a Jew haggling over the most sacred possessions. Immediately afterward, Serrano appeared in Rome, where in turn he complained of the Germans, while Mussolini showed little enthusiasm for Spain's early entrance in the war, probably because it might reduce Italy's role, though otherwise his attitude merely showed good sense.

More important was the attempted landing by the Royal Navy and De

Gaulle's Free French at Dakar, in French West Africa, between 23 and 25 September, while Serrano was still in Berlin. The Vichy forces fought off a weak attack, but the whole operation gave Hitler second thoughts about handing over any French African territory to Spain. Since he resolutely resisted any full southern strategy of his own, for the time being he relied on Vichy to defend the Axis perimeter in northwest Africa. Thus when he met Mussolini at the Brenner Pass on 4 October he declared that giving the Spanish any French territory at the present time was out of the question, just as he had told Ciano a few days earlier. Mussolini agreed that this matter would have to await the final peace, especially because, as the Italians saw, Hitler clearly had ambitions of his own in Morocco. Negotiations with the Spanish government now slowed, at least momentarily.

When one focuses on Hitler's rhetoric, as Norman Goda says, it is easy to overlook how much Franco and Serrano were offering Germany. They were willing to enter the war directly, guaranteeing the conquest of Gibraltar and elimination of the British from the western Mediterranean, a secondary goal of Hitler's but nonetheless desirable. In addition, they offered major economic concessions—all French mining businesses in French Morocco and joint ownership of nearly a score of French and British mining companies in Spain, plus all production not needed for the Spanish economy. They were willing to compromise on Spain's own economic demands and make delimited arrangements for two German bases in Morocco. These bargaining chips were at least plausible, though whether the entry on Germany's side of a country as weak economically and militarily was really desirable was another story.[62]

What would make a deal impossible was Germany's territorial demands—a Canary island, the cession of Spanish Equatorial Guinea and Fernando Poo—and the unfeasibility of stripping Vichy of Morocco so long as the war lasted. Though for some time the Spanish leaders would fail to understand it, the kind of deal that they expected was already becoming impossible.

CHAPTER **6**

The Meeting at Hendaye and Its Aftermath

On 16 October Franco named Serrano Suñer foreign minister in place of Beigbeder, whom Serrano had been keeping under police surveillance. Though Serrano had very little experience in foreign affairs, his role was now more prominent than ever, for the Ministry of the Interior remained under his assistant minister, enabling Serrano to keep a hand in that key area as well. Moreover, the army officer who served as minister of commerce and industry was replaced by Serrano's Falangist associate Demetrio Carceller. All these developments served to signal that the Spanish government was becoming increasingly fascist, and Serrano announced as much when he took over the Foreign Ministry. He would have liked to appoint more Falangists to important posts in the ministry or the diplomatic service, yet could make only limited changes because of the lack of qualified personnel. The panegyrics over Serrano reached their height as the press praised his "extraordinary intelligence" with the grandiosity typical of the dictatorships of that era.

Serrano's first public pronouncements hailed a new activist era for Spanish foreign policy, in which "we cannot waste a minute, for this is a matter of Spain's destiny," promising to expand "the place of Spain on the world map and the implementation of its rights."[1] He made no effort to adopt a stance of neutrality with the British and American representatives, expressing to the American ambassador, Alexander Weddell, Spain's "moral solidarity" with the Axis. His declaration that Berlin had not pressured him to enter the war was, as Javier Tusell observes, true in one sense, since the Spanish government had freely offered participation as a bargaining chip. Though by this point Germany had already lost the aerial Battle of Britain (something of which Serrano seems to have been unaware, despite reports from London that his government passed on to Berlin), he offered his services to Hoare as mediator for peace terms with Germany.[2]

Serrano's arrogance knew few bounds, and resentment against him, already considerable, mounted steadily. His behavior was often as undiplomatic as that of Ribbentrop, and during the following year personal relations with the American ambassador were virtually broken off, while Hoare required the utmost self-control to deal with him. One of his keenest critics was the Portuguese ambassador, Pedro Teotónio Pereira, who wrote that his combination of excitability, arrogance, harshness, megalomania, fascist taste for flashy uniforms, and lack of scruples could lead Spain to a catastrophe. Pereira reported that during one conversation he could barely resist the temptation to smash him in the face, and was well aware of Serrano's resentment of and possible designs on Portugal.[3]

Serrano had proposed to give the Spanish state a more organized one-party structure through a set of constitutional laws, which Franco, however, had rejected, because the Caudillo did not wish to limit his personal power or commit himself more explicitly to any fully developed state model. Eventually Serrano would begin to criticize Franco himself and become somewhat more abrupt in his dealings with him. He aspired to be the real political leader of a more genuinely fascist Spain, but despite all his overweening pride and arrogance, he held no independent power whatever, as he later would become mortifyingly aware.

For some time Serrano was so impressed by clippings from his controlled press and his conviction of his own genius that he was often inattentive, not appearing at the foreign ministry for days at a time. Such behavior was due not to laziness but to a combination of arrogance, multiple responsibilities (he continued to devote much time to domestic politics) minor health problems, and fairly elaborate social activity. Long weekend hunting parties were a special feature of the high life of the new regime. Even the Italian ambassador told him that he should devote more time to foreign affairs, as Serrano tried, in his own way, to dominate many of the key aspects of Spanish government.

In mid-October Hitler, Ribbentrop, Franco, and Serrano—though in differing ways—all believed that the differences aired in Berlin could be worked out and that Spain's entry into the war could still be arranged. Of the five strategies that had been open to Hitler the preceding summer, three had been ruled out. There would be no invasion of Britain and the aerial offensive was ending in failure. Hitler was indeed pursuing a blockade strategy against Britain, though the means to implement it remained uncertain, while a broader Mediterranean strategy, never a priority, was resisted by Mussolini, determined to pursue his "parallel war" without German interference. Hitler was more interested than ever in developing an African and eastern Atlantic strategy (a southwestern as opposed to a more general southern strategy). This was where Spain came in, though the strategy was at first conceived partly as a defensive scheme to bar the route to American expansion while Hitler liquidated the European war. The key issue was ultimately not Great Britain but the Soviet Union, which Hitler could deal with either by expanding the present relationship into a broader alliance, a possibility he would continue to toy with through the end of November, or simply by direct conquest, which had always been his preferred goal. Planning for an invasion was already under way, though no final decision had been made, and Hitler was still willing to consider alternatives.

By the time of his meeting with Mussolini at the Brenner Pass on 4 October, Hitler had already formed the outline of his southwestern strategy. Italy would continue to play an exclusive role in the main part of the south, but the Vichy regime would temporarily have an important place in the defense of French Africa, and Spain would be brought into the war to facilitate the conquest of Gibraltar, a stronger German position in northern Morocco, the preparation of German bases first in the Canaries and later in southern Morocco, and also a position from which to control Portugal, even if the Portuguese islands could not yet be occupied. The competing interests of Spain and France would have to be finessed for the time being by means of what the chief of the German staff, General Franz Halder, had termed in his diary the day before as a "a great deception,"[4] though as it would turn out, Hitler made no attempt at direct deception, believing that neither Vichy nor Madrid would be able to keep secrets. For the moment, Vichy France would not be threatened with significant colonial losses, though with the understanding that at the end of the war there would be minor colonial adjustments at the expense of Great Britain. The Spanish leaders would simply have to be more realistic, contenting themselves with Gibraltar and a limited advance in Morocco at war's end. Hitler seemed confident that Spain's ambitions could be reduced to terms more commensurate with that country's extremely limited means.[5] To this end, the German government drew up the draft of a very detailed economic agreement concerning items of interest to Germany in Spain and Morocco.[6]

The news from Madrid was seemingly reassuring. Serrano (at that moment not yet foreign minister) wrote Ribbentrop on 10 October that he had thoroughly discussed the points of the Berlin meeting with Franco, and that the Spanish government would soon be sending new economic proposals to facilitate its entry into the war, as well as possible terms for a ten-year alliance. Two more divisions of infantry were dispatched to the Spanish protectorate, bringing its components to seven full divisions, a huge component for such a small, barren territory. Similarly, what little Spain could spare—four batteries of artillery, machine guns, more obsolescent aircraft—was sent to beef up the defenses of the Canaries, all this to make Spain's southern perimeter as resistant as possible to British counteraction once Spain had entered the war. Franco was probably also hoping to be able to advance in Morocco as soon as possible.[7]

All the while British policy clung tenaciously to its goal of keeping Spain out of the war. Churchill was not at all averse to playing the Morocco card, letting it be known to the Spanish government that Britain would look favorably on a major adjustment of Morocco's border that would enhance Spain's status. Madrid then passed the news on to Berlin to encourage concessions. On the eve of the meeting between Franco and Hitler, Churchill declared encouragingly that he looked "forward to seeing [Spain] take her rightful place . . . as a great Mediterranean power."[8]

On 20 October Hitler set out by rail on his southwestern tour to talk successively with Pétain, Franco, and Mussolini, first meeting with Pétain in central France and then arriving at Hendaye, on the Spanish border, on the afternoon of the 23rd for his one and only meeting with Franco. This visit later became perhaps the most mythified event in the Caudillo's very long career, the occasion on which supposedly he had outtalked Hitler, turning the conversational tables on the loquacious Führer, adroitly frustrating him so as to keep Spain out of the war.[9]

The mythification begins with the explanation of the late arrival of the Spanish delegation, supposedly engineered by Franco to keep Hitler waiting for him. In fact, it was due simply to the disastrous state of the rickety Spanish railroads and was a source of embarrassment and irritation to Franco. The element of truth in the myth is that, whereas Hitler was expecting an easy ratification of his prior understanding, Franco had come for serious negotiation, since, as he wrote in his preparatory notes that morning, "Spain cannot enter just for fun [*por gusto*]."[10] The terms had to be guaranteed in advance. He began what became a three-hour conversation by thanking Hitler warmly for all that Germany had done for Spain and by affirming Spain's sincere desire to participate in the war on Germany's side, although he apparently did not reiterate Serrano's emphasis on the importance of Spain's participation in completing the political transformation of the Spanish regime.[11]

Hitler then launched his standard monologue, declaring Great Britain already beaten but still dangerous on the periphery, where, with possible American intervention, the main trouble spots were Africa and the Atlantic islands. Hence the crucial importance of the Gibraltar operation. A "broad front" of all the continental powers, including Vichy, must be organized against the Anglo-American world. The French must not be discouraged by having severe territorial losses in Africa imposed on them at this time; such matters would be worked out for Spain at the end of the war.[12]

What was unusual about this encounter was that Franco did much of the talking. In later years, Parkinson's disease made Franco appear stiff and increasingly terse, an effect that has served to obscure the fact that for most of his life he was extremely talkative. His long discourse on the history of Spain in Morocco, interspersed with the manifold petty digressions that formed the typical substance of his private conversation, bored Hitler to tears. Franco went on and on about his personal military experiences and many petty facets of Moroccan history and of military affairs; Hitler later said that he would rather have three or four teeth pulled than sit through another conversation with Franco.[13]

Franco's goal was to outline Spain's needs, but here it was the Führer who refused to engage in more serious discussion. Hitler declared that Spain's most pressing wants would eventually be satisfied and that he did not wish to consider specific territorial concessions, for he was now unwilling to grant any so long as the war lasted. Similarly, there was no further discussion of the cession to Germany of one of the Canary islands. Franco observed that he did not think the war was nearly over, but that, if necessary, Britain might continue the war from Canada with American assistance. When he made the sensible observation that seizure of the Suez Canal would be very important, Hitler rejected the point, saying that Gibraltar was considerably more significant as the gateway to western Africa and the Atlantic. Not surprisingly, Franco had no opportunity to make use of the lengthy position paper prepared by Juan Fontán, governor of Spanish Equatorial Guinea, which claimed for Spain a huge territory in west-central Africa.[14] Finally, the long talk ended rather abruptly, followed by a cordial but rather austere dinner in Hitler's restaurant car (soup, fish, fruit salad) and a final late-evening conversation. The newsreel photos taken later that night reveal a smug and self-satisfied Caudillo, perhaps overly conscious of the historical significance of his meeting with the conqueror of so much of Europe. At that point Hitler still expected and Franco still hoped to gain essentially what they wanted.

When Ribbentrop and Serrano met separately, the German foreign minister presented the draft of a secret protocol for Serrano to sign, pledging Spain's imminent entry into the war without setting a date, promising German assistance without citing details, and committing the Spanish government to subsequent signature of the Tripartite Pact, as well as expressing "conformity" with the Pact of Steel military alliance between Germany and Italy. According to Article 5, Spain was to receive Gibraltar and unspecified French African territory, though only to the extent that France could be compensated elsewhere, presumably at the expense of Britain. Spain would thus be totally committed, Hitler would get everything he wanted, and the Spanish would get very little. Economic assistance would be agreed upon through future consultation.[15] The mythic version of the meeting holds that the original text gave Germany the power to determine the date of Spain's entry and that the Spanish leaders changed it to specify a date agreed upon by mutual consultation, but there is no proof that the Germans had originally made such a stipulation.[16]

The protocol was a shock to Serrano and, a few hours later, to Franco. Serrano suggested to Ribbentrop that the concessions to Spain could be specified in a subsequent letter from Hitler to Franco. The Spanish leaders then presented a supplementary protocol on the following morning dealing with economic relations, but referring also to "the French Zone of Morocco, which is later to belong to Spain."[17] Because of that terminology, it was never accepted by the Germans. The only change in the protocol that they would make merely reiterated the vague promise that Spain would obtain further territorial compensation in Africa so long as France could be adequately compensated and German and Italian interests protected. The final version of the protocol was prepared only on 4 November, after the Italian government added further clauses involving respect for Italian interests. It declared:

Hendaye, 23 October 1940
The Italian, German, and Spanish governments have agreed as follows:

1. The exchange of views between the Führer of the German Reich and the head of the Spanish state, following conversations between the Duce and the Führer and among the foreign ministers of the three countries in Rome and Berlin, has clarified the present position of the three countries toward each other as well as the questions implicit in waging the war and affecting general policy.

2. Spain declares its readiness to accede to the Tripartite Pact concluded 27 September 1940 among Italy, Germany, and Japan and for this purpose to sign, on a date to be set by the four powers jointly, an appropriate protocol regarding the actual accession.

3. By the present protocol Spain declares its accession to the Treaty of Friendship and Alliance between Italy and Germany and the related Secret Supplementary Protocol of 22 May 1939.

4. In fulfillment of its obligations as an ally, Spain will intervene in the present war of the Axis Powers against England after they have provided it with the military support necessary for its preparedness, at a time to be set by common agreement of the three powers, taking into account military preparations to be decided upon. Germany will grant economic aid to Spain by supplying it with food and raw materials, so as to meet the needs of the Spanish people and the requirements of the war.

5. In addition to the reincorporation of Gibraltar into Spain the Axis Powers state that in principle they are ready to see to it, in accordance with a general settlement that is to be established in Africa and that must be put into effect after the defeat of England, that Spain receives territories in Africa to the same extent as France can be compensated, by assigning to the latter other territories of equal value in Africa, but with German and Italian claims against France remaining unaffected. [A typewritten footnote on the document at this point reads: "The original text reads: 'thus protecting any German claims to be made against France,' and was corrected as above by the hand of His Excellency Minister Ciano."]

6. The present protocol shall be strictly secret, and those present undertake to preserve its strict secrecy, unless by common agreement they decide to publish it.

Done in three original texts in the Italian, German, and Spanish languages.[18]

This final revised text was dispatched from Berlin in triplicate on 6 November and, contrary to mythic versions that circulated later in Spain, Serrano signed three copies in Madrid, two of which were returned by special courier, as reported by Stohrer on 11 November.[19]

Hitler had apparently gotten what he wanted, and Spain had pledged itself to become a full military partner of the Axis and a complete participant in what soon would be called the Second World War. The protocol seemed to be decisive, yet that would prove not to be the case. Franco then quickly wrote another letter to Hitler, along the lines of Serrano's suggestion, specifying once more Spain's claims to all of Morocco and the Oran district, to which Hitler paid not the slightest attention, assuming that he had gotten all that he needed.[20]

The Spanish Plan to Seize Gibraltar

Another source of disagreement, never fully discussed, was the differing concepts of the Gibraltar operation. The German evaluation of the combat readiness of Spanish forces was extremely low and Hitler not surprisingly was firm in his contention that Gibraltar would have to be seized by German forces, with the Spanish playing no more than a very secondary supporting role. For Franco, conversely, it was a point of both honor and national interest that Spanish forces carry out the operation, with the Germans in the role of assistants.

Planning of a sort for this operation had begun in the summer of 1939, as noted earlier, and when German specialists entered Spain during the summer and autumn of 1940 to undertake precise assessments, they found that Spain had already completed a great deal of preliminary work of military photography and technical measurements. The Spanish plan, "Operación C," was presented to Franco in October, either just before or just after the meeting at Hendaye. It proposed a lengthy three-phase artillery bombardment, followed by aerial attacks from 100 combat planes. In the final phase, Spanish infantry would attack behind a curtain of tanks and under the cover of a dense smokescreen, led by General Agustín Muñoz Grandes, commander of the local military district. The use of Spain's reserves of poison gas was also discussed. The Germans would not be directly involved, though in the event of a strong counterattack in the Straits by the Royal Navy, the Luftwaffe would be asked to provide concerted assistance. Apparently at the time of the signing of the additional protocol between Spain and Portugal in the summer of 1940, Salazar had given his oral agreement that Portugal would remain neutral in the event of such an operation.[21]

On 12 November the General Staff presented to Franco a plan for carrying out the full mobilization initially discussed thirteen months earlier, which would more than double the size of the army to fifty divisions and nearly 900,000 men. Weapons would apparently have to be supplied by Germany and Italy. This plan was to be followed by the massive mining of the Straits to close them to the Royal Navy.[22]

When could such an operation take place? Franco had emphasized to Hitler the importance of a vigorous North African offensive that could seize Egypt and the Suez canal. Though Hitler had brushed off this suggestion at Hendaye, the most important sector of the Italian army was committed to an offensive against the British position in Egypt. Admiral Salvador Moreno, the minister of the navy, submitted a report on 11 November, prepared by Captain Luis Carrero Blanco, which stressed that taking the Suez canal would be the blow to convert the Mediterranean into an Axis lake, making possible large-scale Axis supplies to Spain and enabling the latter to undertake the Gibraltar operation. So long as the war continued, however, the Royal Navy would completely isolate the Canaries and Equatorial Guinea. This fact would initially have to be accepted, for any attempt by the weak Spanish navy to defend the islands would mean that the Spanish ships would simply be blown out of the water, "exactly as in the case of Santiago de Cuba [in 1898]."[23] In subsequent discussions Franco would reiterate the importance of Spanish forces' undertaking the Gibraltar operation, though this problem, never resolved, was not the chief reason why the Spanish government later chose not to honor the Hendaye protocol.

Invasion of Portugal?

On 28 October, four days after leaving Hendaye, Hitler was in Florence to report the outcome to Mussolini, who casually informed him that earlier that day Italian troops had launched an invasion of Greece from bases in Italian Albania. This was part of Mussolini's ongoing policy of parallel war, whereby he sought to carve out his own sphere of conquest in southern Europe and the Mediterranean. German intelligence had long since informed Hitler, who took the news with equanimity. It was a complication that did nothing to improve Germany's situation, but he trusted that Mussolini could pull it off.

In Madrid Franco and Serrano also took note. Franco could not at all be so complacent about the outcome of the meeting at Hendaye as Hitler, but, like Mussolini, hoped yet to be able to go forward with his concept of national interest. Hopefully Hitler would still be forthcoming. In the meantime, there was the possibility that Spain might act on its own, like Italy. Hitler had vetoed an invasion of French Morocco; moreover, the French forces there were numerous and much better armed than the Spanish.

Franco's chief goal was Gibraltar, but the Spanish could act on this goal only when there was complete agreement with Germany and massive assistance had been provided.

There remained Portugal, which might now become Spain's Greece, its army small and weak. In Berlin Serrano Suñer had hinted several times about his designs on Portugal. There is no record of what was said about the country at Hendaye, which may not have been much, but Hitler may have alluded to the ongoing German military plans, which did not necessarily involve the invasion of Portugal but did assign German units at least temporarily to screen the frontier. Despite its special relationship with Spain, Portugal was an ally of Britain and there was no German veto against its invasion. Moreover, its forces were so weak that it could conceivably be conquered by Spain's own arms.

Judging from the "Estudio para el Plan de Campaña No. 1," prepared by the Supreme General Staff (AEM) in December (no specific date),[24] Franco ordered his staff officers to draw up a contingency plan for the invasion of Portugal, which might either precede, accompany, or follow the operation against Gibraltar. Conceivably this might be part of Franco's own parallel war, equivalent to Mussolini's invasion of Greece.

The "Estudio" referred to Portugal as "the enemy," and began with a brief study of various invasions of Portugal from Spain throughout history, including the French campaigns of 1807–10. It emphasized the central invasion route between the Duero and the Guadiana rivers, for "Lisbon being the general center of resistance, there is no doubt that the decisive invasions will always be those aimed at dominating the central region," with the Alemtejo offering the most favorable terrain. The calculation was that army troops in mainland Portugal numbered no more than 20,000, though with time Portugal could mobilize 300,000 men, of whom half might be placed on the front lines.

"The conquest of Portugal" should be considered only in terms of broader strategy, for, given the country's "intimate connection with England, it represents one aspect of the struggle against the latter nation." It involved the problem of defending the Portuguese coastline, as well as communications with the islands and Morocco, from British reprisals, and, if Spain acted on its own, there was also the problem of how to "conquer, or at least neutralize, the Gibraltar region." The AEM judged that the Spanish arsenal was adequate in machine guns and light mortars, but its main artillery was "very worn out," inadequate even for defense, only four regiments of low-caliber anti-aircraft guns were available, "by any standard inadequate." The quantity of ammunition might be sufficient, but the last field exercises demonstrated that "there are many defects in the cartridges." There were not enough horses, radios, field tents, or even blankets. The army had 12,000 trucks of varying quality, but no reserves or replacements for the four meager tank regiments. Thus "according to the study by the Ministry of the Army for carrying out an arms plan, the calculation is that until 1946 the necessary equipment for all the units formed" "by the first doubling of the permanent divisions" would not be completely available.

Fifteen days would be needed for mobilization, after which each of the three battalions of the Motorized Regiment could provide the means to move one infantry division into combat. All this was discouraging, but the AEM observed that "the negative and painful impression stemming from the above has been set aside in the preparation of the study-proposal for a plan of operations, on the supposition that even if this had to be carried out under present conditions, we would receive material assistance from the group of allied countries [meaning primarily Germany], since in today's world wars are carried out by groups of nations." In toto, an invasion would employ ten infantry divisions, the one existing cavalry division, the four armored regiments, and various smaller units, supported by one division in reserve, two divisions masking Gibraltar, and the seven existing divisions in Morocco.

This force would be at least twice the size of what Portugal could put in the field, even though Portugal would declare general mobilization "and the inhabitants will be hostile to us," to put it mildly. The goal would be to reach Lisbon and the Atlantic coast as soon as possible, so that for the entire operation it would be desirable to expand the Spanish army in the peninsula to approximately twenty-five divisions; in addition to the eleven to be employed in the invasion, five more could support the operation, while another nine remained in reserve and on the defensive. Speed and a rapid decision would be key factors, for a fully mobilized Portuguese army might field fifteen divisions (though where they would find the weapons was not explained).

A brisk invasion should be carried out in two phases, the second of which would trigger the broader Spanish mobilization (though how all this was to be done rapidly was not clear). The two main invasion routes would be westward from Ciudad Rodrigo through the Mondego valley and from Extremadura, accompanied by two diversionary attacks, one in the north and the other in the far south. No exact timetable was proposed, though speed was emphasized, which would permit "resistance to be rapidly overcome." It was nonetheless calculated that Lisbon could be taken only during the second and broader phase of operations, so the two diversionary attacks would also take place in that phase. In addition, "a project to neutralize or occupy Gibraltar" was being drawn up, which at minimum would require two divisions, since no concrete military agreement had been reached with Germany.

One of the worst problems was that "the immediate consequence of war with England will be total loss of Atlantic naval communications and loss of contact with the Canaries, the Sahara and Guinea." The United States could be expected to assist England, while "the action that our surface fleet could take" against British shipping was "nil." A pious but unconvincing hope was expressed that British forces might be kept at bay by the meager Spanish submarine fleet and the small obsolescent air force.[25] But these units had little in the way of parts and supplies, only enough for an initial attack. Since the British could rapidly reinforce Portugal, "our allies" would need to provide Spain with no fewer than six bomber groups, three fighter groups, and three reconnaissance squadrons.

A vital priority would be to "ensure the protection of communications between the peninsula and the Moroccan protectorate, keeping in mind that submarines can always cross the Straits." What Spain currently imported from the western hemisphere would have to be provided by rail from Germany or from the Black Sea, though the latter route would probably be cut by the British Mediterranean fleet. Somehow that fleet would have to be neutralized, though the means were not specified.

This whole dubious enterprise could be placed in motion by an order from Franco that would declare that "the delicate situation of Portugal" was being exploited by British expansionism, requiring him to "prepare the invasion of Portugal." The operation would begin "with a surprise attack, immediately followed by mass action," though preceded by "an ultimatum to Portugal."

Was this a serious plan? All military establishments draw up contingency plans, but a major difference between the five British contingency plans for Spain and the three later drawn up by Germany was that all of them were essentially defensive operations, to be triggered only by an enemy incursion into Spain, whereas the Spanish plan contemplated a gratuitous act of aggression. The time taken to prepare this 130-page study seems to have taken care of any possible execution of it, for by December it was clear that Mussolini's invasion of Greece was a total disaster and that, at least for the moment, Spain's entry into the war must be placed on hold.

Hitler's Plans Advance

Franco had made a poor impression on Hitler, to whom he seemed petty and provincial, a rigid and narrow-minded chatterbox "with the manners of a sergeant major." "With me such a man would not even have become a *Kreisleiter* [local leader]."[26] In one sense, this was not new; foreigners had never been impressed by Franco, and the first German and Italian representatives had reported back to Rome and Berlin that Franco was a disappointment in appearance and manner and did not look like a great leader.

As Goebbels wrote in his diary:

> The Führer's opinion of Spain and Franco is not high. A lot of noise, but very little action. No substance. In any case, quite unprepared for war. . . .
>
> Landesgruppenleiter Thomsen of the AO [Nazi Party abroad] in Spain reports conditions there simply unbelievable. Franco and Suner [sic] are completely the prisoners of the clerical faction, totally unpopular, no attempt made to deal with social problems, enormous confusion, the Falange totally without influence. All areas of the economy in ruins, a lot of grandiose posturing, but nothing behind it. Germany is looked upon as a wonderland.[27]

Hitler was used to dealing with mediocrities and considered the meeting a success. The Spanish were signing the protocol and would enter the war; Gibraltar would soon be taken. Franco had been a disappointment on the personal level, but had not yet become the "Latin charlatan" that Hitler would later dub him. Moreover, Hitler was apparently reassured by the receipt of Franco's letter on 1 November, which repeated all the Spanish requests and reiterated his intention to enter the war.[28] Hitler largely ignored the former and accepted the latter. He later told Mussolini that Spain would receive "a substantial enlargement of Spanish Morocco," but that no concrete promises could be made at that time.[29] He planned a meeting of the three dictators in Florence that would announce Spain's signing of the Tripartite Pact and its formal entry into the Rome-Berlin Axis.

German military plans were developing rapidly. On 16 October, a week before the meeting, General Franz Halder, the chief of staff, had detailed troop requirements for the Gibraltar operation. It would involve one regular infantry regiment, a mountain infantry regiment, twenty-six medium and heavy artillery battalions, eight supporting specialty battalions of various kinds, and various logistical units. Within another week, this projection had been increased to include an armored division to guard against a British landing, and stood at a total of 65,383 men, with sizable supply requirements. By early November, the key units were undergoing special mountain-assault training at a camp in France.[30]

At his staff conference on 4 November, Hitler was more expansive. Though his main interest was becoming directed toward an eastern offensive, he was determined to seize Gibraltar as soon as possible. If Franco delayed very long, Germany would force his hand. Hitler now talked of building German air bases in Spain and of occupying the Canaries, Azores, and Cape Verdes. For a brief period he seems to have pondered a broad southern strategy, bailing out Mussolini with an offensive against Greece and committing the troops in North Africa necessary to take the Suez Canal.[31]

On 12 November he signed Military Directive no. 18, outlining his military strategy at that moment. Preparations for an offensive against the Soviet Union would continue, while dispositions for Operation Sea Lion, the assault on England, should not be abandoned. Some German forces would have to be sent to North Africa to assist the Italian drive into Egypt, which had bogged down, while German forces would also have to invade Greece, which had stymied Mussolini. The main part of these instructions, however, treated the Gibraltar operation, now code-named Felix, in detail. Four phases were specified: (a) initial reconnaissance; (b) German air attacks on Gibraltar, accompanied by the movement of army units into Spain; (c) the direct assault; and (d) consolidation of the conquest and the closing of the Straits. Two days later, the plans became yet more elaborate: in addition to assigning the SS Totenkopf panzer division to guard against any British landing, a second armored division and a motorized infantry division would enter Spain to screen Portugal or, if necessary, to invade that country, though an invasion was a complication to be avoided if at all possible.[32] Very little military assistance was expected from Spanish forces, a German staff report concluding that "Spain's economic readiness will not permit it to sustain a war by its own means, even for a brief period of time."[33]

That month Hitler would induce Slovakia, Hungary, and Romania to join the Tripartite Pact, and Hitler wanted Spanish participation as soon as possible. He believed that he had created a united front in western continental Europe, with Germany, Italy, and Spain as military allies and Vichy France associated with them. This arrangement settled territorial disputes in Africa for the moment, he thought (though in fact it had resolved little), and when the Soviet foreign minister, Viacheslav Molotov, arrived on 12 November for a crucial series of talks, Hitler informed him that he had just established his form of Monroe Doctrine for the main parts of Europe and

Africa. The Soviet Union was then given one last chance to join a "continental bloc" on German terms.

To expedite the military process, Ciano and Serrano Suñer were then summoned to meet with Hitler at Berchtesgaden on 18 November. The mood in Madrid, however, was shifting. Economic problems had reached a point of crisis, with grave shortages, the situation having deteriorated considerably during the autumn. Most of the military commanders were losing their enthusiasm, and probably not merely because of the British bribes. The proposal of the naval leaders, presented on 11 November, recommended postponing action until the Axis had seized Suez. José Enrique Varela, the minister of the army, was one of the least Germanophile generals and strongly anti-Falangist, and recommended that the trip to Germany be postponed, but it was not thought possible to defy Hitler in such a manner.[34]

At Berchtesgaden Hitler initiated another monologue, stressing the importance of rapid action by Spain. According to the German account, "Serrano Suñer replied," with seeming ingenuousness, "that he had not known exactly what the Führer wanted to talk to him about, and therefore could present only his personal opinion on the questions raised." Serrano emphasized the gravity of Spain's economic problems and the need for major German assistance, while stressing that Spain had had to seek more provisions from Britain and the United States simply to avoid famine. He also admitted that there was a problem of "public morale" and that "a war was always unpopular." Serrano declared that "after their return from Hendaye, he and Franco had been quite depressed and worried about the secret protocol, because Spain's demands were treated, especially in article 5, in a form that was much too vague." He dwelt once more on Spanish demands in Morocco, to which Hitler responded that Germany did not want Morocco for itself and that he would soon reply to Franco's letter in that regard. "When Germany had reached her goal, Spain could be satisfied in Morocco." The official German memorandum then observed that "these statements of the Führer and of the Reich Foreign Minister on Gibraltar and Morocco appeared to dispel the objections raised by Serrano Suñer. At any rate he did not revert to them later, but turned to the subject of the military commissions." The conference ended with a discussion of military assistance for the defense of the Canaries, to which Hitler attached great importance, and the kind of artillery that would be installed at Gibraltar. Serrano pledged to import as much grain as possible in order to prepare Spain. A conversation between Serrano and Ribbentrop followed the same lines, with the Spaniard pointing out all the weaknesses and problems to be resolved, avoiding concrete discussion of the date for entering the war.[35] The highly pro-Nazi Spanish ambassador, General Eugenio Espinosa de los Monteros, later criticized Serrano for contradicting Ribbentrop on the question of the productive potential of the United States, for Serrano "refuted Minister von Ribbentrop in a manner certainly not pleasant for the latter, telling him that according to absolutely reliable reports the data about the United States were accurate, and I must say that I heard this with astonishment, since it was absolutely unnecessary to bring up anything so disagreeable."[36]

In subsequent discussions during the next two weeks with German diplomats in Madrid, these matters were further debated, the Spanish officials protesting that they were proceeding as rapidly as they could. They also requested that Hitler send a senior military officer to discuss the numerous military problems involved. On 5 December, Stohrer reported with satisfaction that the Spanish government had also consented to the clandestine refueling of German destroyers "by German tankers in remote bays along the Spanish coast."[37]

Another special meeting of the Supreme War Council was held in December, though the exact date cannot be determined. It was apparently a somber gathering that discussed the manifold problems and weaknesses facing both the military and the country, and there clearly was no enthusiasm for any early entry into the war.[38]

As German preparations proceeded apace, Hitler convened what would be his last major Gibraltar planning session on 5 December. Since he wished the assault to take place no later than early February and the German leaders calculated that the buildup would take twenty-five days, Spain being relatively large and its transport system very poor, German troops would have to enter Spain starting on 10 January. The entire operation should have been fully consolidated and nearly all the troops ready for service elsewhere by May. No fewer than 800 German planes were being assigned to what was becoming a sizable operation. The British defenses were reported to have 98 pieces of regular artillery and 50 anti-aircraft guns, against which the Germans would employ 210 pieces of heavy artillery with more powerful shells. An artillery specialist calculated that these guns would need to fire 20,000 rounds in order to neutralize the defense, but Hitler, who had experienced quite a few bombardments in World War I, ordered that figure to be increased considerably. By now he had given up his unrealistic goal of seizing the Portuguese Atlantic islands, but directed that one armored and one motorized division would have to proceed temporarily to Spanish Morocco to consolidate the whole operation.[39]

Meanwhile he had ordered Admiral Wilhelm Canaris, the Abwehr commander with a broad Spanish background, to go to Madrid to obtain Franco's final acquiescence. Canaris, who had good personal relations with the Caudillo, met Franco on 7 December, telling him that Hitler wanted to begin moving German forces into Spain on 10 January, and that at that time large amounts of German supplies would begin to flow into the country. For the first time, Franco directly dug in his heels. In addition to all the economic and military supply problems and the absence of firm guarantees about Morocco, Spain would at least temporarily be inundated by German troops, which had never been Franco's intention. Though the large German assault force was not necessarily the main reason for his demurral, it constituted a problem. Franco did not say so to Canaris, but he did state that Spain could not enter the war so long as the British navy remained so strong, the Canaries so exposed, and Spain's own economic and military problems so great. When Canaris asked what other date might be acceptable, Franco refused to give a concrete answer. Telegraphed to try again to get a firm date, Canaris replied on 10 December that he had done his best, but that the real problem was that Franco would not enter the war so long as Britain was in a position to inflict great damage on him.[40] Hitler, increasingly preoccupied with other problems, at last gave up and ordered that preparations for Operation Felix cease for the time being.[41]

The mythic version has attributed to Canaris, who had covertly begun to oppose Hitler's endless aggression and eventually joined the conspiracy against him, a subversive role, warning Franco of the dangers of Hitler's war and advising him to stay out. There is no evidence to support this interpretation.[42] At that time, Germany was very much on top and Canaris fulfilled his responsibilities. The decision was made by Franco and his closest associates, and it was not a political rejection but a military and economic decision. Spain still remained nominally bound by the protocol, but now the date of its entry in the war receded. Almost everything that happened during the next year would indicate that Franco and his closest associates (though not necessarily all the regime's elite) believed that Germany would eventually win the war and still wanted Spain to participate at some date in the future, but under more positive conditions. Despite all the haggling in which they engaged, the Spanish leaders were relatively frank and sincere with the Germans. They wanted Hitler to win, they identified with his cause and wanted to enter the war, but they knew the weakness of their position and were absolutely forthright about the assistance they needed, as well as about their determination to win a major territorial advance in Africa. The myth holds that Franco cleverly deceived Hitler, but in fact at least until 1942 the main Spanish leaders were surprisingly honest in their dealings with the Germans.

In his memoirs, Serrano insisted that "the truth is that between Franco and myself . . . there was always perfect agreement and *identical points of view* concerning *foreign policy*" (italics Serrano's).[43] By December, both brothers-in-law were agreed that Spain's participation in the war must be postponed, though Serrano would in the future show more interest in it, in part because more than Franco he associated it with a fascist regime. Since about the middle of 1940 Serrano had begun to press for a more unified and Falangist government, though the more he did so, the more the military and some other sectors showed their opposition. Serrano seems generally to have felt that entry into the war was needed to complete the establishment of a fascist regime (doubtless a correct analysis), which would in fact cement his own personal political power. Subsequently much of the documentation of this process, however, was either destroyed by the regime or sequestered and withheld by Serrano.

By the close of 1940 military opposition to any change in war policy was becoming more fixed and direct, and there is absolutely no doubt that the vast majority of the population approved. Nowhere in the world during World War II, not even in Nazi Germany, was the great bulk of the population eager to be involved in war, as Göring rather cynically admitted during the Nuremberg trials. In Spain, which had just survived the ordeal of the Civil War and where, by the last months of 1940, people were seen occasionally to faint in the streets from hunger, this was even more the case. British diplomats reported during the second half of 1940 that even among the working classes, generally antifascist and sympathetic to Britain, there were expressions of annoyance that Britain had not made peace so as simply to put an end to war in Europe.[44]

The Anglo-American Carrot and Stick

The British government meanwhile also made its own military contingency plans regarding Spain. Brief consideration was given to an Operation Challenger, which would have seized Ceuta on the coast of Spanish Morocco to strengthen control of the Straits, though that idea was soon abandoned. Other plans ranged from seizure of the Canaries to building a bigger bridgehead at Gibraltar, especially if German forces entered Spain. Subsequent plans in support of Gibraltar bore the names Ballast, Blackthorn, and Sapphic.[45]

Relations between Hoare and Serrano were hostile but correct. Hoare cultivated a wide range of conversationalists, especially among the military, and considered himself well informed. He practiced a carefully calculated form of appeasement in regard to both maritime traffic and Spain's territorial aspirations, which received varying degrees of verbal support from the Churchill government. His reports had been generally reassuring, insisting that politics and propaganda were one thing, serious national interests another, and that Franco was too canny to go to war under present conditions, even averring that so long as Franco remained chief of state, there was no danger that he would enter the war.

By the end of 1940 several leading generals had become more direct in their contacts with the British, led by Aranda, who now was probably receiving large amounts of money. The Anglophone Carlos Martínez Campos, head of the Supreme General Staff, was also active. The generals gave Hoare a somewhat clearer view of the gravity of the situation, urging generosity in economic supplies and emphasizing the importance of avoiding any internal disruption that might provoke Hitler or provide an excuse for direct German intervention. A new Anglo-Spanish commercial treaty somewhat improved the desperate problems of food and fuel supply. Spanish authorities assured the Germans that the treaty had been signed purely out of economic necessity. Churchill's government did not particularly fear Spanish military might, and indeed appreciated better than Hitler what an economic burden Spain would be on Germany if it entered the war, but at the same time wanted to avoid the further strategic complications its participation would present.

American policy roughly paralleled that of Britain, though sometimes with differing emphases. Ambassador Alexander Weddell was not well informed and was often ingenuous in his recommendations, seeing Franco as a noble figure opposed to war and Nazism, in contrast to the sinister Serrano. This was an extreme form of the way Hoare viewed the situation. From the autumn of 1940, nonetheless, Washington began to take a tougher line on economic assistance than did London, which was a course easier for an American government, so far from Europe, to pursue. American shipments also expanded to reward good behavior, though humanitarian policies also played some role.[46] Increasing provisions from the democracies in turn angered the Germans, who seem particularly to have held it against the "Jesuitical" Serrano, though he was surely as good a friend as they had in the Spanish government.

Renewed German Pressure

In December Hitler committed the German military machine to an offensive against the Soviet Union by the end of May. It was the most frustrating month for him since the fall of France. The British were successfully on the offensive against the Italians both in East Africa and, more seriously, in Libya, while the Greeks held the upper hand on the Albanian frontier and the operation against Gibraltar had to be canceled. Even so, Hitler had not given up all hope that Franco could soon be persuaded to enter the war and proceed with the Gibraltar operation.

On 28 December Ribbentrop talked with the Spanish ambassador, General Eugenio Espinosa de los Monteros, who had been extremely supportive in his dealings with the Germans and seems to have been well regarded in Berlin. Ribbentrop observed that he had been receiving diverse reports from Madrid, some of which attributed Franco's reluctance to simple lack of enthusiasm, others to the opposition of the generals, and others to the disastrous economic situation. He insisted to Espinosa that it was an error to think the economic problems could ever be resolved with British assistance and that with regard to the issue of territorial concessions, it was, as Espinosa reported, "materially impossible to specify this right now. Germany wants Spain to have not only Gibraltar, but also as large an empire in Africa as possible, which will be granted to it at the end of the war."[47]

What Ribbentrop did not grasp was that Espinosa was a military man who had been perhaps the last major appointee of Beigbeder (in consultation with Franco) and that he was detested by Serrano, who saw him as a member of a military clique in opposition to the foreign minister. Thus until nearly the middle of January Serrano refused his request to honor the wishes of the Germans by returning to Madrid to report directly to Franco. When he did appear, Serrano chewed him out for being overly ambitious and denied him access to the Caudillo. Espinosa attempted to resign on the 25th.[48]

The report about the situation in Spanish Morocco filed at the end of the year by Herbert Georg Richter, the consul in Tetuán, was also not encouraging. His two main conclusions were "1. The Spanish inability to do anything positive for Morocco. 2. Spain's systematic fight against any German influence in the country." Richter assured his superiors that "the natives respect and love us because we are militarily strong and are the only European Great Power that does not rule over any of their coreligionists in the Arab-Islamic world." He insisted that Spanish Morocco was dominated by "corruption, misery, and famine," while "the Spanish effort to exclude us from Morocco has been evident in the course of the year on unimportant occasions as well as in matters of principle." This was "a bad sign for the future, if Spain should really succeed in gaining possession of the French zone. . . . Spain would have only one aim: she would never rest until the last German had left the country." Moreover, "the disproportionately strong garrisoning of Spanish Morocco is a constant proof of aggressive intentions." If Spain should dare to invade the French zone, its forces would probably be smashed by the well-armed French, but that could also create a crisis for Germany, throwing the "whole area" "into the arms of De Gaulle." And, if the United States were to enter the war, "French Morocco would then become the base for American operations in Europe."[49] This was the same sort of thing that Hitler worried about.

At military meetings on 8–9 January, the Führer reiterated that Felix was for the moment a lost cause, but that it was so important he would still try to gain Franco's permission and participation, now ruling out an idea he had broached in November, that if necessary Spain could simply be forced into war. The priority was to bail out the Italians in Greece and Libya before the Soviet campaign, so that Felix could be done only in agreement with Franco. Therefore at his next meeting with Mussolini on 19–20 January, he asked the Duce, in view of the very friendly relations between Rome and Madrid, to meet with Franco and persuade him to cooperate.[50]

Reports received in Berlin were conflicting but nonetheless contained signs of hope. On 8 January, for example, Stohrer reported a conversation he had just had with Francesco Lequio, the Italian ambassador. The Spanish leaders always spoke more freely with the Italians, and Serrano had allegedly told Lequio "to tell Count Ciano that Spain would enter the war even at this time if she had grain to prevent a famine; he keenly regretted this hindrance and still hoped that it could be eliminated."[51] Stohrer also enjoyed close and friendly relations with Serrano, who often intimated that he was more keenly in favor of entering than was Franco, though by 1941 this may not have been the case. Stohrer was impressed by what he saw as Serrano's good faith, and always reported quite favorably about him to Berlin.

On 11 January Erich Heberlein, the German chargé, reported a conversation that Pedro Gamero del Castillo, acting secretary of the FET and at that time a leading pro-Nazi activist, had with Hans Lazar, the German press chief in Spain. Gamero stressed the internal political conflict between Franco on the one hand and Serrano and the FET on the other. Whereas Franco wanted to maintain a broad government representing the various sectors of the national movement of 1936, Serrano and the Falangists pressed for a unified "activist, homogeneous" government, which they implied would be necessary to bring Spain into the war. Gamero stressed that in this struggle "German intervention with Franco would be of decisive importance. . . . This would be to the advantage of Germany herself, because she could collaborate militarily only with an activist, homogeneous government group and otherwise would have to resort to ruthless intervention."[52]

Stohrer was briefly recalled to Berlin for further instructions and, while the Axis dictators were meeting, had another discussion with Franco on 20 January, in which he claimed to have employed "ruthless candor." At that moment in Spain "everything was moving speedily toward a catastrophe which only Germany could prevent." He emphasized that for Spain to wait until the war was almost over would be too late and of no use to Germany, repeating Hitler's insistence on the importance of the Gibraltar operation and stressing that the Germans would do all the fighting, not grasping that this last consideration was a major negative for Franco. "Spain would hardly be called on to make any great sacrifices," but would receive major economic assistance. He quoted Ribbentrop's urgent request for a response within forty-eight hours.

Franco remained calm, reiterating his confidence in Germany's ultimate victory and his desire to enter the war as soon as circumstances permitted, protesting that "Spanish policy had undeviatingly followed a straight line." (From Franco's point of view, this was undoubtedly so.) There followed the usual litany of problems and shortages, to which Stohrer replied that as soon as Spain entered the war, Germany would make good these deficiencies. Franco again emphasized, according to Stohrer, that "it was not a question at all of whether Spain would enter the war; that had been decided in Hendaye. It was merely a question of when. He was still [striving] to bring that moment to pass, namely by economic measures, which admittedly had not yet been very successful, and by far-reaching military preparations. . . . Supported by the [Foreign] Minister, Franco then protested sharply against the assumption that he had told Admiral Canaris he would enter the war only when England had already been laid low. Spain intended to participate in the war fully and not obtain anything as a gift."

Stohrer stressed several times that the opportune moment was now and that if Spain waited longer it would miss its chance. When Franco insisted that it would be crucial that his country receive major economic assistance in advance, Stohrer replied that he was authorized to say that "we might perhaps consider such a prepayment but that it would come into question only if Franco gave the assurance *in advance* that Spain would then enter the war at a time to be determined *by us*" (italics Stohrer's). Serrano and Franco both then stated that this put a new construction on the matter that required further consideration. In a follow-up telegram the next day Stohrer reported on a subsequent conversation with Serrano, who stated that he completely agreed with the German view, the only question being the exact timing of Spain's entry into the war, which the ambassador believed that the foreign minister planned to take up with the Supreme War Council.[53]

On 21 January, even before receiving the last message, Ribbentrop fired off an abrupt communiqué to Stohrer, which he instructed the ambassador to read to Franco verbatim. It consisted of six points, which may be summarized as follows:

> 1. Franco could never have won the Civil War without Hitler and Mussolini.
> 2. "The English, French, and Americans have one aim: the destruction of Franco and of Nationalist Spain."
> 3. Spain's future is bound up with Germany, which alone can provide "really effective aid."
> 4. "The war for the Axis is today already won," but "the closing of the Mediterranean by the capture of Gibraltar would contribute toward an early end of the war and also open up for Spain the road to Africa. . . . This action would be of strategic value only if carried out in the next few weeks."
> 5. "The Führer and the Reich Government are deeply disturbed by the equivocal and vacillating attitude of Spain," which makes no sense.
> 6. "The Reich Government is taking this step in order to prevent . . . a catastrophe for Spain." If Franco does not enter the war now, "the Reich Government cannot but foresee the end of Nationalist Spain."[54]

When this message was read to Franco, he replied "that these communications were of extreme gravity and contained untruths. . . . Franco very heatedly asserted that he had never taken a vacillating position and that his policy was unswervingly on the Axis side, from gratitude and as a man of honor. He had never lost sight of entry into the war. This entry would come," but extreme economic weaknesses must first be overcome, which he again elaborated upon. Serrano eventually chimed in that he had made this problem clear from the beginning, so that Germany, by not responding this far, was "co-responsible for the fact that Spain was still so little ready for war."[55]

This message brought a curt reply from Ribbentrop on the 24th, demanding that Franco immediately set a date, promising 100,000 tons of grain as soon as he did so. Serrano answered him one day later, patiently repeating all the standard arguments, insisting on Spain's full devotion to the cause of the Axis, though also again reproaching Germany for not yet having provided economic assistance. On the 27th Stohrer was able to present Ribbentrop's message directly to Franco, who launched into his customary explanation. "The only noteworthy item in this recital was that the Generalissimo did emphasize much more strongly than hitherto that Spain would undoubtedly enter the war, . . . which, he felt, would still last for many months." In addition to all the economic problems, Franco brought up the question of 200,000 French and colonial troops in Africa, as well as the problem of the "Portuguese frontier," since Portugal might not "resist an English landing." This time he managed to win Stohrer's attention by asking for the dispatch of German economic and military experts, suggesting a visit by Field Marshal Wilhelm Keitel, head of the high command (OKW). Ribbentrop shot back on the 28th in a tone of outrage, demanding that his ambassador explain what was going on, whether he had carefully followed instructions, and how he was permitting Franco and Serrano to turn the tables by blaming the situation on Germany. Stohrer protested that he had carried out instructions to the letter and that Franco's reply could read either as a rejection of immediate entry or as a ploy to gain immediate economic assistance; in the latter case, he asked what was the last date that Germany could accept.[56]

All this was totally infuriating to Berlin.

When Hitler and his staff officers next spoke of the Gibraltar operation on 28 January, it had slipped even further away. Even if Franco were suddenly to agree, the assault could not now begin until April, meaning that the sizable contingent of troops involved would not initially be available for the invasion of the Soviet Union, so Hitler ended any further military discussion of the Gibraltar operation.[57]

Even so, he still had not given up altogether. On 6 February he received a report from Stohrer that the situation in Spain was worse than ever, with great internal division, resentment, mass hunger, and signs of banditry and social breakdown, although Franco did not seem gravely worried. Serrano had once more stated his agreement with the German ambassador that only entry into the war could rectify the situation, "but we must receive the means beforehand to alleviate quickly the worst need to some extent." The present government, Stohrer concluded, was so divided that Franco might receive an ultimatum from his generals to form a strictly military government, but such a government "would perhaps . . . take a more positive position with regard to the matter of the date of the entry into the war."[58]

That same day Hitler prepared for Franco the longest letter he had ever sent him. Though Ribbentrop had never directly threatened Franco, Hitler's communication was considerably more diplomatic, emphasizing the ideological dimension of the war and the fact that the future of the Spanish regime depended on Nazi Germany. "Jewish-international democracy" would never forgive the fact that their regimes were based on "national conditioning and not on bases obligated to capitalism [*nach völkisch bedingten und nicht kapitalistisch verpflichteten Grundsätze*]." Hitler declared that in such a desperate struggle Franco should understand that "*we cannot offer any gifts*" (underlined in Hitler's text) ahead of time, but Germany was ready to send 100,000 tons of grain and other assistance as soon as Franco set a date to enter the war. Hitler emphasized that Spain was united with the Axis by "the most implacable force of history" and that Spain's "broad territorial claims" would be satisfied "according to the way in which they are coordinated with, and to some extent complement, an acceptable new order of African colonies for Europe and its states." Hitler underlined quite a few phrases and added exclamation points for emphasis.[59]

After Stohrer presented this message to Franco on the 8th, he reported that the Caudillo insisted that he was in full agreement with all of Hitler's "fundamental ideas. . . . I identify myself completely with them," and that it was a misunderstanding to think that he intended to delay entry into the war until the autumn or winter. He promised a complete reply after his imminent meeting with Mussolini, but in the meantime had just sent off the longest list of Spain's needs that the German government had received yet. This one specified not 100,000 but a million tons of grain, 16,000 boxcars of food and strategic goods, and an additional small navy—two cruisers, thirteen destroyers, and four submarines—to protect against the

British fleet. After examining this list Emil Wiehl, director of the German Economic Policy Department, concluded it was "so obviously unrealizable" that it was clearly a "pretext" to avoid entering the war.[60]

By this point Franco was relying on Mussolini's assistance to obtain better terms. On 31 December Hitler had written to him that Franco had just committed "the biggest mistake of his life," and three weeks later Ribbentrop said that it was up to Mussolini and Ciano to try to convince him.[61] This led to the one and only meeting between Franco and Mussolini, which took place at Bordighera, on the Italian Riviera, on 12 February. In arranging this meeting, Serrano had emphasized the absolute ideological identity between the three regimes, but complained of German pressure and the disastrous Spanish domestic conditions. Since Franco had refused to fly after the deaths of two generals in plane crashes during the first year of the Civil War, he traveled across southern France in an elaborate motorcade.

If Hitler had been unable to convince the Spanish dictator, it was doubtful that Mussolini would be more successful, though he played his role as best he could. The Italian army had been stymied by the Greeks and massively defeated in Africa by the British, but he assured Franco that measures had been taken to set these things right. Mussolini rehearsed the German arguments that the survival of Franco depended on Italo-German victory, though he made the concession that Franco himself would have to decide exactly when Spain would be ready to enter the war. Some members of Mussolini's entourage were apparently unable to disguise the discouragement that was beginning to take hold of much of the Italian leadership.

Franco gave Mussolini the same assurances that he had provided to Hitler. One Italian diplomat described his performance as "verbose, disorganized and losing itself in petty details or long digressions about military issues," all of which sounded like a typical Franco conversation. He claimed to be "more convinced" than the Duce himself of final Axis victory and assured Mussolini that he did not want to delay Spain's entry until it was "too late." Mussolini observed that the war was likely to be a long one, and Franco was of the same opinion, lamenting that shortages of every kind made it impossible to expand the Spanish army beyond 300,000 indifferently equipped troops, while Serrano observed that the internal situation was so dire that if Spain were to enter the war at that moment, it would be more a liability than an asset to Germany, an assessment that was surely correct. Franco declared, truthfully enough, that Germany was not creating the proper conditions for Spain to enter, because of the very limited assistance and lack of guarantees. When the time came, Franco still wanted to seize Gibraltar with Spanish forces (an ambition that the Germans thought ridiculous, as indeed it probably was). Franco seems to have been pleased with the meeting, which generated little pressure and confirmed his impression that Mussolini was truly a great man.[62] The Duce in fact was of two minds about the Spanish issue. On the one hand, he wished to have the maximum influence in Madrid, an influence inevitably usurped by Germany; on the other, he wished to avoid Spanish competition in Algeria, all of which he wanted for Italy.

After receiving Mussolini's report,[63] Hitler finally gave up for good. Though Germany would continue to enjoy the close collaboration of the Spanish government in many areas (as detailed in the next chapter), the German representatives made no more direct efforts to obtain Spain's entry into the war. On the 22nd Ribbentrop telegraphed Stohrer: "Please do not take any more steps whatever in the question of Spain's entry into the war. . . . You should act, in principle, in an objective and friendly manner, but be cool and reserved." By the same token, there would be no special economic assistance.[64] Nonetheless, it would not be quite right to say, as sometimes has been suggested, that the relationship reverted to that of May 1940, for Spain remained a nonbelligerent, not at all a neutral, and would continue to be closely associated with the Axis.

Later the German leaders would become convinced that the "Jesuitical" Serrano and the "Latin charlatan" Franco had deceived them all along, but an examination of the evidence supports Javier Tusell's conclusion that the Spanish leaders were basically honest in their dealings, telling Hitler and the German diplomats what they considered to be the truth about their situation at the time. They were not feigning allegiance to the Axis cause, but sincerely believed in it, and they wanted very much to enter the war, if only the proper conditions could be created. These things were repeated over and over, and the Spanish leaders were usually sincere in their enunciation, just as they were truthful in their description of Spain's massive economic and military needs. Well might Juan Peche, Serrano's undersecretary in the Foreign Ministry, later write that "we did not enter the war because Franco resisted German pressure, but because Hitler did not want us to or make the necessary calculations," and what he offered was simply inadequate to make it an attractive proposition.[65] Every indication, however, was that both Franco and Serrano were still hoping that these conditions would change. Neither was aware, as of February 1941, that henceforth—with perhaps one exception—such opportunities would continue to recede.

CHAPTER 7

The Zenith of Collaboration

By December 1940, Franco and Serrano had decided that entry into the war was simply not desirable at that time, and that Spain must wait until the situation improved both internally and strategically and until Hitler was more forthcoming on territorial demands. This second phase of nonbelligerence would last approximately two years, until December 1942, when the success of Torch, the Allied invasion of northwest Africa, convinced the Spanish leaders that—unless the war suddenly changed drastically in Germany's favor—Spain should stay out of it altogether. There followed a shorter phase, from December 1942 to October 1943, when Franco was still expecting some sort of German-dominated continental Europe to emerge from the war, even though the Spanish government no longer planned to enter the fight. Only in the summer of 1944, after the success of Overlord, the Allied invasion of France, did Franco accept that Germany was simply going to lose the war, and that European affairs would be dominated by its enemies.

Thus the decision to postpone Spain's entry in the war had not been due to any slackening of enthusiasm for the German cause, as Franco and Serrano constantly and truthfully reassured Berlin. The following year of 1941 would in fact expand the broad-based Spanish collaboration with the German war effort. Germany's longest-established service in Spain was intelligence, but at first it was modest and scarcely went beyond the services of other major powers. In the summer of 1939, as war loomed, Admiral

Canaris, since 1935 chief of the Abwehr (military intelligence), undertook to establish an advanced series of intelligence units called *Kriegsorganisationen* (KO—war organizations) in ten major neutral countries, including Spain and Portugal. KO-Spanien would grow to become the largest, with a staff of 220, a roster of approximately two thousand agents and collaborators, and a network of observation and transmission stations throughout the country. Like the Abwehr itself, it was organized in three sections. The first dealt with gathering intelligence, the second with organizing sabotage of enemy forces, and the third with counterintelligence and disinformation. It became the largest single agency of the Reich outside German-occupied territory, its personnel also including 171 staff members of the huge Madrid embassy (with more than 500 personnel, the largest German embassy in the world), 21 members in the office of the police attaché, 74 under the military attachés, and Wehrmacht staff—a grand total of nearly 500 under diplomatic immunity, to which might be added the services of the 180 German employees of the thirty consulates in Spain.[1] Walter Schellenberg, Hitler's last intelligence chief, has testified regarding the great importance of German intelligence activities of all kinds in Spain.[2]

The most important single focus of activity was, of course, Gibraltar, for which German intelligence activity continued to expand throughout 1941, until by the end of the year at least eleven observation points were being manned along the southern coast and in Spanish Morocco, the station at Algeciras alone transmitting twenty messages per day. Late in 1941 nine new stations were constructed on the north shore and five on the south, equipped with powerful new infrared ray technology. Franco gave his final approval in March 1942 and the new network (Operation Bodden) went into operation the following month.

Just at this point, in December 1941, the British code-breaking operation Ultra at Bletchley Park succeeded in breaking the Abwehr radio code and soon learned much about Bodden. The British naval command considered launching a commando operation to destroy some of the key stations, but decided this idea was too bold and risky. Instead, Hoare presented a detailed aide-mémoire to Franco at his residence in El Pardo on 27 May 1942, describing German activities and demanding that they be ended. Coming on the heels of the supply operation for German submarines and destroyers, this latest German initiative in Spain was doubly exasperating. Bodden had required not merely Spain's approval but its active complicity in construction, logistical support, and auxiliary personnel. Franco denied everything, the official Spanish response alleging that

German personnel had been brought in for technical assistance with the placement of new Spanish artillery on the coast. Since the operation had been discovered, however, the Spanish government decided on 25 June that it was too risky and closed it down, though a minor share of the observation facilities were reestablished elsewhere.[3]

Spanish authorities and agents also provided extensive intelligence services from British soil. During the Battle of Britain the embassy and its military attachés, with the assistance of the Spanish government, provided sometimes daily reports on damage inflicted and the state of British morale, though the assistant press attaché, Juan Brugada, was turned by MI5 and provided false reports. The most notorious Spanish agent working for Germany in England was the Falangist press attaché Angel Alcázar de Velasco, who was uncovered and later banned by the British, but there were a good many others. The Spanish government considered this activity so normal that when a new air attaché, the monarchist Juan Antonio Ansaldo, refused to collect intelligence data for the Germans, he was summarily dismissed and prosecuted for insubordination.[4] Altogether, forty or more Spaniards worked for German or Japanese intelligence outside Spain.[5]

After Japan attacked the United States, the Japanese found themselves virtually bereft of sources of intelligence on their new enemy, and turned to Serrano Suñer for assistance in Madrid. He authorized Alcázar de Velasco to set up a network of Spanish agents, mainly journalists, in the United States to provide intelligence for Japan by way of Madrid between 1942 and 1944. It became the principal conduit of Japanese intelligence on the United States during these years, but the information provided was of poor quality, some of it pure fabrication.[6] When U.S. counterintelligence learned of these activities, as it soon did, the image of the Franco regime became blacker than ever and stimulated the very strong pressure that Washington exerted against Madrid in the later stages of the war.

British and Allied intelligence later responded quite effectively, using the waters and territory of Spain for major deception operations that confused the Germans with regard to the Allied invasions of Italy and France.[7] Equally useful was the remarkable work of Juan Pujol ("Garbo"), who has been called the most important double agent of the Second World War. During the Civil War he had been a convinced Francoist, appalled by the excesses of the revolution though forced briefly to serve in the Republican army. During 1940–41 Pujol's reading of Nazi literature convinced him that Hitler was a grave menace to the world and he offered his services to the British, who set him up as a double agent. Recruited by the Germans, he was sent to Britain ostensibly as a Spanish businessman; there he fed the Germans crucial false information for three years.[8]

The Abwehr's sabotage organization (SO) was organized in Spain in September 1940 to function as an auxiliary of the Gibraltar operation. It relied on the assistance and participation of a considerable number of Spanish agents, who in fact were largely in charge of active operations, making use of Spanish workers employed in Gibraltar to plant and set off a variety of explosive devices. These devices caused not inconsiderable damage, and one calculation has it that the SO was responsible for sinking somewhere between 70,000 and 100,000 tons of Allied shipping from the beginning of 1941 until its operations were largely closed down in March 1944.[9]

A series of Italian sabotage operations against Gibraltar were also carried out with Spain's approval and complicity, many of them organized from the Italian tanker *Olterra*, interned in the Bay of Algeciras.[10] After repeated Allied protests, these operations were finally ended in September 1943. In addition, fifteen Italian air raids launched against Gibraltar had to make use of Spanish air space for belligerent activities, some of the planes having on occasion to land at Spanish airfields for refueling on their way home. Only on the occasion of the final raid, launched from Mussolini's puppet Salò Republic on 3 June 1944, were the planes that stopped over at Spanish airfields interned, along with their crews.[11] All these attacks and acts of sabotage, mounted with Spain's complicity, never came close to crippling Gibraltar, but they hampered its operations and complicated the work of the Allied forces in the Mediterranean.[12]

In addition, in mid-1940 the Luftwaffe was permitted to establish two stations for weather reporting and navigational guidance near Lugo and Seville. These stations continued to operate until the very end of the war, using German planes with Spanish insignia. They also provided technical assistance to the Spanish air force, and clearly acted in violation of international law in time of war.[13]

Armed Spanish warships first began to provide escort protection for German shipping along the northern and southern coasts of Spain in January 1940. This activity was very risky, however, and was soon brought to an end. In addition, German diplomatic correspondence and intelligence information were carried across the Atlantic in Spanish ships under the cover of Spain's own diplomatic correspondence for much of the war. In 1941, as Franco postponed Spain's entry into the war sine die, naval collaboration with the Germans increased. Not merely did the resupply of German submarines operate at its highest level during that year, but new forms of naval collaboration developed. The war in northeast Africa quickly achieved a new intensity and importance, with Axis forces logistically handicapped by British naval and air dominance in the Mediterranean. As Erwin Rommel's newly formed Afrika Korps went from victory to victory, despite its small size, it became clear to the German command that Rommel might eventually fail, not because the British would defeat him in battle but because they might succeed in blocking the flow of vital supplies. Therefore the German command turned to SOFINDUS, the German holding company in Spain, which in August 1941 created a new German enterprise in Spain, Compañía Marítima de Transportes, S.A., which would be commonly known as Transcomar. This firm was registered not as a German but as a Spanish company under the names of Spanish intermediaries and obtained authorization from the Falangist Demetrio Carceller, minister of industry and commerce, to operate five ships to engage in trade in the western Mediterranean. These vessels would spend part of their time in the covert shipment of supplies to German forces under cover of the Spanish flag, which freed them from the danger of British interdiction. Within a few months more ships were added to this operation, known to the Germans as Aktion Hetze, credited with moving 125,000 tons of supplies to North Africa within a period of ten months during 1941–42.[14]

The British soon learned of these activities and took two countermeasures: ships of 500 tons or more were prohibited from entering the Mediterranean without British approval and the Spanish government was pressured into requiring that Spanish ships leaving Spain return directly, without engaging in other activity. In addition, the British decided to buy up as much Spanish shipping as possible; by 1942 they had dedicated £3 million to this enterprise, most of it loaned by Juan March, who was later repaid in gold at the end of the war and earned a great profit.[15]

During 1942 the problem of supply to Rommel became increasingly desperate, and the Germans intensified their efforts to make use of nonbelligerent and neutral shipping. To exploit Spanish resources further, a German shipping company purchased 50 percent of the Compañía Naviera Levantina, using counterpart funds from the sizable unpaid debt owed to Germany by the Spanish government. Within months it was soon operating a larger number of Spanish ships than Transcomar had done, while the Germans also purchased a controlling interest in the Bilbao shipping company Bachi, again employing Spanish front men as shareholders. Five of this company's six ships were then moved to the Mediterranean, where they were also used for German supply operations and to shield regular German supply ships. The British eventually sank two of Bachi's ships and pressured the Spanish government into suspending the operations of the remainder. An undetermined number of the boats employed by the Compañía Naviera Levantina were also sunk, as these operations gave rise to a whole series of incidents and protests. Yet a further Spanish-fronted German shipping company, Naviera Ibérica, was formed in 1944 to construct small boats for the German trade, but by this time the military advance of the Allies largely put an end to such efforts. A further minor dimension of naval collaboration was the covert use of Spanish ships to South America to repatriate the most important crewmen of the pocket battleship *Graf Spee*, interned in Uruguay and Argentina.[16]

Another significant form of collaboration involved the Spanish and German police. The Franco regime had first sought technical assistance from the Gestapo in methods of combating communism in November 1937, and they signed an agreement to cooperate on 31 July 1938. This measure provided for broad exchange of information and collaboration. Heinrich Himmler made an elaborate four-day visit to Spain, more for high-level tourism than police activity, in October 1940, on the eve of the meeting at Hendaye. The friendship treaty of 1939 provided for assignment of special police representatives to the embassies in Berlin and Madrid, and a verbal agreement at the time of Himmler's visit transformed these assignments into the novel posts of police attachés, giving the German police a direct presence in Spain for the remainder of the war to control German nationals.

As the first major police collaboration, Germany provided a list of Republican notables trapped in German-occupied France, as requested by Madrid in August 1940. The people sought were then handed over by the Germans, who would also have been happy to return all the 50,000 or more Spanish émigrés initially in their zone of France, but Franco had no interest in the return of large numbers of hard-core leftists. The notables who were repatriated were immediately placed on trial, and some of the most prominent were quickly executed. The executions, however, led the Vichy government to refuse to hand over other notables resident in unoccupied France.

When the Germans occupied Vichy territory in November 1942, all the remainder of the 140,000 Republican refugees in France passed under German control. At least 7,288 were eventually deported to the concentration camp at Mauthausen in Germany, where at least 64 percent of them died.[17]

German propaganda in Spain expanded considerably during 1941. To that point it had been represented by an information bulletin published three times a week by the embassy in approximately 50,000 copies, a satirical weekly that reached 300,000, and a propaganda-based crossword puzzle sheet, *Crucigramas*, of which more than 150,000 were distributed weekly.

In the summer of 1941 the German embassy reached the conclusion that British propaganda was having a significant effect and that Germany, with the assistance of the Spanish government, should become much more active. Stohrer and the press attaché drew up the outline of what became known as the Grosse Plan of German propaganda in Spain. It was officially approved in Berlin at the beginning of 1942 and immediately won the personal endorsement of Franco and Serrano. It was designed to expand German propaganda while controlling that of Great Britain, and, given the close collaboration between the two governments, would be conducted as much as possible by Spanish personnel, without the official participation of the embassy.

The Grosse Plan set up five sections. Group A was composed of Spaniards sincerely committed to the German cause, of whom a list of approximately 500,000 had been compiled by July 1942. They would be organized into local sections, each led by a local Spanish leader, drawn from 15,000 core collaborators. The local groups would receive the embassy's information bulletin, as well as special leaflets and pamphlets published by Spanish intermediaries. Group B was to be formed within the Spanish postal service, with the goal of facilitating the introduction and passage of German propaganda and intercepting the flow of Allied propaganda through the mail. Group C would be created within the FET, with the assistance of the latter's national delegate of propaganda, Federico de Urrutia. It would facilitate the distribution of German propaganda, spread rumors favorable to the German cause, and identify Allied propaganda and its sources, channels, and recipients. Group D was to be set up within the Dirección General de Seguridad, using the Spanish police system to gather information about Allied propaganda and the means, both official and unofficial, of combating it. Group E was probably the least important, to be organized among supporters in the Association of Ex-Captives of the Civil War. This group had a membership of 28,000 former prisoners in Republican jails, 20,000 of whom were judged to be pro-German.[18]

Stohrer reported in March that half the extensive amount of Allied (mostly British) propaganda in the mails was being intercepted and eliminated. During the course of 1942 German propaganda, in turn, published 56 leaflets with a total distribution of 9 million copies, though financial

support never went beyond ESP150,000 per month, forcing German officials to collect additional funds from German businesses operating in
Spain. Propaganda material was prepared in a wide variety of categories
designed for different sectors of the Spanish population. This plan remained in operation until virtually the end of the war, inundating the
country with German propaganda, while, at least until the last year, restrict-
ing the flow of Allied propaganda. Diplomatic protests by the British and
American embassies about the irregularities in the Spanish mail at first
achieved only limited effect, for the Spanish government referred to its own
decree of June 1940 which theoretically restricted drastically the circula-
tion of foreign propaganda; only official bulletins were to be sent, and they
only to government agencies. By 1942, Spanish police at least on some
occasions arrested Spanish citizens who tried to enter Allied embassies,
with resultant diplomatic protests. These restrictions on Allied propaganda
continued, though with diminishing vigor, until the middle of 1944.[19]

Yet, as Franco and Serrano observed many times to the Germans, the
Spanish government could not be an entirely free actor, for it was heavily
conditioned by Allied control of the seas and of vital imports. Thus, even as
the regime cooperated with and helped to implement the Grosse Plan,
Serrano would have to tone down the expression of German propaganda
and German-slanted news in the Spanish media from time to time in order
to maintain the flow of imports. Similarly, though Falangists collaborated
avidly with German propaganda and publicly chanted Nazi slogans, the
FET was given orders in 1941 and 1943 that forbade party members to
work for or merely align themselves with foreign organizations. These
contradictions were never fully resolved until the final destruction of the
Reich in 1945.

In addition to waging this vigorous propaganda and counterpropa-
ganda campaign in Spain, the German government made a major effort to
influence and control the Spanish press. These efforts had begun to a
limited degree in 1935, but they ratcheted up during the Civil War when
propaganda personnel from both Goebbels's ministry and the Nazi Party
Auslandsorganisation (AO) were sent to the Nationalist zone, though in
fact Nazi press and propaganda activity during most of the conflict was
somewhat limited.

It expanded with the arrival in September 1938 of the suave, sophisticated Austrian Hans Lazar, who would cut a wide swathe in Spain virtually
down to the end of World War II. He came as representative of Transocean,
the Nazi Party overseas propaganda agency. Becoming press attaché in

September 1939, he enjoyed a monthly budget of ESP200,000, most of which seems to have been used to bribe Spanish journalists. Influencing the Spanish press was all the easier because of the draconian Spanish censorship law of April 1938, which established tight central control, with a sizable part of the press owned and operated by the FET. Ramón Garriga, who was one of the leading journalists and state information officers of that era, later judged that "in no other country did the press behave in such a servile manner during the war years."[20] As Manuel Ros Agudo says, it reached a paroxysm of Germanophilia during the second half of 1940, when its task was to prepare Spanish opinion for a short war.[21] Generally speaking, Spanish news coverage was heavily slanted in favor of the Axis until the later stages of the war.[22]

Nazi leaders believed that Latin America was a fertile field for their propaganda, but also feared that the major anti-Nazi campaign begun by the U.S. government might eventually close the western hemisphere to them. Therefore at the time of Serrano Suñer's mission to Berlin in September 1940 it was suggested to Vicente Gállego, director of the newly created Spanish state news agency Efe, that the German government was greatly interested in helping Efe expand its operations in Latin America, where it might serve as conduit for Nazi propaganda. When Gállego refused to be bought, the Germans strove, though unsuccessfully, to have him dismissed from his post.

Franco's decision to postpone entry into the war in no way diminished German enthusiasm for using the country as a propaganda stepping-stone, and by the spring of 1941 Stohrer and Lazar had begun to negotiate directly with Serrano and with Antonio Tovar, the German-speaking and Naziphile undersecretary of press and propaganda. In June Paul Schmidt, press chief for the German foreign ministry, came to Madrid to sign what became known as the Schmidt-Tovar agreement, which stipulated that funding would be made available for Efe to set up branches throughout Latin America. The branches would send to Madrid by radio full reports of developments in Latin America, and Efe would dispatch large amounts of material, including much Nazi propaganda, for them to disseminate as widely as possible. Sophisticated new technology would be provided, including an extremely powerful transmitter to be set up in Madrid. Nonetheless, implementation was largely stymied by the opposition of Gállego. German financial and technological assistance was never accepted, and of thirty pro-German Efe agents to be dispatched to the western hemisphere under diplomatic cover to work for German propaganda and intelligence interests, no more than four were sent.[23] One Spanish journalist who agreed to work for the Nazis in Latin America in fact served as a British double agent. The Germans continued their efforts to expand their foreign propaganda through Spanish sources in 1942–43, though once more with limited effectiveness. Negotiations were also begun in Berlin in the autumn of 1940 to create a joint German-Spanish espionage service in Latin America, in which the Spanish foreign ministry was deeply involved, but this operation never went into effect. The goal of Spain's effort to influence the policies of Latin American countries in 1941–42 was to discourage cooperation with the United States and a pro-Allied policy in favor of a pan-Hispanism opposed to the United States, oriented toward Spain and neutrality, and a policy more favorable to the Axis. These efforts failed almost totally and were largely abandoned before the end of 1942.[24]

At the same time it must be recognized that the policy of *hispanidad* was not primarily the result of any Axis strategy but represented basic goals of the Spanish regime itself. The effort to gain influence in Latin America was a fundamental strategy, though it was also aligned with Axis interests, but it was a general failure, with the exception of relations with Argentina.[25]

How significant was Spanish collaboration with the Axis during the war? Such activities were generally marginal to the German war effort, with the exception of the submarine refueling, Mediterranean supply-running, and Gibraltar sabotage operations. These activities were all direct contributions to the German war effort. Collaboration in propaganda and intelligence had considerably less direct effect, but in general Spain's collaboration was more extensive and long-lasting than that of any other nonbelligerent or neutral country.

Nonetheless, pressure by the Allies increasingly forced Spain to reduce key aspects of its collaboration, and thus pointed up how gratuitous and voluntary most of this collaboration was. It should also be kept in mind that the Germans were not given a blank check. They asked for things they did not get, such as Spain's direct entry into the war. Moreover, in each area the Germans would have liked to carry collaboration considerably further, but Spanish authorities refused. Attitudes also varied on the part of individual Spanish officials. Some, such as Vicente Gállego of the Agencia Efe, refused to be exploited. At the highest level of the government, the entry of the Count de Jordana as foreign minister in place of Serrano Suñer in September 1942 brought significant pressure for change, as will be seen in later chapters.

Such extensive collaboration was not the Spanish equivalent of Sweden's temporary permission for passage of German troops across Swedish territory, but followed a systematic pattern reflecting the political sympathies and identity of the Spanish regime. It was also sometimes intended as compensation for the fact that Spain had not actually entered the war. Though collaboration was substantially reduced by mid-1944 as a result of Allied pressure, it was never completely terminated until the end of the Third Reich itself.

Economic Collaboration

Economic collaboration was also extensive, but in this area collaboration by the Spanish regime was no greater than that of neutral countries such as Switzerland and Sweden. During the war the Swiss economy was broadly cooperative with that of the Reich in industrial production and finance,[26] which Hitler accepted as a valid alternative to military occupation, a project with which he had toyed in the summer of 1940. The difference was that Switzerland was eventually entirely surrounded by German-occupied territory, and Sweden also found itself completely enclosed within the German sphere, whereas Spain's geographic location potentially gave it greater independence, which Franco and his associates did not attempt fully to exercise.

The regime looked to Italy and Germany for technical assistance in war industry and in some other kinds of technical and industrial development, and was also hoping for capital investment. Such assistance was considered compatible with the declared program of autarky, which was not to be confused with isolation. The Spanish leaders did not fully grasp that the Italian and German economies were becoming so totally devoted to their own military production that there was little assistance to be had, and no surplus capital was being accumulated.

After the war began, the German government became eager for a new commercial agreement that would guarantee imports of raw materials. An agreement signed on 22 December 1939 provided for mechanisms of exchange, with the goal of equilibrium in the mutual trade balances of the two states. There was no agreement with regard to the large debt owed by Spain, and Madrid rejected a German proposal to use that debt as credit for the purposes of investment in the Spanish economy. An interministerial delegation to negotiate final terms of the debt arrived in Berlin in August 1940, and a confidential protocol eventually signed on 28 February 1941 formally recognized a debt of 372 million reichsmarks (RM).[27] The

Spanish had hoped for a major reduction, perhaps equal to the nearly 40 percent rebate granted by Mussolini. José Larraz, the finance minister, took a persistently tough line, arguing that the Civil War had been part of an international conflict, "precursor of the present world conflict," and emphasizing both the military advantages and the "great advantages of a political nature" that Germany had gained from it. Franco stressed these same arguments at a major meeting on the problem at El Pardo on 14 November.[28] There was no general agreement on repayment, and in fact this issue would lapse until 1943–44.

The problem was that the Spanish economy desperately needed to import sizable quantities of petroleum, fertilizers, machine tools, and food, most of which Germany was unable to provide. Consequently, as mentioned earlier, the German agreement was quickly followed by new trade agreements with France in January 1940 and with Britain in March, which provided for extensive commerce, a British credit of £3 million, and also the requirement that no imported goods be re-exported. The Spanish government nonetheless was slow to make full use of these opportunities, even though they were desperately needed. Politics trumped economics, to the deteriorating well-being of the Spanish population.[29]

During the first half of 1940 German officials negotiated what was called the Wagner-Aktion (named after the naval attaché in Madrid), a scheme to import ESP60 million of vitally needed Spanish raw materials. They were paid for by Spanish currency made available in return for earlier imports, as well as the sale of German airplane parts, and were transported by Italian ships and other blockade runners, as well as in a few cases by airplanes, the OKW providing five large Junkers and ninety transport planes, which flew 300 tons of key Spanish and Portuguese raw materials, mainly wolfram, to Germany during the first eight months of 1940. Germany also made use of the services of Juan March to purchase 25 percent of the shares in a key Spanish oil company, CEPSA. In general, however, imports from Spain declined from RM22.5 million in the third quarter of 1939 to RM1.6 million in the second quarter of 1940, before rebounding after the fall of France, with restoration of direct rail service, to RM12.4 million in the final quarter of that year.[30]

Italy and Germany were able or willing to provide only limited technical assistance, extracted rather than provided capital, and could not supply the bulk of Spain's vital imports, so the Spanish government increasingly came to request the export of military matériel from the Reich. Since Spanish military production was so limited, arms were also requested from the Allies, who not surprisingly were very reluctant to supply them. Spanish representatives or delegations sought German arms and technical assistance, primarily for the air force, in May 1939 and in January and May 1940, but little was achieved before the fall of France.[31]

A series of negotiations went on throughout 1940 in which the Germans sought to extract maximal imports against minimal exports. Spanish negotiators made concessions on individual items, but the Germans never obtained the global agreement they wanted.[32] Imports from Germany in 1941 would amount to only ESP52 million, against ESP161 million in Spanish exports, some of it foodstuffs, such as citrus and almonds, desperately needed at home.[33] Altogether the trade deficit in favor of Germany rose from RM122 million at the close of 1941 to RM249 million by 30 June 1943.[34] As the situation deteriorated in Spain, the government even sought, unsuccessfully, to negotiate a $100 million loan from the United States in September 1940. The British credit was exhausted soon afterward, and a second loan was requested from London in November. Anglo-American economic relations only gained in importance.

The key German interests were concentrated in mining, but an audit at the end of 1940 found that 76 percent of the German investments in that sector had to be considered a loss. In April 1941 ROWAK, the German import consortium, "decided to close down all mining enterprises except all wolfram mines because of their importance for the war effort, and those iron ore, lead and tin mines which were making a profit by producing for the Spanish domestic market."[35] New mining investments were nonetheless being made in fluorspar in 1943 and the preceding guideline was never fully applied.

The regime passed a new mining law on 21 September 1942 which completely reserved to the state new claims on wolfram and tin in certain designated areas. Everywhere else all new claimants had to be either Spanish citizens or companies wholly owned by Spaniards. This requirement did not stop either the Germans or the Allies from filing new claims through Spanish front men. The most important new German effort was the Compañía Española Somar, S.A., devoted to vital wolfram. In fact, Germany's lack of foreign exchange, the steep rise in the prices of wolfram and other necessities due to Allied competition, and inefficient mines with bloated overhead and personnel costs all created great difficulty for the German mining companies and the import program, for which the Spanish government would later provide a partial bailout through an advance of RM100 million on its Civil War debt in the autumn of 1943.

Germany was so hard put to satisfy Spain's economic demands that by 1942 news of larger Anglo-American supplies was received with some relief. By 1943 Berlin would find that the easiest way to provide exports was through the war matériel eagerly desired by Madrid, even though it was in short supply in Germany.

CHAPTER **8**

Temptation Continues

Despite the decision not to enter the war immediately, the Spanish government was theoretically committed to make public at some future date its adherence to the German-Italian military alliance and to the Tripartite Pact with Japan. Its continued nonbelligerence was intended to be pre-belligerence, which explains why collaboration with Germany only increased during 1941.

Public expression of expansionist goals, building since mid-1940, was louder in 1941. The most notable publication was *Reivindicaciones de España* (Claims of Spain), a book with scholarly pretensions by the Falangists José María de Areilza and Fernando María Castiella, which appeared in April. It laid historical and cultural claim to large sections of Africa, and was followed during the course of the year by such books as *El estrecho de Gibraltar* by General José Díaz de Villegas, writing as "Hispanus"; Captain Luis Carrero Blanco's *España y el mar;* Alberto Cavanna Eguiluz's *Nuevo iberismo: Notas sobre política geográfica;* and José María Cordero Torres's *La misión africana de España,* followed the next year by others, such as Tomás García Figueras's *Reivindicaciones de España en el norte de Africa.* The book by Areilza and Castiella, clear and systematic but not shrill, initially attracted the most attention and is most commented on by historians, but the book most widely circulated and read was Cordero Torres's very brief *Aspectos de la misión universal de España,* issued in 1942 by the newly created Vicesecretaría de Cultura Popular. How all this was supposed to fit within the Nazi New Order was the theme of Juan Beneyto's *España y el problema de Europa: Contribución a la historia de la idea de imperio*, which would also appear in 1942, though its concept of European civilization remained distinct, since it affirmed a major role for Catholicism.

These works varied somewhat in their expansionist claims, but the tendency was to claim all those territories requested of Hitler by Franco and Serrano, while the most expansive included a large chunk of the western Sahara as well, and also much of eastern Nigeria. Cameroon was sometimes included, as it extended inland from Equatorial Guinea, but in most cases this territory was left out, since it was formerly a German colony, and it was sensed, correctly, that Hitler would want it back. Moreover, there were sometimes public as well as private references to French territory earlier seized from Spanish principalities, such as the French Basque departments, Roussillon, and Cerdagne, and also Andorra. The annexation of Portugal was not demanded publicly, but only expressed privately. At most Cavanna and Cordero Torres would refer to "federation" with Portugal, which would increase the power and influence of the Iberian peninsula abroad. As to the means, some were more diplomatic than others. Areilza and Castiella affirmed, "Perhaps by this point there is no viable peaceful solution for the problem of Gibraltar," while the mild-mannered Cordero Torres observed more discreetly that he was only outlining "general guidelines . . . not intended as an inflexible mandate for immediate execution in every detail"; the duplicitous Aranda also participated in this enterprise, publishing his own booklet on Morocco, which declared that "the present moment is historically unique for the interests of Spain."[1]

The general concept was a common one in history, that of a specially chosen people with a special mission to expand its dominion and its cultural and spiritual values to the less fortunate. As has been common in modern (as possibly distinct from some ancient) imperialism, this belief was predicated on a kind of higher authority, or in the Spanish case spirituality, which supposedly lifted Spanish imperialism beyond the level of materialism and self-seeking. These arguments were not new, dating in some form back to the Middle Ages.

The strongest claims were made with regard to Morocco, which, it was held, was really not foreign territory, but a geographical and in some sense cultural extension of Spain itself. This literature extensively elaborated on the interaction between the peninsula and Morocco, dating back to Roman times. In its strongest form, it held that there was really no difference between the two countries, except for religion, since they represented a common territory whose natural boundaries were the Pyrenees on the north and the Atlas range on the south. Thus Morocco was no more than "a part of Spain, extended to the far side of the Straits." The most extreme echoed the orientalist themes of "romantic Spain" and placed the home country outside the core of Europe, as García Figueras called Spain itself a territory of "Eurafrican transition," possibly even "African land." In this final phase of European imperialism, no other set of imperialists went quite so far in going native on their own claims of transnational identity, probably reflecting the confused debate on national identity in modern Spain itself. The Spanish Arabist Rodolfo Gil Benumeya even insisted on basic similarities in Spanish and Moroccan culture and social psychology, pointing to the salience in both societies of "controversy, social circles and the group of friends," the "tendency toward atomization in society and customs," "extremism and the absence of compromise" and the tendency toward "either petty domestic goals or grand and chivalrous ideals."[2]

German geopolitical theory had had considerable influence on Spanish geographers as well as on political and military essayists in recent years. All relied on the standard arguments of a relatively high Spanish birth rate and a natural zone for expansion, with emphasis on the need for territorial security, holding that control of Gibraltar and Morocco were necessary to provide a defensive framework for the peninsula.

Government leaders still hoped that Hitler would change his decision in favor of Vichy, so that Franco was alarmed by a report from Colonel Antonio Barroso, his military attaché at the French capital, sent on 20 February 1941, informing him that the Vichy authorities were determined to preserve all their empire and talked of general "European cooperation," meaning above all cooperation with Germany, to make that possible.[3] The Spanish continued to press the issue. In May 1941 the main Spanish news magazine, Mundo, declared that "the French African empire can and should undergo serious reduction, and not merely to the benefit of the Axis. Proven friendship must be worth something," with the clear implication that Spanish collaboration should be rewarded.[4] Since Britain was in these months defined as Spain's number one enemy, Franco would probably not have been surprised to learn that the British ambassador, Hoare, would later privately inform his American counterpart that, in Hoare's view, it would be best for all concerned if Britain and possibly the United States took responsibility for Morocco after the war.[5]

By the late winter of 1941 the Spanish regime was once again trying ineffectively to catch Hitler's interest, which was turned elsewhere. The embarrassing fact was that the Anglo-American countries were providing the vital supplies that Germany could offer only in very small measure. While Serrano tried to prevent a new emissary from Roosevelt from talking with Franco directly, Hoare took the initiative, following earlier efforts by his American counterpart, Weddell, in providing new assistance, signing a new commercial credit for Spain in April and urging the Americans to do likewise.[6] This was not possible, partly because of the Roosevelt administration's hard line, which made assistance dependent on a public pledge by the Spanish state renouncing collaboration and declaring that it "does not contemplate extension of aid to the Axis powers."[7] Worse yet, relations had completely broken down between Serrano and Ambassador Weddell, who waved at Serrano a postcard received by Mrs. Weddell bearing a German censor's stamp. When he declared that statements in the collaborationist Spanish press read as though written in a foreign language, Serrano responded that he had offended Spanish dignity.[8]

In March 1941 Franco acceded to one German demand in Morocco, expelling from Tangier the *mendub* (representative of the sultan in the French zone) and on the 20th the caliph of the Spanish zone made his official entry into the city as native overlord. The German consulate, closed in 1914, reopened some days later. It became a large legation and a significant espionage center for the next three years.

Meanwhile, Hitler still could not bear to abandon his Gibraltar fixation, even though he remained firm that he could not afford to satisfy Franco's maximal demands. By the end of February the plans for Barbarossa, the invasion of the Soviet Union, had been set, and optimism was high that the USSR could be finished off almost as quickly as France. Hitler therefore ordered that planning for Felix be resumed, the operation to take place as soon as troops could be spared from Barbarossa. This order produced Operation Felix-Heinrich, presented to Halder by his staff on 10 March, which posited that as soon as the troops invading the Soviet Union had reached the approximate line Kiev–Smolensk, hopefully by 15 July, units could begin to be withdrawn to prepare for the Gibraltar operation, which would then begin on 15 October. Felix-Heinrich would largely follow the original plan, with the same key forces involved, though the supporting units would be new. How ambitious this was was shown by the fact that it would still involve at least two full panzer divisions, as well as 29 of the total of 111 artillery battalions to be engaged on the eastern front. It was decided to reduce supply requirements for Felix-Heinrich, which nonetheless remained very sizable. The whole concept was so expansive that it never became an active plan, but was held on file pending developments. Nonetheless, the grandiose mood into which Hitler had entered after the fall of France lasted through the autumn of 1941. On 11 June, on the eve of Barbarossa, he still spoke of returning to Gibraltar and sending troops to Morocco and west Africa as soon as events in the east permitted.[9]

In the meantime, Hitler made a further effort to obtain concessions from Vichy. In March Admiral Raeder had attempted once more to impress on Hitler the importance of military bases in northwest Africa, and by early April the Führer decided to meet with Admiral Jean-François Darlan, new strongman of the Vichy government. This decision was apparently motivated by several factors: ambitions in Morocco and French Africa, interest in sending military aid through French Syria to the pro-Axis government of Rashid Ali, which had taken over Iraq on 3 April, and also the hope of using French North Africa as a source of supply for Rommel's logistically hard-pressed Afrika Korps. Hitler offered Vichy certain military concessions in return for closer collaboration, German naval facilities in west Africa, and the opening of a supply route to Rashid Ali. Darlan accepted some initial German military concessions and in turn agreed to permit transit of military assistance to Iraq. Though a partial agreement was completed at the end of May, Vichy's position hardened, and a month later British forces began to overrun French Syria.[10]

Meanwhile, Franco had not responded to Hitler's letter of 6 February for twenty days, finally writing on the 26th, a full two weeks after the meeting with Mussolini at Bordighera, and the letter does not seem to have been hand-delivered to Hitler until 6 March. It restated the Spanish position, protesting that "you, the Duce, and I" "are indissolubly linked in a historic mission," and that at Bordighera he "gave proof before the world of [his] determined attitude." He stressed, however, the importance of seizing Suez at the same time as Gibraltar, for otherwise "Spain's position in a prolonged war would become extremely difficult." Franco also emphasized Spain's many and grievous needs, with regard to which the Hendaye protocol was "rather vague," to put it mildly. He then boldly stated that "the facts in their logical development have today left far behind the circumstances which in October brought about this Protocol, so that it can be considered obsolete at the present time." Thus Franco virtually declared Spain free of any obligations, though he insisted that he must stress "my readiness to be completely and decidedly on your side, united in a common destiny," reiterating "my faith in the triumph of your cause, of which I shall always be a loyal supporter."[11]

Berlin maintained its policy of not trying directly to interfere in Spanish domestic affairs. Thus when Don Juan, pretender to the Spanish throne and resident in Rome, approached a German intermediary to try to gain support for the restoration of the monarchy (an indication of how broadly different Spanish factions at this time were trying to play the German card), Ribbentrop telegrammed Stohrer that Berlin had shown no interest and that this fact should be relayed to Franco.[12]

The Wilhelmstrasse was being less than frank and may have wanted to put pressure on the Caudillo. It has been alleged that Ribbentrop had first made contact with Don Juan in December, when Franco had initially dug in his heels.[13] At any rate, further contacts developed during the early months of 1941, though at that time the German government had little interest in trying to promote a political change in Madrid, for Hitler was anticipating that after the swift success of Barbarossa, he would have no difficulty in dealing with the Mediterranean, possibly before the end of the year.

The blitzkrieg that he launched into Yugoslavia and Greece on 6 April was another smashing success, overrunning both countries in three weeks. This victory turned heads in Madrid, as it did elsewhere, and once more ratcheted up enthusiasm for entry into the war. Even as the new commercial agreement was being signed with Great Britain, the Spanish press launched a new series of attacks on that country.

On 22 April Stohrer filed a lengthy report on the political situation in Spain, saying that the country was suffering from disastrous leadership, profound internal division, and near-famine conditions, with Franco increasingly isolated. Under these conditions, the leftist opposition was growing stronger and stronger. "Foreign Minister Serrano Suñer saw clearest of all; he recommended Spain's immediate entry into the war," but Franco would not agree. The military detested Serrano, however, so that "a coup d'état in the form of an ultimatum to Franco is possible at any time." "A few days ago General Aranda, the most politically active of the generals, declared to the Military Attaché that Spain certainly had to take part in the war." Amid this confusion and discontent the monarchists were gaining strength and "are endeavoring to win our interest. Don Juan is said to have promised in Berlin to adopt a thoroughly pro-German policy." Despite Franco's hesitation, "it may consequently be asserted that both the Foreign

Minister and the generals' party consider Spain's entry into the war necessary." If the supply question can be solved and "if we fulfill certain military wishes of Spain, on about 1 July the entry of Spain into the war must be expected even without any influence from us." A basic problem, nonetheless, is that "at present the generals say that they will not enter the war with Serrano Suñer." Stohrer concluded by inquiring whether Berlin was still interested in encouraging Spain's immediate entry. If that was the case, he asked further whether it was advisable to continue Germany's policy "of noninterference in Spanish domestic affairs." Should that policy change, he suggested, there were three alternatives: the first was to help Serrano become completely dominant. The second was "to help the generals to come into power. The generals are all friendly to the Germans (except, perhaps, for the present War Minister, Varela). . . . The formation of a military cabinet would represent an important step toward the restoration of the monarchy, because the generals are monarchists almost without exception and to some extent even now inclined to create a transition period by means of a regency." The third alternative was to "try to achieve a truce between the two opponents . . . . Our influence in Spain makes it entirely feasible to try all three possibilities," though since "relations with the Foreign Minister are good and trusting . . . too close relations with the military party have been avoided, although indirect contact is being kept with it continuously."[14]

In a lengthy conversation with Serrano, the Italian ambassador, Francesco Lequio, got the impression that Serrano regretted that Spain had not acted earlier, for the foreign minister declared that "only war can achieve the goals of the Falange" and resolve the internal political crisis. The combination of the Balkan blitzkrieg and Rommel's advance in North Africa once more made the option very attractive, and Serrano declared that after Spain entered the war, it would fulfill the protocol and announce its adherence to the Tripartite Pact.[15] Stohrer reported to Berlin a similar statement by Serrano that only entry in the war could solve Spain's domestic political crisis.[16] That month there was a new police crackdown on the opposition, which was opposed to participation, and the papal nuncio feared that Spain was once more about to enter the conflict.[17] A sign that this might indeed be the case came on 28 April, when the Ministry of the Navy ordered captains of all Spanish merchant ships on the course they should follow if their country suddenly found itself at war.[18] Serrano may have wished to enter the war at that point, but Franco decided otherwise, because increasingly serious internal division was now added to the other obstacles.

The British government again became alarmed, and during April Churchill mentioned the danger of Spain's entry twice in letters to Roosevelt. The British drew up two contingency plans, Puma and Pilgrim, which envisioned seizing the Canaries, if it came to that,[19] while a month later Roosevelt secretly ordered preparation of an American force that could be prepared to take over the Azores. Hitler feared that the British might seize the initiative in Portugal, northwest Africa or the Atlantic islands while the Wehrmacht was engaged with the Soviet Union. He had a brief chat with Gen. Espinosa, the Spanish ambassador, on 28 April, expressing his concern and warning the Spanish to be on their guard, again lamenting that Gibraltar had not already been taken and that German troops were not already in Morocco. This in turn aroused apprehension in the Spanish government, completely unaware of the imminent invasion of the Soviet Union, that Germany might act unilaterally to intervene in Spain.[20]

Hitler had no such intentions, and showed his lack of immediate concern for the western Mediterranean by ignoring Admiral Raeder's plea that Germany seize the key island base of Malta. Instead he ordered the costly invasion of Crete in the eastern Mediterranean on 20 May, the largest offensive by airborne troops in history. There was no equivalent in the west, nor did Hitler send any significant reinforcements to North Africa, for his attention was fixed on Barbarossa.

Ribbentrop had not even bothered to reply to Stohrer's query on how to deal with the mounting political problems in Spain, so the ambassador reiterated his question just as the longest and most serious political crisis in the history of the regime began to unfold in May. Ernst von Weizsäcker, state secretary to the Foreign Ministry, replied on 11 May that German policy toward Spanish internal affairs was unaltered.[21] Doubts had been raised in Berlin about Stohrer's effectiveness and his accuracy in evaluating Spanish affairs, but a recent Foreign Ministry investigation had judged him reliable.

On 2 May Serrano gave an unusually aggressive speech that demanded power for the Falange, but Franco was under considerable pressure from his generals, so his only response was to appoint the conservative monarchist (and anti-Falangist) Colonel Valentín Galarza to the Ministry of the Interior, a post technically vacant for months. This appointment outraged the Falangists and prompted Serrano's remarks to Lequio and Stohrer that only a decision for war would shake things up enough to give power to the FET. On 5 May ten provincial party chiefs resigned in protest, as did several other officials, creating a major crisis for Franco that he did not resolve until 20 May.

This was the most difficult internal political situation he ever faced, but he moved carefully step by step, maneuvering his pieces well. He made three major new Falangist appointments, all of loyalists on whom he could count not to generate dissent. One of them, José Luis de Arrese, became the new secretary general of the party, and would prove the most effective person ever to hold that office in the history of the regime. He immediately created a rival polarity to that of Serrano, so that henceforth the *cuñadísimo* would face a major antagonist within the party itself. Galarza remained minister, and Franco appointed an invaluable new assistant in the naval officer Luis Carrero Blanco, who became his new secretary of the presidency, or chief personal and political assistant, and within a year would begin to exercise some of the influence once wielded by Serrano. As in 1939, this reshuffling seemed at first to give more power to the Falangists, but in fact rebalanced the government in such a way as to reinforce Franco's personal authority. It did not resolve the tensions between the Falange and the army, which would remain acute through the summer of 1942 and then provoke one more crisis, but it gave Franco slightly greater control of the situation.[22]

This development, however, was not apparent in the immediate aftermath of the cabinet reorganization, which some observers understood to have increased the power of Serrano and the Falangists and thus to have the effect of hastening entry into the war. Stohrer reported on 30 May that "it is evident . . . that Serrano Suñer urgently desires entry into the war. As long as he does not fall, he will adhere to this view." The prospect of this outcome was much more favorable now than it had been a few months ago, especially "because of the unexpected easing of the food situation and because of the operation against Suez," which Franco had always hoped would coincide with his entry into the war. Stohrer urged greater military supplies for Spain, and recommended that a more precise decision be taken with regard to promises of territorial acquisition, though the Spanish leaders had not been pressing the latter point recently.[23] Though Hoare was alarmed, the British Foreign Office read the situation in Madrid more accurately than Stohrer, and concluded correctly that the political changes would not be likely to encourage Franco to enter the war.[24]

At the end of May, after the crisis had ended, Hans Thomsen, chief of the Nazi Party in Spain, suddenly appeared in Berlin to say that a group of generals was planning a coup to eliminate Serrano and form a new government of generals and Falangists under Franco, but feared that Hitler might forcibly intervene. According to Thomsen, they sought guidance as to how to coordinate their initiative with German policy. Ribbentrop correctly gauged the superficiality of the contacts and plotting involved, and saw to it that no German political intrigue destabilized the situation in Spain while Barbarossa was being developed.[25]

Mussolini, Ciano, and Ribbentrop met at the Brenner Pass on 2 June, and seven days later Serrano received a hand-delivered letter from the Italian foreign minister. In this missive Mussolini and Ciano urged the Spanish government at least to take the step of immediately making public its signing of the Tripartite Pact. Serrano replied immediately that Franco would be willing to consider doing so, adding that "our goal is to act militarily as soon as possible." He went so far as to tell Lequio, when handing him his response, that the question of Spain's territorial claims might be settled through a "completely private letter" that would offer the necessary guarantees, presumably kept secret so as not to alienate Vichy.[26] The chance of Hitler's reaching any such decision on the eve of Barbarossa was in fact nil, though at that moment even the Italian Fascist leaders knew nothing of the imminent offensive.

News of the massive invasion of the Soviet Union on 22 June, accompanied by Germany's announcement that its goal was to defend "our European civilization," touched off a great wave of enthusiasm in Madrid and in other parts of Spain. Ideologically, Hitler's war now made perfect sense to the supporters of the Spanish regime, to some for the first time. The German embassy found itself deluged with messages of enthusiasm, and the diplomats were surprised by numerous expressions of support from Carlists, hitherto the sector most reserved with regard to the German cause, though their support owed more to anticommunism than to enthusiasm for the Nazis. The FET immediately proceeded to capitalize on the situation by organizing a series of pro-German meetings and demonstrations all over the country. Even in neutral Portugal the invasion aroused an unprecedented wave of sympathy for the German cause, though it would soon wane.

The government met on the 23rd, producing a tense encounter between Serrano and Varela, the army minister, as Serrano promoted the idea of sending a group of Spanish volunteers to fight alongside the Wehrmacht. Varela, apparently supported by Galarza, the interior minister, vehemently opposed the dispatch of a Spanish army force (taking the same position as had German, Italian, and Soviet military leaders vis-à-vis Spain in 1936). Varela and Galarza insisted that, however desirable it might be to see the Soviet Union destroyed, the war had now become more complicated and the German army was now in a weaker strategic situation, making that of Spain more dangerous.[27]

The concept of a volunteer unit was therefore approved as a means of repaying Germany for its contribution to the struggle against communism in Spain and of affirming Spanish solidarity with Germany in its war against the common enemy of the human race. Once more the Spanish government identified its own battle in the Civil War with the military initiatives of Germany. Its official press release, which appeared in newspapers on the 24th, declared that "God has opened the eyes of statesmen, and for the past 48 hours *the beast of the apocalypse* has been under attack in the most colossal struggle known to history, to strike down the most savage oppression of all time." It stressed that the first blow in this struggle had been struck in the Civil War by "the glorious soldiers of Spain, commanded by their blessed and ever-victorious Caudillo, the world's first crusader in unceasing struggle against the Comintern and its diabolical machinations."

Falangist enthusiasts saw the new volunteer unit, soon baptized the Blue Division from the color of the Falangist uniform shirt, as their great military and political opportunity, but in a long discussion with Serrano on the 24th, Franco made it clear that the army insisted that all commanders and officers be regular army men. Immediately afterward, Serrano met with Stohrer, who suggested that the Spanish government accompany this gesture with a declaration of war at least against the Soviet Union. Serrano replied that such an act might bring a declaration of war from Great Britain, or at least a British and American blockade of Spanish commerce that could have devastating consequences. Of course, said the foreign minister, even sending the Blue Division might have this effect, "but if so, the course of events could no longer be changed." The Spanish cabinet met again late on the 24th, the Falangist ministers urging that the ideal moment to enter the war officially had arrived, though they were effectively challenged by the more conservative ministers. Stohrer was convinced that a decisive change had begun, reporting to Berlin on the 28th that Serrano was dead set on entering the war, and was exaggerating differences with Britain to prepare the political climate, though he still had to face the opposition of many of the generals and could not bring Spain into the war until conditions had been more fully prepared.[28]

In Madrid the university postponed final examinations, and toward noon on the 24th a large demonstration of students and other Falangists marched down the Gran Vía to the FET headquarters. Serrano was summoned from the Foreign Ministry, and from the balcony delivered an ex tempore speech to the ardent crowd: "Russia is guilty! To blame for our Civil War! To blame for the death of José Antonio [Primo de Rivera], our founder, and for the deaths of so many soldiers fallen in that war due to aggression by Russian communism! . . . History and the future of Europe demand the extermination of Russia!"[29]

The crowd then marched to the British embassy and tossed rocks through several windows, vandalized embassy cars, and ended up in front of the German embassy to cheer Hitler. Other demonstrations took place in various parts of Spain that day and the next, and on the 25th Spanish batteries at Gibraltar fired at a British plane and then exchanged rounds with British batteries that fired back. Around four o'clock on the afternoon of the 24th Hoare and the three British military attachés appeared at Serrano's home to protest the assault on the embassy. Serrano has claimed that when Hoare said that such things could occur only in a land of savages, he summarily dismissed them without further discussion.[30]

The immediate consequence was temporary new economic restrictions by the British, though those already imposed by the Roosevelt administration were more stringent. As Willard Beaulac, the new American counselor of embassy who arrived in Madrid in July 1941, wrote forty years later, American attitudes were "more emotional, more ideological, and more influenced by what they read in the press" than were those of the British.[31] Washington had cut oil supplies to only about 60 percent of the 1935 level, a restriction that remained for much of the war. Beaulac helped to establish better relations between Washington and Madrid by the fall of 1941, but the British government had difficulty persuading its American counterpart to add more carrot to the carrot-and-stick policy that London pursued.[32]

Intense enthusiasm for the Russian campaign, particularly among Falangists, continued into the summer, as some called for the organization of at least one additional volunteer division. Franco saw that this was too dangerous a time for Spain to enter the war, but there is no doubt that the invasion of the Soviet Union resonated strongly with him on a political and emotional level, and further stimulated his sense of identity with Hitler's cause. On 17 July, the anniversary of the rebellion of 1936, he delivered before the National Council of the FET the most outspokenly pro-German speech that he ever made. He denounced the "eternal enemies" of Spain, with clear allusions to Britain, France, and the United States, who still engaged in "intrigues and betrayal" against it. Franco boasted that "on our fields were fought and won the first battles" of the present conflict, and insisted, "Not even the American continent can dream of intervening in Europe without subjecting itself to a catastrophe. . . . In this situation, to say that the outcome of the war can be changed by the entry of a third country [against Germany] is criminal madness. . . . The issues of the war were wrongly presented and the Allies have lost it." He ended by hailing Germany for leading "the battle sought by Europe and Christendom for many years, in which the blood of our own youth will be united with that of our Axis comrades in living expression of our solidarity."[33]

Even the Axis ambassadors commented on the imprudence of these remarks. Stohrer reported that Serrano himself had termed the speech "premature," because, as Stohrer summarized Serrano's remarks, "It suddenly opened the eyes of the English and the Americans about the position of Spain. Previously the English Government especially kept on believing that only he [Serrano] . . . was pushing for war, while the 'wise and thoughtful' Caudillo would preserve neutrality unconditionally. That illusion has now been taken from them. They had come to realize that Spain, in understanding with the German Government, would enter the war at a suitable moment." Serrano observed that the speech might provoke either direct British intervention in Portugal or American action in Spanish Morocco.[34]

The following month an agreement was signed with Germany to provide 100,000 workers for the increasingly strained German industrial force,[35] though none left Spain for months. In the long run, only 10,569 were sent,[36] compared to nearly as many Spanish workers who worked daily for the British in Gibraltar throughout the war. Spanish consulates in France managed to recruit nearly 40,000 unemployed Republican émigrés for German jobs, whom Hitler, by the final year of the war, would dream of converting into pro-German revolutionaries to overthrow Franco.[37]

The Spanish government remained concerned about a British initiative against the eastern Atlantic islands, and indeed the four months from mid-April to mid-August 1941 were the second period of the war in which heightened apprehension about the danger of Spain's entry into the conflict led London to plan active countermeasures. After the German invasion of the Soviet Union, followed by Franco's notorious remarks on 17 July, the British contingency plan for seizing the Canaries was expanded and on the verge of being implemented, and temporarily was accompanied by consideration of an offensive operation from Gibraltar to gain broader and more secure defensive positions along the Straits. At that point the Madrid leaders considered the Portuguese Azores equally at risk, and Serrano announced on 29 July that the Spanish government would consider Britain's seizure of the Azores a hostile act. Only in mid-August was British planning deactivated, the embassy in Madrid convincing London that at present there was little danger of Spain's entry into the war.

British policy thus continued to offer a carrot along with a stick, as evidenced at a private dinner in the Spanish embassy in London on 2 October, when Churchill and other British figures once more expressed their support for an expansion of the Spanish protectorate in Morocco after the war was over. Churchill repeated this position at a British Defense Committee meeting two weeks later. The Churchill government soon concluded, however, that to encourage any further speculation along these lines would be a mistake, and directed Hoare to offer no further verbal support, however vague, for Spanish ambitions.[38] More successful was the strong British protest, accompanied by direct evidence, about the provision of refueling facilities for German submarines (Operation Moro), which had been under way more actively since March 1941. Franco reduced the submarine arrangements in October,[39] and then, probably not uninfluenced by the frustration of the German offensive in Russia and the vigorous Soviet counteroffensive, terminated them in December.

Internal political divisions remained pronounced. The government reorganization in May had the effect of somewhat strengthening Franco's personal authority but had resolved none of the points at issue. The basic rivalry between military leaders and Falangists was still intense. General Kindelán and certain other military leaders condemned Franco's July speech in private conversation, and in discussions with British diplomats Kindelán indicated at the end of August that he thought that Germany had no more than a 50 percent chance of winning the war, though some of the generals were temporarily dazzled by the initial success of the Russian campaign.[40]

The leader of military opposition to the Germanophile policy was not one of the murmurers who took bribes and chattered to British diplomats, but the minister of the army, José Enrique Varela. General Carlos Asensio, chief of the General Staff, reported to the German military attaché that Spanish army leaders were concerned about the idea being circulated that the Spanish would have to carry out the Gibraltar operation on their own, and Stohrer was convinced that this idea was being propagated by Varela to reduce enthusiasm for the whole operation. "Varela, as reported at various times, is probably the only important Spanish general who is considered to be our enemy; he leans strongly toward England, and holds the opinion that the war will not be won by us. Varela is on the point of marrying into a rich Bilbao family that is strongly Anglophile," Stohrer reported. He lamented that "Franco thinks a great deal of Varela." Stohrer was quite wrong to believe that Varela was the only Spanish general to hold such views. At the beginning of September, nonetheless, both Stohrer and Lequio had convinced themselves that Franco was now ready to enter the war or permit the Germans to carry out the Gibraltar operation, if only he were approached again with firmness and vigor.[41]

They misread the situation. Though Franco still felt committed to the German cause, his new political alignment was beginning to rein in the FET, always the prime source of Naziphilia, rather than reinforce it. José Luis de Arrese, the new secretary general, was in a general way Naziphile, but was opposed to Serrano and was also the champion of a more Catholic orientation of the party, of what would later be called the *fascismo frailuno* or friar fascism of the regime. The most ardent pro-Nazi in a high position was Gerardo Salvador Merino, the head of the state trade union organization, who had been in Berlin at the time of the May crisis and there intrigued unsuccessfully for German support, promising intense economic collaboration and entry into the war.[42] Franco and Serrano learned something of this promise, and Salvador Merino was soon undermined by a coalition of regime conservatives and Falangist rivals. He was purged during the summer and the trade unions were placed in more disciplined and obedient hands. In September the main functions of press, propaganda, and censorship were taken from Serrano's henchmen and placed under the new Vice-secretaría de Educación Popular, headed by the right-wing Catholic Gabriel Arias Salgado. Thus the summer of 1941, despite the new pitch of enthusiasm created by the invasion of the Soviet Union, also paradoxically marked the beginning of the downgrading of the most radically fascistic elements of the regime.

By September it had become clear that the changes considerably reduced the power of Serrano. To the intense animosity of the military was added the rivalry of new leaders in the FET, climaxed by the purge of Salvador Merino and the appointment of Arias Salgado. As Stohrer reported to Berlin, Serrano had become something of a scapegoat for all the ills afflicting Spain. It was rumored that the generals had again demanded his ouster in September, and that Serrano had even offered to resign. He told Lequio that he hoped to flee to the ambassadorship in Rome, which had been vacant for some time. Certainly from the time of the change in the direction of the press he received less attention and less flattery, and was no longer referred to pompously as the "minister-president."[43] Serrano's great weakness was that he had developed no major allies, and had come to depend too much on foreign policy and his relations with the Axis powers.

In a discussion with Stohrer on 10 October, Serrano expressed great bitterness against the generals, singling out Aranda as the most active critic and someone who maintained close contacts with the British embassy. The foreign minister repeated his conviction that a German victory was necessary for the future of Spain, which otherwise would be partitioned to the benefit of the Catalan and Basque nationalists.[44]

If there was one figure in the current government who stood out as the greatest master of duplicity, it was the opportunistic Falangist Demetrio Carceller, whom Serrano had arranged to become minister of commerce and industry in September 1940, as support for Serrano's policies. He probably realized that Serrano's position was already beginning to weaken, and in a discussion with the new American embassy counselor, Willard L. Beaulac, at the beginning of August described the foreign minister as "perverse" and "ambitious." He declared that Serrano tried to use the German connection to advance his own political interests—which was true enough —but declared that in fact Spain's collaboration could be described as minimal, that sending the Blue Division was no more than a gesture to relieve pressure by the Germans, and that it was a mistake to think of Franco as a dictator.[45]

In Berlin to discuss economic relations a month later, Carceller took exactly the opposite tack, insisting that the Spanish regime was fully committed to Germany, "was ready for anything," and that "the German General Staff had to determine whether it fitted in with its plans for Spain to enter the war or not," though the latter statement was made in conversation with a lower-ranking official. In a more practical vein, Carceller pointed out what he called "a certain contradiction in Germany's attitude toward Spain," since over the past two months the press section of the German embassy had incited an enormous amount of incendiary anti-British and anti-American statements in the Spanish press which had the effect of worsening the country's economic condition and weakening its military potential. He "mentioned . . . several times" that the U.S. ambassador had been persona non grata to Franco for several months, but that even a brief fifteen-minute conversation between the two could help to improve Spain's economic situation.[46] In fact, to a greater degree than any other cabinet minister Carceller would continue to play both sides throughout the war.

With the invasion of Russia still proceeding satisfactorily, Hitler had not lost interest in Gibraltar. In a memorandum issued at the beginning of September, he directed that the present level of relations with Spain be maintained with this goal in mind, though no military action could be contemplated before the spring of 1942. Therefore any economic measures to support it were premature, and further direct reconnaissance activities should be avoided for the moment. Field Marshal Keitel repeated these orders on 13 November, stressing that German officials must "refrain, as in the past, from discussing with members of the Spanish Government the preparation of any sort of joint military actions or the entry of Spain into the war." In a meeting with Ciano on 30 November, Hitler continued to lament the instability of the situation in the western Mediterranean and northwestern Africa, which he blamed on Franco. He declared that after taking Gibraltar he would have stationed two German divisions in Spanish Morocco, thoroughly controlling the region.[47]

The renovation of Hitler's Anti-Comintern Pact was the occasion for Serrano's last meeting with Hitler and Ribbentrop in Berlin, on 29 November. There he stressed the importance of a quick Axis victory in North Africa, adding that "Spain . . . performed every possible service to the Reich to the modest extent possible to her." He once again lamented the country's economic dependence on foreign powers, and declared that the news of his trip to Berlin had led Washington to cancel the departure of two oil tankers for Spain. Serrano confessed that in Spain "only the Falange was pro-German," for the country was still infested by "a tremendous number of Reds." He therefore requested that a number of young Falangist leaders serving in the Blue Division be sent home to generate political support, and Hitler agreed to that.[48]

In general, the second half of 1941 was the quietest period for Spanish foreign policy since the war began. With the shift of Germany's attention to the east, pressure to enter the war had virtually disappeared, while economic extremities had forced a de facto rapprochement with the British and Americans. On the one hand the formation of the Blue Division aligned Spain even more fully with the Axis than before, but on the other hand the new circumstances of the summer and autumn made participation in the war less likely than it had been at the end of April. With the main German war effort committed in the east, southwestern Europe and North Africa were more exposed to the British, the Gaullists, and potentially the Americans. Whatever Serrano may have wished, Franco had no intention of going further at that time, and some of the most important generals were taking a stronger stand against entering the war. Mid-1941 marked the apogee of the Spanish alignment with the Axis, but also a plateau beyond which for the moment there was no inclination to advance, and from which after another six months a very slow withdrawal would begin.

CHAPTER 9

The Blue Division

The Blue Division marked the height of Spanish collaboration in the German war effort. No other nonbelligerent country raised an entire reinforced division of troops to fight on a major front in World War II for two years. The Blue Division was therefore unique, and it has seized the imagination of so many writers and historians that the total amount of publication about this unit is greater than that concerning any other division of any of the belligerent powers.[1]

After Hitler defeated France and seemed about to do the same to Great Britain, Franco, Serrano Suñer, and their associates had no hesitation in labeling Britain and France the chief hereditary or "eternal" enemies of Spain. This was true enough in a historical sense, and France had supported the Republic in the Civil War, but British policy, if stiff and formal, had generally been rather benevolent toward Franco's regime. The Spanish government's attitude toward Britain was a question not of recent injuries but of historical memory and the Gibraltar enclave, whereas France held territory that Madrid coveted.

The animus toward communism and the Soviet Union was more intense. If Britain and France were historical enemies and imperial rivals, the Soviet Union was the ideological enemy number one, blamed for the Civil War and the nation's massive suffering. The Soviet regime was held responsible for the economic devastation from which the country suffered and which prevented it from playing a significant role in the current war.

Whereas Britain and France were believed to have frustrated Spain in the past, the Soviets were held to have tried literally to destroy it in the present, and hence the enormous wave of enthusiasm that the invasion of the Soviet Union roused among Franco's followers. This seemed to be a truly "just war," a crusade in the fullest sense.

The German government tried to present its invasion as a pan-European crusade against communism, and achieved some response in that regard. In later stages, as the war became more difficult, the theme of the Third Reich's effort as a defense of European civilization against Soviet barbarism became ever more prominent. Initially the German forces were joined by military units from Italy, Romania, and Slovakia, while Finnish forces also attacked to regain the territory stolen by the Soviets little more than a year earlier. The Finns would subsequently refer to this as the Continuation War (that is, a continuation of the defensive struggle against the Soviet invasion of 1939–40), and went over to the defensive after regaining their lost territory. Hungary also joined the Germans on 27 June, the day that the organization of a "legion of Falangist volunteers" was announced in Spain. The newly created German satellite state of Croatia also participated, while units of volunteers were also organized in most of the national and ethnic groups of continental Europe. There is no question that the invasion provided the Nazi regime with an international propaganda windfall, at least in its early months, and even roused considerable enthusiasm in neutral and largely pro-British Portugal. Of all the independent nonbelligerent states, however, only the Spanish government organized its own military force to fight beside the Germans.

Rafael Ibáñez Hernández has synthesized the motivations for its formation under four headings: (1) the pressure of the strong Germanophiles in the regime; (2) the felt need to repay the Civil War tribute in blood to Germany; (3) an example to mitigate Spain's long delay in entering the war; and (4) the expectation of a quick German victory, thus positioning Spain to participate in the spoils.[2] To these motives may be added the reason mentioned earlier, the desire to pay back the Soviet Union and help defeat the Communists.

The Blue Division was especially important to Serrano Suñer and the FET, who were responsible for the initiative and the recruiting, and for whom it played a significant role in guaranteeing a fascist future for Spain and for Europe. For Serrano it was an important link in the chain of events that would eventually bring Spain into the war at the right moment, and in an interview published in the *Deutsche Allgemeine Zeitung* on 2 July 1941 he declared that this was the beginning of a change in Spain's policy. Serrano even endorsed the conquest of territory in the east to guarantee the solidity and prosperity of the New Order and its revitalized society throughout Europe.

On the first day of recruiting, quite a few workers were noticed among the volunteers, yet the bulk of them came from the middle classes and especially from the universities. As in Italy, Germany, and Romania, the fascist movement in Spain had been especially strong among students, so easily drawn to any new radicalism. Indeed, without them it might not have survived its first years, and the Blue Division, particularly in its initial period, probably had the largest quotient of students, intellectuals, and writers of any military unit in Spanish history. An examination of the social origins of 4,500 volunteers from Madrid and Barcelona revealed that no less than 17 percent were students, followed by white-collar employees (*empleados*), with 14 percent.[3] Many Falangist leaders volunteered, so that among the initial recruits were five members of its National Council, the head of its student syndicate, and eight provincial chiefs, as well as a considerable number of lesser luminaries. One of Franco's youngest cabinet ministers, the decorated Civil War veteran José Antonio Girón, the regime's first minister of labor, also volunteered but was not permitted to leave his ministry. Twenty-nine members of Soviet nationalities who volunteered were accepted, as well as one German Jewish officer, Erich Rose, who had lengthy experience in the Civil War after earlier being expelled from the German army by Hitler.[4] There were also a number of Portuguese as well as a few Moroccans, the latter among the noncommissioned officers.

The official designation was División Española de Voluntarios (DEV), but from the beginning the unit was generally known as the Blue Division, from the color of the shirt worn by the Falangists who accounted for so many of the first recruits. In many parts of the country there were more volunteers than could be accepted, but exceptions were most notable in Catalonia and in the Basque Country, and also in highly anticommunist and normally militant Navarre, where the Carlists tended to boycott a primarily Falangist enterprise. At the University of Deusto, then the only full-fledged Catholic university, not a single student volunteered. There was considerable pressure on very young, low-level leaders of the FET to present themselves, and failure to do so cost some of them their posts.[5] Altogether, 18,000 volunteers were initially accepted. At the insistence of army leaders, all officers came from the regular army, as did two-third of the NCOs, a requirement that gave the division greater coherence. The core was composed of three full infantry regiments of three battalions each plus one battalion of mobile reserve. The additional fourth ersatz or cadre and training regiment would also be committed to combat duties. All the troops would receive the regular pay of German soldiers from the German government, but would also be paid by the Spanish government at the elite rate of members of the Spanish Legion, ESP7.5 per day. The division would be accompanied by a single squadron of fighter pilots, the Escuadrilla Azul.[6]

The commander presumably had to be drawn from the very small pro-Falangist sector of senior officers. Most of these men were either unsuitable or not trusted fully by Franco. The choice therefore fell on the experienced Agustín Muñoz Grandes, veteran of combat in Morocco, who had been responsible for organizing the Republic's special riot police in 1931–32. Arrested by Republicans in the Civil War, he managed to avoid execution and eventually made his way to the Nationalist zone, where he served as a divisional commander for the second half of the Civil War. Muñoz Grandes had been radicalized by the conflict and espoused a militant Falangism, performing rather ineffectively as secretary of the FET for a brief period in 1939–40. Most recently he had been military commander of the Campo de Gibraltar district, where he had pressed for offensive action and entry into the war.

Muñoz Grandes was an astute choice. He was a tough, hard-bitten professional, austere, hardworking, and resistant to corruption. He possessed administrative talent as well as the capacity to command. His combination of military intelligence, courage, and resoluteness would soon bring him the respect and even the admiration of the Germans.[7]

The division began basic training under German instructors at the Grafenwöhr barracks in Bavaria, where all ranks had assembled by 23 July. Training was accelerated as much as possible, and the first sections left by rail for the east on 19 August. The route to the front provided the first test of the Spanish volunteers, as they found that the now world-famous "blitzkrieg army" in fact had few trucks but moved primarily by rail and on foot. The odyssey involved nine days by train at a very slow pace, a march to the east of thirty-one days, and thirteen more days by very slow train. The length and slowness of the journey were due to a decision by Hitler and the German command to concentrate strictly German units for the decisive drive on Moscow and therefore to shift the Spaniards to the north, where they would initially play a defensive role. As Division 250 of the Wehrmacht, though internally under strictly Spanish command, it took up a position at Novgorod, advance units first coming under Soviet artillery fire on 7 October.[8]

The Spaniards were not initially subjected to major military pressure, but winter conditions on the eastern front came as something of a shock to them, and so did the muddy spring. That first winter the division registered more than 2,500 cases of illness and 1,235 cases of frostbite. The Spanish troops soon learned to strip Red Army corpses of their superior winter clothing. The Soviets also enjoyed air and artillery dominance in the Blue Division's sector, but deteriorating weather limited the planes' effectiveness and reduced the accuracy of the guns. The division's first offensive action, a limited advance beyond the Volkhov River, just to the north of Novgorod, was executed successfully at first but bogged down against superior Soviet numbers. During November the new position, at one point an absurd perimeter nearly 110 kilometers long, was subjected to very heavy counterattack. By early December the Spanish units had to retire to the west of the river once more, but never broke under stiff pressure. At the end of the year the division reported 1,400 dead.[9]

Hitler was impressed by the combat reports and on 4 January 1942 observed to one of his favorite commanders, SS General Sepp Dietrich, that the Spanish troops, though unkempt and "wildly undisciplined," "a crew of ragamuffins," had "never yielded an inch of ground" under attack. "One can't imagine more fearless fellows. They scarcely take cover. They flout death. I know, in any case, that our men are always glad to have Spaniards as neighbors in their sector."[10] His description was validated by the next Spanish combat, the suicidal dispatch of the 200-man Spanish ski company across the frozen expanses of Lake Ilmen, to the south, to support a German position that was nearly surrounded. The company was virtually wiped out in the attempt—moving in temperatures of $-52°C$ ($-61°F$), it suffered 94 percent casualties and eighteen of the Spaniards eventually had to undergo double leg amputations—but a small nucleus got through to support the Germans.[11]

During January and February the main part of the Blue Division helped the German units to its north seal off a Soviet offensive on the west bank of the river. During March and April the Spaniards participated in an offensive to eliminate this bulge, the operation in which Soviet General Andrei Vlasov was captured. The summer months were relatively quiet by comparison, and at the beginning of September the division was taken out of line in the Novgorod sector to a new position farther north, on the edge of the southern suburbs of Leningrad, exchanging a completely rural environment for an at least partially suburban one. Its mission was to anchor the southern end of a German offensive to seize Leningrad, but instead had to fight desperately to blunt the most massive Soviet counteroffensive yet during September and October. The German offensive was canceled, and in the last four months of the year the division lost 257 more men.[12]

The Soviet winter offensive of 1943 brought more heavy fighting, including the massive assault at Krasny Bor, near the center of the Spanish line, on 10 February. For the first time the division buckled and began to give way. One regiment crumbled, though a desperate counterattack managed to seal off the Soviet advance after some ground was yielded, restoring a continuous defensive line. This was the most costly day of the war for the heavily outnumbered Spanish troops, as they suffered 2,252 casualties in less than twenty-four hours, including at least 1,125 dead—one-fourth of all their fatalities in more than two years of combat. Soviet casualties for the day were estimated at 7,000–9,000. Other stiff Soviet assaults had to be fought off during February and March, but the last seven months of the division's existence, until it was formally disbanded in October 1943, were more calm, producing only minor actions.[13]

A kind of hagiographic literature has developed around the Blue Division in Spanish, crediting them not merely with a valiant combat record—an obvious fact—but also with having shown great chivalry and generosity to Russian civilians, in marked contrast to German arrogance and racism. While the "White Legend" of the Blue Division in this regard is overdrawn,[14] it seems to have a degree of substance. Spanish soldiers also sometimes committed crimes, but on balance they seem to have shown greater humanity, and when surviving veterans or their descendants visited the Novgorod district after the war, the older inhabitants of the region who remembered them often spoke relatively favorably of their deportment.

By 1942, when the length and harshness of the campaign became evident, it grew harder to find replacements for the division. There were always volunteers, but by 1943 it became necessary to have recourse to a certain number of regular army troops, so that the division was no longer an all-volunteer force. When it was finally disbanded, 2,133 men remained behind in November 1943 to continue to fight against the Soviets, most of them volunteers but a few the objects of coercion. This group had a higher desertion rate than the division itself. They were called the Legión Española de Voluntarios (LEV) or Blue Legion, initially assigned to the German 121st Division, but Franco dissolved the legion in March 1944 as his general policy turned increasingly defensive. Whereas the return of the initial veterans was met with enthusiasm among the public in 1942, the final return of the volunteers in the autumn of 1943 was denied all publicity and was received with apathy, international conditions having greatly changed.[15]

Even in March 1944 a number still remained behind and were organized into a small "Spanish Volunteer Unit" of 243 men. There were also very small Spanish units in the Waffen SS, and a few Spaniards enlisted directly in the regular German army. A handful of former Republican Spanish workers, recruited in France (sometimes forcibly) for work in Germany, apparently also volunteered for the German army to escape their drudgery. A small trickle of volunteers presented themselves for clandestine recruitment in the Waffen SS or the German army, the embassy in Madrid holding a list with 130 names as of 18 January 1944.[16] As late as the late spring and summer of 1944, possibly as many as 300 Spaniards clandestinely crossed the Pyrenees to enlist in the German forces.[17] These men were mainly veterans of the Blue Division, fanatical young Falangists of the Frente de Juventudes, or in a few cases simply adventurers. One veteran who claims to have gone back that summer, Miguel Ezquerra, enlisted in the German army and quickly rose to the rank of colonel of a very understrength regiment of foreign volunteers, and found himself with the remnants of his unit helping to defend the center of Berlin at the close of April 1945. Captured by the Soviets, he soon escaped and managed to make a clandestine return to Spain.[18] Most of these final volunteers were not so fortunate. Moreover, they were not recognized by the Spanish regime but threatened with loss of citizenship.

The total number of volunteers in the division itself may have been as many as 45,500. Statistics of the Fundación División Azul, organized many years later in Madrid, list 4,954 dead, 8,700 wounded, 2,137 cases of amputation (mutilados), 1,600 victims of frostbite (congelados), 372 prisoners, and 7,800 cases of sickness. Thus casualties were high, though proportionately considerably less than those of either the German or Soviet forces as a whole on the eastern front. The majority of Spaniards served enlistments of no more than a year or so, their front never collapsed, and so the great majority survived. The heaviest price was paid by the Ruiz Vernacci family, two of whose sons were killed fighting in the division. The division registered few deserters and comparatively few volunteers were taken prisoner, though of the 372 men who fell into the hands of the Soviets, the three-quarters who managed to survive served extremely long terms in the Soviet Gulag, ranging from nine years to in a few cases as many as fifteen years. The main group of 248 division prisoners, plus fifteen downed pilots of the Escuadrilla Azul, were returned to Spain in 1954, the very last five years later.[19]

Though the Germans provided the division's arms and equipment, the Spanish government punctually paid for its maintenance, a cost that eventually totaled ESP613.5 million. According to one computation, this was equivalent to 39 percent of Spain's Civil War debt to Germany. Invalid survivors later qualified for German army pensions, for which the postwar Federal Republic paid a total of DM80 million between 1965 and 1995,[20] though in toto the Spanish state paid much more.

Xavier Moreno Juliá, the most thorough historian of the division, concludes that its mobilization served temporarily to revitalize the FET at a point in 1941 when its decline had already begun. The FET at first monopolized recruitment, though the division always remained under regular army command and was always subject to the Spanish Code of Military Justice. General José Enrique Varela, minister of the army during the division's first year, was intensely anti-Falangist and always sought to keep the division on a short leash, but his successor, Carlos Asensio, was one of the few pro-Falangist generals and was more supportive. All members of the division swore the personal military oath of loyalty to Hitler, but as commander of the armed forces and not as head of the National Socialist Party.

Most of the Spanish volunteers went to the eastern front to combat and destroy communism, while a much smaller group of approximately 800 Spanish Communists served in the Soviet forces.[21]

Their high motivation explains their generally strong morale and combat spirit in difficult circumstances. The Blue Division fought on the most deadly major front in World War II and was exposed to the most severe extremes of climate. Not only was it almost always outnumbered, but it found itself inferior in firepower as well. Throughout its campaign it enjoyed little air support, and its artillery was almost always weaker than that of the enemy. Moreover, unlike all German divisions without exception, the entire division was never withdrawn for rest and rehabilitation. The German command furloughed only small units and, primarily, individual soldiers. Hitler was so impressed by the division's combat spirit that he had a special medal created to award its members, something that he did for no other foreign unit. In addition, the Spanish volunteers won many regular individual German and Spanish decorations, including two German Knight's Crosses, two Gold Crosses, 2,497 Iron Crosses (138 of the first class), and 2,216 Military Merit Crosses (16 of them first class).[22] To some extent they saw themselves as liberators of the Russian people, one factor, though not the only one, in their slightly more harmonious relations with the civilian population in their areas. Franco and the regime leaders, in turn, interpreted the intervention of the Blue Division as Spain's contribution to a broader conflict, the European resistance to Soviet communism, a common European enterprise of which the Spanish Civil War marked an earlier high point. During the three decades of the Franco regime that followed, professional officers who had served in Russia would tend to play elite roles in the army and the security forces, holding many significant commands.

Formation of the division in one sense helped temporarily to stabilize an uncertain domestic political situation, pacifying Falangists and also making it possible to ship out some of the most ardent and fanatical to fight abroad. Yet there was some danger that this tactic might backfire, for the division was a site of extreme Germanophilia and zeal for Spain's entry into the war, and, as will be seen in the next chapter, Hitler sought to use Muñoz Grandes to put pressure on Franco.

Serrano Suñer insisted to the Germans that the Blue Division inaugurated a new level of collaboration, yet in his later writings he contended the very opposite—that it was a ploy that enabled the Spanish to limit collaboration. Curiously, both interpretations hold an element of truth. The division initially marked a new peak of collaboration, but later it served as a kind of bargaining chip and pledge of good faith that was used to limit or avoid other collaboration. Its 5,000 combat deaths repaid the blood debt stemming from the role of the Condor Legion, which suffered 300 dead in the Civil War, a proportion of approximately 16 to 1. It turned out not to complicate relations with Britain and the United States to any great degree. After the initial sharp reduction in oil shipments, Washington generally went along with British policy for two years, until the whole course of the war began to change, at which point policy toward Madrid would have tightened in any event. From the summer of 1943 pressure mounted for dissolution of the division, but from that point Allied pressure against the regime in general was steadily increasing.

10

Temptation Abates

The turning point in the European and East Asian wars came with Japan's attack on the United States, followed four days later by the declarations of war by Germany and Italy. The attitude of Hitler and Mussolini toward the United States had been contradictory, at first somewhat friendly but changing into mounting hostility as the 1930s advanced and Roosevelt became more outspoken in his opposition to the Axis aggressions. It might be thought that memory of the impact of the United States on World War I would have given them pause, especially since both Hitler and his generals were concerned to avoid the mistakes of that war. They saw Germany's chief handicap in the earlier conflict as having to fight on two fronts, aggravated by internal weakness, producing the Nazis' favorite accusation of a "stab in the back." At the outset Hitler had promised his generals that Germany would not make the mistake of fighting a war on two major fronts at the same time. Before 1942 he had partially kept that pledge, but would do so in the long run only in the paradoxical sense of a war on three or four fronts.

Hitler was aware that the United States would eventually be capable of large-scale military production, but he knew from his own experience that it would take some time to mobilize and that the United States would not be able to put a major combat force into Europe before the spring of 1943 at the earliest. This calculation proved correct, and he planned to have won the war in continental Europe by the end of 1942, a calculation that failed miserably. On the one hand, since the summer of 1940 he had fretted over the aggressive initiatives of the Roosevelt administration, though he tended to interpret them as indications of the U.S. government's desire to inherit the position of a mortally wounded British empire. He relied a great deal on intuition, and it did not necessarily fail him when he intuited that the Americans, or the British and Americans, might attempt to seize the eastern Atlantic islands or attempt a landing in northwest Africa, as indeed they did in November 1942. That concern played a role in his negotiations with Franco during the fall and winter of 1940–41. On the one hand, his understanding of the United States was refracted through his racial doctrine, which led him to conclude that its multiracial society was hopelessly mongrelized; on the other, he could not ignore its vast resources, even if he thought they represented more quantity than quality.[1]

This belief lay at the root of the relationship with Japan, the Tripartite Pact of September 1940 being designed specifically to encourage the Japanese not to back down in their confrontation with the United States in the Pacific. If it came to all-out war between Japan and the United States, Hitler calculated that the Americans would at least be tied down long enough in the Pacific to enable him to liquidate the war in Europe. A German-led Europe would then be impregnable, victorious in the final contest for world dominance. Conversely, if the diabolical Roosevelt were to achieve his goal of maneuvering the United States into an immediate war with Germany while maintaining peace with Japan, Hitler realized that he would be presented with a serious complication, to put it mildly. Hence his instructions to submarine commanders during the summer and autumn of 1941 to avoid any confrontation with the American naval units that had, on Roosevelt's instructions, engaged in an undeclared war with German forces while protecting British convoys in the northwest Atlantic.

The Japanese onslaught, followed by the United States' declaration of war one day later, at first began to develop the scenario that Hitler had in mind. Though a state of war existed between the United States and Japan, Roosevelt found that he could not, at least for the moment, ask the U.S. Congress for a similar declaration of war against Germany. The Reich had not attacked the United States or even done anything to provoke it directly, and there was very strong sentiment both among the American public and within the Congress not to become involved in another European war. As of 8 December 1941, it looked as though Hitler were winning and Roosevelt losing, for the United States was at war with what Roosevelt judged to be its number two enemy, while his administration seemed helpless to maneuver the country into a state of war against its number one enemy. Then on 11 December Roosevelt's problem was miraculously solved by the German and Italian declarations of war, even though the terms of the Tripartite Pact did not require the other two powers to come to the assistance of the third power in a conflict that the latter initiated. Why did Hitler do it?

As far as can be determined, he did it without the slightest hesitation, and found almost no doubters among his chief henchmen—unlike the situation before the invasion of Russia—or on the part of Mussolini. There seem to have been several factors that influenced Hitler's thinking. One was that he thought it made little difference, since the United States was doing all it could to help Great Britain anyway, whereas, with the new Pacific war on its hands, it would be able to assist Britain much less than before. Second, Hitler seems to have had the idea that the Japanese navy was superior to the American fleet, so the latter would have its hands full. A third factor was the aforementioned calculation that even under the best circumstances the Americans could not put a significant force into Europe before 1943. A fourth was his conviction that Soviet resistance would largely be broken before the close of 1942. A fifth factor probably had to do with his annoyance at the policy of restraint that he had felt forced to follow in recent months, particularly in view of Roosevelt's numerous provocations and his undeclared naval war against German submarines. Hitler apparently felt that Roosevelt was making a fool of him, especially after an unusually provocative speech by radio that the U.S. president directed against Nazi Germany on 9 December.[2] Hitler believed that war with the United States had become inevitable, and that an official state of war was now in Germany's best interests, since it would guarantee that Japan would not weaken or come to terms with the United States in a separate peace.[3]

Ribbentrop then asked the other European signatories of the Tripartite Pact similarly to declare war on the United States. Those that lay under German guns in east-central Europe did so (with the exception of Finland), but Franco politely demurred, though Serrano immediately informed the German ambassador that he considered Germany's and Italy's initiative correct, and that he fully shared the sentiments behind it, as he no doubt did in fact.[4] The Spanish leaders professed not to be impressed by America's entry into the war and at first this may have been the case, though they understood that it would complicate the situation and discourage any major new initiative on their part. Franco and Serrano continued to believe in

German victory, but it would now take longer and be more difficult. It might also be less complete. They told their Axis counterparts that the Spanish position remained unchanged, as Franco announced in the *Boletín Oficial del Estado* on 19 December. Serrano said to the Italian ambassador, Lequio, that in fact Japan's offensive would now reduce American aid to Britain and the Soviet Union, reflecting the trend of Hitler's thinking and drastic underestimation of American capabilities. Spain would merely wait until this situation played itself out, and then within its own sphere could "dictate terms." Serrano added that "Spain will evidently not be able to avoid joining the European united front when the development of the war requires it," and offered to transmit the Italian diplomatic correspondence from Latin America in the official Spanish valises.[5]

Captain Luis Carrero Blanco, Franco's undersecretary of the presidency, was now becoming a key adviser and offered his evaluation in a written memorandum of some length. He judged the war now to be a struggle between "the power of evil incarnated in the Anglo-Saxon/Soviet coalition managed by the Jews" and a reaction that was vigorous but not guided by the principles of Catholic Christianity, which was also a problem, creating a war "whose duration is hard to predict but inevitably lengthy." Both circumstances were reasons for Spain not to alter its present policy. There was no question of ever joining the Jewish-dominated Allies, so Spain's choice would inevitably have to be Germany, though its paganism was distasteful. When the time came, entry into the war should be secretly negotiated for some future date by the military leadership, not by the overly ambitious foreign minister.[6]

The immediate concern was the danger of an Anglo-American incursion into the Canaries or Spanish Africa. At the beginning of the new year Franco reinforced military units in both the Canaries and Morocco, and placed all the Spanish African territories under his personal supervision. There was ample evidence of increased activity by the Allies in Tangier and in Dakar, while Allied propaganda against the Spanish regime was growing in both volume and intensity. Matters were further complicated by Hitler's decision to expand German activity in Tangier, where the consulate was elevated to the rank of general consulate and its staff increased from fifteen to fifty, somewhat to the annoyance of the Spanish.

Though Spanish publications on politics and strategy continued to endorse the Axis and the goal of imperial expansion, the new year of 1942 nonetheless brought the very slow beginning of a process of marking some ideological distance. The first straw in the wind came from the Instituto de

Estudios Políticos, the recently created brain trust of the regime. Its director was Alfonso García Valdecasas, once a liberal Republican who had
been a co-founder of the original Falange in 1933. Frightened by its fascism, he had quickly abandoned that enterprise but subsequently reestablished himself in the good graces of Serrano and the new regime during the
Civil War. García Valdecasas liked to stress José Antonio Primo de Rivera's
denial in 1935 that the Falange was a fascist movement.

In the issue of the new *Revista de Estudios Políticos* that came out in
January 1942, García Valdecasas published under his own name a lead
article titled "The Totalitarian States and the Spanish State," carefully dif-
ferentiating the character of Spanish totalitarianism:

> In the original Points of the Falange, the state is defined as a "total-
> itarian instrument at the service of the integrity of the fatherland." It
> is, then, deliberately expressed that ours is an instrumental concept
> of the state. Every instrument is characterized by being a medium
> for something, by a task that it serves.
>
> No instrument is justified as an end in itself. It is worthwhile inso-
> far as it fulfills the end for which it is destined. Therefore, the state is
> not for us an end in itself, nor can it find its justification in itself.
>
> . . . The state ought not to pursue ends or undertake tasks that
> are not justified as a function of the integrity of the fatherland. On
> the contrary, its forces are dispersed and wasted in improper enter-
> prises, which, when attempted, aggravate the problem of bureaucra-
> tization to which we have previously referred.
>
> . . . In order to justify itself in a positive sense, the state must act
> as an instrument for the achievement of ultimate moral values.
>
> . . . Genuine Spanish thought refuses to recognize the state as the
> supreme value. This is the meaning of the polemical attitude of all
> classical Spanish thought against the reasons of state enunciated by
> Machiavelli.

This article was no more than a straw in the wind, but it reflected the
nuances in some aspects of Spanish political thinking that would slowly
become more pronounced.

Erich Gardemann, the German counselor of embassy, reported that
Franco had begun to hint in November 1941, a little over a year after the
meeting at Hendaye, that he would like to talk to Hitler again. In the
middle of December Ribbentrop dispatched a top aide, Rudolf Likus, to
Madrid to investigate the situation. Likus was also given the task of setting
up a separate German information network apart from Stohrer, whom
Ribbentrop did not trust. Likus reported that Gardemann's information

might be correct, that Franco seemed to have some interest in coming to Germany and reviewing the Blue Division as commander in chief, while discussing closer relations with Hitler. There was speculation that Franco wanted to gauge German support on his own, without Serrano Suñer, and also learn if Serrano had engaged in any special conversations and made any promises when he had visited Berlin to renew the Anti-Comintern Pact at the end of November. Since returning to Madrid the *cuñadísimo* had engaged in a new round of bragging, insinuating that the Germans would guarantee his role in Spanish government. In order to obtain a more frank opinion, the Germans arranged to have the matter taken up with Franco on 3 January by his old boyhood friend and now industrial chief Juan Antonio Suanzes, at which time he declared that the domestic political situation was too tense to permit him to leave the country.[7]

As early as 10 January 1942, after the Blue Division had been in action only three months, Franco became somewhat alarmed by early losses, though there would be worse to come, and by the Russian spaces involved, with the division at that point technically holding a 100-kilometer perimeter. This first experience with the eastern front was unsettling, and he feared a major Soviet assault might break the Spanish position. Therefore the Conde de Mayalde, a Serrano associate who had replaced General Espinosa as ambassador in Berlin though he spoke no German, was ordered to request the temporary withdrawal of the Spanish division for reinforcement and reorganization, but the German military command did not agree. Mayalde repeated his request, emphasizing that some of the young Falangists were needed to maintain political zeal and a strong pro-German orientation at home. By the end of the month, Franco's close associate General Pablo Martín Alonso was sent to Berlin to press the issue, followed by General Carlos Asensio, head of the General Staff, six weeks later.[8] Arrangements were worked out for rotation and replacement of troops, but no temporary withdrawal.[9] Mayalde was nonetheless ordered to continue to press the point, as he did in Berlin on 21 February, saying that withdrawal and reorganization were needed both for military reasons and because of political pressures in Spain. German authorities replied that the Spanish division could not be spared on the front line, that it was in no danger of being overwhelmed, and that any necessary reorganization could be done piecemeal.[10]

As the war continued and grew more complicated, Franco seems increasingly to have lost enthusiasm for being personally identified with the Blue Division, and was notably absent from the large ceremony in honor of the first returning veterans held in Madrid's Retiro Park in May. By that time plans were under way to replace the division's commander, Muñoz Grandes, who had earned Hitler's esteem, with General Emilio Esteban Infantes, non-Falangist, politically conservative, and more representative of the military hierarchy.

The widening of the war encouraged the anti-Serrano military commanders to become more vocal in their criticisms. On 6 January a delegation of generals led by Kindelán visited the Generalissimo, demanding the removal of Serrano and insisting that the present pro-German policy impeded vital imports from the western hemisphere, without which Spain could not survive. Kindelán went so far as to begin to say that the combination of the positions of chief of state and president of government was too much for any one man, though Franco cut him short in mid-sentence and dominated the conversation. By the second week of January there was an explosion of rumors that Serrano and other Falangists might be ousted in favor of a new military-led cabinet that would return Spanish policy to simple neutrality. Serrano assured the German ambassador that this was just talk, as was indeed the case, but a lot of talk there was, as the internal tensions within the regime showed little sign of abating.[11] Serrano sought support from the Axis powers, but neither the German nor the Italian ambassador received instructions to intervene, and the rumors soon quieted. At this point pressure from the military was more of a problem than the FET, and Franco was using the latter to counterbalance the former.

Relations with Portugal

The United States' entry into the war heightened the war's Atlantic dimensions and encouraged closer cooperation between Lisbon and Madrid, with regard to both Latin America and the security of the Atlantic islands. The Spanish military also urged closer relations with Portugal, and an initiative from Lisbon was expanded into a visit by Salazar to Seville in mid-February. There Franco, rather than Serrano, dominated the Spanish side of the discussions.

Salazar greatly distrusted the United States but feared the Soviet Union even more, and was not pleased to see his British ally lined up with the Soviets. In a major speech on 25 June Salazar denounced the Anglo-Soviet alliance, which had been announced on 26 May, along with the weaknesses and proclivities of democratic systems in general. This outburst temporarily strained Anglo-Portuguese relations.

Invasion of the Soviet Union stimulated enthusiasm for the Axis cause among a considerable portion of the Portuguese military, the police, and the country's militia and youth movements. Salazar, however, continued to have few illusions about Hitler, and since the spring of 1940 secret conversations had been ongoing between London and Lisbon about arrangements for the evacuation of the Portuguese government to the Azores in the event of a German invasion of Portugal. There was nonetheless more than a little disagreement about the terms of such an operation, and early in 1942 the Portuguese government took great offense when it uncovered a secret British organization in Portugal that included Portuguese Communists, aimed at committing acts of sabotage should the Portuguese end up by giving in to Hitler.

The occupation of Portuguese East Timor in the South Pacific by Australian and Dutch forces on 17 December 1941 had been received with outrage in Lisbon, and momentarily produced the threat of a break in relations with London.[12] Salazar was also concerned about the announced desire of the Roosevelt administration to promote the liquidation of the European empires, since his regime considered retention of the large African colonies indispensable to the well-being of Portugal.

Before the Allied victories that would begin during the second half of 1942, Salazar's outlook was that the war was likely to end in a sort of draw or compromise peace. In such a future, he looked to the possibility that right-wing Latin Catholic regimes such as those of Spain, Portugal, and Vichy France "might come to play a decisive role, one that would be politically, culturally and strategically extensive to South America."[13] Though he did not at all support Franco's policy of nonbelligerence, Salazar would cooperate as much as possible with Spain to keep foreign troops out of the peninsula and, though he did not agree with the pro-Axis character of the Spanish policy of *hispanidad* in Latin America, he would cooperate with it in the interest of keeping South American countries purely neutral and out of the clutches of the United States, a goal to which he attached great importance.[14]

In Seville the two leaders apparently agreed, at least in a vague and generic way, on Spanish military assistance, supported in some fashion by the Germans, in the event of an Allied invasion of Portugal or its islands. This was no more than a general understanding, not a plan, and the agreement was reached without difficulty because for the moment Salazar was more equidistant from both sides than was Franco. There was equally vague agreement about the need to collaborate in Latin America, as well as closer cooperation between the two countries' internal security forces.[15]

Ribbentrop had informed Stohrer on 17 January that Germany requested simply that Spain see that Portuguese policy remained "strictly neutral," promising German support in the event of any Allied incursion. Serrano assured both Axis ambassadors that his government was working to increase Portugal's independence from the Allies, and went so far as to tell Stohrer that the additional protocol signed in 1940 contained a secret clause that would enable Portugal to draw on Spanish military assistance in the event of any British landing, even to the extent that it authorized Spain to send troops into Portugal automatically, which in fact was not the case.[16] The Axis governments therefore considered the meeting in Seville something of a victory, and believed that any Allied landing in the Azores would bring the two Iberian states into the war on their side. What Portuguese diplomats told Allied representatives was nearly the opposite, that the significance of the meeting in Seville was not any movement of Portugal toward the Axis, but rather some loosening of the ties of the Spanish regime in that direction.

Franco quickly reinforced the Germans' positive impression with his speech before the army garrison of Seville on 14 February, in which he declared, with regard to the Anglo-American alliance with Stalin: "Europe is being offered as a possible prey to communism. We have no fear that will actually happen; we are absolutely sure that things will not end thus, but if there should be a moment of danger, if the road to Berlin were left undefended, it would not be merely a division of Spanish volunteers who would go, but a million Spaniards who would offer themselves."[17] This was one of his most extreme pro-Axis statements, but was also an indication of his position in the "just war" against the Soviet Union, one that to some extent even Salazar might agree with.

Serrano, as was his wont, went even further in an interview that he granted a Scandinavian news agency on 22 April, in which he insisted that Spain should not be considered neutral, since its two major friends were at war with countries that had been the enemies of Spain in the Civil War. Spain was not entering the war at present, but he stressed that "those powers and Spain have the same ideology and are united by many other bonds. . . . Today the democracies are fighting in practice for the triumph of bolshevism. . . . The war policy of the Allies has been made subject to the Soviet dictatorship. Spaniards cannot be indifferent as to who will end up the victor. We have every reason to want our friends to triumph."[18]

The German embassy reported that Serrano's position had momentarily, at least, been strengthened by the events of February, followed by discovery of the British clandestine organization in Portugal, which was said to have some counterpart in Spain.[19] In fact, the only person whose position had been strengthened in Madrid by the maneuverings of early 1942 was Franco, who had withstood the pressure of the military, encouraged the FET once more as a counterbalance, and continued to make use of Serrano as a lightning rod. As the chief target of the regime's dissidents, Serrano reduced pressure on the Generalissimo.

Relations with Germany

Before the meeting in Seville, Stohrer had warned his superiors that even if Anglo-American action forced Spain into the war, its weakness might produce an extremely difficult strategic situation. He urged attention to the problem of military supply for Spain,[20] but German resources were stretched so thin that it could not be given priority. Though German discussion of Operation Felix against Gibraltar had continued even during the first months of the Russian campaign, since May 1941 the principal concern in Berlin had been to use German forces to counter any British strike at the Iberian peninsula while most of the German army was committed in the east. A new contingency plan, Operation Isabella, originally issued on 7 May 1941, provided for the entry of German forces to drive out the British, followed by the German occupation of the most important ports on the Atlantic coastline of the peninsula. It originally envisioned the use of seven infantry divisions and one armored brigade, all drawn from occupied France. For a time, as the initial invasion of Russia went well, there had been speculation that if Isabella became necessary, it might be combined with Felix, enabling a quick move on Gibraltar. There was no absolute certitude in Berlin that the Spanish would vigorously resist a British landing, which could complicate the entire strategy. By the end of 1941, the ever-increasing demands of the eastern front showed that Isabella was too ambitious, and it was revised with a smaller commitment of troops designed simply to hold the Pyrenees, with the possible contingency of defending Bilbao and Pamplona as well. In July 1942 Isabella was replaced by Operation Ilona, which was slightly more ambitious, envisaging holding a broader position in Spain running from Santander to Zaragoza.[21] The German leadership was also comforted by Franco's assurance to Stohrer in mid-April 1942 that an Allied invasion of French Morocco would be grounds for Spain's entry into the war, and that the Allies therefore presumably would make no such move unless or until they could muster massive resources.[22]

Economic issues remained vitally important, with an increasingly dominant role played by the United States. Threat of an oil embargo forced the Spanish government to agree that no imported goods could be re-exported to third parties, and to accept the establishment of American observers in ten districts across the country to monitor the movement and consumption of oil. Britain and the United States became increasingly active in buying up key raw materials, to deny them to Germany. The supply situation had improved somewhat by the spring of 1942 but re-mained extremely tight.

Roosevelt decided that a new ambassador was needed who might have a more delicate and effective touch with the Spanish. His choice was the distinguished Columbia University history professor Carlton J. H. Hayes, at that time probably America's leading scholar in the field of modern European nationalisms. His extensive work on France had never taken him to Spain, but Hayes was an experienced Europeanist with a reputa-tion as a moderate liberal, and was also a devout convert to Catholicism who was said to attend mass daily. Washington deemed him to possess the right combination of talents for the job, and he served for the next three years as a more competent ambassador than his predecessor, Alexander Weddell, despite his lack of diplomatic experience.

Hayes's task was to execute the American hard line with greater deft-ness and efficiency. He was given a considerably expanded staff, though the United States' embassy in Madrid never reached the size of Germany's. He never got on well with the supercilious Serrano and his initial impres-sion of Franco was negative, but that soon began to change. As a per-spicacious scholar, he rejected the standard propaganda images of the Spanish Civil War, later writing that "it was not a clear-cut struggle be-tween democracy and fascism, or merely [as Franco claimed] a first round in the Second World War." By 1943 he was beginning to think that the Generalissimo might gradually be brought all the way over to the Allied camp. Hayes always executed the letter of the increasingly hard American line, but his personal spirit became increasingly conciliatory, something that Franco came to appreciate. After he returned to the United States in 1945, he worked to encourage greater tolerance and understanding for the Spanish regime.[23]

Despite the increasing reliance on American imports, Spain's wartime economy continued to be oriented toward Germany as much as possible. Throughout the war years approximately 40 percent of total Spanish exports went to the Third Reich, concentrated especially in iron ore, wolfram, lead, zinc, hides, olive oil, citrus fruits, and textiles. Germany provided manufactured goods, metal and chemical products, and eventually military weapons, but always in lesser volume, by the end of the war leaving a trade balance of more than $116 million in favor of Spain.[24] Until 1943 total imports, concentrated in foodstuffs, were greater from Argentina than from the United States. Though Germany could provide neither oil nor food, the two key desiderata, total imports from Germany in 1942, at ESP117 million, were twice as large as those from Argentina, and rose further to 171 million in 1943, compared with 92.6 million from the United States. Even though the Reich could not provide the goods most needed in Spain, total exports to Germany rose from ESP146 million in 1941 to 226.6 million in 1943.[25]

The first part of 1942 was a time of intense economic negotiation, with a role now being played by the Spanish regime's new Instituto Nacional de Industria (INI), designed to become a giant state holding corporation of new state companies to complete the country's industrialization. As was usually the case when foreign inspiration was to be found in Franco's regime, the nearest model was not German but Italian, Mussolini's Istituto di Ricostruzione Industriale (IRI). Founded in 1933 to cope with the Depression, the IRI came to hold approximately 19 percent of the industrial and financial capital of Italy, proportionately the largest state sector outside of the Soviet Union. Yet, though the IRI served as a precedent, it had been an emergency response to a national crisis, while the deeper inspiration for the INI came from the military nationalism that was one of the most important political and ideological bases of the new regime.

The INI had its roots in the industrial mobilization commissions, composed mainly of artillery and engineers officers, that had surveyed potential Spanish industrial mobilization for war in 1916, initiating a military-technocratic concern with industrialization that had endured, the successors of the original commissions continuing down to the Civil War. This orientation was more important than fascism or Falangism. The INI would emphasize development of energy and of the chemical and major metallurgical and industrial resources vital for the nation's strength. Its founding was a product of the political change of 1941, reflecting the increasing role of sectors of the military. Whereas economic policy between 1939 and 1941 had tended to privilege the Falangist unions and a greater role for private business initiative in national reconstruction, the elimination of Salvador Merino and the growth of military influence privileged the formation of an institution that would directly develop state capitalism. The Instituto Nacional de Industria would become a key institution of the regime, absorbing 34 percent of all public investment in 1950 and 42 percent in 1955. The INI's origins thus lay in the political voluntarism of the regime and its goal of autarky, featuring accelerated industrialization for import substitution and military production.[26]

For director, Franco chose his old acquaintance the engineer and industrial administrator Juan Antonio Suanzes, ardent nationalist and industrializer, who had been minister of commerce and industry in his first regular government of 1938. Reflecting the dominant economic thinking in the regime, he looked to Germany for technical and financial assistance, telling German representatives that one of his major goals was the "elimination of the influence of British capital" in the Spanish economy.[27] Suanzes traveled to Germany in February 1942 to seek assistance, which was promised to him, first in the form of expanded German exports. The problem that Suanzes and all the Spanish economic negotiators faced with Germany was simply the decline in the marginal capacity of its economy due to the war.

The closeness of the relationship between Madrid and Berlin was shown by the fact that when Serrano received Washington's new economic memorandum specifying the requirements for obtaining increased American exports, he showed it to Stohrer and asked for advice.[28] Stohrer had none to offer, since Germany could not possibly meet Spain's energy requirements, so that the American demands were accepted on the following day.

In a major meeting of diplomatic and economic officials in Madrid on 3 February, the Germans complained that the Spanish government continued to export crucial raw materials for war production to the Allies; the Spanish representatives replied that this was their only means to import indispensable supplies of oil, coal, and rubber. The Germans had little to answer, save to offer the Spanish government use of German commercial and industrial holdings in Argentina; the Spanish replied that any such use was likely to be embargoed by the Americans. The Germans agreed theoretically to "balanced accounts" in their bilateral trade (though this goal was never achieved), and the Spanish insisted on including wolfram and other vital exports for war production within the standard framework of accounting, rather than giving the Germans separate privileged terms for these items.[29]

Though German exports increased, they did not equal the volume of Spanish exports, and German authorities offered a new proposal on 30 March: a new round of RM200 million of imports of wolfram and other Spanish products, to be compensated by export of RM120 million of German arms, coal, and finished goods, the difference to be either covered by a commercial credit from Spain or credited against Spain's Civil War debt. The Spanish government failed to respond for months, other than to indicate that the export of German arms was the most reliable way of reducing Anglo-American influence in Spain, all the while reducing somewhat Spanish exports. German officials declared on 16 May that their own military requirements made it impossible to send arms to Spain.[30]

This slowdown brought an energetic protest from the embassy in Madrid at the end of May, leading Carceller, the commerce minister, to promise that half the goods requested would be released, but this pledge was not completely fulfilled. The Spanish insisted that commercial relations must be balanced or otherwise directly paid for, and during June Stohrer, to the annoyance of officials in Berlin, repeatedly insisted that Germany must provide a more adequate counterpart, asking for a visit by Walther Funk, the Reich's minister of economics, which seems to have been vetoed by the Foreign Ministry, Ribbentrop seeking a more dominant role for his ministry in commercial relations.[31] This contretemps delayed further negotiation long enough to permit new trade relations between Madrid and the Allies to become fully established, weakening the German position. Instead of a new general agreement between the two governments, there followed sectoral agreements negotiated by German individual entities or ministries, particularly the Luftwaffe and the Navy.

In the absence of a general agreement, Stohrer was directed to meet with Franco, the resulting conversation taking place on 14 July. Without conceding on general principles, the Generalissimo agreed to increase exports, particularly of wolfram. He lamented the lack of German support for the expansion of Spanish military industry and protested Germany's failure to send arms. This seemed to indicate a more accommodating policy by the Spanish government, as indicated in a further discussion by a German trade representation with Carceller on 14 August.[32]

The Monarchist Offensive

All of Franco's efforts to achieve internal political equilibrium had succeeded only in maintaining his personal authority, not in resolving internal conflict, which became even more heated during 1942. The monarchists were now the beneficiaries, as the candidacy of the heir to the throne, Don Juan, received increasing attention from diverse parts of the political spectrum. Juan Yagüe, one of the two most notable Falangist generals, had spent a year and a half in internal exile, and in January told German representatives that the only decent way out of the present impasse was to replace the failing authority of Franco with a restored monarchy working in accord with the FET and aligning Spain more directly with Germany.[33]

Meanwhile, monarchist representatives, having failed in their efforts to gain German support during the preceding year, approached the Italian government in February 1942. Though Ciano had insisted earlier that Don Juan (still resident in Rome) and the entire royal family were strongly Anglophile,[34] he decided that this connection was worth cultivating, and invited the Pretender to join him in a hunting party in Italian-occupied Albania in early April, setting off further speculation. Tensions in Madrid were nearing a climax, with army officers being instructed to carry their side arms when off duty to protect themselves from Falangists, while the physical assault by Falangist toughs on a young monarchist aristocrat in March led to the reassignment abroad of the latter's chief antagonist, a Falangist leader who had served as press chief of Serrano's foreign ministry.

Franco himself dispatched a letter to the Pretender in mid-May 1942, explaining that only the Caudillo would be able to introduce the "revolutionary totalitarian monarchy" (allegedly in the tradition of the "Catholic monarchs," Ferdinand and Isabella) that Spain required, but that Don Juan should in the meantime identify himself fully with the FET and wait for the Generalissimo to complete his task.[35] Meanwhile plans were under way for a visit to Berlin by General Juan Vigón, Yagüe's replacement as minister of the air force. Since Vigón was a moderate monarchist, some of the pro-monarchist generals hoped that this occasion might be used to clarify the German attitude toward a restoration. Though Vigón had always been loyal, this was a risk that Franco did not care to take, and the trip was abruptly canceled on 4 June.[36]

Even Serrano began to conclude that a monarchist restoration, properly prepared, might be the best solution. As he put it to Stohrer in June, a restoration must either be resolutely combated or else properly shaped to reinforce the structure of the new Spain and a strongly pro-Axis policy. "To ignore or merely tolerate the monarchist movement is no longer in question."[37] Serrano spent three days in mid-June in northern Italy, always more at ease with his friend Ciano than with the Germans. There he insisted that the right kind of monarchist restoration was the best solution, since Franco had been unable to build a coherent and unified system or to carry out the national revolution. He averred that Franco still had some popular support but had lost that of the elites, and referred to his brother-in-law's political ineptness in the most scathing terms, saying that every speech that he delivered was more clumsy and ineffective than the last. Serrano urged the Italians, whom he trusted more than the Germans, to take the initiative in winning Don Juan to the Axis cause, in order to carry out a restoration on terms that would unify the country politically behind the Axis.

Serrano further declared that though he had firmly supported Spain's entry into the war in the past, he was now convinced that Spain lacked the military strength and political unity to engage in the conflict and would only be a liability. Within the country there was support for the Axis but also much sympathy for the Allies. Had German troops entered Spain in the winter of 1941, they would have touched off guerrilla resistance, as in the Soviet Union. Serrano declared that though he himself still supported the Axis, Spain should enter the war only if threatened with immediate invasion, such as an Anglo-American landing in Morocco. Serrano affirmed this position to the Germans.

When he went on to speak briefly with Mussolini in Rome, Serrano found the Duce totally hostile to restoration of the monarchy. Mussolini pronounced Don Juan and the Spanish royal family to be hopelessly Anglophile and declared that the Pretender, if he had a chance, would "drown Falangism."[38] Ribbentrop agreed, firmly ordering Stohrer on 4 July to have nothing to do with monarchist machinations.[39]

Hitler's Attitude toward Spain in Mid-War

Whereas Hitler had once spoken approvingly of Spaniards as "the only Latins willing to fight," his irritation with Franco and his regime only increased with the passage of time. In his after-dinner conversations with subordinates during 1942, he touched occasionally on the theme of Spain, which he found disgustingly associated with Catholicism. He justified a leftist revolution in Spain as the response "to an interminable series of atrocities. One cannot succeed in conceiving how much cruelty, ignominy and falsehood the intrusion of Christianity has spelt for this world of ours." Hitler lamented that the Communist menace had forced him to intervene in Spain, for otherwise, happily, "the clergy would have been exterminated," in the best interest of the country. Though he admitted that in general religious activities in Spain were no different than elsewhere, on 5 June he declared himself stupefied by the religious obscurantism of Franco and three months later added gratuitously that Spanish women, whatever their formal educational accomplishment might be, "are outstandingly stupid," expressing amazement at reports that Franco's wife attended mass daily.[40]

Hitler's attitude toward Spain was ambivalent, for he prized Spanish valor, but his principal remarks were negative. Hitler was generally ignorant of the country, approaching it through his standard racial and modernist fantasies, pontificating that "in the Spanish people there is a mixture of Gothic, Frankish and Moorish blood," the native Celtic-Iberian population being presumably nonexistent. He harbored the notion that Isabella the Catholic queen was "the greatest harlot in history" and thought that she lived sometime during the nineteenth century, apparently confusing her with Isabella II. Hitler judged that the Islamic hegemony had produced "the most intellectual and in every way the best and happiest epoch in Spanish history," the Golden Age being presumably nonexistent. Hitler generally had a high opinion of Islam and once proclaimed it the best of religions because of its theological simplicity and emphasis on holy war. In Spain, however, after the Muslims came the curse of Christianity. Hitler expressed regret that Islam had not swept over all western Europe. Had it replaced Christianity in Germany, the innate racial superiority of the Germans in conjunction with Islam would have enabled them to conquer much of the world during the Middle Ages.[41]

In Hitler's judgment, conflict between the Catholic Church and the Franco regime was inevitable, "and a new revolution thus comes within the bounds of possibility. Spain may well have to pay with her blood, in the not too distant future, for her failure to carry through a truly national revolution, as was done in Germany and Italy." After he was informed that during a recent Corpus Christi procession in Barcelona only a few Falangist leaders had been permitted to wear their blue shirts, Hitler imputed the restriction to the growing influence of clerical and monarchist reactionaries, so that "the Spanish State is rushing towards fresh disaster. . . . If a new civil war breaks out, I should not be surprised to see the Falangists compelled to make common cause with the Reds to rid themselves of the clerico-monarchical muck." He singled out for particular denunciation the "Jesuitical" Serrano Suñer, whom he fantasized as hyperclerical. "From my first meeting with him I was conscious of a feeling of revulsion."[42]

In his after-dinner conversation on 7 July, Hitler declared, "One must be careful not to put the Franco regime on the same level as National Socialism or Fascism. Todt, who employs many so-styled 'Red' Spaniards in his workshops, tells me repeatedly that these Reds are not red in our sense of the world. They regard themselves as revolutionaries in their own right and, as industrious and skilled workers, have greatly distinguished themselves." He wished to retain the services of the nearly 40,000 Republicans currently laboring for the Reich, to "keep them as reserves in case a second civil war should break out. Together with the survivors of the old Falange, they will constitute the most trustworthy force at our disposal." Field Marshal Wilhelm Keitel chimed in, remarking that the Spanish honor guard at Hendaye carried rifles so rusty as to be laughable, and reminded Hitler that Admiral Canaris had warned the Führer that the physical encounter with Franco would be a disappointment, since in appearance Franco was "not a hero, but a little sausage [*statt eines Heroen ein Würstchen*]."[43]

Yet the ambivalence remained. Hitler appreciated the fact that Spain's controlled press, at least through 1942, was giving the Reich more favorable treatment than the press of any other nonbelligerent state, so that at one point he gushed, "Taking it all round, the Spanish press is the best in the world!" Spaniards were also noteworthy for physical courage and for a certain charm and style. Despite the scourge of Catholicism, "Spain is a country for which it is impossible not to entertain feelings of affection. The Spanish are full of *grandeza*, and, in war, of courage. . . . I do not think I have met anyone who is not filled with admiration for the Spanish." He took further comfort from a new book that he was reading about Spain which convinced him there could never be a true entente between Spain and the United States, because the materialist values of the Americans and the heroic ideals of Spaniards were so far apart that the two countries could never understand each other.[44]

A man apparently much nearer the Führer's own heart than Franco or Serrano Suñer was Muñoz Grandes, in charge of the Blue Division, who bitterly resented what he saw as Spain's overly cautious foreign policy. He had complained about it in a letter to his superior, José Enrique Varela, in April, pointing out that Japan's new war in the Pacific would eliminate many European colonies, reducing the available spoils, so that Spain needed to act immediately to gain its share. Muñoz Grandes insisted that Gibraltar, Portugal, and Morocco were all indispensable to Spain but could not be gained if Spain did not enter the war.[45] Soon to be replaced as commander of the Blue Division by Emilio Esteban Infantes, he volun-teered to German officers that Spain was facing a crossroads, observing that he had been made secretary general of the FET on the eve of the Hitler-Stalin Pact of August 1939, which had been highly unpopular in Madrid, but he had worked diligently to maintain support for Germany. Now the offensive of the "monarchists and reactionaries" threatened to undo the new Spanish system, for which the success of a Falangist "social revolu-tionary" triumph in Spain was linked with a decisive pro-German change in foreign policy. Muñoz Grandes repeated these sentiments to a special emissary of Ribbentrop, saying that as he returned to Madrid he needed to know to what extent Germany would support decisive change in Spain, and exactly what place Spain might expect to have in Germany's New Order.[46] He was quoted as declaring that "next to my friendship with Ger-many, my driving force is hatred for England, which has oppressed my country for generations." Muñoz Grandes said that he was prepared to lay aside command of the Blue Division temporarily for a "furlough" in Spain, "where I can have the opportunity to negotiate with the government. I am ready to take the risk." There he would totally reject the monarchists in favor of a radical new pro-German ministry.[47]

Hitler grew more angry with Franco and Serrano Suñer with each passing month, and seized on this report concerning the political queries of Muñoz Grandes, whom he had already awarded an Iron Cross. He was doubtless aware that various intrigues by low-level German diplomats and Nazi Party activists in Madrid with radical Falangists were continuing, but had produced no results. Hitler wished to prevent a takeover in Spain by the "clerico-monarchical muck," and dispatched Canaris to talk with Franco on 22 June, at which time the admiral explained that it was the Führer's personal wish that Muñoz Grandes retain command a little longer. Franco had little choice but to agree.[48]

During his after-dinner divagations on 7 July, Hitler observed: "Whether a General possesses the political acumen necessary to success, the future alone will show. But in any case, we must promote as much as we can the popularity of General Muñoz Grandes, who is a man of energy, and as such the most likely one to master the situation. . . . The Blue Division may well once more play a decisive role, when the hour for the overthrow of this parson-ridden regime strikes."[49]

Hitler summoned Muñoz Grandes to his headquarters at Rastenburg on 11 July, and the crusty Spanish general seemed overwhelmed. The "mere mention" of Serrano's "name sent Muñoz Grandes into a paroxysm of rage," and he claimed that Serrano and Varela, the reactionary, Anglo-phile army minister, were planning to subvert the Blue Division in "direct sabotage against Germany." Muñoz Grandes proposed that he retain command momentarily but that he soon return to Spain with German support to promote a decisive political change that would make the general chief of government and in charge of Spanish policy under a Franco who would lose most of his power. This move would enable him to align Spain's policy completely with that of Germany. Hitler liked the idea, though he did not totally commit himself, indicating that the time for action would come after the success of Germany's summer offensive in Russia. He made arrangements with the general to maintain direct personal communication outside normal military and diplomatic channels. Muñoz Grandes swore "eternal friendship" to Hitler, though he was somewhat chagrined when he realized that Spain could not gain equality with Italy in the Führer's affections.[50] Meanwhile, Esteban Infantes was kept waiting in Germany for several months and not allowed to proceed to the front.

Strategic Change and Domestic Politics

During the summer plans were developing for the first Anglo-American offensive in the European theater, to take the form of a major landing in northwest Africa. In August Churchill traveled to Moscow, where he and Stalin agreed that such an operation would scarcely be threatened by Spain, which it would simply neutralize further. Some American leaders, with their less pragmatic, more ideological approach, did not at first agree. Before leaving Madrid, Weddell had recommended an Allied landing in the Canaries, while the most left-wing members of Roosevelt's administration, such as Vice President Henry Wallace (a great champion of the Soviet Union) and Harold Ickes, urged the invasion of nonbelligerent Spain. The U.S. military command was also leery of Spain, preferring to avoid the Strait of Gibraltar and concentrate the landing on French Morocco, but the Americans finally accepted the British conclusion that Spain would not interfere, so that Allied forces could also land simultaneously in Algeria.[51]

Since German military intelligence was quite poor, these plans were known to neither Berlin nor Madrid. Franco continued to complain that Germany would neither provide Spain with German weapons nor lend technical assistance to develop Spain's own arms industry. Nevertheless,

Stohrer was optimistic that the Grosse Plan for greatly expanding German propaganda would soon pay dividends, though to his alarm, Franco expressed little concern about the effects of British propaganda.[52]

Meanwhile Franco took the most important action since the end of the Civil War to institutionalize his regime with the start of what critics would later term "cosmetic constitutionalism." The second of the regime's "Fundamental Laws," the "Law of the Cortes," was promulgated in July, establishing the terms for appointing a new corporative parliament in Madrid, vaguely analogous to the Chamber of Fasces and Corporations in Rome. Significantly, Franco had assigned the drafting to the secretary general of the FET, José Luis de Arrese, a bitter rival of Serrano, who was succeeding in bringing the party ever more firmly into obedience. Moreover, in his annual speech to the party on 18 July, Franco was more moderate than usual and did not refer to Germany and Italy by name.

Soon after, Serrano mounted an offensive that proved to be his swan song. He prepared new legislation to regain control of all censorship of news from abroad, which he had lost to the new leadership of the FET a year earlier, claiming this step was necessary for the proper conduct of foreign policy. Then early in August the Spanish press reprinted an article by Serrano, "Spain and the World War," which had earlier appeared in a Nazi journal in Germany. It reaffirmed the Spanish government's solidarity with the Axis and against democracy and communism.[53] At that very moment German and Japanese expansion was reaching its farthest points in the Soviet Union, North Africa, and the South Pacific, and Serrano seemed determined to take advantage of the international situation to recoup his position in Madrid and with the Axis leaders, even though he no longer wanted Spain to enter the war directly.

In mid-August the regime's second political crisis suddenly began to unfold. On the 16th, Carlists celebrated a memorial mass for their troops fallen in the Civil War at a church in the suburbs of Bilbao. It was attended by two Carlist government figures, General Varela and the undersecretary of the interior, Antonio Iturmendi. As the throng began to leave, a handful of Falangists hurled two grenades, injuring a great many, and Carlist sources later claimed two fatalities. Varela, who happened to be inside the sanctuary at the time of the incident, immediately seized on it as evidence of a Falangist attack on the military, possibly even an assassination attempt. He sent telegrams in this vein to all district captains general of the army and protested vehemently to Franco, seconded by Colonel Valentín

Galarza, minister of the interior, who dispatched similar messages to provincial governors throughout Spain. Six Falangists arrested in the incident were then prosecuted before military tribunals.

Franco was greatly displeased by what he considered the overreaction of Varela and Galarza, but hesitated to intervene in the military justice system. Several of the Falangists under indictment were veterans of the Blue Division who sought a fully Falangist regime and entry into the war on the side of Germany. All six were convicted and two received the death penalty; Juan Domínguez, national sports director of the Falangist student union (SEU) and the person allegedly responsible for throwing the one grenade that exploded, was eventually executed on 29 September. The fact that Hitler was induced to award him the Cross of the German Eagle for his service on the eastern front had no influence on the outcome.

Varela also demanded of Franco direct political satisfaction against the FET. According to one version, their conversation became so hostile that Franco realized he would have to dismiss his army minister, of whom heretofore he had been relatively fond. He also decided to remove Galarza, whom he blamed for having run a slack ship and for having withheld information, as well as one secondary FET leader.[54]

When Franco communicated these decisions to his undersecretary, Luis Carrero Blanco (who had for some time been conniving with Arrese to eliminate Serrano), Carrero pointed out that firing two army ministers without discharging someone important on the other side could create serious complications. Serrano had done much more than Arrese to try to save Domínguez, and Carrero warned that if Serrano were allowed to remain, the military and all other non- and anti-Falangists would say that Serrano and the FET had won a complete victory, that Franco was no longer in full control.[55] Franco seems to have required little convincing, for he was increasingly impatient with his brother-in-law, who tended to contradict and criticize him more and more, and who had already suggested resigning.[56] Domestic relations were equally strained due to Serrano's intense extramarital affair with the wife of an aristocratic lieutenant colonel of cavalry, which had just produced an illegitimate daughter and was being referred to in diplomatic reports. Equally important, Franco now had trusted and reliable personnel in Carrero Blanco and Arrese to fill the roles earlier held by Serrano.

The cabinet reorganization that Franco carried out on 3 September 1942 sought to achieve a more fully pragmatic equilibrium than those of 1939 and 1941. Serrano Suñer was dismissed, never to return to the Spanish government. The conservative and practical General Francisco Gómez Jordana returned to Foreign Affairs, while Varela was replaced by Carlos Asensio, chief of the General Staff, pro-German and much less hostile to the FET than Varela, but a trusted and disciplined subordinate who may not have been the first choice and whom Franco had to press vigorously to accept the appointment.[57] Galarza was replaced by Blas Pérez González, a prewar University of Barcelona law professor who was a neo-Falangist but also, perhaps more important, a member of the Military Juridical Corps. He would direct his ministry effectively for many years.

These changes proved astute, giving Franco the best combination of ministers he had enjoyed to this point. None of the major political contestants was fully satisfied, but the military gained rather more than the Falangists, which would prove useful during the remainder of the war. The military's gain by no means stilled its criticism of the FET,[58] but it ended the crisis and relaxed the state of political tension for almost the first time in two years.

The most important consequence was the return of the extremely diminutive but eminently sensible Gómez Jordana to Foreign Affairs. He had quietly watched with dismay the drift of Spanish foreign policy toward the Axis[59] and for two years had been a prime candidate of the generals to replace Serrano Suñer. Change in foreign policy was not, however, Franco's intention in appointing him. The Generalissimo considered other candidates but could not avoid the obvious conclusion that Jordana was honest, experienced, and reliable. The first statement released by the new government on 21 September declared there would be no basic change in foreign policy, declaring that it "reaffirms the orientation maintained during the past six years, consistent with the spirit of our Crusade, with the anticommunist character of our Movement, and with the imperatives of the European New Order." Italy and Germany were not specifically mentioned. Jordana's influence was probably evident in the reference to "our close friendship with Portugal," the only country specified among "the Hispano-American countries" with which "our historical solidarity" was affirmed.[60]

Franco used the contacts of Arrese and other FET leaders with the German embassy to assure the latter that Spanish policy would not change. Canaris was immediately sent to Madrid to evaluate the situation and reported that the replacement of Varela by Asensio would mean a more pro-German attitude on the part of the military. Most Reich officials were not sorry to see Serrano go, and Stohrer reported that though Jordana might be less "brilliant," he would probably be steadier and easier to work with.

Though he had detested Serrano, Hitler was not pleased with the change, for he did not see it as benefiting Germany and decided he would finally have to relieve Stohrer for failing to provide adequate information. Ever since March Stohrer had been reporting that Serrano remained in a strong position (whereas in fact he had become somewhat isolated), and on occasion had requested permission to intervene in Spanish affairs to strengthen the foreign minister. Permission had always been denied. As recently as 13 August Berlin had received word from FET's German contacts that Arrese was on the verge of persuading Franco to make a major change that would reduce the Generalissimo's authority in favor of the FET and unify the Spanish government behind a pro-German policy that would soon bring Spain into the war.[61] Such reports had been wildly optimistic.

All the while the Führer retained Muñoz Grandes in command of the Blue Division, deferring any political move until the Spanish troops could participate in the final victorious offensive (Northern Light) against Leningrad in September. That offensive was preempted by a powerful Soviet assault before the end of August. Moreover, Muñoz Grandes also looked for major colonial compensation from Germany, though he asked for no more than "a word" of Hitler's, assuring the Germans that he had refused to respond to purported overtures from the Pretender. After the cabinet change in Madrid, he reiterated his willingness to promote a radical alteration of the Spanish government, but also judged that the elimination of Serrano was a step forward and that it probably meant that Spain would soon declare war, though he admitted he could not be sure.[62] Muñoz Grandes therefore proposed that he soon return to Spain to rouse political support. If Hitler were then prepared to order German troops into Spain to defend the country and announce his recognition of Spain's colonial claims, Muñoz Grandes would see to it that they were greeted as comrades, so that Franco would have to declare war on the Allies, while Spain rallied opinion in Latin America to oppose the United States. The catch with this plan from Hitler's point of view was that it required a commitment of troops he could not make. He fretted and grumbled, but in September the German offensive continued to press toward Stalingrad and the Caucasus, and at that point he was not disposed to complicate German strategy or diplomacy by intervention in Spain, on 8 September dismissing Muñoz Grandes's plan as "fantasies."[63]

He was further beguiled when the embassy counselor Erich Gardemann arrived in Berlin on 26 September with word that Arrese, encouraged by Franco, sought an invitation to visit Germany in order to tighten relations. Arrese reportedly recognized Hitler as "the chief opportunity for a new ordering of Europe." Manuel Valdés Larrañaga, FET's undersecretary, had told Gardemann that Spain would enter the war as soon as Germany could provide adequate supplies, emphasizing the importance of the current German drive on the oil of the Caucasus: "As soon as you arrive in Batum [now Batumi, a Black Sea port connected by pipeline to the Baku oil fields], we shall go into action."[64]

Though the Germans had grown increasingly skeptical of such assurances, the constant conversations and intrigues with Falangists and a handful of pro-German military officials had a disconcerting effect. Captain Hans Hoffmann, liaison officer with the Blue Division, reported that Muñoz Grandes had been offered the new post of minister of supplies or, alternately, that of ambassador in Berlin, but had rejected both because of their seeming unimportance. Yagüe, who remained in internal exile in Burgos, told German contacts that Franco had rejected an earlier plan proposed by Yagüe, which would have called for the Spanish government to use every means at its disposal (even closer economic relations with London) to build up enough supplies to enable it to enter the war on Germany's side. Yagüe insisted that it was important for Muñoz Grandes to return to Madrid immediately, where he might once more assume leadership of the FET (though it was absurd to think that Franco would have given him such a post). Yagüe held that Muñoz Grandes, in conjunction with himself and the new army minister, Carlos Asensio, could bring the Spanish government to a decisively pro-German policy, as soon as Germany provided the necessary economic assistance. The Germans, however, were well enough informed to realize this plan made little sense, especially since Asensio was quite hostile to Arrese's proposed trip to Germany, which Asensio saw as a ploy to restore the primacy of the FET. What made the plan even less convincing was that both Yagüe and Asensio indicated that the most viable solution in the long run was a restoration of the monarchy under proper conditions, Yagüe having written to Don Juan urging him to work more closely with the Reich.[65] This "reactionary solution" was abhorrent to Berlin, and on 5 November Ribbentrop firmly vetoed any German encouragement.[66]

The existing policy stalemate thus continued until the early morning of 8 November, when Franco was suddenly awakened with word of the Anglo-American invasion of French Morocco and Algeria. On several occasions Spanish officials had privately defined this action to Axis officials as a casus belli.

CHAPTER 11

Temptation Ends

The architect of change in Spain's foreign policy was the new foreign minister, General Francisco Gómez Jordana y Souza, conde de Jordana. Son of a leading general, the sixty-six-year-old Jordana was a generation older than Serrano and considerably more conservative. For most of his career he was a staff officer and military academy professor; as a young man he had fought in Cuba and had twice served as high commissioner in Morocco. Alfonso XIII had given him his title of count for his achievements there. He was not a political general, however, and though the Republic had removed him from military service, he had played no role in the military conspiracy of 1936. Barely five feet tall, Jordana made Franco seem large by comparison, but the little general stood out for good judgment, administrative efficiency, and reliability. Franco had made him president of the Junta Técnica during the Civil War and then his first regular foreign minister in 1938.

He had played no role in the increasing fascism of the regime between 1937 and 1942, but neither had he overtly opposed it, so that Jordana had no very distinct political profile when he was reappointed foreign minister in September 1942. In private, however, his opinions were clear and sharp, as he had recorded in his diary that the outbreak of the European war was due to the "inordinate ambition" of Hitler, adding, "May God protect Spain, helping it to avoid involvement in this conflict, which would be a catastrophe for us."[1] As foreign minister in 1938–39, he had been careful to avoid any step or statement that might appear to involve Spain in a broader war.

Spanish policy had become more cautious during 1942, but there is no indication that the Generalissimo had any specific change of policy in mind when he appointed Jordana, merely having confidence that he would be prudent and reliable. Franco was not aware that his new foreign minister disagreed categorically with the policy of nonbelligerence and would work steadily to turn Spanish policy toward a neutrality that would be more complete and genuine than that of 1939–40. Jordana was not an Anglophile, but by the autumn of 1942 he had formed the conviction that the Allies were likely to win the war and that Spanish policy should be adjusted accordingly. He was, after Franco, the most important figure in Spanish government during World War II and beyond all doubt the one to whom Spain owed the most. Jordana had to wage, sometimes almost single-handedly, a bitter, persistent, and thankless battle against powerful forces within the regime, and stands in perspective as the Spanish government's most positive leader of the war years.

Jordana was personally loyal to Franco and knew better than to challenge him directly, while he also showed the integrity that Serrano had lacked in not criticizing Franco in discussions with foreign diplomats, even those most hostile to the Generalissimo. At the same time, he showed great determination in pursuing a more constructive policy, working assiduously and tactfully to influence Franco. Several times he carried that determination to the point of offering his resignation.

Jordana retained as undersecretary Juan Pan de Soraluce, a professional diplomat who was both competent and moderate. He reduced Falangist influence in Latin American policy and upgraded relations with the Vatican, which had often been rather tense under Serrano. His new ambassador to Berlin, Ginés Vidal de Saura, was, unlike the two preceding ambassadors, a competent professional.

Anglo-American diplomats were quite pleased with the appointment of Jordana, who made a good impression on Myron Taylor, Roosevelt's special representative to the Vatican, who passed through Madrid at the close of September en route to Washington, apparently to report on the possibility of Italy's leaving the war. Franco asked Taylor to come to talk with him at his residence, El Pardo, on 30 September. There Franco laid out, for Roosevelt's ears, what would become known as his three-war theory. The Caudillo held that the world war was made up of three separate conflicts. In the Pacific war Spain was completely neutral. Despite having earlier accepted responsibility for representing Japanese interests in Latin America, for several months the Spanish government had been taking steps to distance itself from Japan.[2] In the West European imperial contest between the haves of Britain and France and the have-nots of Germany and Italy, Spain did not take sides but hoped to receive its fair share in the readjustment of colonial territory, an idea that Franco would not give up. In the East European struggle between Christian civilization and "barbarous and oriental" communism, Spain was a belligerent. His concern was that with the United States in the war, the conflicts were being merged and communism might triumph. Franco seemed to imply that the Western powers should make peace among themselves so that Hitler could destroy the Soviet Union. He suggested that Germany's frontiers should advance to the Volga and that Germany should dominate greater Central Europe, even while conceding some autonomy to the countries in its sphere.[3]

During October Jordana made several gestures of greater independence. He obtained an apology for German submarine action against Spanish shipping, and twice protested to Rome about Italian claims to have discovered America, as well as, for the first time, protesting the violation of Spanish air space by Italian planes bombing Gibraltar. He was also concerned to firm up Spain's weak defenses, and renewed pleas to Germany for arms shipments.[4]

Jordana was seen to be very nervous the first week of November, when he informed the Council of Ministers that the Allied second front might be expected any day and might well involve Spain or its possessions.[5] There had been an intense American press campaign against the Spanish regime, with calls to break relations and rumors of the preparation of a new Republican army of exiles, though finally on 30 October Hayes had been authorized to give formal assurance, as Hoare had done earlier, that the United States had no hostile plans regarding any Spanish territory.[6]

It was no secret that an Anglo-American offensive buildup was under way during the summer and autumn of 1942, but German intelligence was unable to discover the target of what the Allies would call Operation Torch. The Germans concluded that it was likely to be the Atlantic islands, or possibly Libya or even Spain; Italian intelligence seems to have been somewhat better informed. In selecting French Morocco and Algeria, Allied leaders hoped for the cooperation of the French and the neutrality of the Spanish. French Morocco was included to protect Gibraltar and, if necessary, to screen off Spain. In his final assessment with the Germans before leaving the Foreign Ministry, Serrano had specified that an invasion of Tangier and Spanish Morocco would automatically bring Spain into the war, but this time French Morocco had been left out of the equation.[7] Though seven divisions of troops, totaling slightly more than 100,000 men, were stationed in the Spanish zone, they were poorly equipped, with a small and weak armored force and sixty obsolescent airplanes. The greater danger for the Allies was German intervention by way of Spanish territory. To counter such a move the British designed Operation Backbone, a plan to seize control of Spanish Morocco and the area around Gibraltar only if the Germans entered Spain. The hope was that the Germans would not interfere, and General Dwight Eisenhower, the American commander in chief of Torch, seems initially to have speculated about offering Spain a slightly larger slice of Moroccan territory to win it to the side of the Allies, though at no time did that become a practical issue.

The most impressive aspect of the initiation of Torch was the relative secrecy with which it was carried out. The Allies knew that Franco had cooperated in the development of highly sophisticated German detection posts on both sides of the Straits, against which Hoare had lodged stiff protests in April and again in October, which prompted Franco to issue an order for partial dismantlement. The British launched a major disinformation campaign that stressed the heavy reinforcement of Malta as a diversion, and much of the Algerian invasion convoy passed Gibraltar without drawing special attention. Only a few hours before the landing did the Axis command learn that the objective might be Algeria, Tunisia, or western Tripolitania, and by then it was too late.

Despite Anglo-American assurances, when Jordana received a telephone call from Hayes at his home about one o'clock on the morning of Sunday, 8 November—one hour before Torch was to begin—his first reaction was to assume that he was being officially informed of an invasion of Spain, which he knew had probably been discussed by the American government. Hence his relief at being told the target of the operation, followed by a friendly letter of reassurance from Roosevelt and, soon after, an equivalent British guarantee.

Franco's Council of Ministers held two long meetings on the 9th and 10th. It discussed calling up the army recruitment classes of 1938 to 1942, a few members of which had served in the Civil War, but decided to wait for fear of seeming provocative to the Allies. A pro-German posture was strongly championed by Asensio, the new army minister, and by the two chief Falangist ministers, Arrese and Girón, though they did not demand entry into the war at that moment. Jordana vigorously argued for complete neutrality. Three days later the Spanish embassy reported a rumor in Berlin that Hitler would demand passage for German troops through Spain, though there was no sign of any German action in this direction. Franco convened his ministers once more; they agreed that any such request must be refused and that partial military mobilization would begin the next day, momentarily increasing the Spanish armed forces to 700,000 very poorly equipped troops.[8]

When Franco replied officially to the Allied governments on the 12th, he did not use the term "neutrality," which would have been contrary to Spanish policy, but employed language equivalent to that of Roosevelt's letter, speaking of friendship and peace with the Allies. Partial mobilization was then publicly announced on the 18th, and was presented, and correctly seen, as a normal defensive measure. On 15 November the press was given orders, for the first time in more than two years, to be more impartial in the treatment of war news.

The war had now entered its most dangerous phase for Spain, with the danger of hostile action from either side. On the morning of the invasion Jordana had given Stohrer a letter asking the Germans to reply "with all possible speed" concerning their response to the new strategic situation.[9] Only five days before Torch began, the new British offensive in Egypt had thrown Rommel's forces into full retreat, so that complete disaster threatened the Axis in North Africa. Hitler's immediate response to Torch was to occupy all of France and begin to seize control of Tunisia, which was to be built up as the final Italo-German redoubt, since both Libya and Algeria were as good as lost. To make matters even more grim for the Germans, on 19 November, only eleven days after Torch, the Soviets launched their powerful counteroffensive at Stalingrad, but the need to pour troops into Tunisia severely limited reinforcements for the eastern front.

Germany's military occupation of the entire Pyrenees frontier provoked concern in both Madrid and Lisbon. Salazar was particularly anxious for a declaration of complete neutrality in the peninsula, but he knew that Franco held a position from which he could not immediately extricate himself, for fear of offending the Germans. The Portuguese dictator therefore tried to force the issue by having the Lisbon press announce that the German ambassador in Madrid had promised the Spanish government that the Reich would respect and protect Spanish neutrality. This clever if misleading announcement did force Hitler's hand, so that on the following day Jordana finally received the clarification that he had requested. The

German government expressed its understanding of the need for Spain
to accept the Anglo-American guarantees for the time being, but urged
Franco to make no deals and to continue to tilt toward the Third Reich.
Franco was asked only to give the appearance of being ready to take military action, so that the Allies would have to divert part of their forces to
mask the Spanish.[10] When Franco's official reply to Roosevelt and Churchill was made public one day later, the German embassy criticized its very
friendly tone, but Jordana shrugged off the criticism as nitpicking at the
simple courtesy of using language equivalent to the original Allied letters.
Some days later Stohrer apparently told Jordana that Germany and Italy
were willing to give Spain a formal guarantee that they would not invade
its territory, but the foreign minister replied that it was not necessary.[11]
Stohrer reported to Berlin on the 20th that Franco had termed the Allied
guarantee no more than a piece of paper but judged that it was in the
interest of the Allies to honor it, at least for the time being. The Germans
also warned of the danger of an Allied landing in the Balearics; Franco
replied that the Spanish were reasonably well prepared to defend against
such an invasion,[12] though that was probably not the case at all.

The new strategic situation exacerbated internal conflict. Perhaps for
the first time there were a number of pro-Allied political incidents in Spain,
and Basque nationalists became more active in efforts to promote an Allied
partition of the country. Several sharp encounters took place between Jordana and FET leaders, who were determined to maintain their position. A
circular distributed by the party's Secretaría General declared that the FET
held as "permanent and irrevocable" "our antidemocratic position," "our
imperial ambition," and "our territorial claims."[13] The standard intrigues
were continued by SS and other Nazi activists in Madrid, but when the
Foreign Ministry in Berlin received an SS intelligence report that it might
be possible to promote a military takeover in Madrid, Rudolf Likus, Ribbentrop's right-hand man, spurned such manipulations as merely likely to
lead to restoration of the "reactionary" monarchy.

Franco made no political concessions. Contrary to the SS report, the
strategic danger had the effect of rallying the military around him more
firmly than before, so that both Asensio and Yagüe informed their German
embassy contacts that the military would not support any sort of "political
experiment" amid the current crisis.[14] Franco in turn once more rallied the
Falangist and hard-core elements. New appointments to the FET National
Council included Serrano Suñer and his pro-Axis colleagues, while Franco's speeches before the council and at the military academy in Zaragoza

were strongly pro-Falangist. For the first time in more than two years, Yagüe was reappointed to active command and placed in charge of the military district of Melilla, in eastern Spanish Morocco. There Yagüe publicly condemned liberalism, praised Italian Fascism and the Duce, and made statements that almost sounded as if Spain were about to enter the war, all a calculated ploy on the part of Franco, to the disgust of Jordana.

The best reflection of the basic thinking of Franco and his new alter ego, Luis Carrero Blanco, was expressed in two memoranda written by Carrero. The first, penned on 11 November, only three days into Torch, condemned previous German strategy, alleging that Germany and Spain together should already have gained full control of northwest Africa. Since Germany had not acted in time, the situation had grown much more complicated, but Germany still possessed great reserves of strength and might yet win a clear-cut victory. Thus Spain should still have the "decided will to intervene on the side of the Axis," but in view of present complications should continue to delay, planning its future policy secretly with Germany while continuing to "mislead" the Allies.[15]

Carrero Blanco's subsequent memorandum of 18 December, nearly six weeks later, presented quite a different perspective. Germany seemed unable to counter very effectively either on the eastern front or in the Mediterranean. It looked like a long war without a clear German victory, one in which Hitler might even make a new deal with Stalin. Carrero observed soberly that there was nothing in Nazi ideology to prevent him from doing so, since it must be recognized that Nazi Germany "presents no fundamental religious or spiritual divergence" from the USSR. To avert a catastrophe in the east, Spain should try to persuade Great Britain to change its policy and deal with Germany.[16] The strategic condition had become so dire that from December 1942 there were no longer any plans to arrange Spain's entry into the war at some future date.

Franco's policy for the moment was to stand pat. He was apparently still convinced that one way or another the war would yet produce major new developments that his regime could take advantage of. On the first anniversary of the Japanese attack on Pearl Harbor, his speech to the National Council of the FET declared: "We are witnessing the end of one era and the beginning of another. The liberal world is going under, victim of the cancer of its own errors, and with it collapse commercial imperialism, finance capitalism, and their millions of unemployed." After once more praising Fascist Italy and Nazi Germany, he insisted: "The historic destiny of our era will be realized either by the barbarous formula of Bolshevist totalitarianism or by the spiritual patriotic one that Spain offers, or by any other of the fascist peoples. . . . Those who dream of the establishment of demo-liberal systems in Western Europe delude themselves."[17] Another of Franco's disastrously false prophecies, it indicated that he still believed the Third Reich would survive the war in a reasonably strong position, something that at this point he considered necessary for the survival of his regime. Therefore on 18 December he declared before the Senior War College that "the destiny and future of Spain are closely tied to a German victory."[18]

There was some new collaboration, though aspects of previous collaboration were being reduced. An invitation from the German navy at the close of 1942 brought twenty-six Spanish naval officers and noncommissioned officers for training with German ships in the North Sea, and three small German torpedo boats would subsequently be purchased for the Spanish fleet.[19] Throughout the autumn of 1942 the FET leadership was eagerly promoting a formal visit by Arrese to Berlin, though Jordana did everything he could to delay or cancel it, possibly even threatening resignation. On the more positive side, Jordana was able to inform the Germans at the close of December that they must put an end to radio transmissions from Spanish soil that were used for operations against the Allies, though not all such transmissions immediately came to an end. By that time German agents had received orders to abandon external sabotage against Allied shipping in Spain; henceforth the main tactic would be internal sabotage by bombs placed within cargoes.[20]

German Planning

On 19 November, with disaster looming in both east and south, Hitler held a conference with Admiral Raeder. He was determined to hold Tunisia, knowing that if it were lost, southwestern Europe would lie open to Allied invasion. In such an eventuality, Hitler thought, the Iberian peninsula was a more likely target than Italy or the Balkans. It was nearer the sources of Allied supply in the Atlantic, while the invasion of Spain would make Gibraltar secure and connect with Portugal, giving the Allies a base from which to proceed to either France or Italy. He therefore ordered measures to prepare to activate Operation Gisela, the new name for Ilona,[21] which now envisioned no more than the defense of the Pyrenees, together with seizure of a few key ports and cities in the far north of Spain, though a small armored force was made ready in southern France. Hitler ordered his commander in France, Field Marshal Gerd von Rundstedt, to be prepared to mine the Pyrenees passes, and indicated that some attention should now be given the persistently denied Spanish requests for German arms, so that Spain would stand a better chance of defending itself against the Allies. Stohrer had been urging this measure for some time, and by the beginning of December a lengthy list of Spanish desiderata had been assembled.[22]

Admiral Canaris made another of his frequent trips to Madrid at the beginning of December, ostensibly to discuss the Spanish request for arms, though it has also been claimed, without clear evidence, that he was charged with gaining approval for the possible entry of German troops into northern Spain under Operation Gisela. Canaris spoke with two top generals, Juan Vigón and Carlos Martínez de Campos, who allegedly told him that the only situation in which Franco would permit German troops to enter the country would be a direct Allied invasion of Spain.

According to certain of his biographers, Canaris was invited to lunch with Jordana at the home of Martínez de Campos. Though no copy of such a document has been found, Canaris then purportedly filed a report to Berlin concluding that there was no hope of Spain's entering the war unless the situation on both the eastern and southern fronts was stabilized (with the buildup of German forces to drive the Allies out of Algeria and Morocco), unless German peace goals for Europe were formalized (and recognized the claims of Spain), and unless the Reich government established better relations with the Vatican, provided assurance that National Socialism would not make another deal with the Soviet Union or lapse into a form of "western bolshevism," and provided major economic assistance.[23]

On 3 December Hitler notified Ribbentrop that he had firmly decided it was not desirable for Spain to enter the war, for both military and economic reasons. At this point, therefore, attitudes in Madrid and Berlin were to some extent converging. Hitler declared that he would not provide arms unless he could be certain that, if necessary, the Spanish would use them against the Allies, and repeated that he did not want to release Muñoz Grandes, but would send him back only when there was an absolute political need for his presence in Spain. Two days later he received Vidal y Saura, the new ambassador, who expressed continued hopes for German victory, asked for the sale of German arms, and particularly pressed Franco's request for the return of Muñoz Grandes. Hitler replied that the Finnish troops and the Blue Division were the best of the allied forces on the eastern front and, somewhat surprisingly, reversed himself a

few days later and agreed to let Muñoz Grandes go.[24] This decision probably reflected the diminished status of Spain in Hitler's thinking.

On 13 December, Muñoz Grandes departed his command and was
flown to meet Hitler at Rastenburg. The Führer greeted him warmly, declared that the Blue Division was equal to the best of its German counterparts and informed the Spanish general that he was adding the coveted
Eichenlaub (oak leaves) to his Iron Cross, a distinction very rarely con-
ferred on non-Germans. Then they took up the question of Spanish policy
and the possible role of Muñoz Grandes in Madrid. Hitler showed no interest in any scheme to overthrow Franco, which he did not think was realistic. Instead he asked that Muñoz Grandes work vigorously to resist the
Allies, fight with all determination should they invade, and do all he could
to influence Spanish policy further toward the Axis. Hitler indicated that
he was now ready to recognize Spanish ambitions in Africa and was prepared to send German weapons, but first asked Muñoz Grandes to learn
exactly how Franco planned to use them. Secret direct communications
with the Führer would be established through Ribbentrop's special office,
bypassing the embassy in Madrid.[25]

On the following day Ribbentrop assured Muñoz Grandes in Berlin
that the next German summer offensive would throw back the Red Army
and stabilize the eastern front; German reinforcements would then be able
to drive the Allies from north Africa. He further insisted, falsely, that Germany had always supported Spanish territorial ambitions. On the 15th
Muñoz Grandes met with Vidal, who sought to learn the scope of the
general's discussions with Hitler, and was assured that they only had to do
with the problems of the eastern front.[26]

Muñoz Grandes returned to Madrid on 17 December to a hero's welcome by a huge crowd, though Franco was not present. The Generalissimo
immediately promoted him to lieutenant general, a rank that had the advantage of making him ineligible for any further active divisional command. Franco then invited Asensio and Muñoz Grandes to dinner on New
Year's Eve, but, according to Muñoz Grandes, was evasive about adopting
a more strongly pro-German policy. Muñoz Grandes reported to German
contacts that Franco was wary of him but that he, Asensio, and Yagüe were
prepared to take measures—unspecified—to bring Spain into the war by
the summer of 1943. That could happen, he said, only if Germany successfully assumed the offensive in both Russia and North Africa.[27]

For two and a half months, Franco left Muñoz Grandes without assignment, then on 3 March named him head of his personal military staff.

This move was intended to seem an honor that would please Berlin, but in fact left the Blue Division's former commander without command of troops and under Franco's thumb, where he could cause least trouble. Muñoz Grandes continued to maintain secret contact with Berlin for some time, but military and political events increasingly undercut his pro-German posture, and as a political factor he was effectively neutralized.

Meanwhile, at a meeting of Hitler and Raeder on 22 December, the German naval commander insisted that the Allies' invasion of Spain was an imminent danger, almost a "strategic necessity" for them. Hitler came to agree, and on 7 January 1943 ordered Rundstedt to prepare to activate a more ambitious version of Gisela. The hastily revised plan now called for one German corps of three divisions to move past Hendaye and Ronces-valles in the western Pyrenees to seize Bilbao and Pamplona, whence it might fan outward toward Galicia, if desirable, while a second corps of three divisions would occupy Catalonia. The operation would employ seven divisions in all, including at least one armored division and one armored artillery regiment, with other sizable units in reserve. German forces might advance as far as Valladolid and Madrid. Apprehension concerning Allied plans was intense, and the final orders for this revised and expanded version of Gisela were issued on 10 February. Almost simultaneously, the Führer ordered that preparations be both accelerated and expanded.[28]

Allied concerns exactly mirrored German apprehensions. Some American units had been held in reserve to cover Spanish Morocco in the event of hostile action by Spain, while several very small American paratroop units, which had landed there by mistake, were interned for the duration of the campaign. As the major phase of the Tunisian campaign began to develop in the first weeks of 1943, a new Allied contingency plan for Spain, Backbone II, was drawn up by the British. In the event of either Spanish hostilities or a German invasion, the new scheme called for a three-pronged invasion of Spanish Morocco, perhaps to be accompanied by the establishment of a bridgehead in southern Spain around Gibraltar. If need be, Backbone II would have included a new task force proceeding directly from Great Britain and would probably have easily overwhelmed Spanish forces, but, like each of the fairly numerous contingency plans involving the peninsula or the Spanish and Portuguese islands, it never had to be brought into play.[29]

Amid this uncertainty and danger, a priority of Jordana was to strengthen relations with Portugal to assist in moving Spain toward neu-trality. On 18–22 December 1942 he paid a visit to Lisbon, where he and Salazar got along very well together. They seemed to develop a genuine liking for each other, based on similar values and personal philosophies. In Lisbon Jordana declared publicly that Spain's status of nonbelligerence should not be interpreted as equivalent to that of Italy in 1939–40, because at that time Italy had been an official military ally of Germany, whereas Spain was not. By comparison, he said, Spain and Portugal were constructing similar regimes based on Catholicism. On returning to Madrid, Jordana had to reassure German diplomats that the Lisbon visit was intended solely to renew the common determination to maintain the integrity and independence of the peninsula, and pointed out to them that closer relations between Madrid and Lisbon were a means to balance and loosen Lisbon's ties with London.[30] This was nonetheless Jordana's first notable initiative to create an alternative orientation in foreign policy and led to the announcement in February 1943 of the Bloque Ibérico to maintain the peninsula's independence. Franco accepted this as normal prudence, but refused to do anything to follow up on it, while closer relations with Portugal were strongly opposed by Falangists, who still hoped in some fashion to swallow up the neighboring country.[31]

The last months of 1942 had completed the discrediting of Stohrer in Berlin, where the veteran diplomat was judged to be naive, inept, and hopelessly ill informed, a sometime stooge of Serrano Suñer. The new ambassador, Hans Adolf von Moltke, arrived in Madrid on 11 January 1943. He was a seasoned professional, but his main service had been in Eastern Europe and he knew little of Spain, whereas Erich Heberlein, the best and most experienced of Stohrer's subordinates, had also been recalled. Moltke plunged into his new assignment, making contact with many Spanish officials, but he was more careful than Stohrer to avoid involvement in Spanish political intrigues. After a conversation with Franco on 24 January, he reported: "Franco underlined with clear words the political position of Spain in this war: Germany is the friend; England, America, and bolshevism are the enemies. To the extent of its political capabilities, Spain is ready and willing to assist Germany in its decisive battle. It would be grateful for any suggestion as to how this might be done." Franco pointed out that the longer the war lasted, the more destructive it would be for all Europe, and that "he must also say that his information on the mood in Italy worried him." Franco pointed up the importance of trying to exploit the contradictions between the Anglo-Americans and the Soviets. Moltke could only respond somewhat lamely that this was a good idea, but that given the attitude of their enemies, the German people were determined to see the war through to victory.[32]

Moltke's arrival virtually coincided with the last high-level Spanish political visit to the Reich. The journey of Arrese to Berlin, where the FET secretary general would technically be a guest of the Nazi Winter Relief social organization, was a Falangist project designed both to raise the profile of the party in Spain and to tighten connections with the Reich, and had been in gestation for several months. Though the trip would anger the Spanish military, Franco finally overruled Jordana and gave his approval on 7 January,[33] but before the FET chief left Franco held a six-hour conversation with him to be sure that he did not exceed instructions. Accompanied by his two top aides, Arrese arrived in the German capital on 17 January, amid maximal pomp and publicity in all the Spanish media. For the next six days he talked with a variety of government and party officials and visited various Nazi social organizations. The visit was formal, superficial, and ultimately without significant political content. Following instructions, in his visit with Ribbentrop "Arrese became inaccessible. Any attempt to engage in serious discussion was blocked, ending in mutual assurances of anticommunism and phrases without concrete meaning. . . . The conversation between Hitler and Arrese . . . was carried on by Hitler with a degree of excitement. Just as in his conversation with Ribbentrop, Arrese did not show, along with his courtesy, the slightest interest in a political dialogue," though he did issue a public statement that the Blue Division would fight "until final victory" over Communism. Later, when he met with Goebbels, the conversation descended to bullfights.[34]

From Franco's point of view, the trip was a great success; from the German perspective, disappointing. Though Muñoz Grandes and Asensio continued to meet with German representatives during the first months of 1943, assuring them that they were working to persuade Franco to enter the war, the German leaders had given up any hope of a significant change in Spanish policy, and only asked that Franco maintain a posture that might keep the Allies off balance. The usual set of German intriguers in the SS, the party, and the embassy nonetheless remained active, and floated the rumor early in February that Churchill would stop in Lisbon on his way back from the Casablanca conference for a secret meeting with Franco. They also spread stories of imminent Allied intervention in the peninsula, all in the interest of provoking some drastic new move by either Madrid or Berlin. Moltke, however, had all these rumors checked out, and arranged to send home Erich Gardemann, the leading political intriguer in the German embassy.[35]

Jordana had already sent one letter of resignation to Franco, perhaps at the very end of 1942. He declared that he was carrying on a "titanic" effort to make Spain's policy more neutral, in the best interest of all. The main opposition came from the FET and from Asensio's pro-German section of the military command. Soon after Arrese's return, Jordana complained once more to Franco that his own efforts to achieve "a position of neutrality" were not being supported, and that "to achieve that I have had to fight, and continue fighting, with the state party, which still, certainly without the slightest instinct for self-preservation, has not digested such a policy." The best that could be said for Arrese's trip was that it was completely futile, "and on returning Arrese himself publishes a pamphlet that talks about the policy of Arrese and the party in fundamental disagreement with that formulated by the government," or at least by Jordana. The foreign minister was correct that in the first half of 1943 most activity of the FET and its press and propaganda continued to align Spain completely with the Axis, while, he observed, "against me they wage a maximal propaganda effort." Nonetheless, Jordana concluded that this effort had only limited effect because the great majority of Spaniards supported his policy (as undoubtedly they did).[36] The FET's stubbornness in maintaining its strongly pro-German line was due to its own ideological priorities, not to any pressure from Berlin. The German government had long since ceased to pay much attention to the FET, realizing that it held little power.[37]

Jordana insisted that he could not continue unless foreign policy was concentrated in his hands and not dispersed among the party radicals. He complained that Franco did not respond to the foreign ministry's planning papers and demanded the firing of Arrese and several other top Falangists. Though Jordana failed to get them dismissed, he did succeed in establishing with Franco that all foreign policy issues must be channeled through his ministry. Nonetheless, he later learned that the Spanish trade union organization had signed an agreement with the Deutsche Arbeitsfront, the Nazi labor organization, without informing the foreign ministry, and Jordana again complained that the FET was conducting its own foreign policy. He slowly made headway, because by that time the Axis position in Tunisia had totally collapsed, and even Arrese finally began to change his tune. In June Arrese finally held a special dinner for Jordana and the Axis ambassadors "to give the appearance of unity," at which he behaved with greater prudence. Jordana wrote in his diary that on this occasion the Falangists "were very nice to me and seemed ready to change tactics on international affairs."[38]

To Jordana's disgust, collaboration with Germany nonetheless continued. During the first months of 1943, German sabotage activities against Gibraltar continued to be planned and carried out from Spanish territory. By the end of March he was about to resign once more because of a new decision by Franco to close the Spanish frontier to downed Allied airmen and others escaping from occupied France. Jordana canceled his personal appointments for a day or two in protest, but on 5 April he finally got his way, as the frontier was quietly reopened.[39] Moreover, after the British foiled a major sabotage effort against Gibraltar in June, Franco was finally moved to order a partial dismantling of such activities.[40]

During February the Germans pressed for military staff discussions with the Spanish concerning the defense of Spain and Portugal against the Allies, but Franco avoided any such conversations. Martínez de Campos was scheduled to go to Berlin in March to discuss the arms situation, and Moltke stressed to his superiors the importance of taking advantage of this visit to conclude an arms deal. Though the Spanish continued to avoid formal staff talks, on 17 April General Rafael García Valiño, who had replaced Asensio as chief of staff, assured a German diplomat that in the event of an Allied attack on the Balearics or any other part of Spain, the two countries would have to proceed to joint military action. The German diplomat then reported that "so far as I know, this is the first time that a Spanish military commander in a major position has clearly affirmed the need for military discussions," but that was to exaggerate the tenor of the remarks.[41]

In the meantime, after scarcely more than two months in Madrid, Moltke suddenly died of acute appendicitis on 22 March. Within a month he was replaced by another experienced senior diplomat, Hans Heinrich Dieckhoff, since the Germans always sent their top personnel as ambassadors to Spain. He presented his credentials on 30 April amid what he termed "the customary Castilian-African pomp" of Spanish ceremonies. Franco assured Dieckhoff of continued support for Germany, though he expressed a rational fear that American resources might simply be too great to be overcome. At this point Franco professed no further concern about invasion by the Allies, though he recognized that they might try to take over the Azores and declared that he was determined to strengthen the Spanish armed forces as much as possible. A week later Jordana diplomatically repeated the same pro-German sentiments but made the same observation about American strength, against which Dieckhoff strongly protested.[42]

The New Trade Treaty and Arms Deal

The only thing that Jordana wanted from the Third Reich was the delivery of arms, since the Spanish military was so poorly supplied and Spanish industry was not prepared to produce the more complex weapons systems. A Foreign Ministry planning report by José María Doussinague on 18 September 1942 had stressed the importance of obtaining better weaponry since war would inevitably expand in the Mediterranean, either because the Allies would seize the offensive or because the Germans might gain a victory in the east that would allow them to give full attention to the south. In less than two months this forecast was amply fulfilled, and the question of arms supply, under negotiation with the Germans since the preceding July, assumed new urgency.

It was common practice for the Third Reich to use arms as an economic bargaining chip with neutral countries, because this was the only major desideratum that the German economy might be able to provide. The Spanish government, however, also wanted technical assistance for its own arms industry and orders and assistance for the INI. In 1943 military expenditures reached 63 percent of the Spanish budget, a high point for the entire war, but it had become very difficult for the German economy to provide assistance abroad, a prospect made the more discouraging in the Spanish case because of the prevailing economic disorder and the danger that, given internal divisions, some part of any new weaponry might end up in the hands of the Allies, or so the Germans feared. Conversely, whereas Spanish firms received a large volume of French contracts during World War I, they got few new German contracts in World War II. In 1942 the German government did place an order for RM2 million of ships to be constructed in Spain, of which seven small merchant ships had been completed by the summer of 1944. In 1943 another contract was signed for the manufacture of pistols in Spain, but few were produced.[43]

All economic discussions between Madrid and Berlin moved with great slowness. The size of the German trade deficit was a major obstacle, to which was added the Germans' reluctance to provide weaponry already in short supply in the Reich, as well as the tendency of various Spanish ministries to try to negotiate separate deals on their own, a practice that Jordana managed to bring to an end. The short-term trade agreement signed on 16 December 1942 was the first official trade agreement in more than five years, and was valid until 30 November 1943.[44] During its first three months Madrid was to provide RM130 million in export credits, against which the German government promised to ship at least RM60 million of goods to Spain, followed by a sufficient volume during the remainder of the period to guarantee that Germany's deficit for the period would not be more than RM70 million. It also promised to honor separate ministerial deals negotiated during the preceding year in which the Luftwaffe and Kriegsmarine would provide RM40 million in supplies, as well as 6,000 machine guns. As it developed, however, Spain provided the RM130 million of goods on credit, while Germany delivered only RM20 million of the RM60 million of goods pledged.[45]

When Vidal Saura left as ambassador to Berlin at the close of 1942, Jordana stressed that his main priority would be to obtain arms. Vidal began by asking for 125 late-model German airplanes. This was impossible, but because of Spain's difficult strategic situation and the large trade imbalance, the German government decided it would have to do something, so that in the long run about 20 percent of all German arms exports during 1943 went to Spain.

To expedite negotiations, on 10 February Jordana signed a secret protocol with Moltke whereby the Spanish government pledged to resist vigorously Allied military assault on any part of its territory.[46] Serious bargaining was begun in Berlin on 15 March 1943 by a Spanish delegation led by General Carlos Martínez de Campos, who presented three tiers of requests. Hitler took a hand in the negotiations, finally offering 15 fighter planes, 10 bombers, 30 tanks, 150 antitank and anti-aircraft guns, plus other smaller weapons and supplies.[47]

When the negotiation of terms began on 5 May, the Spanish were taken aback to find that German prices ranged from 200 to 400 percent higher than the last German arms prices that they had seen in 1939. Their reaction was indignant, and even German arms industry officials admitted that the prices were too high. When terms were finally agreed on 18 August, the Spanish negotiators had managed to reduce the total price increase to approximately 20 percent, a huge improvement.[48]

The first shipments in June 1943 of what the Germans called Programm Bär included 65 boxcars of air force equipment and 293 boxcars of other arms, in addition to 25 fighter planes. Final terms provided for another 670 boxcars of weapons, shipments of which proceeded on schedule down to the end of 1943. After that the rate began to decline sharply, so that down to August 1944, when rail connections with Germany ended, little more than RM20 million of arms had been sent in 1944, compared with RM115 million during the preceding year. Small shipments continued by air during the remainder of 1944; altogether they amounted to RM158.4 million of the RM216.5 million of arms promised.

A new trade agreement was negotiated to run from 1 December 1943 to 30 November 1944, according to which Germany could import RM335 million of goods from Spain, of which vital wolfram would make up at least RM127 million. Financing would come from an advance of RM100 million of credit by the Spanish government against the Civil War debt, while RM179 million would be paid for Programm Bär, though all but RM5 million of the latter would be drawn from the debt accrued by the German commercial deficit. In addition, Spain would accept a trade deficit from Germany up to an additional RM70 million, and RM50 million would be paid by regular German exports to Spain. This arrangement provided Germany with a total Spanish balance of RM225 million on which to draw, but still left it RM110 million short, which could come only from more arms shipments, so in 1944 Berlin proposed Programm Ankara, which was to include sixty-seven tanks, sixty-two pieces of artillery, and a number of airplanes. This offer was accepted by Madrid in mid-July 1944, by which time, of course, it was too late. All that was received from this final agreement was equivalent value from the possession of fifteen German planes that had had to make forced landings in Spain.[49]

Though some successes were achieved, German economic ambitions in Spain were in general never fulfilled. The desired penetration of the Spanish economy was for the most part resisted effectively, while the limited number of mines and other companies that had passed into German ownership produced less and less under wartime conditions. While Germany became increasingly dependent on Spain for wolfram (which will be discussed in Chapter 14), it proved altogether incapable of closing the large trade deficit.[50]

Diplomatic Repositioning

From his first weeks as foreign minister, Jordana had personally termed his policy "neutrality," yet he did not dare use such language officially, since it would have contradicted Franco's official posture and since German forces still remained militarily dominant on the continent. Even Franco, however, recognized by the beginning of 1943 that things had changed and that there needed to be some realignment among European states. To that extent the Duke of Alba, ambassador in London, had been instructed in January to offer the British government the good offices of

Madrid to attempt to mediate peace between the Allies and Germany, a ploy that was summarily rejected.

A new scheme developed in the Ministry of Foreign Affairs during January and February as Plan D, apparently the brainchild of José María Doussinague. He was an experienced professional who had been strongly pro-German during 1940–41, when Hitler was winning, but now realized that conditions were changing drastically. As head of long-term planning, he came up with a scheme that reflected his own thinking more than that of Jordana, not so much a precise plan of action as a new general orientation, based on the notion that the war would continue for some time, with neither side winning a complete victory. Hence the need for "an arrangement" based on a "policy of just and benevolent reconciliation." Spain's goal should be to intervene at the right time to bring about this arrangement. Representing a country unscarred by the present conflict, the Spanish government might, if it used its influence at the right time and in the right way, "make of Spain a great power."

It might be possible for Spain to do so because it was "the most important of all the neutral nations" and also the "number one Catholic country," and could in a different form create an analogue of Salvador de Madariaga's policy a decade earlier by building an entente of Catholic states such as Portugal, Ireland, Hungary, and Croatia. This idea of course overlooked the fact that Hungary and Slovakia were satellites of the Third Reich, while Croatia was virtually a puppet. Without opposing the United States, Spain should make an effort to draw Latin American countries into the scheme. Doussinague acknowledged that this proposal "does not fully fit our friendly relations with Germany and Italy," but was nonetheless designed to assist them. The plan might be initiated through contacts with the Vatican and with other Catholic governments.[51]

Doussinague referred to this proposal as "a neutralist probe," but it was quite unrealistic. Doussinague dreamed of making Spain a dominant mediator without having fully altered its skewed policy of pro-Axis nonbelligerence, and hoped to make use of a Vatican with which relations remained somewhat shaky and which did not necessarily see Spain as the "number one Catholic country." The notion that a congeries of German satellites, puppets, and occupied territories might enjoy the autonomy to follow a separate Spanish foreign policy merely reflected delusional thinking. In this scheme, Hitler was to give up all conquests except the city of Danzig (now Gdansk), while Spain would be rewarded by significant colonial cessions in Africa. Though Spanish diplomats would float the idea of a mediation scheme in various European capitals between January and July, the only interest shown was in Helsinki and Budapest, whose governments were increasingly interested in a separate peace. Even the Vatican, which in general had made the greatest efforts toward mediation, did not find the scheme attractive or viable.

Nonetheless, on 8 March Franco emphasized to Moltke Spain's strong desire for peace and its determination to persist in the defense of "European culture and Christian civilization." On 1 April he told a German diplomat that the Spanish government still had faith in Germany's strength and resolve and would never do anything to harm German interests, but that the war was so long and destructive that Spain had a responsibility to work with other neutrals toward a reasonable peace. As the Axis position in Tunisia crumbled, even Muñoz Grandes became a qualified convert to the new policy, as he explained in a rather convoluted way to a German representative on 21 April.[52]

Franco moved one step further in his orientation toward "cosmetic constitutionalism" when he convened the first session of his new appointive and controlled Cortes, or parliament, in mid-March. This move was intended to give a more representative gloss to the Spanish dictatorship, though in fact it probably made it look more like Fascist Italy, with its Chamber of Fasces and Corporations. Franco used his inaugural address to stress the danger of the advance of Soviet communism and Spain's desire to work for peace. At the beginning of May, as Axis forces were on the verge of surrender in Tunisia, Franco reminded a military audience in Seville that Spain was still a nonbelligerent, possibly as an act of defiance to the Allies, lest they think of invading Spain. That gesture, however, would never be repeated, and only a few days later in Almería Franco gave his most categorical public peace speech to date, which he deemed so satisfactory that it was immediately circulated widely as a pamphlet. Dieckhoff, the new German ambassador, lamented that his own protests had not managed to convince Franco of the harm his emphasis on peace would do and promised Berlin to try harder, chalking it up to Franco's need to strengthen his domestic position, given the pacifist sympathies of most of the Spanish population.[53]

Since the beginning of 1943 the Allies' diplomacy in Madrid had been much more active than that of the Axis. Both Hayes and Hoare enjoyed increasingly good relations with Jordana, who privately used the term "neutrality" in discussing Spain's policy with them. By May even Franco was expressing some skepticism to German diplomats about an eventual

German victory. In some desperation, Muñoz Grandes suggested through his secret channel to Berlin that a new meeting between Franco and Hitler should be arranged, but Ribbentrop curtly rejected the proposal because he saw no sign of interest by Franco.[54] The German foreign minister saw Spain as a lost cause, though any basic change in its policy would only accentuate the isolation of the Reich.

Dieckhoff had a more substantive discussion with Franco and Jordana on 16 June, in which he requested that the Caudillo cease efforts to mediate and especially to avoid giving the impression that Germany was using Spain to alleviate a position of weakness. Franco replied with his usual self-righteousness that he was merely seeking to create "a psychology of peace also useful to Germany" and pointed out that the tone even of German propaganda had begun to change. He observed that if Mussolini had followed the same policy as Spain, Italy would not have been a "heavy burden" for Germany but instead might then have been able to help in the present situation, as Spain was trying to do now. For the first time Franco condemned Hitler's persecution of the churches as "profoundly mistaken," and repeated again that Germany could never hope to win a complete victory over the United States.[55] These last points were not included in Dieckhoff's report, which did record Franco's statement that the Axis's collapse in Tunisia had made a serious impression on him. The Generalissimo complained strongly once more about the prices Germany was charging for its arms, but the ambassador concluded that he believed that Franco was sincere when he said that Spain and Germany had the same enemies and thought that "in his heart" Franco was on Germany's side, but he simply felt that Spain was too vulnerable strategically and economically to the Anglo-Americans.[56]

Immediately after the Axis collapse in Africa, the Supreme General Staff (AEM) prepared a brief assessment, recognizing that it was a "small disaster" for the Axis, and that if Hitler was not able to resume the initiative soon, he would have to seek peace. Otherwise, the most likely result was the defeat of Germany, leaving the Soviet Union dominant in continental Europe. It pointed out that Portugal did not support the Spanish mediation policy but was leaning seriously toward the Allies.[57] In Argentina, the most pro-Spanish Latin American state, a partly pro-American military coup at the beginning of June installed a new government more hostile to Germany and Spain. Another report from the AEM later that month warned that an Allied invasion of Spain might be imminent, though Jordana considered this too alarmist.[58]

Jordana declared on 1 June that it was high time to control the pro-German propaganda which still dominated the Spanish press, even as he officially protested the counter-propaganda revealed in the new American newsreel special *Inside Fascist Spain*, which was being shown all over the United States. This documentary was full of lurid wartime hyperbole, such as the claim that under Franco there had been "over a million executions of Republican prisoners during the Spanish Civil War," that there were still "over half a million Republican prisoners" in 1943, and that the Spanish regime was a totalitarian state in which "banking and finance have passed under the complete control of the Falange," and so forth.

Though both the American and Spanish left would have been only too happy to see an Allied invasion of Spain, such speculation was useful to the Allied command primarily as a diversion. Spanish collaboration with the Axis was employed by Allied intelligence to carry off one of the most effective deceptions in the war to date, known to the Allies as Operation Mincemeat. The corpse of a recently deceased British derelict (a suicide without relatives to claim him), dressed in the uniform of a British navy officer, was cast ashore near Huelva by a British submarine on 30 April. The corpse bore documents indicating that the next Allied invasion would be directed against Greece and Crete, with only minor diversionary gestures toward Sicily and Sardinia.[59] This material was translated for Franco and then passed on to the Germans[60] and Italians, who accepted it as valid, though they had previously thought Sicily the most likely target. The deception greatly facilitated the invasion of Sicily, which began on 10 July, for otherwise the island would have been more heavily reinforced. In this case Spanish collaboration proved to be something of a boomerang for the Axis (as also in the case of the false espionage of Juan Pujol in England). In the meantime Hitler had canceled Operation Gisela altogether, replacing it with Operation Nürnberg, a simple plan to fortify the Pyrenees.[61] Later, after the Allied deception had become obvious, the embassy in Madrid was asked to conduct an inquiry as to whether the Spanish had served as an innocent conduit or whether Spanish personnel had collaborated in the deception.[62]

The Fall of Mussolini

Franco first received a report on declining morale in the Italian military and the beginning of war-weariness in the Italian population on 11 July 1941,[63] and after that the news slowly became more and more negative. After Serrano's trip to Italy in June 1942, relations grew more distant, for

Jordana completely lacked his predecessor's Italianist orientation. Several figures in the Italian regime developed an interest in using nonbelligerent Spain as a channel through which to pursue a separate peace, but Mussolini completely reorganized his government at the beginning of 1943, eliminating his son-in-law Ciano and anyone else likely to show independence. Though Mussolini apparently thought and occasionally even spoke in private of trying to regain freedom of action, he was too bound to Hitler's chariot to break free. In February he warned the new Spanish ambassador, Raimundo Fernández Cuesta (former secretary general of the FET), that if the Allies succeeded in seizing all North Africa, they would next invade Spain. During February and March Mussolini repeatedly urged the Führer to turn the flank of the Allies by attacking them through Spain, which he mistakenly thought was now ready to enter the war, while also urging him to make peace with Stalin so that Axis forces might be concentrated in the Mediterranean. Fernández Cuesta, however, was under strict instructions not to encourage the slightest speculations of this sort, while Hitler showed no interest in changing priorities.[64]

When the Duce named a new ambassador to Madrid in April 1943, he gave him two charges: to try to arrange a meeting between Mussolini and Franco, and to make secret contact with the Allies concerning their terms for a separate peace. Neither effort was successful. Franco replied, no doubt honestly, that he sincerely hoped for Axis victory but that Allied pressure was too stringent to permit a meeting, while the Allies, after the Casablanca conference in January, insisted on unconditional surrender.[65] That spring major Allied bombing of Italian cities began and made a considerable impression in Spain, for it showed how deeply the war had penetrated the heart of southern Europe.

Reporting from the Spanish embassy was nonetheless weak, and Franco and most of his associates were not prepared for the sudden collapse of the Italian Fascists late in July. Dieckhoff reported on 14 July that Franco had just told him that he took the news of the Allied invasion of Sicily with "complete calm," though even Muñoz Grandes pointed out that Spain was so similar to Italy that if things went badly there, they might have a major impact on Spain.[66] Franco's address to the FET on the 18th registered a ringing endorsement of Falangism and once more denounced capitalism and liberalism in the best fascist style, though some thought it was directed more against the monarchists, who again were becoming increasingly active.

Six days later came the overthrow of Mussolini by the Grand Council of the Italian Fascist Party itself, in collaboration with the king and the Italian army command. Many in Madrid were stunned, and a police report submitted to Franco three weeks later, on 17 August, observed that within the FET there was great alarm for fear of similar developments in Spain and lament that foreign asylum was so difficult, though after the first days a new determination emerged not to give up, but even to organize squads of twenty men in each neighborhood to keep political dissidence under control.[67] Jordana was soon beside himself once more, because the FET leaders seemed suicidal, continuing to wrap themselves in the banner of the fallen Italian Fascists.[68]

The Spanish government initially responded with a new police crackdown, but so dramatic a change inevitably sparked debate. At the next meeting of the Council of Ministers on 29 July, the air force minister, General Juan Vigón, even suggested that the time had come for Franco to appoint a prime minister.[69] The Caudillo would have none of that, but another of the periodic orders did go to the Spanish press to treat the war news more fairly.[70] Dieckhoff was alarmed by such signs, and though Jordana later assured him that this betokened "no change in Spanish foreign policy," he was not fully convinced.[71]

For the first six weeks after the fall of Mussolini, Franco was determined to present an image of calm and equanimity to the Germans. During the intermission at a concert by the Berlin Philharmonic in San Sebastián on 9 September, Franco invited Dieckhoff to his box and unburdened himself on the present situation. According to the German ambassador, he was "indignant" about the overthrow of Mussolini and blamed it on subversion by his bête noire, Freemasonry. Nonetheless, Franco opined that Germany was in a stronger position now that it did not need to shore up the Italians. "He expressed his astonishment at the fortitude of the German people and said that he hoped we would soon strike back against the British air attack in the sharpest way." He also expressed considerable interest in the neo-Fascist regime in northern Italy, and Dieckhoff found him "open as never before," "quite indignant over Italy but quiet and determined."[72]

For the time being, Franco virtually froze contact with Italy, Fascist or post-Fascist. Whereas for six months his government had been maneuvering to present itself as a peace negotiator, when the first concrete opportunity presented itself the Spanish regime refused all involvement, ignoring feelers from the new Italian government about helping to arrange a separate peace, for fear of being tarred with the Fascist connection by the Allies on the one hand and of offending the Germans on the other. Those

Fascist notables, led by Mussolini's daughter Edda, who sought refuge in Spain, were brushed off, and Franco would not at first even allow an Italian representative to come to Madrid to negotiate directly with the British and Americans. Dino Grandi, a Fascist hierarch who had led the coup, was finally permitted to proceed to Madrid to negotiate under a false name, but by that point much time had passed. Grandi later alleged that the Italians' failure to negotiate a more effective withdrawal from the war was due to the delays imposed by Franco. The one time that he had a chance to help negotiate peace, Franco feared to seize the opportunity.[73]

On 12 September, three days after the Generalissimo's complacent conversation with Dieckhoff, the army minister, General Asensio, delivered to Franco a letter signed by nearly all the lieutenant generals. For the first and only time in the history of the regime, the military hierarchy collectively suggested—with the utmost respect and obsequiousness—that the time had come to step aside and restore the monarchy. The so-called German faction had virtually ceased its conspiratorial conversations, and while many looked to Don Juan to restore the monarchy and liberalize government, some of the pro-Germans in the military and the party now looked to the Pretender to form a strong new Spanish government that could preserve national independence and follow a sort of middle course, not a merely pro-German posture.[74] There was even some speculation about an all-military, basically nonfascist, government led by the monarchist General Luis Orgaz, as a step in this process.

In this internal crisis, Franco displayed his customary calm and stubbornness, making no concessions whatever. He received the lieutenant generals one or two at a time, explaining that the international situation was too dangerous to permit any political change; at the same time he promoted a number of his most stalwart supporters to lieutenant general in order to guarantee himself stronger support among the military hierarchy. By the end of September, he was even disposed to recognize Mussolini's new puppet Italian Social Republic, but Jordana dissuaded him by another threat to resign. Only a semi-official representative, not an ambassador, was sent to northern Italy.[75]

The End of Nonbelligerence

The first significant sign of change came in August as Franco and the FET initiated a slow and very limited process of disencumbering the Spanish state party of its fascist accoutrements, though it would take some time to have any effect. On 20 August Franco told Hoare with a straight face that the FET was merely an instrument for social programs, not a fascist-style state party. Arrese announced the new line in a major speech at Burgos on 8 September. All invocation of the totalitarian state was long gone; the line now was that "Falangism subordinates the state to man as its supreme goal."[76] On 23 September official instructions henceforth forbade anyone to refer to the FET as a "party"; it was to be exclusively termed a "movement," the "National Movement." Slowly a series of measures were undertaken to redefine doctrine in a more moderate and conservative direction.

At the same time, Jordana seems to have gained Franco's agreement to announce the return of Spain's policy to neutrality, as well as the withdrawal of the Blue Division. Similarly, Allied pressure increased markedly after the fall of Italy. By the end of September restrictions were placed for the first time on German activities in Tangier,[77] which would lead to the first expulsion of German agents the following month. The decision to withdraw the Blue Division, threshed out in two very long meetings of the Council of Ministers on 24–25 September, was one for which German officials in Berlin were already prepared.

The status of nonbelligerence was never officially renounced, but when Franco addressed the National Council of the FET on 1 October, he defined Spain's policy as one of "vigilant neutrality," the first time in more than three years that he had publicly referred to that policy as neutralist. On the following day Dieckhoff was informed of the Spanish government's decision to withdraw the Blue Division. In accord with Berlin, the dissolution of the unit was formally announced on 12 October. Strict orders to the Spanish media to be more neutral were not given until nearly the end of 1943, and the term "neutrality" did not begin to appear regularly in the media until February 1944, but the first steps had been taken.

On 8 October Franco had a friendly meeting with Salazar near the border, and four days later was officially informed by Hoare of the arrangement negotiated by the British to establish bases in the Portuguese Azores. At the pan-Hispanic fiesta of the Día de la Raza on the 12th, Franco's speech made not the slightest reference to fascism or the Axis, but emphasized the Catholic and humanitarian mission of the historic Spanish empire, principles now declared to motivate Spain's foreign policy. The beginning of the new line was set.

PART III
The Struggle to Escape the "Axis Stigma"

CHAPTER **12**

Spanish Diplomacy and
the Holocaust (I)
A Spanish Paradox: Traditional
Prejudice and Philo-Sephardism

The Spanish government's policy concerning Jewish refugees during World War II was noteworthy for several reasons. One was the extent of collaboration between the Franco regime and the Axis, though not in this area; the second was the physical proximity of Spain as a relatively large nonbelligerent country that from 1940 bordered German-held territory; and a third was the fact that Spain was the only West European country to have generated a distinct major Jewish community historically identified with it—the *sefardíes,* Sephardic (formerly Spanish) Jews.[1]

During the fifteenth century Spain had gone from being the West European land that had the largest Jewish community enjoying the greatest degree of tolerance to one of forced conversion and assimilation, climaxed by the expulsion of all those who refused to convert in 1492.[2] Jewish refugees found shelter in the Ottoman Empire and in smaller numbers in West European countries, but the largest single group moved across to Morocco, where they led a difficult and checkered existence, but generally managed to survive.[3]

After that there were officially no unconverted Jews in Spain for approximately three centuries, though there were tens of thousands of converted Jews, or *conversos,* and their descendants in the country. At least half, probably more than half, of the Jewish population apostatized, so that 100,000 or more formerly Jewish people were slowly assimilated into a population that at that time may have numbered 7 million. In more recent times, assimilation of Jews has become common in Western countries, but the Spanish anomaly was the eventual complete absorption of a formerly Jewish population into the general society, though this was a slow and highly discriminatory process. On the one hand, conversos held many elite positions; on the other, they were bitterly resented as new and false Christians.

The Inquisition had been instituted in 1482 by Ferdinand and Isabella to deal with the issue of "Judaizers," false converts who secretly practiced Judaism, whose actions allegedly hindered the full Christianization of other conversos and the conversion of those who remained Jews. In its first decades the Inquisition targeted individual conversos almost exclusively (it had no jurisdiction over Jews and Muslims) and turned over thousands to the civil authorities for execution, while at the same time much of Spanish society resented the assimilation and absorption of tens of thousands of conversos. The appearance of conversos in elite roles led to the notorious *limpieza de sangre* (racial purity) statutes of the sixteenth and seventeenth centuries, which, though occasionally denounced by church leaders for their racist implications, often succeeded in barring the descendants of conversos from elite positions, until the statutes finally died away in the eighteenth century.

After much travail, the conversos were eventually fully assimilated and in Spain Jews remained only a memory. The images and associations connected with Jews, however, were almost universally stereotypical and negative, stemming from the traditional social and religious attitudes of the fifteenth and sixteenth centuries. A small number of crypto-Jewish families may have survived, and among others there was some memory or legend of past Jewishness, but Jews again appeared in Spain only with the liberalization of the nineteenth century, and then only a handful.

The edict of expulsion may be considered to have been annulled, at least de facto, by Spain's democratic constitution of 1869, one of the first democratic constitutions of modern Europe, which recognized complete freedom of religion. It was modified by the subsequent constitution of 1876, which denied the public practice of religion to non-Catholics, but permitted them to practice their religions freely in private. The first Jews entered modern Spain even earlier, around 1840, consisting of Ashkenazim who came as representatives of Central European firms and a number of small businessmen who moved to southern Spain from Morocco. By 1900 approximately 2,000 Jews resided in the country, overwhelmingly middle-class and in some cases quite affluent.[4]

The image of Jews in modern Spain remained negative. Though the image of Moroccans was also bad[5] (at least before the rise of a nationalistic pro-Morocco movement by the early twentieth century), it was not quite at the level of anti-Jewish feeling, so that the first Jewish shopkeepers who moved from Morocco to Seville in the mid–nineteenth century found it preferable to identify themselves simply as Moroccans. Nineteenth-century liberals sometimes strove to reduce prejudice against Jews, though primarily as part of their progressive politics in general and their opposition to the Catholic Church, not so much out of any specific concern for Jews.[6]

The direct re-encounter with Sephardim was a result of the Spanish-Moroccan war of 1859–60, which stemmed from the liberal nationalism characteristic of Spain in the mid–nineteenth century. From this campaign came the growth of late nineteenth-century Spanish Africanism and modern Spanish imperialism, a new romantic sense of relationship with Morocco and the Islamic world, and also a new awareness of Sephardic Jews. It was also the first modern Spanish military campaign in its use of public relations, supported by the strongest, most united single outburst of patriotism seen in modern Spain since Napoleonic times, and attended by a sizable number of Spanish and even foreign journalists, such as Karl Marx. The result was a considerably heightened awareness of Muslims and Jews,[7] which had previously almost died away.

Though the initial reaction to ordinary poverty-stricken Moroccan Jews was more negative than positive, the Spanish military and the accompanying journalists were in some respects impressed by a community that had retained its own archaic version of Spanish (the Moroccan Sephardic dialect known as *haketía*), as well as an ancestral memory of Spain. The entry of French and Spanish colonialism into Morocco had generally beneficial effects on the Jewish population, improving their status.

Modern Hebraic studies began very slowly among Spanish scholars during the second half of the eighteenth century, then expanded steadily during the century that followed. The first chair in Hebrew was established at the University of Madrid in 1915, a Jewish scholar being invited from abroad to fill it.

The first initiative of a modern Spanish government to assist foreign Jews was taken under the Liberal leader Práxedes Mateo Sagasta in 1881, when it offered asylum to Jewish refugees, generally not Sephardim, fleeing pogroms in Russia. Most Russian Jews sought to get to the United States or other more prosperous countries, but a small group of fifty-one moved to Spain.[8] Long before, Spain had joined other countries in negotiating "capitulation" or special-status agreements with the Ottoman government, whereby it could extend protected status to selected members of affiliate religious groups, the first such agreement having been signed as early as 1782. This relationship lay largely dormant during the nineteenth century, when only a very small number of Balkan Sephardim sought protected status from Spain, but the Balkan wars of 1912–13 created serious problems, especially for the large Sephardic population of Salonica. This city had just been seized by Greece, which agreed to recognize existing Spanish protection rights, 2,000 Salonica Jews petitioning successfully for that status. During World War I Zionist leaders asked Spain to urge the German government to restrain the persecution of non-Muslim peoples so savagely unleashed by its ally Turkey. As head of state of the largest European neutral, King Alfonso XIII attempted to do what he could, though it amounted to little.

By far the best-known though generally misunderstood Spanish state gesture on behalf of Jews during the early twentieth century was the limited Sephardic citizenship decree of 20 December 1924, promulgated by the military dictator Miguel Primo de Rivera. Many writers have presented this decree as an offer of citizenship to all Sephardim who petitioned for it, but it was much less than that. The offer of Spanish citizenship was limited specifically to "those under Spanish protection or their descendants" who petitioned the Spanish government. Thus it could not encompass more than a few thousand people, and by the time the six-year limit stipulated by the decree expired at the close of 1930, scarcely as many as 2,000 Sephardim had taken advantage of it.[9]

A certain philo-Sephardic policy had thus developed which was not so much philo-Semitic as pan-Hispanic in inspiration. That is, the goal was not so much to promote Jewish interests as such as to promote a broader Hispanic identity among all Spanish-speaking people, just as Spanish policy in the early twentieth century reached out increasingly to the Spanish-speaking Americas. This qualification does not gainsay the fact that the Spanish policy could be genuinely helpful to Sephardic Jews.

The climax of modern Spanish progressivism was reached during the first years of the Second Republic, by which time the Jewish population had increased to 6,000. The Republican constitution expressed a kind of ecumenical pan-Hispanism, facilitating terms of double citizenship for Latin Americans and the opportunity of citizenship for all people of Spanish origin living abroad. Concrete legislation to implement this provision, however, was never completed, though hundreds of new "certificates of nationality" for Sephardim were issued during the Republican years, mainly in Greece, Romania, and Egypt.[10]

Traditional anti-Jewish prejudices persisted on the right, and were sometimes expressed in a new form on the left. The concepts of modern racism ("mystical racism") and of racial anti-Semitism also entered Spain in the late nineteenth century and found a limited number of champions. Different kinds of racial ideas might be found, but the common attitude among anthropologists, historians, and other scholars was rather similar to racial ideas in Italy,[11] that the population of Spain was composed of a mixture of races, and that this very hybridity was an advantage to Spain, creating a stronger and more durable race. In Spanish the term "race" continued to be used primarily in the traditional sense, referring to language, culture, or national group, not to a distinct biogenetic entity. In this sense the journal founded in 1922 to re-associate the Sephardim with Spain was titled *La Raza*. Basque nationalism developed the only racist doctrine in the German sense, for a good many years holding that Basques were a distinct, pure, and superior race. Basque nationalists were also strongly anti-Jewish and even anti-Semitic in the modern sense,[12] though these attitudes later changed.

Fascism in Spain, as in Italy, was not developed as an anti-Semitic movement, and most of its chief leaders did not express anti-Semitism and even occasionally gestured against it. The Italian Fascist Party had a disproportionately Jewish membership—in that Jews formed a higher percentage of its membership than they did of the Italian population as a whole—at every stage of the party's development from its founding in 1919 until Mussolini's sudden adoption of quasi-German-style anti-Jewish legislation in 1938.[13] There were, of course, anti-Semites within both groups and some anti-Jewish propaganda, and in Spain the party's number three leader, Onésimo Redondo, was strongly anti-Semitic. Nazi Germany did not spend a large amount on propaganda in Spain, but it suborned the Madrid newspaper *Informaciones,* probably the principal conduit for Nazi and anti-Semitic propaganda before the Civil War.[14]

During the Civil War Jewish opinion generally favored the Republican side, and Jews were numerous in the International Brigades; according to the best estimates they accounted for 6,000 to 8,000 of the 41,000 volunteers for the Republic. By comparison, only a tiny handful of foreign Jews volunteered to fight for Franco, though apparently most of the Sephardim with Spanish documentation in Romania, for example, supported the Nacionales. Jews with Spanish citizenship in the Moroccan protectorate were regularly drafted by and served in the Nationalist army. Affluent Jewish businessmen in Morocco and Spain, and often elsewhere as well, supported Franco,[15] but in addition members of the Jewish communities in the larger cities of the protectorate and Seville were forced to make "voluntary" contributions. A number of Sephardim active in leftist associations were shot in the repression in Morocco, though Franco made a public statement there opposing racism and anti-Semitism.[16] He had apparently maintained personal friendships with several Moroccan Jews, and during the Civil War he was careful to avoid, and even on occasion to disown, racial propaganda. The most noted anti-Jewish publication of the Civil War was the book *Comunistas, judíos y demás ralea* (1938), if for no other reason than that its author was the noted novelist Pío Baroja. Even Baroja differentiated Sephardim from Ashkenazim, however; the former were held to be virtuous and assimilable, the latter disorderly and spreaders of communism.

Franco shared at least some aspects of the common anti-Jewish prejudices of the Spanish right and believed that an international conspiracy of leftist Masons and Jewish financiers pulled the strings in the liberal capitalist "plutocracies." On the other hand, Franco was not a racist in the Central European sense, so that his use of the term *raza* was strictly a traditional usage referring to ethnic or cultural group. That it was an important cultural concept for him he demonstrated in encouraging the production of and writing part of the script for the film *Raza* (1942), which glorified fallen Spanish heroes of 1898. This movie was undoubtedly the only one produced by a collaborator of Hitler's during World War II that includes favorable references to Jews, for it suggested that the cultural and spiritual force of the Spanish "race" was so great that it had even purified Spanish Jews. Franco did not believe that there was any unique Spanish biological race. He shared in the romantic, paternalist attitude of many in the military concerning Maghribi Muslims, believed in Spain's "civilizing mission" to uplift Africans, whether tan Muslims or black pagans, and showed little or no animosity toward ordinary Jews as distinct from the big financiers that he believed pulled the strings in Paris, London, and New York. Anti-Jewish in a certain traditional sense, he was not anti-Semitic in the manner of Hitler, as Mussolini had not been before 1938. More specifically, his experience in Morocco had developed in him a positive appreciation for Sephardic Jews, as he himself expressed it in print as a comparatively young officer.[17] This probably helps to explain his relative immunity to the full force of Nazi anti-Semitic propaganda.

All the same, the association with Germany during the Civil War had the almost inevitable effect of opening Spain more and more to that propaganda, though the Vatican and the church hierarchy managed to block Franco's cultural treaty with the Reich in March 1939. As has been seen, by the time of his final victory Franco had developed a certain intoxication with his own power and broadly imitated the fascist style. Thus in his speech before the victory parade of 19 May 1939 he denounced "the Judaic spirit that encourages the alliance of grand capital with Marxism," which he claimed had allied "grand capital" with Spain's revolutionary left.[18] He used rather similar language on at least six other public occasions between 1939 and 1943, the last instances occurring on 4 May and 18 July 1943, after which they disappeared from his public lexicon. Because the last of these references took place at such a late date, there is no reason to think that they involved any opportunistic gesturing toward Hitler. Such remarks instead reflected his genuine view regarding the nefarious influence of Jewish grand capital, though he excluded ordinary Jews from its "conspiracy."

The massive antireligious violence in the Republican zone during the Civil War that closed all Catholic churches and destroyed many of them sometimes spared small Protestant churches but not synagogues, which were also sacked and closed. Franco's regime permitted only Catholic churches to function openly, so the synagogues would long remain closed. No public Protestant or Jewish ceremonies were allowed, but otherwise no special repressive measures were taken against the small number of Jews in Spain, a few of whom even converted to Catholicism. Those Jews arrested and prosecuted were indicted for political or criminal offenses, not for religion or ethnicity. Nonetheless, at the height of the regime's collaboration with the Third Reich, on 5 May 1941 the Dirección General de Seguridad ordered the civil governor of each province to prepare a file on every domestic or foreign Jew residing in his province, resulting in a nationwide set of Archivos Judaicos, which were maintained at least through 1944.

From 1941 Jewish identity was stamped on national identity or residence cards, though there is no evidence of any specific discriminatory treatment.[19] Like much else in the regime, this would depend on the course of the war. Between 1939 and 1943, the FET engaged in more than a little anti-Jewish propaganda, though one critical study of such material found that this sort of message was always secondary and never a dominant feature of its ideology.[20] Perhaps most tellingly, German diplomats noted with dismay that Spain enacted no specific anti-Semitic legislation.

During its long collaborationist period, the regime in fact had it both ways. In 1941 the official Consejo Superior de Investigaciones Científicas organized a new research unit, the Instituto Arias Montano, which featured an Escuela de Estudios Hebraicos. It supported the work of distinguished Spanish Hebraists and published the respected scholarly journal *Sefarad*. The official Spanish news weekly *Mundo* regurgitated Nazi anti-Semitic propaganda on the one hand while praising the character and culture of Sephardic Jews in Morocco and in the Balkans on the other. It specifically rejected "models" in this regard, declaring that Sephardic Jews "do not serve the goals of universal Judaism."[21] This stance seemed to square the circle of being philosophically anti-Semitic and concretely philo-Sephardic. During the North African campaign in 1942–43, there was eventually a crackdown on a number of Jews in the protectorate, and especially in Tangier, for being dangerously pro-Allied or subversive, though the nearly four hundred arrested were not kept in detention very long. There were various assaults on individual Spanish Jews during World War II but we find no record of any homicide, and two Falangists guilty of one attack in 1944 were arrested, prosecuted, and sentenced to lengthy prison terms.[22]

During the final phase of the Civil War the question arose of what should be done regarding Spaniards living abroad or Balkan Sephardim with citizenship or nationality cards who had outspokenly supported the Republic. Spanish consulates were left to deal with the issues of withholding services or denying documentation strictly on an individual basis, with no regard to race or religion, even in the cases of German Jewish refugees who had been issued papers by Republican consulates. Similarly, Spanish consulates were ordered to protest formally and provide protection to Jews with Spanish papers who were being expelled from Italy under the Fascist regime's new anti-Semitic legislation. A line was nonetheless drawn at any significant immigration of Jews into Spain itself, though no categorical measures were taken in this regard so long as the Civil War lasted.[23]

Wartime Refugees and Travelers in Transit

The return of peace to Spain, followed by the outbreak of the European war, opened the question of a neutral Spain as the goal of refugees and, even more frequently, as an exit route to Portugal and other countries. In this area the contradictions between anti-Jewish prejudice and positive consideration for Sephardim became more acute.

The first direct discrimination against Jews in the policies of the new

Spanish regime appeared in a decree of 11 May 1939 which regulated foreign travel into and out of Spain. Entrance and passage were denied to five categories of undesirables: opponents of the Movimiento Nacional, persons who had engaged in business dealings with the Republican government, Freemasons, persons who had played leading roles in firms in the Republican zone, and those "of a markedly Jewish character" and Jews in general, unless they had shown a specifically friendly attitude toward Spain or the Movimiento Nacional. The great majority of foreign Jews were affected, but there were no restrictions in this regard concerning Spanish Jews.[24] Foreign Jews were not desired in Spain, though their transit through the country was freely permitted if their papers were in order.

The development of these restrictions is confusing, for those concerning Masons and Jews would seem to have been temporarily rescinded by a modified decree of September 1939, but were apparently reimposed by a further decree of 1 May 1940, while a directive of the Foreign Ministry restated their validity in December 1942. The ruling of 1 May 1940 directed that all Spanish consulates must first submit documentation to Madrid before issuing visas or transit cards, though exceptions would be permitted in cases of emergency.[25]

One of the most important features of Spain's situation during the war was its position as a tilted nonbelligerent that possessed an open frontier with a genuinely neutral Portugal. Despite certain designs of the Spanish leaders on their neighbor, relations with Portugal, as we have seen, were positive, and Spanish consulates received authorization to approve automatically transit visas to Portugal for persons with legitimate Portuguese documentation.

The Salazar regime was not anti-Semitic. Salazar had at one time shown a rather high opinion of Jews, but still the Portuguese government was not eager to be overrun by wartime refugees. A decree issued in Lisbon in November 1939 denied to Portuguese consuls the right to issue transit visas directly to various categories of travelers, including Jews who had been expelled from their native lands. The war was ruining prospects for the Lisbon Exposition and the two special centenary celebrations that the Portuguese regime had planned for 1940. It had hoped for a million visitors, and now apparently would get an unknown number of refugees.

The principal Portuguese hero of the Holocaust was the consul in Bordeaux, Aristides de Sousa Mendes. As France was collapsing in June 1940, Lisbon was at first not responsive to his requests to approve transit visas, and then ruled categorically that he should issue no more visas unless the person involved had a sponsor or had guaranteed accommodations in Portugal, and was not Jewish.

Sousa Mendes quietly rebelled, deciding that his Christian conscience and profound sympathy for the refugees required him to act otherwise. First opening the premises of the Bordeaux consulate to provide shelter to Jews and to other refugees, he then began to sign transit visas by the thousands, with no questions asked. When he found that his vice consul in Bayonne, near the Spanish frontier, was not cooperating, Sousa Mendes promptly went to Bayonne and instituted the same policy there. So many visas were issued within a few days that he deputed his power of signature to others, since he was unable to sign all the papers himself. Then, when one group of refugees to whom he had granted papers was denied entrance at one Spanish border post, Sousa Mendes personally led them all to a second one, where they were admitted. Most of those who benefited from his largesse were Jews; the identity of the rest varied widely. They included Archduke Otto of Habsburg and his family and various members of the French and Belgian governments. There is no record of the number of Jewish refugees who received papers from Sousa Mendes, but the most common estimate is of the order of ten thousand.

Once it became clear what Sousa Mendes was doing, he was recalled to Lisbon in disgrace at the beginning of July for having deliberately disobeyed orders. Some months later he was separated from the Portuguese diplomatic service, so that the fate of Sousa Mendes would seem to indicate the truth of the maxim that "no good deed goes unpunished." Father of a large Catholic family, he was unable to find adequate employment in wartime Portugal, though he later worked briefly for a Jewish refugee agency. He progressively had to sell off all the properties he owned to support his family; his children also suffered discrimination. At the end of the war most of them emigrated and two of them, born in Berkeley and thus U.S. citizens, volunteered for the U.S. Army in 1943. When Sousa Mendes died in 1954, the only property said to be remaining to him was the family burial plot. This remarkable man was eventually recognized by the Israeli government, which planted twenty trees in his honor in 1961, and by Yad Vashem (Holocaust Martyrs' and Heroes' Remembrance Authority in Jerusalem) six years later.[26] The Spanish equivalents of Sousa Mendes would emerge only in 1944.

During the fall of France, thousands of refugees entered Spain through the border posts at Hendaye and the western Pyrenees, so long as they fulfilled the Spanish requirements or possessed Portuguese visas. The

Spanish consul at Hendaye estimated that at one point he had issued 2,000 transit visas within eight days, but many others were turned back, particularly Central and East European Jews without French passports or Portuguese visas. Subsequently, new Spanish regulations, issued partly to please the Germans, restricted the issuance of transit visas, beginning in October 1940, by denying them to citizens of belligerent countries, a category that included France, since French citizens lived under terms of armistice rather than a peace treaty. The German authorities had pressed for such a restriction, not to limit the emigration of Jews (for at that date Jewish emigration was still encouraged by German policy) but to prevent the flight of young men from military or labor service. The measure was therefore modified by the end of 1940 to apply only to men between the ages of 18 and 30 from belligerent countries.[27]

What remains unclear is to what extent, if any, a direct effort was made to exclude Jews individually on the basis of religion. A curious order of 23 October 1941 by the Ministry of Industry and Commerce prohibited the passage of Jews on Spanish ships bound for the western hemisphere. The reason given was that some Jews, having reached safety in this way, then sued Spanish shipping companies for overcharging them.[28] As a result, this means of escape was closed to the vast majority of European Jews.

The question of smuggling and illegal crossing of the frontier became acute when the roundup of Jews began in France in 1942. In August, after the U.S. embassy intervened directly, the Spanish foreign ministry promised that no illegals would be returned against their will. It cannot be determined that all Spanish authorities followed that guideline, though in general it seems to have been upheld. German occupation of all French territory in November greatly accelerated the flight of illegals, particularly those of labor-service age, and the following month the Spanish government bowed to the request of the Vichy ambassador that these people not be handed over to the Germans. By this time Allied fliers downed over France, sheltered and transferred by the French resistance, were beginning to appear in larger numbers as well.[29]

German pressure, the increasing proximity of the opposing armies to Spain, and the continuing large numbers of illegal refugees led Franco to do what he often did in times of difficulty—take a hard line and lie low. On 25 March 1943 he ordered that the border with France be strictly closed to anyone without a transit visa. The Allied governments and the papal nuncio immediately protested and succeeded in reversing the new policy within a short time.[30]

An untold number of Jews and other refugees lacking papers were turned back at the border, and during the course of the war approximately 500 illegals were returned. Yet the great majority of those who appeared at the border made it across, and the vast majority of the illegals were not returned. Some 10,000 or more non-Jewish refugees crossed the Spanish border legally. The estimated number of 70,000 Jews who reached safety in Spain is undoubtedly too large.[31] Haim Avni, who conducted the first major research in this area, originally concluded that the best approximation was 30,000,[32] though he later reduced his calculation to 20,000. Emilienne Eychenne, author of the best study of illegal émigrés from France, estimates their number as somewhere between 15,000 and 35,000, the lower figure being the more likely; Jewish refugees who arrived illegally possibly amounted to as many as 3,000.[33] Bernd Rother has thus concluded that the best that can be said is that the total number of Jews who gained safe passage across the Pyrenees was somewhere between 20,000 and 35,000.[34] Accurate statistics in the century of mass atrocity are hard to come by.

Spain's policy is not easy to summarize. Its rule was to deny simple entrance visas to Jews, as most other countries did, yet it routinely granted very large numbers of transit visas, and it is not clear how systematically the exclusionary decrees on Jews were enforced. Most illegal Jewish refugees were not handed back to the Germans. A fair conclusion would be that Spanish policy discriminated against Jews less than did that of most European countries, but there was no plan to especially favor or assist them, except with regard to Sephardim who could claim citizenship rights, as will be seen in the next chapter.

CHAPTER **13**

Spanish Diplomacy and the Holocaust (II)

Given the idealized version of the Third Reich that prevailed in Spain, it is appropriate to ask how much was known in Spain about the Holocaust. Obviously everyone knew that Jews were discriminated against and treated harshly, but initially word may not have spread rapidly concerning mass killings in Poland and the great slaughter carried out by the SS in occupied Soviet territory in 1941. Nazi policy had previously encouraged emigration, a policy unsuccessful not so much because of German obstructionism as because few countries were willing to accept many Jewish refugees. Spanish policy in this regard was unexceptional.

It is clear that the decision to adopt a "final solution" of mass liquidation was taken by Hitler and other Nazi leaders in the autumn of 1941, plans being formalized at the notorious Wannsee conference in Berlin at the close of January 1942. News of systematic liquidation, as distinct from arrests and ghettoization, was brought by the first returning veterans of the Blue Division, who, despite their pro-German fervor, were often appalled. Though they did not see the *Vernichtungslagern* (extermination camps), which were just beginning their gruesome work, they observed numerous murders of Jews and Polish and Russian civilians, as well as the wasting away of hundreds of thousands of Soviet POWs. The Dirección General de Seguridad, in its regular reports to Franco, observed on 28 April that returning veterans denounced "cases of barbarism, especially in Poland, Lithuania, and Russia. They point out particularly that for a German the life of a Pole or a Russian means absolutely nothing, and have seen them shot down in the middle of the street (in the cases of Poland, Lithuania, and Czechoslovakia) or interned in isolated camps where they receive only a miserable gruel of boiled potatoes and that only once a day."[1] By 1943 some of the best-informed Spanish officials were the diplomats in the Berlin embassy, who complained to Germans that they could not abandon Sephardic Jews in the Balkans and elsewhere to be liquidated en masse. The Germans formally denied that such a danger existed.

Spanish diplomacy vis-à-vis Germany and other states dealt primarily with issues concerning Sephardic citizens and followed a complex, meandering, and uncertain course. During the first year of the war, resident Spanish diplomats sought to intervene with several Balkan governments concerning their treatment of Sephardim, but achieved little.

Soon after the occupation of northern France in 1940, German officials ordered the registration of all Jews and then confiscated their businesses. The Spanish consul general thought the two thousand Sephardim in France with Spanish citizenship should be immune to practices not recognized by Spanish law, but the Foreign Ministry under Serrano Suñer responded in November that these German measures must be complied with. Earlier the Foreign Ministry had even ruled that fifty German "non-Aryan" Catholics seeking passage to Brazil would not be issued transit visas through Spain.[2] Madrid did negotiate an understanding with regard to confiscation of Sephardic businesses, arguing that they were part of Spain's national wealth and arranging that they be placed under the administration of non-Jewish Spaniards.[3]

The first petition by a group of Sephardim to be allowed to move to Spain was presented in Paris in June 1941, but some petitioners did not have Spanish passports. The ruling in Madrid was that if they possessed any kind of Spanish documentation and were people of good reputation (*honorabilidad*), they could be admitted. Several months later, the consul general in France, Bernardo Rolland, declared that persecution of Jews in occupied France was becoming so severe that the only solution was mass emigration, and proposed that Sephardim in France be allowed to emigrate to Spanish Morocco, since the Spanish government sought to avoid increasing Spain's permanent Jewish population, Sephardi or not. German authorities refused, since by that point German policy on emigration had changed drastically. The Foreign Ministry in Madrid took no initiative. As Bernd Rother notes, "the fundamental contradiction was that on the one hand Spain did not want to tolerate the persecution of its Jews but on the other hand it was not ready to allow their immigration," and had no clear policy.[4]

Tension developed between the Spanish ambassador, José Félix de Lequerica ("the ambassador of the Gestapo"), and Rolland. The ambassador, a pronounced Naziphile, argued against any responsibility for Sephardim, even if they possessed Spanish passports, while the policy of Rolland was much more humane. The issue was seemingly resolved by a position paper prepared within the Foreign Ministry in February 1941 which concluded that "Spain could not tolerate the persecution of its Jews by foreign powers,"[5] but the initial beneficiaries would be Sephardim in Romania, subject to the severe persecution then ongoing in that country. Many of these people had supported Franco in the Civil War, and the Foreign Ministry ruled that they could be issued Spanish entrance papers, on a case-by-case basis. This process proved complicated, Romanian policy softened, and no Romanian Sephardim at that point entered Spain. Spanish passports were sent to Sofia for a small group of Bulgarian Sephardim, though whether they were used is not clear. Eventually, during 1942, further documentation was issued to Sephardim in France who did not possess Spanish papers, but these documents were issued only to protect their status in occupied France, not to permit them sanctuary in Spain. Some Sephardim in France who already possessed passports managed to enter Spain in the periodic repatriation convoys arranged by Madrid for Spaniards in occupied France, and down to the beginning of 1943 a total of forty-seven Spanish Jews from France gained legal residence in Spain. When this was brought to the attention of the Foreign Ministry, Jordana, who was in charge by then, ruled in January 1943 that Spanish passports or other documents issued to Sephardim were not valid for full rights of citizenship or entry into Spain, but constituted only a secondary class of documentation issued to protect Sephardim abroad.[6] Jordana proved to be a titan in reorienting Spanish foreign policy, but his attitude toward Sephardim abroad was only a little more generous than that of Serrano Suñer.

From the beginning of 1943 the Germans issued a series of repatriation ultimatums to all neutral and nonbelligerent governments concerning foreign Jewish nationals in occupied territory. Foreign states were given three months to repatriate their Jewish nationals, after which they would be subject to deportation to the east (that is, to the extermination camps). The initial German ultimatum came only a little over a month after an official communiqué from the Allied governments of 17 December 1942, which for the first time denounced the German extermination policy and also began to apply pressure on neutral governments to cooperate in rescue and repatriation.

By the spring of 1943 the British embassy calculated that there were approximately 25,000 international refugees in Spain, made up of 14,000 French citizens, 3,000 Czechs and Poles, and possibly as many as 8,000 others of diverse categories, perhaps half of whom were Jews without legal status. Many of the latter were maintained in a special camp in Miranda del Ebro. The Spanish government was very reluctant to add to their number, refusing to accept Jews, even Sephardim with Spanish nationality papers, as permanent residents. José María Doussinague, director general of foreign policy in charge of Foreign Ministry planning, presented a report concluding that the Spanish state must nonetheless act to repatriate Sephardim because if it did not, Allied pressure would only increase, and because their repatriation would permit recovery of goods belonging to Spanish nationals. Jordana agreed, but the government refused to grant permanent residence, insisting instead on transit to third countries. This effort failed because all three possible third countries—Turkey, Switzerland, and Portugal—refused to admit any Jews, and the German government officially refused to permit transit to third countries.[7]

Doussinague therefore proposed to grant Sephardim temporary residence rights in Spain and then to move them on to third countries as soon as possible. This plan was accepted in modified form when the Foreign Ministry, apparently with Franco's personal approval, informed the German embassy on 15 March 1943 that Spain would accept immediately 100 Sephardim for residence in Spain. The plan apparently proposed that as soon as arrangements had been made for this group to move to a third country, another group would be accepted in Spain. Only Jews who had Spanish passports were eligible, while it would be up to international agencies to find third countries for Jewish refugees, as well as to help pay for their maintenance in Spain, before more would be admitted.[8]

Rother has written that the Spanish government presented this policy in three guises: the Germans were told that Spain was accommodating permanent repatriation of the Jews it admitted; Falangists and other opponents of this policy within the Spanish government were assured that all Jewish refugees would be in Spain for only a brief time; and Allied representatives were assured that Spain was granting new papers to Sephardim for the purpose of rescuing them but that they would be expected to exit Spain as soon as possible. The deadline for repatriation was eventually extended to 20 August 1943, but the means for qualifying were made very complicated. Only Sephardim with currently valid Spanish passports were directly eligible, while those whose passports had expired, who had other kinds of documentation, or who had earlier inquired about such possibilities but not acquired passports were placed in a series of secondary categories. People in the latter categories, however, were almost universally denied eligibility, though they continued to enjoy whatever extraterritorial protection their local Spanish consuls could provide, so only a very limited number of Sephardim could in fact qualify. Ultimately, after much delay and back and forth, by August eighty-seven Spanish Jews had been repatriated to Spain from France, ten from Belgium, and a few additional individuals from elsewhere.[9]

The largest single case involved a sizable number of Sephardim in Greek Salonica, at least 550 of whom had Spanish papers. Sebastián Romero Radigales arrived in Athens as Spanish consul in April. He was said to be married to a Sephardi, and showed genuine humanitarian zeal, though, unlike the Portuguese consul Sousa Mendes in Bordeaux three years earlier, he was careful not directly to disobey orders. Romero Radigales immediately set to work to prepare for repatriation of Spanish Jews in Salonica, and found the chief German administrator for Jews in Athens to be, unlike most of his counterparts elsewhere, relatively moderate and cooperative. The Foreign Ministry was slow to provide authorization, however, and communication between Athens and Madrid was wretched, letters sometimes taking a month or more to arrive. Romero advanced the obvious humanitarian and diplomatic arguments on behalf of repatriation, observing that even Fascist Italy was actively arranging the repatriation of Italian Jews in Greece, the Fascist regime never having proposed to expose Italian Jews to extermination.[10] On 20 May the Foreign Ministry authorized repatriation of Spanish Jews in Greece who had their papers fully in order, but denied its consul's proposals for swift action and a very broad interpretation of adequate credentials. Only two weeks later, however, on 4 June, this authorization was temporarily canceled, apparently after the realization that a large number of Spanish Jews had their papers in order, and that immediate repatriation might involve 500 or more. Even Günther Altenberg, the German administrator in Athens, tried to persuade the Spanish government to be more cooperative, for German authorities on the one hand wanted to be rid of foreign Jews but on the other did not want to be accused by foreign powers of violating their diplomatic rights.

Unable yet to effect repatriation, the energetic Romero Radigales busied himself trying to protect Spanish Jews in Greece. His efforts were apparently not appreciated in Madrid, for on 1 July Jordana sent a telegram to Vidal Saura in Berlin, saying, "Indispensable neutralize excess zeal consul general Athens, freezing this matter (which could create serious difficulties in Spain)." He repeated to Vidal on the 14th, "At no time has the Spanish government intended to repatriate a mass of Sephardim, but only to resolve exceptional cases."[11]

Romero refused to give up. He arranged with the Italian authorities, always more benevolent in such matters, to move Spanish Jews from Salonica, in the German zone, to Athens, which was in the Italian zone, but this move was partially blocked by the Germans. He also tried to gain approval from Madrid for the repatriation of a number of special cases, since that was apparently more what the Foreign Ministry had in mind. Madrid's vacillation was exasperating to German officials, one of whom pressed the first secretary of the Berlin embassy, Federico Díez Isasi, for a firm decision. Díez replied that he understood the Germans' concern, but the Spanish government "could not give its agreement to the liquidation of Spanish citizens in Polish camps," and Vidal wrote to Jordana that if Spain permitted the Sephardim to be deported to Poland, the consequences for them would be "tragic."[12] This was also reiterated by Fernando Oliván, the newly appointed consul in Vienna, who wrote to Doussinague that denying repatriation to such a large quantity of people "automatically condemns them to death. . . . I cannot believe that there exists no possibility of saving them from the horrible fate that awaits them." Even setting up a concentration camp for them in Spain, he wrote, would be preferable.[13]

Since Madrid still had not made a final decision, on 29 July the Germans moved 367 of the Spanish Jews in Salonica to a local ghetto, pending their shipment to Bergen-Belsen, a less drastic fate than an extermination camp. Of the other 200, Romero had managed to move some to the Italian zone in Athens, while others had apparently succeeded in fleeing on their own. Romero wrote to Madrid that its behavior was creating a negative image of Spain, since all the other governments had repatriated their Jews in Greece, even the Italian Fascists, and wrote further in a second missive that the matter was even challenging his own sense of patriotism and honor. On 3 August, the group of 367 Spanish Jews were deported to Bergen-Belsen. The main thing that had kept this group of Spanish Jews from the Polish death camps was not the policy of Madrid but the zeal of Romero Radigales and the Third Reich's curious concern for international legality.[14] The Germans offered reasonable means for saving these Jews, but the

Spanish government dithered, still seeking an interim formula that would not require it to provide permanent residence.

Before learning of the deportation from Salonica, the Council of Ministers in Madrid agreed on a new Spanish policy on 4 August: Spain would accept repatriation of all Spanish Jews from Greece and from all other German-occupied territory, but for interim transit only, and only in batches of 25, each new group to be accepted only after the preceding group had left. German authorities naturally found this an absurd way to deal with the group in Bergen-Belsen, since in batches of 25 per month the entire operation would take fifteen months, and Vidal Saura added that in the meantime the majority might end up in death camps. The Foreign Ministry finally agreed to receive them in batches of 150. Just when it finally seemed that something was about to happen, the repatriation was once more paralyzed before it could begin. On 17 August Jordana declared this plan could not proceed because David Blickenstaff of the American Friends' Service Committee, who headed a consortium of humanitarian agencies in Madrid to assist in the problem, was not obtaining enough entrance visas from third countries.[15] Three groups of repatriated Jews were, however, received from France in October, bringing the total entering from France since the German repatriation ultimatum to about 335.[16] Moreover, the costs of caring for them in Spain were borne not by the Spanish government but by Blickenstaff's agencies and Jewish relief groups.

On 6 December the embassy in Berlin was finally able to tell the German government that repatriation could proceed, though Madrid still held to the arrangements defined above. Spanish officials continued to be slow in completing arrangements, but during February 1944 the Salonica Jews held in Bergen-Belsen arrived by train in two batches totaling 365, two elderly refugees having died in the camp. They were delighted by the treatment they received on crossing the Spanish border, though generally disappointed to find that they could not remain in Spain.[17]

There remained the issue of the approximately 300 Spanish Jews still in Athens, whose interests Romero Radigales continued to represent with vigor and courage. They were eligible for repatriation under the Foreign Ministry ruling of 4 August theoretically authorizing passage in groups of 25. Romero Radigales thought this absurd, for, given the snaillike pace of wartime civilian transport, even if repatriation began immediately, it would take at least two years, in the course of which most would doubtless be deported to death camps. In December Madrid finally declared that it would accept them all, but only after the entire group from Bergen-Belsen had passed through Spain, which the Germans said was unacceptably slow. On the night of 24 March 1944 they rounded up most of the Jews in Athens, including 155 Spanish Sephardim. Romero immediately petitioned for their release, which was denied. Instead they were deported to Bergen-Belsen, where, like their Salonica predecessors, they were held in the section for "neutrals." Conditions were better there than in other parts of the camp, and nearly all eventually survived.

The Spanish Foreign Ministry then carried on its usual back-and-forth minuet, soliciting repatriation but failing to initiate concrete steps to carry it out. Since rail contact between Spain and Germany was cut off by the Allied military advance in August 1944, during the following month American diplomats made arrangements with the Swiss government for the Spanish Jews from Athens to be accepted by Switzerland. Since they were Spanish nationals, however, Madrid had to take the initiative in making this request of Berlin, which it did not do until November, and nothing came of it. The Spanish Jews from Athens remained in captivity until the end of the war, when they were finally liberated by American troops.[18]

In the first months of 1944, several hundred other Spanish Jews remained in German-occupied territory. Some of them had already been arrested, a very few had voluntarily chosen to remain, and the largest share was composed of a sizable but undetermined number who had applied for protection or citizenship in the past but had not received valid papers. In November 1943 the Foreign Ministry in Madrid received word that some fifty had recently been arrested in Paris, and so on 1 December Jordana wired the Spanish embassy to petition for their release so that they could be repatriated to Spain. This plan accorded with the Spanish guidelines because the relief agencies had recently been able to move approximately that number of Jewish refugees to North Africa. On 22 December Díez Isasi even informed the Foreign Ministry in Berlin that Spain was now ready to repatriate all remaining Spanish Jews, but Berlin replied that it was too late. The Spanish government had for the most part dawdled for eleven months, and conditions had changed. Verbal pressure by Díez Isasi got the German authorities to agree that Spanish Jews still in France could yet be repatriated. As usual, the arrangement proceeded very slowly. A total of 170 more Sephardim in occupied France were recognized as eligible for repatriation in 1944, and most, though probably not all, had been repatriated by early August. Smaller numbers of Spanish Jews in Bulgaria and Romania also petitioned for repatriation during 1943–44. Though they received a certain amount of support and protection from Spanish diplomats, no organized repatriation was ever carried out.[19]

Sanz Briz and Perlasca in Budapest

The most widely publicized and also the most dramatic and extensive work by Spanish diplomats during the Holocaust was the rescue efforts by Angel Sanz Briz and Giorgio Perlasca in Budapest during the autumn and winter of 1944–45, though, as in the case of Spanish policy as a whole, its extent has sometimes been exaggerated. Even so, Sanz Briz and Perlasca fully deserve the recognition they have received (belatedly, in the case of Perlasca) as genuine heroes of the Holocaust.

The Hungarian case became the final great Holocaust drama because, when Germany abruptly occupied Hungary in March 1944 and forced the appointment of a subservient government, the population of 800,000 Jews in greater Hungary was the largest to be found anywhere in Europe except the Soviet Union. Very few of them were Sephardim, and fewer still had ever obtained Spanish documentation. Of the latter, forty-five lived in Budapest.

The first initiative with regard to Hungarian Jews after German occupation began came not from Budapest or Madrid but from Spanish Morocco. On 15 June 1944, General Luis Orgaz, the high commissioner, approved a request from Moroccan Jews to bring 500 Jewish children from Hungary and care for them at their own expense. This move was authorized by Madrid, and Angel Sanz Briz, the acting chargé d'affaires in Budapest, gained the approval of the Hungarian government, but since the Germans refused transit to Spain, 500 children were placed in special residences under Spanish protection.

The dapper, handsome Sanz Briz, a young career diplomat who had served in the Nationalist army, had taken over the legation in June after a diplomatic incident that brought the expulsion of the senior Spanish representative.[20] After the German occupation, United States diplomacy pressed neutral governments to protest actively and to increase their own delegations in Budapest. Several did so, Sweden sending Raoul Wallenberg as special representative to undertake a massive humanitarian task that ultimately proved fatal to him. Madrid, however, at first did nothing in particular and Sanz Briz was largely left on his own.[21]

Moroccan Jews proposed to sponsor another 700 Hungarians, though it is not entirely clear whether the additional Hungarians were taken under Spanish protection. That summer Sanz Briz issued transit visas for another 1,500 Jews, all of whom seem to have been detained in Germany, though some of them eventually reached Switzerland. When the papal nuncio on 21 August organized a strong protest against the deportation of Jews, Sanz Briz signed the protest, along with the representatives of Sweden, Switzerland, and Portugal. Instructions from Madrid to take a softer line fortunately did not arrive in time.[22]

The Germans ousted the incumbent Hungarian government on 15 October, installing a puppet National Socialist regime. To that point the large Jewish population in Budapest had largely been exempt from deportation, but a much harsher policy was now enforced. To Sanz Briz's request for instructions, Lequerica, now foreign minister, for the first time sent firm and forthright guidelines: the first priority was to protect Jews who were Spanish citizens; second, to protect those Sephardim who did not have complete papers; third, to do whatever could be done to assist the remaining Jews.[23] After becoming foreign minister in August, Lequerica had eventually grasped the importance of gaining credit from the Allies by presenting the Spanish regime as rescuer of Jews, and this might be the last major opportunity.

Within less than a month Sanz Briz issued 352 provisional passports and approximately 1,900 letters of protection. Transportation out of Hungary was no longer possible, so those under Spanish protection had to be housed in special extraterritorial residences rented or diplomatically protected by the Spanish chargé. In addition, he issued 45 regular passports to Sephardim for transit to Spain (these were apparently all the genuine Sephardim that he could find), but they were forced into the prison-like ghetto instead. The Hungarian fascists then began to raid some of the special residences under Spanish protection and send their inhabitants on forced marches to Germany, but Sanz Briz was able to follow and quickly gain the release of more than 100. Altogether, he managed to protect about 2,300 Jews in Hungary, while issuing transit visas to between 500 and 1,200 others who were able to escape abroad.[24] This was a notable humanitarian achievement, by far the most outstanding of anyone in Spanish government during World War II. Yet it should be remembered that the Swedes, led by Wallenberg, and the Swiss saved many more, and Sanz Briz also might have accomplished even more had he received greater assistance from Madrid.

In the climactic phase of the rescue effort, he found a key assistant in the Italian purchasing agent Giorgio Perlasca, whose work subsequently was for many years virtually ignored. The intrepid Perlasca was a lifelong Fascist who had volunteered for the Italian forces in both the Ethiopian war and the Spanish Civil War. During the European conflict he became a purchasing agent in Hungary for foodstuffs for the Italian army, and by 1944 found himself in a dangerous situation, since he did not support Mussolini's puppet regime. Perlasca's military experience in Spain gave him easy entrée to Spain's Budapest legation, where Sanz Briz provided him with a Spanish passport and apparently made him his chief assistant. When the chargé was ordered to leave Budapest in the face of the Red Army advance at the end of November, he turned over the legation (without official authority) to Perlasca, who continued to cooperate with Wallenberg in the rescue of Jews. Sanz Briz left him with passport forms and other kinds of documentation, and it is not clear how many Jews Perlasca was subsequently able to rescue. At that point, he was in greater personal danger than Wallenberg or than Sanz Briz had been earlier, for he lacked authentic diplomatic credentials and the immunity they brought. In the hellish conditions of besieged Budapest during December 1944–January 1945 Perlasca showed greater personal courage than any other person involved in Spanish diplomacy during World War II, and managed to gain formal recognition from the puppet government of Hungary, directing the Spanish legation for a month and a half, until mid-January 1945. He might have suffered the same fate as Wallenberg, who disappeared forever into Soviet captivity, but fortunately did not, and was allowed by the Soviets to return to Italy in May 1945.[25]

Sanz Briz went on to a brilliant career, eventually becoming delegate to the United Nations and the first Spanish ambassador to Communist China. Four years after his death in 1980,the Israeli Holocaust memorial center Yad Vashem recognized him as one of the "Righteous among the Nations," and in 1994 his widow received in his name the Grand Cross of Merit of the Republic of Hungary. Giorgio Perlasca became a modest Italian businessman, his heroic work long unrecognized, until in 1989 the Hungarian parliament awarded him the Grand Star of Hungary, and two years later in the Spanish embassy in Rome he received similar recognition from Spain for his efforts on behalf of Spanish diplomacy and the Hungarian Jews.

Legend and Reality

During 1943 the Spanish Foreign Ministry became increasingly aware of the importance of presenting itself to Allied representatives as a champion of the Jews, though this did not at all bring the government to expedite repatriation of Spanish Jews or to give them permanent residence in Spain. As will be discussed in the following chapter, once the Anglo-American powers forced a virtual end to collaboration with Germany in the spring of 1944, Spain fell more and more into the Allied sphere. After Lequerica took over as foreign minister in August, playing the Jewish card became an obsession with him, the Spanish regime having few other credentials of that sort to present after its long collaboration with Hitler.

The first important personage to publicize—and exaggerate—Spanish efforts on behalf of Jews was Maurice Perlzweig, head of the political committee of the World Jewish Congress. He developed a close relationship with Juan de Bárcenas, the Spanish ambassador in Washington, who showed genuine zeal in transmitting Jewish requests to Madrid. Even Jordana thought Bárcenas too favorable to the Anglo-American point of view. Though not uniformly, American Jewish organizations generally expressed gratitude for Spanish efforts, and their praise reached its apotheosis in the lengthy report that Perlzweig delivered to the meeting of the World Jewish Congress in Atlantic City in November 1944. In Madrid Ambassador Carlton Hayes promoted this point of view, while Nicolás Franco, the Generalissimo's rather more congenial and bon vivant older brother who served as ambassador to Portugal, also developed very good relations with representatives of Jewish associations in Lisbon. Nicolás Franco was particularly assisted by the Falangist writer Javier Martínez de Bedoya, a leader in the effort to redefine Falangist doctrine in a more moderate direction,[26] who was sent by Jordana to Lisbon as press attaché in November 1943 especially to expand contacts with Jewish organizations.

The theme was taken up energetically by the Spanish government during the period of ostracism that it underwent after 1945, but, though increasingly accepted in the United States, it made little impression in Israel, where the Franco regime was generally viewed as a collaborator with Hitler.[27] After the government of Israel joined others in voting against Spain's entry into the United Nations in 1949, the Spanish Foreign Ministry quickly whipped out two slightly different pamphlets, *Spain and the Sephardic Jews* and *España y los judíos*, portraying Franco as the savior of the Jews. These representations often met a positive response, and various Jewish spokes-men and writers have continued to echo Perlzweig's sentiments down to the present time, most prominently the American rabbi Chaim U. Lipschitz, author of the book *Franco, Spain, the Jews, and the Holocaust* (1984). Before Franco's death, Federico Ysart had published a book in the same vein, *España y los judíos en la segunda guerra mundial* (1973), on the basis of selected documentation made available to him by the Foreign Ministry. More recently there has appeared the very brief work by David Salinas, *España, los sefarditas y el Tercer Reich (1939–1945)* (1997). The bibliogra-phy of articles and short periodical pieces in this regard is considerable.[28]

The key research in this area by Haim Avni, Antonio Marquina Barrio, Gloria Inés Ospina, Bernd Rother, and others has made it clear that the reality was rather different. The Franco regime propounded no racial pol-icy and did not discriminate directly against Jews, but to some extent the regime itself, and to an even greater extent some of its chief followers, presented a traditional anti-Jewish discourse tinged with, and sometimes directly echoing, the "Protocols of the Elders of Zion." There is no particular indication that Nazi persecution of the Jews disturbed the Spanish leaders and their followers before 1942, even though such policies were not copied in Spain.

Thanks in considerable part to the open Portuguese exit at their rear, Spanish borders generally remained open to Jewish and other refugees in 1940 and after, so long as they possessed the right documents. This was primarily a matter of transit, for Jewish immigrants and refugees, whether Sephardim or not, were no more welcome in Spain than in most other countries. An unknown number were turned back, though several thou-sand refugees who succeeded in making their way into the country were not sent back but allowed temporarily to remain, most of them interned in the camp at Miranda del Ebro.

Once the character of the Holocaust became clearer and the Foreign Ministry began to be besieged by reports and requests from its representa-tives abroad, Franco and his government did agree to repatriation of Span-ish Jews, but this policy was painfully slow and halting. It was initiated only after the star of the Third Reich had begun to decline. Gaining respect in the eyes of the United States government, whose forces at this time were be-coming increasingly influential in the European theater, seems to have been a major consideration. It is legitimate to question whether the Span-ish government would have lifted a finger had the Axis repelled Torch and won the battle of Stalingrad. The Germans were willing to permit repatriation of Sephardim with any sort of documentation that Spanish authorities would recognize, but the latter were much more demanding. In each case, the Spanish Sephardic background of each Jew given a passport had to be carefully identified. There was no concern for Jews in general, save in the final phase in Budapest. Thus only a fraction (Rother estimates about one-fifth) of the Spanish Jews resident in France as of 1940 ever obtained Spanish passports, a proportion that in Greece, however, rose to more than two-thirds. Even Jews with Spanish passports were not generally accepted for residence in Spain, and their repatriation in the vast majority of cases was made dependent on passage being obtained, usually by third parties acting on their behalf, to other countries. Spanish policy was so dilatory and sometimes contradictory as to border on indifference. When the neutrals finally began to get themselves together for more extensive initiatives in the final great drama in Budapest, the policy makers in Madrid did not at first participate. Sanz Briz initially received little in the way of instructions, and was fully encouraged only in October 1944. This was also the only occasion on which Spanish diplomacy carried out a major initiative on behalf of non-Spanish Jews. The final stage depended on the improvisation of Sanz Briz and the heroics of an Italian ex-Fascist.

An examination of the final balance sheet is appropriate. In toto, the Spanish government did not repatriate directly more than a thousand Sephardim. Approximately 3,500 Jews were protected and saved in Hungary and very small numbers in other countries. To this total of possibly 5,000 persons should be added the large number who crossed the Pyrenees, primarily in direct transit to Portugal, a figure it will never be possible to calculate precisely but according to the best research was somewhere between 20,000 and 35,000. The Blue Division employed and protected several hundred Jewish civilians in its rear guard, but was not able to give them permanent sanctuary.[29] Rother points out that, by comparison, Sweden repatriated 10,000 Scandinavian Jews and, through a maximally concerted policy, distributed 20,000 international passports in Hungary. The difference between what Sanz Briz and Perlasca accomplished in large measure on their own and what Wallenberg and the Swedes achieved was the difference between complete and systematic government support and the lack of it. Switzerland is said to have denied asylum during the war to approximately 40,000 people, mostly Jewish, but provided asylum to 230,000 others, of whom nearly 10 percent were Jewish. The Salazar regime in Portugal accepted repatriated Portuguese Jews without requiring them to move on as soon as possible and treated more generously other Jewish refugees who could not find shelter abroad. Rother's conclusion seems just: "More than a few of the persecuted found safety by means of Francoist Spain, which scarcely anyone had expected to assist Jews. Yet, if it had really wanted to, the Madrid government could have saved many more."[30]

CHAPTER **14**

Neutrality by Compulsion

The continuing transition in Spanish diplomacy after 1 October 1943 was not intended to signify adoption of full neutrality, but rather a return to something like the tilted neutrality that had existed during the first nine months of the war. Madrid still sought to be a special friend of Berlin. Franco and some of the other Spanish leaders could not conceive of the total defeat of Germany, and believed that, though Germany might no longer be able to win a clear victory, it would somehow escape the war with its Great Power status intact, and thus be in a position to help Spain and the Franco regime in the future. Spanish policy remained somewhat tilted, though no longer "nonbelligerent," with the goal of being the last friend of Germany among the neutrals, maintaining a bond that would continue to be useful in the future.

Franco was never able to understand the moral and ideological commitment of the Western Allies to the war against Hitler, but continued to interpret it in traditional terms of the balance of power, according to which it seemed to make little sense. Pressure from the Allies all the while continued to increase. In November Washington asked for a complete embargo on all shipment of wolfram to Germany, which Franco refused. Market competition was already denying most Spanish wolfram to Germany, for American agents bought up about 75 percent of Spanish production that year.

Ambassador Dieckhoff had a long meeting with Franco in El Pardo on

3 December. Dieckhoff began by saying that during his seven months in Spain he had been struggling to "form a clear portrait of Spanish foreign policy," which he perceived "in recent times had begun to change." He ticked off a series of complaints about concessions to the Allies: free passage of French refugees to North Africa, withdrawal of the Blue Division, internment of several German submarine crews, disposal of German and Italian ships in Spanish harbors in favor of the Allies, and so on.

Franco replied that "there could be no question of Spanish policy changing. He knew quite well that Germany sought to strengthen Spain, while the traditional British and American policy had been to weaken Spain. He also understood very clearly that only victory by Germany would make possible the continuation of his regime," despite Anglo-American assurances to the contrary. "He hoped for Germany's victory with all his heart and his greatest wish was that this victory would come as soon as possible." Franco then launched into his list of Spain's problems and weaknesses, concluding that he had done Germany a great service by following his own policy of collaboration but staying out of the war. He trivialized all recent concessions to the Allies, pointing out that the senior U-boat commander among the internees had already been sent back to Germany. He pledged that Spain would give no more than token concessions to the Allies, and maintained that a "neutral Spain" shipping wolfram and other necessities to Germany was more useful than a weak belligerent partner would have been. Spain's greatest need was advanced weapons, of which he asked that Germany provide more.[1]

Though certain changes had taken place in Spanish policy, Jordana still received little cooperation from some of his fellow ministers, particularly the commerce minister, Carceller, who wheeled and dealed on his own, insisting on the advantages of exporting maximal quantities of wolfram to Germany. It was not clear that Franco was willing to shift to a completely neutral policy, and Jordana presented a second letter of resignation to Franco on 20 January 1944, but he had indeed become irreplaceable and was persuaded to remain on the job.[2]

Hoare complained that German sabotage and intelligence operations carried out from Spanish territory had cost the Allies 50,000 tons of shipping, folding together a limited number of small ships sunk by direct sabotage with the larger number destroyed as a result of intelligence from Spain. On 30 January Ribbentrop sent Hitler an Abwehr report on German sabotage in Spain, which declared that sabotage against Gibraltar had been temporarily discontinued but that direct acts of sabotage against

Allied ships in Spanish ports still went on, in one recent instance allegedly employing Spanish Communists who had been deluded into believing they were acting on orders of the Third International.[3] In a new tactic developed at the close of 1943, the Germans placed bombs in crates of oranges bound for Britain, and in January Jordana protested that this practice must stop.[4]

During the early winter of 1943–44 there was some indication that Franco was digging in his heels, as his remarks to Dieckhoff indicated. For a time Doussinague, whom the Portuguese ambassador called "Franco's shadowy diplomat," may have exercised considerable influence.[5] The Soviet winter offensive did not begin until January, while the Allied advance in Italy seemed bogged down for the winter. There was strong resistance in Madrid to going more than partway on the key Allied demands: an arrangement to return the interned Italian boats, dissolution of the small remaining Blue Legion on the eastern front, an end to all German espionage and sabotage in and from Spain, a total embargo on wolfram to Germany and limitations on other exports.

On 27 January, the Argentine government, which had seemed to be Germany's last remaining friend in the western hemisphere, broke relations with Berlin. Two days later the Spanish government suddenly learned from the radio that the United States had suspended all petroleum exports to Spain. By the beginning of 1944, the Allied governments, particularly Washington, were determined to bring Spanish collaboration with Germany to an end, and to extend their own influence in the peninsula. If Spain had always been an important center for German intelligence, the same might be said for its significance for Allied intelligence, for which Spain was the most important country in continental Europe before D-Day, as the Allies developed new sources of information without the benefit of any state collaboration. Moreover, U.S. military intelligence had penetrated the code system and intelligence network of the Alto Estado Mayor and was well informed on Spain's own military intelligence.[6] The Allies were determined to use these advantages and their increasingly dominant strategic position to bring Franco's collaboration with Nazi Germany to an end.

Exporting Wolfram

The most prominent issue in the crisis of 1944 was the export of wolfram to Germany. Wolfram, or tungsten, became the most intensely sought Spanish mineral because of its key uses in major categories of military production. One of the strongest metals and very adaptable to refinement, it was indispensable for production of the hardest steel tools, hardened armor, certain kinds of ammunition, and, because of its light weight, airplane engines and propellers. Germany's principal prewar source, China, was totally interdicted after mid-1941, leaving the chief continental European sources: first Portugal, then Spain, and Sweden a distant third. Before the war, wolfram had been of only modest export importance for Spain, as the two Iberian countries combined provided approximately 9 percent of world production.

German interest in Iberian wolfram accelerated during 1941 and 1942. Well before that, German agencies had begun to purchase sources of production in both countries, though German ownership always remained limited. Portugal retained its lead in wolfram production throughout, producing more than 3,500 tons per year in 1940 and 1941, compared with only a fraction of that amount in Spain. As German military production increased rapidly in 1942 and 1943, so did the demand for wolfram, so that both sides in the war found themselves engaged in a competition for Iberian exports. The Germans needed the ore for themselves, while the Allies had adequate sources of supply in the United States and Bolivia but sought to buy up Iberian production—whether actually exported or not—in order to deny it to Germany. As the bidding went higher and higher, prices increased exponentially. Foreign exchange was a problem for Germany, and eventually, as prices went through the roof in 1943, became a minor problem for the Allies as well. In 1942 Portuguese production passed 4,500 tons, while that of Spain increased to nearly 1,500 tons. Portugal's output hit a peak of nearly 6,800 tons in 1943 and Spanish production topped 3,600 tons.[7]

Portuguese production tended to be centrally organized in larger mines (the largest of which was British-owned) and also controlled and regulated by the government through the Portuguese state corporative system. On 24 January 1942 Germany signed an agreement with Portugal, and ten days later Salazar set up the Portuguese Metals Commission to deal with exports. According to Portuguese regulations, each country could enjoy the full output from mines owned by its citizens; that arrangement favored the British, who owned the majority of foreign-owned mines in Portugal. The original understanding was that in Portuguese-owned mines 75 percent of production would go to Germany, though this was later reduced to 50 percent. Portuguese wolfram sold in 1941 at little more than $1,000 per ton, but by the end of 1942 the price had gone up to $6,000, including a $1,200 export tax. At that point Germany was receiving 2,800 tons per year, and was sending to Portugal much larger amounts of steel and fertilizers.

Spanish production rose very rapidly during 1942–43 on more of a wildcat system. There were fewer large Spanish mines and most production came from small peasant landowners who had deposits on their properties. Moreover, the government prohibited further foreign purchase of wolfram-producing properties on 21 September 1942. Such concessions could henceforth be purchased only by Spanish citizens or wholly owned Spanish companies. An average Spanish site did not produce more than six or seven tons, but that had the effect of spreading the wealth.[8]

British pre-emptive purchasing became increasingly vigorous in Spain during 1942; the British bought more than 50 percent as much as Germany, and, as the price was driven up further, Allied buying overtook German purchases during 1943. Spanish exports were further increased by wolfram that was smuggled from Portugal. The Franco regime sought additional profit from the boom, at the beginning of 1943 imposing stiff production and transit taxes in addition to the existing export tax. As a favor to Germany, however, Spain exempted the Reich from the export tax in February 1943.[9] As a result, by the second quarter of 1943 the total price in Spain rose to $14,612 a ton. Altogether, throughout the war Germany bought about 5,000 tons from Spain and approximately 9,000 tons from Portugal, while with more marginal seams being mined, the quality of the ore dropped by about a third.

To finance their purchases, the Allied governments taxed their own exports to Spain and even shipped a certain amount of gold. The rise in costs was simply too much for German agents, who lacked adequate foreign exchange, and new purchases dwindled during the three summer months of 1943. Spanish commerce suffered as prices declined. Franco then made a major concession to German interests by means of the partial debt-repayment deal negotiated late in 1943, by which a credit of RM100 million, to be credited against the Civil War debt, was granted to Germany, 90 percent of which could be used to pay for Spanish exports, of which approximately half consisted of wolfram. The calculation in Madrid was to get part of this money back from the Allies, because one effect of the deal would be to pump up the price of wolfram once more, as in the month of January 1944 German imports shot back up to 225 tons. Altogether, Spain produced 1,223 tons during the first quarter of 1944.[10]

Carceller, the commerce minister who supervised these operations, was not a committed Germanophile but an overly calculating opportunist who wanted to make as much money as possible from both sides. As Allied pressure mounted, some of his colleagues had begun to doubt the viability of this policy, even before the major American embargo. Thus Doussinague sent a report to Jordana at the end of December 1943 suggesting a way out of the mounting economic conflict. He proposed that Spain ask Germany for another major arms shipment, which the Germans would not be able to provide. The resulting refusal could then be taken as grounds to free Spain of further obligations to Germany, and Spain could turn to the affluent Allied market.[11] This scheme was too Machiavellian and impractical for Jordana and unacceptable to Franco.

The Crisis of 1944

Discussion of a major economic offensive against Spain had been under way in Washington for some time, and a catalyst came in the form of news in mid-January of the RM100 million debt deal, completed nearly two months earlier, which provided Germany with ample new credits.[12] The stiff new American embargo was not a devious British plot, as the Franco regime first thought, but simply reflected the primacy of the United States in the new economic warfare. It threatened the Spanish economy with complete catastrophe.

The Allied embargo came at a time of continued division, growing pessimism, and more than a little disorientation among the lower cadres of the regime. The attitude of the more intellectually sophisticated elements was revealed by a police report from an agent within the Instituto de Estudios Políticos, the think tank of the regime, who declared that "in this center His Excellency is spoken of very scornfully," being referred to as "a simplistic optimist," "vain and pretentious," "a hopeless fellow," and "unwitting." There was much speculation about a major political change, together with the charge that the failure to liquidate the remnants of the Blue Division was "another demonstration that reveals the Caudillo's vacillation." But others said that "there will be no change. He will manage to fool everybody." "It is also held that even though everyone in the Army speaks badly of the Caudillo, they are not likely to lift a finger," because the generals had been bought off and were corrupt. "The general attitude is one of frank pessimism and that any part of our territory might be occupied at any moment, with or without a declaration of war, or with the bombing of Madrid in the same way as Berlin, the difference being that here we have no air-raid shelters but only 'a useless and pretentious Civilian Defense staff with high salaries,' etc." If elections were held in this atmosphere of pervasive corruption, the left would win, but a general conclusion was that "one may perhaps expect to see in Spain a grand 'Competition' of groveling and abasement to win the favor of England and the United States." A similar report the same day on the atmosphere among hard-core Falangists observed that "they are in a state of deep depression," that they frequently charge that Arrese "is a traitor" and should have been assassinated, that the only solution is for the Caudillo "to step down and be replaced by General Asensio."[13]

On 30 January, as official confirmation of the embargo came from American representatives, Doussinague called in a German embassy official to complain that the Spanish regime had "reached the conclusion that England" was trying to destabilize the domestic situation in order to undermine Franco altogether. The Caudillo was determined to stand fast. Spain had reserves of gasoline for three months, which could be stretched to five, by which time conditions would hopefully change. He accused the British of having inspired the crackdown, while Ambassador Hayes "played a double game. . . . Franco and his regime . . . had no illusions" about the long-range goals of the Allies vis-à-vis Spain.[14]

This report probably reflected the Generalissimo's own thinking. Not merely did he not want to abandon the special German connection, but he distrusted the frequent assurances of Hayes and Hoare that the Allies would not intervene in Spain's domestic affairs, and believed that he must maintain an independent posture in order for his regime to survive. The fact that the new Allied hard line coincided with a renewed domestic political offensive of the monarchists, as Don Juan formally broke relations with Franco, only reinforced this attitude.

Yet, despite Doussinague's brave words, Franco also realized that he could not merely sit tight, and the result was another ambiguous course. On 5 February the Spanish government denied new export licenses to Germany, but those already issued remained in effect, so that Germany imported 105 tons of wolfram that month, though hardly any in March. The Germans nonetheless enjoyed many good contacts in Spanish government and business, so that (probably with a certain amount of bribery) it was soon possible to resume imports, which were back up to 198 tons in April. Franco generally approved, because, as he assured Dieckhoff, he wanted to continue to send wolfram to Germany, and Carceller continued to wheel and deal, to the despair of Jordana. Moreover, most of the other ministers tended to support Carceller, one of the reasons that Jordana was always on the verge of resignation.

He won a victory in long cabinet meetings on 2 and 3 February, which authorized him to negotiate an end to the American embargo, without specifying terms. Jordana proposed ending wolfram shipments to Germany in return for termination of the United States' embargo by the close of February, but this proposal was immediately rejected by Washington for its failure to deal with the other Allied demands. Jordana was prepared to go further, having already sent word to Vidal y Saura in Berlin to be prepared for Spain to cede on the issues of the Blue Legion and the German consulate general in Tangier, minimal concessions that would probably be the only way to preserve any remaining autonomy in relations with Germany.

On 7 February Dieckhoff met with what he termed an "unusually worried" Jordana, who insisted that he was not an "Anglophile," and despite the fact that he was following a neutralist policy in the best interests of Spain, assured him that "his sympathies were completely on the German side, not only because of his opposition to communism, . . . but out of gratitude for German assistance in the Civil War and because of his personal conviction that only a German victory could save Europe." He thought it unlikely that the Allies would invade Spain, a step that would bring them no nearer Germany, but should they do so, the Spanish armed forces "would fight against them like a wild animal."[15]

Jordana also informed Dieckhoff that the Spanish police had uncovered subversive conspiracies involving both Spaniards and foreigners, including unspecified Germans. This report particularly concerned veterans of the Blue Division engaged in machinations against the regime, and the ambassador was asked to use his influence to end any German encouragement or the forming of any new organization of Blue Division veterans. Dieckhoff self-righteously disavowed any knowledge of such activities, since he was given no direct evidence, but of course multiple political conversations and intrigues had been carried on, particularly since 1941, by members of the Nazi Party's foreign division, the SS Sicherheitsdienst, the Abwehr, and also embassy personnel, though it also seems that the ambassador usually was not directly informed about many of these activities. The moment for such confabulations had long since passed, and the regime was more sensitive than ever to security problems. Similarly, in recent months German representatives had received more and more critical remarks concerning the activity of Abwehr sabotage operations in Spain, which now seemed to be genuinely resented. Dieckhoff recommended greater prudence and a lower profile, with reduced action.[16]

Jordana's version of the conversation of 7 February was rather different. He wrote that he had asked the Germans to stop "shady intrigues" of "some of their organizations." Dieckhoff replied that these had been brought under control and the worst offenders sent home (which in at least a few cases was perhaps correct). Jordana defined his policy as "strict neutrality."[17]

By February even *Arriba*, perhaps the leading mouthpiece of pro-German sentiment, had begun to define Spain's policy simply as "neutrality," and had the cheek to claim this had always been the case. Jordana was prepared to withdraw the remaining Blue Legion from the eastern front and even to close the large German consulate and espionage center in Tangier, but the Spanish regime stood firm on other points. Even Jordana had doubts about capitulating to the extent of virtually renouncing Spanish sovereignty on key issues.

Diehard elements continued to express strong support for Germany. Even Serrano Suñer may have dreamed of a comeback. In February he sent a letter to Himmler which declared that the war was entering "a new phase that may last a long time." If his "indirect and confidential cooperation" were ever needed, he always stood ready to help.[18] Similarly, despite tentative steps away from fascism in Spain, FET leaders expressed strong support for Mussolini's puppet Italian Social Republic in northern Italy. Though the news reporting in the FET organs had changed, the difference was only relative; Arrese himself published a number of articles denouncing the Allies and their high-handed tactics.

Ginés Vidal y Saura, the ambassador in Berlin, was recalled at the beginning of February for two weeks of consultation. On 16 February, the day before his return to Germany, he met with Dieckhoff and declared that Franco had "said to him with unmistakable clarity that Spain would never break with the Axis powers; there was no question of this." Vidal said that his conversations in Madrid had convinced him "that Spanish policy toward Germany had not changed."[19]

Four days later, Ernst Günther Mohr, counselor of the bloated German consulate general in Tangier, sent his evaluation of the issue of downsizing or closing the consulate. The staff was enormous, amounting to forty-five German nationals, when all the espionage personnel were included, and he admitted that number seemed hard to justify. But if the consulate were closed altogether, an important listening post would be lost, very useful for several kinds of intelligence, which also had symbolic significance for Germany's prestige in the Arab world.[20]

The pressure was felt in Berlin, where Hitler himself had directed on 22 January that wolfram must be assigned the highest priority among German imports, to be guaranteed by further arms shipments to Spain.[21] Conversely, he was ready to accept the dissolution of the Blue Legion, which had no more than the most minor symbolic value. Even while continuing parallel diplomacy and negotiating clandestine deals with Carceller, the German authorities discussed sending some grain of their own to Spain, as well as shipping more arms or negotiating a further deal on the Spanish debt in order to pay the skyrocketing price of wolfram. Canaris meanwhile reorganized the Abwehr's clandestine operations in Spain, in order to get as many operatives as possible under diplomatic cover before what looked like an inevitable crackdown.[22] In March he ordered an end to all sabotage operations conducted from Spanish territory.[23]

By the end of February Jordana had hammered out a tentative deal with Hayes: wolfram exports to Germany would be reduced by 90 percent, the consulate and German military mission in Tangier would be closed, German espionage and sabotage operations would be shut down, all Spanish volunteer units on the eastern front would be dissolved, and all but two of the interned Italian ships would be handed over.[24] This proposal provoked heated debate in three consecutive meetings of the Council of Ministers on 28–29 February and 1 March. Jordana had a long meeting with Franco just before they began and thought he had won the Generalissimo's backing, but the sessions were stormy, with Jordana again in the minority and denounced as "timid" and "a sellout." The Falangist ministers strongly combated his proposals and Franco provided only tepid support. Carceller and Joaquín Benjumea, the finance minister, insisted that ending wolfram shipments to Germany would produce "almost irreparable damage to the Spanish economy," and that under the banner of neutrality, Spain should insist on absolute freedom of commerce with both sides. Carceller and his colleagues seemed oblivious of the drastic change in the strategic situation. When the issue was put to a vote, only the navy minister, Admiral Salvador Moreno Fernández, who had a broader grasp of such things, voted with Jordana, who had annoyed Franco by going so far in his negotiations with Hayes. The foreign minister had to threaten yet again to resign, and the Generalissimo had sufficient sense of reality to understand that he could not afford to lose Jordana. Though Vigón, the air force minister, apparently made the fatuous suggestion that the cynical, shortsighted Carceller take over negotiations, Franco had the wit to support Jordana against nearly all the rest of the council.[25] The deal was not accepted, however, and Jordana's authority was somewhat reduced; henceforth he would be required to submit his negotiations to the council before completing any new arrangement. Franco appointed a commission to decide how much wolfram exports to Germany should be reduced. With each passing week, the foreign minister was subjected to increasing tension, which to some extent began to undermine his health.[26]

All the while Carceller was privately trying to negotiate a grand deal of his own with Berlin. When a high functionary of the Reich Finance Ministry appeared in Madrid in mid-February to settle accounting for the expenses of the Blue Division, Carceller proposed a final liquidation of the Civil War debt. If Germany would apply to the debt ESP347 million from the payments for the Blue Division, ESP24 million already on account in Spain would be applied exclusively to purchases of wolfram. Two conditions attached were that Germany provide as steep a discount on the final reckoning of the debt as Italy had three years earlier, and that Spain would indemnify claims of individual German citizens from the Civil War only if Germany did the same for Spanish citizens in the European war. Carceller's notion was that all these claims would be paid exclusively in pesetas, no foreign exchange would be required, the debt would be finally liquidated, and no money would leave Spain, which would turn a profit on the whole deal. The scheme would show Carceller to be forceful and efficient, while Jordana was supposedly timid and inept. In the process Spain would obtain further arms and other supplies from Germany and stimulate its domestic economy.

The Germans found this proposal promising and continued separate negotiations during March and April. They recognized the remaining Spanish debt as amounting to RM170 million, 70 million of which would be made up by the existing German trade deficit, so that Spain's final obligation was reduced to RM100 million. By the time this proposal was finally presented to the Spanish government in mid-April, however, the Spanish economic crisis was too far advanced and the Allies had gained the upper hand.[27]

The Germans did all they could to weaken Jordana and support Carceller, who persisted in the fantasy that he could balance Allied pressure by obtaining more supplies from Germany. Ribbentrop encouraged this idea, though Dieckhoff more realistically pointed out that Germany could do very little and had no cotton at all, lack of which was about to paralyze the Catalan textile industry. The Germans repeatedly complained that the Spanish were not living up to the terms of the preceding trade agreements. Jordana replied that concessions had been made earlier because of Germany's poor commercial position and Spain's outstanding debt, but with repayment largely accomplished, such trade concessions were "implicitly" annulled, and he added to Dieckhoff on 3 March that the Spanish government had a "duty of supreme vital necessity" to "accommodate itself to existing reality."[28]

At the beginning of April the Department of Commercial Policy of the German Foreign Ministry submitted a report on the consequences of a commercial break with Spain, which were judged to be disastrous. All Portuguese exports (wolfram, resins, cork, canned fish, and turpentine, particularly) came through Spain, while Spain was sending at least 1,200 tons of wolfram per year, a million tons of iron ore, 40,000 tons of zinc, 80,000 tons of pyrites, and 6,000 tons of lead.[29]

On 11 March Ribbentrop telegraphed Dieckhoff to assure Franco that fully reliable German intelligence revealed that the Allies would not break with the Spanish government over the present controversy, and that further concessions would merely lead to greater demands. He held up Turkey's resistance to British and American pressure as an example for Spain to follow, but stressed that it was better to say this to Franco personally, and not to Jordana, "who repeats everything to the English."[30]

Ribbentrop had Dieckhoff go directly to Franco on 17 March. The Caudillo repeated that Spain had always collaborated with Germany as closely as conditions permitted, but that Spain was absolutely dependent on Atlantic commerce, which the Allies completely dominated. Dieckhoff offered 60,000 tons of grain and an unspecified amount of petroleum, but Franco remained skeptical, merely saying that he would obtain the best terms for continued wolfram shipment that relations with the Allies permitted. According to the Spanish version of the conversation, Franco opined that "one cannot expect Germany to win the war, but only to continue it and not to lose it, which is different from winning it."[31] That opinion, however, was more an expression of what Franco preferred than an objective analysis of the situation.

In Berlin Vidal y Saura feared reprisals, but Germany had few cards left to play, and Dieckhoff simply sent Jordana a letter demanding that Spain live up to all its present agreements.[32] Finally in mid-April the Germans made their last best offer: 60,000 tons of grain (to which 30,000 tons of wheat and 35,000 tons of gasoline from Romania would be added), from 200 to 240 tons of synthetic rubber within six months, and from 2,000 to 3,000 tons of artificial fiber to replace cotton. To these would later be added large quantities of substitute fuels and an undetermined amount of arms.

When Franco and Dieckhoff met on 21 April, the Generalissimo reiterated that "he would do everything humanly possible for Germany, whose battle was his own battle and whose victory he saw as absolutely necessary for himself and for Spain," but rejected the offer. He was presumably influenced by the recent visit of the American General Walter Bedell Smith, on behalf of the Allied command, promising officially that the impending Allied invasion of the continent would in no way affect Spain either militarily or politically, though this was not divulged to the German ambassador. Franco realized, he declared, that Washington "was not bluffing," but waging all-out economic warfare, which affected every major sector of the Spanish economy. Moreover, the internal political situation had grown more serious, with the Communists taking advantage of the shortages and agitating to resume the Civil War, aided by Moscow and Washington. If the Allies invaded, Spain would resist, but otherwise there was a limit to its capacity to sacrifice, provided that reasonable terms might be found. Franco assured Dieckhoff that when all was settled, Germany would still receive "reasonable, regular" quantities of wolfram that would be nearly as much as it asked for. The difference was not enough to force Spain to undergo the ravages of all-out economic warfare. Dieckhoff was dismayed.[33]

Though the British worked to soften the terms of the American embargo, it had a drastic effect on the Spanish economy, resulting in the final political and economic settlement of 2 May 1944. Washington grudgingly accepted the principle of limitation, not embargo, of wolfram exports to Germany, set at 20 tons per month for May and June and 40 tons per month thereafter. Franco in turn made major political and military concessions: withdrawal of all organized Spanish units from the eastern front, complete closure of the swollen German consulate in Tangier, and a promise to expel all German intelligence and sabotage agents on Spanish territory (though this last promise was not totally fulfilled). Portugal, meanwhile, had remained faithful to its earlier agreement with Germany until it, too, was threatened with an Allied oil embargo, whereupon all wolfram shipments to Germany ceased on 6 June 1944.

Aftermath

As was typical of its sinuous policy, the Spanish regime did not fully live up to the new wolfram agreement. Carceller made a secret deal to permit additional exports, and other Spanish officials, both senior and low-level, acted in collusion with the Germans, so that, whereas for two and a half months through May, June, and July Spain was supposed to export only 60 tons of wolfram, the Germans actually managed to move a great deal more—according to the American calculation (which may be exaggerated), nearly 500 tons more[34]—for a war economy that at that moment was producing at its all-time peak. This was the last major act of pro-German collaboration during the war, carried out in covert but nonetheless direct defiance of the official agreement with the Allies, proof not simply of venality or greed, though these factors were important, but of Spain's deep and persistent commitment to the German war effort, a commitment that had just led to the near-strangulation of Spain's own economy.

The full extent of the special economic deals with Germany is not at all clear from the formal diplomatic record, but they had a long history. Thus when the Germans occupied all Vichy territory in 1942, they closed all foreign consulates except that of Spain in Hendaye, which was a key to the partly clandestine commercial network that already had been created. Bribery often played an important role,[35] and Carceller remained fully complicit. In mid-May he told the Germans that they would no longer be able to make much use of the existing private network, but provided them with a list of all Spanish producers so that they could continue to make illicit deals on their own. In his diary entry for 26 June, Jordana wrote that "the weakness Franco feels for this truly undesirable man [Carceller], whose departure from the government would be well received both inside and outside Spain, is incomprehensible."[36] Franco nonetheless retained the duplicitous Carceller until the end of the war because he represented a version of Franco's own double game.

The Germans' problem was now moving wolfram across the border, where they were said to have 800 tons stacked by the beginning of May. That month 20 tons crossed legally, 95 illegally; in June 20 more tons were transported legally and 61 tons illegally. At the beginning of June Johannes Bernhardt, head of the German consortium in Spain, took up negotiations with a major private Spanish group to have the latter assume responsibility for moving wolfram. Their price was ESP120,000 per ton, to which Bernhardt agreed, but around the first of July Spanish security forces began to crack down in earnest, and by the close of that month illegal exports had virtually ceased. A large part of the wolfram purchased in 1944 could never be moved to Germany because of severe transport problems, the final Spanish crackdown, and then the withdrawal of German forces from France in August, in retreat from the Allied advance. Thus ended direct land contact with Germany, with hundreds of tons of wolfram still stocked near the frontier for shipment. Subsequently only a small amount could be sent to Germany by air, and when the Spanish authorities finally closed the German embassy in May 1945, they found a great deal of wolfram stored in its basement.[37] As it was, the German war economy never suffered from the cessation of Iberian wolfram exports, for sufficient reserves had been built up to last for the remainder of the war.

The result of Franco's capitulation in May 1944 was to move Spain for the first time to a position of relatively genuine neutrality. A tilt to the Allies had now begun. In Madrid there remained some lingering sense of obligation to Germany, and even Jordana at that point thought it quite important to retain good relations with Berlin, but the general sense was that Spain had done all it could. Though Berlin maintained that more than a third of the Civil War debt was still unpaid, exact figures were in dispute, and Jordana took the position that Spain had paid enough.

The perspective now was that the Allies were likely to win the war, but Franco and most of his government still refused to believe that Germany would be totally defeated. According to Rafael García Pérez, their notion was that

> a defeated Germany would continue to be a great European power with a large industrial and technological base capable of stimulating Spanish economic development. On the basis of this calculation, the Spanish government sought to achieve the status of being the last country still friendly to Germany, after the rupture made by other friendly neutral countries (especially Sweden and Turkey), with the goal of gaining a privileged position in the future reconstruction of Europe. The long-term objective was for the first time to make Spain, not Italy, Germany's chief associate in the Mediterranean.[38]

Franco and most of his ministers continued to believe that they were taking a farsighted approach. The Spanish government granted increasing economic and transit rights to the Allies, but refused to bend completely because it still feared that the Allies would ultimately demand a change of regime in Madrid.

Germany's response to Franco's capitulation was quite angry, with talk of breaking relations. Ribbentrop directed Dieckhoff to lodge a strong protest, and to insist that the Tangier consulate was "not negotiable." The embassy was instructed to limit all contacts, even social ones, with the Spanish government, to whom a "verbal note" was delivered on 8 May. Its two principal charges were that Madrid had unilaterally broken its commercial treaties with Germany and that the closing of the consulate in Tangier constituted a formal act of hostility. It insisted (correctly) that the Allies would now demand even more, while Germany reserved the right to take unspecified countermeasures.[39] At this point Hitler intervened personally, realizing that the Spanish regime still expressed friendship and that it was in Germany's best interest to salvage as much of the relationship as possible. On 10 May he issued instructions to Ribbentrop to maintain good relations.[40]

The Spanish government responded that all that was involved was an adjustment of treaties, as international realities required from time to time, and that it had done the best it could to maintain a certain volume of wolfram shipments to Germany. It reminded Berlin that the German government had taken so revolutionary a step as the Nazi-Soviet Pact of 1939 without consulting the other members of Germany's own Anti-Comintern Pact, and that Germany's closure of many Spanish consulates in occupied France in November 1942 had been a much less comprehensible and justifiable act than the closing of the Tangier consulate.[41] By the end of the month, the time had come for renewal of the Treaty of Friendship of 31 March 1939 between Spain and Germany. This agreement provided for automatic renewal for another five years if neither party denounced the treaty before 29 May 1944, and so it was automatically renewed.

The German government still hoped to gain commercial advantages from final liquidation of the Civil War debt, which Dieckhoff raised again in mid-June. Jordana responded that the previous negotiation by Carceller had no validity whatsoever, but commissioned a new study by the Foreign Ministry's director general of economic policy. Its conclusion was that once all German commercial debts and Spanish credits had been totaled, Germany was now absolutely indebted to Spain, not the other way around. (This conclusion was remarkably similar to that of the Soviet government concerning all the Spanish gold shipped to Moscow.) This new hard line was not so much designed to be tough with Germany as it was motivated by fear that any further commercial concessions to Germany based on the debt would simply lead to another harsh economic crackdown by the Allies.[42]

A final German hope was to lure the Spanish government with the prospect of further arms shipments. In June Berlin offered a choice between three packages, and Madrid accepted a proposal to send sixty-seven Pkw-IVs (Mark IV tanks), sixty 75-mm guns, and two larger cannon. But in less than two months the border with Germany had been completely closed by the Allies, with about 25 percent of Programm Bär still undelivered, so nothing came of the new arms deal.[43]

The struggle over wolfram was General Jordana's last battle. He took some satisfaction in Spain's ability both to stay out of the war and to retain greater independence than either Portugal, which was forced to cede bases to the Allies, or Turkey, which was now being forced into nonbelligerence on behalf of the Allies and would eventually enter the war.

Jordana suddenly died of a brain hemorrhage on 3 August in San Sebastián, only a few days after suffering an injury to his head in a hunting accident.[44] Though he perished technically from the effects of the accident, the man who was arguably Spain's principal hero of World War II was also in some sense a casualty of the war itself, exhausted by his titanic struggle to achieve his country's neutrality.

CHAPTER 15

The End of the Relationship

After the success of the Allied invasion of France, Franco accepted the fact that Germany would definitively lose the war and even become an occupied country, as he admitted in conversations with Allied diplomats. Carrero Blanco's last two strategic evaluations of the war, prepared in August and September 1944, concluded that there was no hope for the Reich.[1]

The final phase of Spanish diplomacy was led by José Félix de Lequerica, recalled from Vichy on 11 August to replace Jordana, who had died eight days earlier, as foreign minister. Ever since the beginning of the embargo crisis, there had been speculation that Jordana might be replaced with someone more attuned to the Germanophile sectors of the regime, but Franco had had better sense than to do that. His subsequent selection of the sometime "ambassador of the Gestapo" in Paris and Vichy seemed at first imprudent and even an act of defiance, but Franco did not view it in those terms. Though Lequerica's past might be held against him, he was clever and sophisticated, and, because of that past, Franco knew that he would be fully loyal.

Lequerica was a cosmopolitan Basque with an international education that had made him fluent in English and French. He had once been known in occupied France as "more German than the Germans," and, according to Serrano Suñer, when in Paris he lunched almost daily with the Paris Gestapo chief, hence his sobriquet. He was also informal, suave, and witty, with good interpersonal skills. He eventually gained the reputation of being the most cynical politician in the regime, despite the considerable competition for that distinction. The reputation of Lequerica in Spanish historiography is that of a consummate opportunist, which seems fair enough. He apparently described himself simply as a *carguista*, sometime who sought the best *cargos* (positions), and despite his wartime Naziphilia, was not an ideological fascist, dismissing the FET as "a loony bin."[2] Though Carrero Blanco thought him crassly unprincipled, Lequerica suited Franco because of his sheer pragmatism and because he had burned all other bridges.[3] Sir Samuel Hoare, who had liked and even admired Jordana, thought that the selection of someone like Lequerica demonstrated that the Spanish regime was beyond redemption, while Hayes expressed a more hopeful view. His was only an interim appointment, to ride out the war, and he would be replaced within a year, once the reorientation of the regime had been completed, but he would continue to play an important role. Several years later Lequerica would serve as ringmaster of the Spanish lobby in Washington that helped eventually to achieve rapprochement with the United States.[4]

The new foreign minister adjusted quickly. To the French and Germans he had denounced Jordana and his chief assistant, Juan Pan de Soraluce, as virtual Republicans, but when he took his new post he immediately saw the wisdom of keeping Jordana's top personnel. Whereas his predecessor's task had been to steer Spanish policy from nonbelligerence to neutrality, that of Lequerica was to prepare Spanish policy for the postwar survival of the regime, distancing it from Germany while attempting to gain the favor of the Allies.

Lequerica proposed to reorient Spanish strategic definitions from a European and African policy to one based on the western hemisphere, hopefully gaining acceptance and support from the United States and Latin American countries. *Hispanidad* reverted to a more benign, primarily cultural and spiritual form, while the attempt to play the North American card was entirely new. With the dominance of the Soviet Union in the east and the Anglo-Americans in the west, there seemed little choice. Lequerica stressed such topics as Spain's supposedly traditional democracy, the regime's Catholic identity (now made the centerpiece), Spain's newly discovered "American vocation," and the need for a policy of "Atlantic cooperation." There was the hope and expectation that the Catholic corporatism of the regime might be able to make a special appeal in the multidimensional postwar crisis that loomed on the horizon.[5]

Like Jordana, Lequerica tried to establish a basic difference between Spanish and Italian nonbelligerence, pointing out that Italy had signed a full military alliance with Germany in peacetime and become "aggressively" nonbelligerent as soon as the war began, even though there was no threat to Italy. Italian nonbelligerence had always been pre-belligerence, whereas that of Spain was described as defensive, adopted only after the war had already spread to the Mediterranean and threatened Spain, and allegedly had referred only to the Mediterranean and ended as soon as Italy had left the war. The official position was that at no time had Spain ever changed its policy regarding the Western democracies from the initial neutrality declared in September 1939.[6]

Spain's response to the Holocaust played a major role. The ambassador in Washington, Francisco de Cárdenas, had already been emphasizing Spanish efforts to Jewish leaders, and Lequerica spurred him on. His telegram of 28 October insisted: "For three years Spain has repeatedly and with the best goodwill responded to any petition presented by the Jewish communities either directly or by means of yourself, the ambassador in London, or other chiefs of mission in America, resulting in energetic initiatives not only in Berlin but in Bucharest, Sofia, Athens, Budapest, etc. At an obvious price to our own diplomatic enterprises, at times producing tense and energetic discussions because of our defense of those interests." He lamented continuing attacks from the more liberal and leftist Jewish publicists.[7]

An extremely lengthy telegram was dispatched on 17 November detailing the current efforts of Sanz Briz in Budapest. Lequerica went on to make extensive claims regarding protection of Jews in Romania and Bulgaria, as well. Cárdenas replied that same day that some of the more sympathetic Jewish leaders had pledged to try to change the attitude of the more liberal Jewish organizations, but this was hard, since there were so many diverse Jewish groups in the United States.[8] Some modest success was achieved, but the struggle to gain greater favor in Washington largely failed.

Relations with Germany steadily grew more distant. Direct rail links began to be disrupted as early as 8 July and the common border disappeared scarcely more than a month later, when the final 275 boxcars of exports were turned back. Mail service dwindled and most commercial contracts had to be canceled. The only remaining direct connection was the Lufthansa flight from Barcelona, which, however, did not operate every day. It nonetheless continued until 17 April 1945, carrying passengers of the highest priority, as well as small amounts of vital cargo for military production or other key items, such as the only small supply of the new Allied wonder drug penicillin to reach Nazi Germany. On 10 October, the news bulletin of the Estado Mayor Central informed senior Spanish officers that the German leaders were still confident that they could force at least a reasonable solution to the war, but that hope had largely waned in Madrid.[9]

Dieckhoff was recalled to Berlin on 2 September and never returned, leaving the German embassy in the hands of its first counselor. The commercial treaty was nonetheless renewed for the second time in November, though this action was largely pro forma, since trade with Germany had virtually disappeared. Moreover, Lequerica required that the final exchange of notes on 30 November remain a strict secret.[10]

One new form of collaboration nonetheless developed in the final phase of the war. At several spots in northwestern and western France German troops had been cut off and bypassed by the Allied advance, forming isolated coastal enclaves. To supply them, in October 1944 the German navy decided to make use of the Spanish ships owned by Transcomar, the German-controlled shipping company set up earlier in Spain. It is not clear how soon the supply service began, but during the three months 1 January–31 March 1945 eighteen small convoys, consisting mainly of large fishing boats (to get past Allied patrols), were dispatched to the coastal enclaves and their cargoes transshipped to either German submarines or French fishing boats in German hands. Two of the Spanish ships involved were sunk by the Allies. At some point the Spanish government ordered that operations be halted, but coastal district army commanders were bribed by the Germans and the supply service continued for some time.[11]

Germanophile diehards were still found in the FET and in the Spanish colony in bombed-out Berlin. There the Spanish-language *Enlace,* a publication of the former ambassador General Wilhelm von Faupel's Ibero-American Institute, on 23 November presented parallel columns contrasting Franco's earlier remarks on his own regime and on Nazi Germany with his recent declaration to the United Press that Spain was "already a true democracy," an "organic democracy," and that there was no reason whatever why it could not cooperate fully with the Allies. Celia Giménez, the voice of Spanish radio in Berlin, had ceased a month earlier to broadcast her mixture of news, propaganda, and entertainment for Radio Nacional de España and German radio.[12]

In December the Spanish government closed the support offices of the Blue Division in Madrid, to avoid further political embarrassment. New pension arrangements for veterans and their families were indefinitely postponed, though the German government still sent small sums to support the veterans' activities. The Allied governments continued to pressure Madrid concerning the small number of Spaniards who had remained as volunteers in the German forces; the government replied that it had forbidden such activities and that whatever continued was beyond its knowledge or control. By the end of the year only a thousand Spanish workers remained in Germany. Spanish diplomats tried to intervene on their behalf and a few were evacuated to Switzerland or Sweden in the final months of the Reich, but most had to be repatriated after its collapse.[13]

The fine embassy building that Hitler had awarded the Spanish government had been destroyed in the heavy air raids of early 1944, and an adequate substitute was never found. Lequerica did not authorize evacuation of Spanish diplomatic personnel until February 1945, leaving only the first secretary and the three military attachés in Berlin. Vidal y Saura, who had been Franco's most competent ambassador to the Reich, then became a symbol of the expiring Spanish-German relationship: he suffered a stroke just before he crossed the Swiss border and died in a hospital in Bern. One of the last Spaniards to remain in Berlin, other than a few volunteers in the German army, was Gonzalo Rodríguez del Castillo, correspondent for *El Español*. He helped to obtain work releases and visas for a number of remaining Spanish workers, and then with a small group lit out on 22 April for the Danish border, which they managed to cross safely.[14]

The last recorded musings of Hitler about Franco and the role of Spain took place on 10 February 1945. He observed that it would have been easy to drag Spain into the war in 1940 because Franco was so eager to participate in the spoils of victory, but that Franco had "very exaggerated ideas about the value of Spanish intervention." Even so, despite the "sabotage" of his "Jesuitical" brother-in-law, Hitler claimed that it would have been feasible to offer Morocco and a slice of Algeria (though that had not been Hitler's position in 1940–41). The Führer now claimed that he had simply concluded that "direct intervention" by Spain was not desirable (though in fact he had not adopted such a position until 1943), because the seizure of Gibraltar was not enough to offset the enormous costs of defending Spain and fending off a new civil war incited by the British.

He then went on to denounce Franco and his regime, partly in line with his usual criticisms and partly in more original terms, declaring that he could never forgive Franco for not having reconciled and reunited Spanish society, for having "condemned" the Falangists "to ostracism," for having treated the Republicans, many of whom were not true Reds (that is, Marxists and Communists), as "bandits." Hitler now had "less sympathy than ever" for a regime dominated by capitalist opportunists and the "clerical gang." Placing half the population outside the law while a small minority looted the country was hardly a solution to Spain's problems. He repeated that he was now sure that "few of the Spanish Reds were really Communists," and, had he known that earlier, he would never have sent his aviators to bomb them.

As it was, however, Hitler agreed that by remaining neutral Franco had provided Germany "the only service" that he could. Having to support Italy was bad enough; Spain would have been even more of a problem. The war had clearly revealed "one thing: the irremediable decadence of the Latin peoples," who had shown they had "no right to participate in the solution of world problems." On the other hand, he mused, it would have been easy to seize Gibraltar with Franco's connivance, even without bringing Spain into the war. That would have solved the strategic problem of Germany in southwestern Europe, while Britain would have been too weak to declare war on Spain itself.[15]

Though Spanish policy was now trying to orient itself more and more to the United States, Franco also hoped for diplomatic support from Churchill. He was cheered by the prime minister's remarks in the House of Commons on 24 May 1944, when he declared, "There is no doubt that if Spain had yielded to German blandishments [in 1940] our burden would have been much heavier." Concerning Torch, Churchill observed: "I must say that I shall always consider a service was rendered at this time by Spain. . . . I have, therefore, no sympathy with those who think it clever, and even funny, to insult and abuse the Government of Spain whenever occasion serves. . . . As I am here today speaking kindly words about Spain, let me add that I hope she will be a strong influence for the peace of the Mediterranean after the war."[16] Churchill had never been a political foe of the Franco regime, and here was probably expressing indirectly his hope that Spain might provide an anticommunist counterweight after the war, and at that moment may also have wished to guarantee a continued neutral attitude in Madrid during the invasion of France, which was about to begin.

Churchill's speech provoked such outrage in the American press, which had largely taken a militantly anti-Franco line throughout the war, that the prime minister felt it necessary to write a letter to Roosevelt explaining his position. He said this was no different from his statements in

1940 and that he sought no unnecessary quarrels, observing evenhandedly that he did not know if there was more freedom in the Soviet Union than in Spain, but that he did not want to fight with either country.

Franco eventually sought to take advantage of Churchill's attitude, writing a personal and rather smug letter to the British prime minister on 18 October that dwelt on the importance of closer friendship between Britain and Spain to save Western Europe from communism. In this he considerably overreached himself; Churchill did not reply for three months, and then only to rebuke him, and a subsequent letter was harsher in tone. The British ambassador meanwhile stressed to Lequerica that the absence of democracy in Spain constituted an almost insuperable barrier to better relations; Lequerica replied with unassailable logic that this surely could not be the case, in view of the Allies' good relations with Stalin.[17]

The Generalissimo tried again in November through an interview with the United Press in which he insisted that his regime had observed "complete neutrality" throughout the war and "had nothing to do with fascism" because "Spain could never be joined to other governments that do not hold to Catholicism as the first principle." He insisted that "institutions that produce excellent results in other countries lead to the opposite results here, due to certain peculiarities of the Spanish temperament." Inaugurating what would become a standard line for the remainder of his long regime, he insisted that despite the absence of direct elections, in its own way his regime constituted a "true democracy," an "organic democracy" based on religion, local institutions, trade unions, and the family.[18]

Churchill in fact largely agreed with Franco about the postwar framework. The Generalissimo had made grievous errors of judgment during the war but had a clearer view of postwar international dynamics than did, for example, Roosevelt, yet so long as the war lasted Churchill dared not respond to Franco's anti-Soviet overtures. Within the British government, however, he argued forcefully against overt intervention in Spanish affairs, reiterating that the Spanish regime had "done us much more good than harm in the war." Though, for diplomatic reasons, he had to give Franco's anti-Soviet letter "a rough reply," he went on to declare:

> I am no more in agreement with the internal government of Russia than I am with that of Spain, but I would certainly rather live in Spain than in Russia. . . . You need not, I think, suppose that Franco's position will be weakened by our warnings. He and all those with him will never consent to be butchered by the Republicans, which is what would happen.

... Already we are accused in many responsible quarters of handing over the Balkans and Central Europe to the Russians, and if we
now lay hands on Spain, I am of the opinion that we shall be making
needless trouble for ourselves. . . . Should the Communists become
masters of Spain we must expect the infection to spread very fast
through Italy and France. . . . At this time every country that is liberated or converted by our victories is seething with Communism. . . .

... I should of course be very glad to see a Monarchist and Democratic restoration, but once we have identified ourselves with the
Communist side in Spain, which, whatever you say, would be the effect of your policy, all our influence will be gone for a middle course.[19]

War's End; Ostracism Begins

Neither the British nor the American government wanted to intervene
militarily in Spain, but their policies, particularly that of the United States,
continued to harden. During the first months of 1945 the Anglo-American
ambassadors lodged repeated protests over what they termed failure to
implement fully the agreement of May 1944. They listed the names of
eighty-three German intelligence agents allegedly still operating in Spain
and protested the continued liberty of other agents initially apprehended,
the continuation of Lufthansa flights from Barcelona, and the persistent
supply shipments to the German coastal enclaves.

The only change in Spanish policy during this final phase was the
breaking of relations with Japan on 11 April 1945, in response to atrocities
committed by the Japanese during the Americans' recapture of Manila in
February. Japanese defenders fortified themselves among the civilian population in the main part of the city, including the old Spanish quarter,
which was largely destroyed during the massive American bombardment.
Manila became one of the most thoroughly destroyed cities in the world,
after Warsaw and Stalingrad. About 50,000 civilians died, not so much
from the bombardment as from mass atrocities by the Japanese. More
than a few of the dead were Spanish citizens, including approximately fifty
people murdered during the wanton destruction of the Spanish consulate
by the Japanese.[20]

During this last stage the FET released an undated "Circular muy res-
ervada" to its sections to dampen the complaints of diehard pro-Germans.
It stressed that "at no time has the Caudillo ever betrayed Germany," but
that he had labored incessantly to save Spain and to try to save Europe. Of
critics it demanded rhetorically: "What is it they want? For Spain to com-

mit suicide because Germany has lost the war?"[21] On 18 April 1945 the party sent instructions to all provincial chiefs that the end of the war should be presented exclusively as a triumph of the regime and of the movement, which had always sought peace and had saved Spain from war. It emphasized the conclusion that *"to celebrate peace is to celebrate the triumph of the Falange and of the Caudillo."* The news of Hitler's death nonetheless prompted *Arriba* to publish a final tribute to a fallen hero.[22]

When Harry Truman took office in April, he seemed if anything more antagonistic than Roosevelt. The Soviets were totally and unremittingly hostile, calling for the overthrow of Franco. The Potsdam conference of July 1945 realized some of the regime's worst fears. Against the wishes of Churchill, it recommended to the United Nations, then being organized, that relations with the Spanish government be broken and recognition transferred to "democratic forces" in order that Spain might have a regime of its own choice.[23]

The founding meeting of the international organization at San Francisco that summer marked a complete victory for the new Junta Española de Liberación, formed by the Spanish Republicans and leftist parties in exile. The government of Mexico, Latin America's most resolute foe of the Franco regime, presented a motion whose terms, excluding the present Spanish government from membership, were passed by acclamation.[24] On 30 June the government of Panama broke relations with Madrid, which braced for similar action by other countries.[25] The postwar tide of the left swept into power new administrations in Western Europe, first in Britain and later in France, whose leaders had already sworn hostility to the Franco regime.[26] The Soviet Union went one step further, launching a campaign against the five neutral governments it accused of favoring Germany during the war—Argentina, Portugal, Spain, Sweden, and Switzerland—urging active measures against them.[27] By the close of 1946, formal ostracism of the regime would be nearly complete. Though there was no economic embargo, political ostracism would continue until 1948, when the consequences of the Cold War slowly began to effect a change.

Liquidation of German Assets

Immediately after the Reich's final surrender the Spanish government adhered to the terms of the Bretton Woods agreement, which recommended seizure of all German property abroad. A Spanish decree confiscated all German public and private property within the country, providing for a careful inventory. The government would apparently have preferred to nationalize this property but had to deal with the Allied Control Council (ACC) in Germany, which claimed jurisdiction over all German property abroad. It refused to recognize the full claims of the council, announcing that all goods stemming from theft or pillage would be handed over, but that German state property would be retained until a peace treaty recognized a legitimate German state to which it could be returned; private property was a separate matter. After further negotiation, Madrid finally recognized the ACC's jurisdiction in October 1946. Nonetheless, it insisted that Spanish claims against German property must be satisfied before anything was handed over, hoping thereby to gain control of most German goods in Spain. Despite the condemnation of the Franco regime by the United Nations in December 1946, the Spanish government continued to negotiate with the ACC, in the following year presenting total claims of all sorts against Germany of slightly more than ESP1 billion. The ACC refused to recognize most of this claim and presented a German counterclaim against Spain of RM377 million, most of which was made up of RM277 million allegedly stemming from the Civil War debt.

Final agreement was reached on 10 May 1948. The remaining Civil War debt was declared liquidated, as well as any other claim of a future German state against Spain. For purposes of settlement, German state enterprises in Spain were valued at ESP100 million and private properties at ESP600 million. The Spanish state was offered 27.8 percent of the sales values of such properties, up to a total of ESP400 million of property sold, and 30 percent of the value of everything exceeding that, amounting theoretically to about ESP195 million, plus ESP30 million more from the sale of the German secondary schools.[28]

Nazi Refugees

During 1945–46, especially, wild and hysterical charges were made abroad concerning the alleged existence of large numbers of Nazi and other fascist refugees in Spain, including preposterous allegations of preparation of a new "Nazi army" and the development of atomic weapons by refugee Nazi scientists, in this fantasy Franco being in the process of accomplishing what Hitler could not do.

During the course of 1944 the Spanish state had begun to comply with Allied demands for expulsion of German espionage agents, though this task was never entirely completed so long as the war lasted. All German state personnel in Spain were then interned at the conclusion of the fighting. There is no evidence of any last-minute appeals to Franco by any major Nazi officials, though there was a forlorn gesture by General Andrei Vlasov, commander of the Russian collaborationist army.[29] No top Nazi found sanctuary in Spain, though some second-level luminaries, such as the SS special operations chief, Otto Skorzeny, did so. The top collaborationist to reach Spain was the sometime Vichy premier, Pierre Laval, but he was soon extradited to France, where he was tried and executed. A number of lesser figures from other countries did reach Spain, perhaps the most prominent of whom was Léon Degrelle, Belgian fascist leader and much-decorated, six-time wounded Waffen SS officer, who was allowed to remain permanently, perhaps in recognition of his combat on the eastern front.

The Allies mounted a special program, Operation Safehaven, in 1944 to track down fleeing Nazis and seize German resources abroad, though its eventual jurisdiction over the latter was limited. The principal countries targeted by Safehaven were Argentina, Ireland, Portugal, Spain, Sweden, Switzerland, and Turkey. The level of cooperation in Spain was about average compared with these other countries. Turkey refused to extradite anyone, and Portugal's Salazar, though dealing with fewer refugees and resources, proved more stubborn than Franco.

In September 1945 the ACC ordered repatriation of all German state personnel abroad. In addition to the hundreds in this category who had already been interned in Spain, approximately 1,200 soldiers and customs personnel had fled across the border in August 1944. By February 1946 1,253 had been repatriated by train and a small additional number by air.

At the close of 1945 Allied officials gave the Spanish government a list of 255 refugee Nazis whom they wanted handed over. Of these, 105 were either extradited to the Allies or declared to have fled Spain, and 77 allegedly could not be located by Spanish authorities; Franco denied extradition for 70. Johannes Bernhardt, the Nazi businessman who had played such a crucial role in German-Spanish relations, was protected by the award of Spanish citizenship in 1946. Altogether, by April 1946 only 74 had been directly extradited. A second and more complete list was presented by Allied officials by the end of March, composed of 492 Gestapo agents, 1,065 German state employees (of whom 332 had allegedly been spies), plus approximately 500 other names listed for diverse reasons. By June, of 734 persons whose names appeared on Allied priority lists, only 192 had been returned.[30]

"Nazi Gold" in Spain?

After the Civil War, the Franco regime was able to recover only a very small proportion of the formerly large gold reserves of the Bank of Spain. During World War II, it found that it could not obtain foreign exchange or equivalent goods for some exports, and accepted payments in gold from Great Britain and several other countries, though apparently not from Germany. These transfers primarily took place during the economic warfare of 1943–44. Altogether, between 1942 and 1945 the Instituto Español de Moneda Extranjera (IEME) acquired 67.4 tons of fine gold from London, Bern, and Basel. Part of it stemmed from ordinary exports to Switzerland, though another portion came from clandestine wolfram exports paid by Germany out of accounts in Switzerland. Of this total amount, according to Pablo Martín Aceña, 38.6 tons came from the Swiss National Bank, 14.9 tons from the Bank of England, 9.1 tons from the Bank of Portugal, 2.5 from the German Transatlantic Bank, less than a ton from the International Bank of Transfers in Basel, and 1.4 tons from the Foreign Bank of Spain. The bulk of the gold came from normal international exchange and payment, though 30.3 tons came in the form of German gold bars. None of the bars proceeded directly from Germany but came mainly through the Swiss National Bank.[31]

Immediately after the war, and then later during the controversy over the use of Jewish assets in Switzerland that developed in the 1990s, it was charged that the Spanish government had obtained gold looted from Jews and other victims of the Nazis. The government of the democratic monarchy that succeeded Franco appointed a commission of economists, led by Enrique Múgica, which filed a 300-page report on 8 April 1998. After a careful search of Spanish records, it absolved Franco's government of having purchased German gold during the war.

As Aceña has explained, "The origins were quite different. These resources stemmed from the Allies and the neutrals." The Germans did use gold in clandestine operations, often changing it into escudos and pesetas in Lisbon, and at the end of the war 1.1 tons of gold was found in the embassy in Madrid, which was turned over to the Allies. Clandestine payments, however, went to individuals and not to the Spanish state, while the German gold bars obtained from the Swiss National Bank, whatever their original provenance, were paid for exports to countries other than Germany. Gold was accepted as payment for exports primarily because the Allies and some others refused to ship the goods in exchange that Spain needed. Directors of the IEME calculated that reserves held in dollars would lose much of their value to wartime inflation, and that the liquidity of gold reserves would make them easy to employ in postwar reconstruction, though such proved not to be the case.[32]

As early as 1943 Allied governments began warning the neutrals not to accept German gold, most of which had been looted, and that it would not be accepted in international payments once the war was over. Even though the Spanish gold had not been obtained from Germany, it was in effect embargoed after the war and could not be used to finance the imports that the Spanish economy desperately needed. The ACC did not complete its investigation of Spanish payments and purchases until 1948, and finally concluded that it could prove acquisition by Spain of a mere 101 kilos of German gold directly, the equivalent of which was handed over by Franco. The Spanish government was then free to use most of the remaining gold as collateral for badly needed loans from New York banks in 1948–49. The gold never returned to Madrid, for repayment was delayed so long that the collateral could never be recovered.[33]

Conclusion

The special relationship between the Germany of Hitler and the Spain of Franco developed as a result of the Spanish Civil War. Though Hitler would later complain that he had been deceived by Franco's representatives and that the communist danger in Spain was not as great as had been described, at the time he had been very pleased with Germany's role in the Spanish conflict and with its political, diplomatic, military, and strategic consequences. This relationship taught the leaders of the Spanish regime to view Germany as the dominant new force in Europe and as the leader in military prowess and technology. Moreover, they saw Nazi Germany as a benevolent influence bent on creating a new order that might help Spain regain the power and prestige that Franco had announced officially as his goal as soon as he became chief of state. It was hoped that German technology and expertise would also be made available for the modernization and expansion of Spanish industry, since industrialization was seen as the motor of the country's economic development.

The relationship sagged somewhat between the end of the Civil War and the fall of France. Hitler had no interest in Spain itself, which he did not see as part of Germany's primary sphere, and the only admirable quality he could find in Spaniards was physical courage. Otherwise, he was a believer in the Black Legend; he abhorred Spanish Catholicism as much as he did bolshevism, and his objective knowledge of the country was nil. Rather than being willing to assist Spain's modernization, he viewed the country as part of the European periphery whose economic relationship to the Third Reich should be semi-colonial; Spain should provide raw materials and absorb any excess industrial products, though such products were in short supply in Hitler's highly militarized economy. Moreover, Germany's goal of deeply penetrating the Spanish economy for its own strategic purposes had been made clear during the Civil War and had been resisted by Franco, though not with complete success. Germany was also much more demanding than Italy with regard to debt payment. Rather than objectively calculating the obvious meaning of all this, together with the Third Reich's dominant values and broader goals, Franco and most regime leaders continued to view Germany in terms of what they saw simply as military superiority and geostrategic advantage. Though they would have preferred a Third Reich less pagan, racist, and extreme, they also preferred to think that the policy of assistance they had experienced in the past would be repeated in the future. The sudden strategic reversal that produced the Nazi-Soviet Pact, followed by outbreak of the European war in 1939, took them by surprise, while the rapid destruction of Catholic and authoritarian Poland, a country friendly to the Spanish regime, was not an agreeable spectacle.

Withal, the new Spanish regime preferred to consider Britain and France, the enemies of Germany, as its traditional foes, responsible for having humiliated Spain in the past and deprived it of its proper imperial role in Africa. The fact that British policy during the Civil War had been rather favorable to Franco was ignored, since that had been accompanied by the usual supercilious British naval tutelage and diplomatic admonitions. France had been on the other side, but in view of its dangerous strategic situation in 1939, it made an increasingly determined effort to win the friendship of the new Spanish regime, an effort that was generally held at arm's length. Even during the period of Spanish neutrality down to June 1940, Madrid's policy was distinctly tilted toward Germany, in the hope that German military success would provide an opportunity to improve Spain's standing at the expense of Britain and France.

Hitler's startling conquest of France convinced Franco—indeed, seems to have convinced most people, at least for the time being—that the Nazi leader had virtually won the war. Certainly he was completely dominant in western continental Europe, and there was intense concern among regime leaders and, at that moment, among virtually the entire military command to join the winning side while there was still time. Beyond that, it should be recognized that during 1940–41 any government in Spain, even a leftist one, would have had to make certain concessions to a victorious Nazi Germany, exactly as did the Social Democratic government of Sweden at that time. The attitude of the Franco regime was not, however, the almost inevitable appeasement normally shown a much stronger power but eagerness to collaborate in military conquest and expansion, which was something quite different. That being the case, Franco's salvation, and that of Spain, was that he refused to proceed in the manner of Mussolini, who had simply plunged in so as to participate in the fall of France, after which the Duce found, to his mortification, that his share of the spoils was minimal, not to say humiliating.

In some ways Franco's policy during 1940–41 was more similar to that of Stalin, something first pointed out by Javier Tusell:

> Undoubtedly Mussolini was more imprudent and grandiose than Franco, the latter having greater scruples (though these seem to have been nonexistent in Serrano) about attacking an adversary without a prior declaration of war. But also decisive for the Spanish Caudillo was the lack of military strength and preparation for taking such a step. Thus it is quite a paradox that Franco's position might be more easily compared with that of Stalin. When Hitler crushed Poland, the USSR intervened only late in the day, obtaining at least as much territory as Germany with scarcely one-twentieth the casualties of the latter. The subsequent occupation of the Baltic countries took advantage of Hitler's victories without any cost. That was the same point at which Franco offered to enter the war, and he undoubtedly wanted to acquire French Morocco in much the same manner as Stalin had acquired those territories.[1]

Indeed, there was more of a parallel between Franco and Stalin in this regard than between the Caudillo and the Duce: both Franco and Stalin hoped to take advantage of Hitler's conquests to expand their own territory on the cheap, without making excessive military commitments of their own.

As Franco said to Serrano Suñer, "Spain cannot enter for fun," but would have to be guaranteed massive military and economic assistance—without which it simply could not operate—as well as enormous territorial concessions in the Maghrib and west Africa. Territory in Africa was the big sticking point, at least at first, for in the autumn of 1940 Hitler could probably have provided, had he wished, sufficient military and economic assistance. Timing is everything, and had the British not seized the initiative in stimulating the Free French movement with the attack on Dakar on 25 September, at the very moment that Serrano was negotiating with Hitler in Berlin, Hitler might have guaranteed Franco sufficient African territory to persuade him to take the plunge before the close of 1940.

Franco, Serrano Suñer, Hitler, and Ribbentrop all went to Hendaye late in October expecting to conclude a deal. The news that Hitler was determined not to alienate Vichy France came as a shock, even though it had already been signaled to the Spanish leaders, and their consternation was simply another indication of their unrealistic expectations. Even so, at that moment they refused to take no for an answer, but for several weeks still hoped and expected to be able to straighten things out; they even attempted to slip recognition of their control of all of Morocco into a supplementary economic protocol, which the Germans rejected. The protocol that was signed, twice, by Serrano pledged Spain to enter the war at a time mutually determined by the two governments, and at some unspecified moment to announce its adherence to both the Italo-German Pact of Steel and the Tripartite Pact with Japan. Though in fact the Spanish government never implemented this agreement by officially joining either pact, the fact remains that no neutral or nonbelligerent government ever went so far in committing itself to the Axis powers.

It was some weeks after the Hendaye meeting that Franco and Serrano began to realize that entry into the war at that time would be a disaster for Spain under any circumstances, even with major German assistance, and by early December told the Germans for the first time that it would have to be postponed. The grave deterioration of economic conditions in Spain during the autumn of 1940 was a major factor, paradoxically a weakness that gave greater strength to Spanish diplomacy. Even so, for two more years the expectation remained that conditions—political, economic, and strategic—would sufficiently improve at some point in the future to make it possible, indeed fully probable, that Spain would enter the war. To quote Tusell once more, "Around May–June 1941 Spanish entry into the war might have occurred, but did not because Hitler shifted the focus of the war to the east. The possibility presented itself once more in the autumn of 1942, but Churchill, against the opinion of the Americans, insisted there be no invasion of Spain, even while some of Franco's own ministers were ready to intervene. . . . One is tempted to say that Spain was never neutral, but on the verge of entering the war during the greater part of the conflict."[2]

To be exact, Spanish policy seems to have been based on the expectation of entering the conflict for approximately thirty months, from June 1940 to December 1942, though the absence of the most crucial Spanish state papers makes it impossible to be absolutely certain regarding the latter date. Only after the success of the Allied invasion of northwest Africa did Franco and his chief associates accept the fact that a clear-cut German victory was not likely, so that there would probably never be any time at which it would be useful for Spain to enter the war. The very opposite was true. Tusell's conclusion seems appropriate: "Spain did not enter World War II not because many of its leaders did not want to but because reality dictated otherwise."[3]

The major counterfactual question is: What difference would it have made if Spain had entered the war in the winter of 1941 and Gibraltar had fallen? The seizure of Gibraltar in itself would not have been decisive, for little traffic was going across the Mediterranean at that time. British forces in Africa had to be supplied by the long route around the Cape of Good Hope or from India, and Britain had the naval resources to continue to do that. Hitler himself later recognized that the fall of Gibraltar alone could not have been decisive. The most important effect might have been political and psychological—a revival of the peace party in Britain—though it seems that Churchill had sufficient support by that time to maintain his policy. The loss of Greece and Crete did not shake it too much, and the loss of Gibraltar might not have, either. The key supply route was not the Mediterranean but the Atlantic, and Hitler never had an adequate strategy for dealing with Atlantic shipping; his main submarine campaign began with too little too late, just as in World War I. Hence the good sense of Franco's urging that the attack on Gibraltar be combined with a German offensive to seize the Suez Canal.

What taking Gibraltar and bringing Spain into the war might have meant, however, was that northwest Africa would have been more effectively sealed against any Allied incursion. The initial opening of a second front might then have had to begin directly with a cross-channel invasion in 1943, with uncertain results, or the invasion of northwest Africa would have had to be replaced by the invasion of a belligerent Spain. The latter operation would probably have sealed the doom of the Franco regime, but, given the difficult geography of the Iberian peninsula, would also have led to a relatively long and difficult campaign. One can construct a scenario in which the entire western front would have remained in stalemate until the first atomic bomb was dropped in 1945 on Germany rather than Japan.[4] Had that been the case, Stalin might well have opted out of the war altogether on Hitler's terms, as he apparently considered on various occasions[5]—always the great fear of Churchill and Roosevelt, and one of the main reasons for their numerous concessions to Stalin. Consequently it might or might not have altered the course of the war, though probably not in so simple a way as Hitler at first imagined.

Even then, the regime maintained its policy of nonbelligerence in favor of Germany, with the prospect of providing whatever practical assistance was still feasible, in the first half of 1943, adopting the goal of mediating some sort of peace that might make it possible for Hitler to concentrate on the annihilation of the Soviet Union, firmly consolidating Germany's position as the dominant, indeed overwhelming, power in continental Europe— a position devoutly believed to be in the best interest of the Spanish regime and of the future of Spain in general. Franco never understood the moral and ideological commitment of the Western Allies to the complete defeat of Nazi Germany, but continued to interpret European relations in terms of traditional balance-of-power concepts, in which case the war between the Western powers made little sense.

Thus it took Jordana an entire year, from the autumn of 1942 to the autumn of 1943, to begin to turn Spanish policy around, the end of non-belligerence conventionally being dated from Franco's rather nonchalant speech of 1 October 1943. Indeed, the very informality of this quasi-announcement indicates that it did not mark any abrupt change of policy but was simply a step in the process of gradual repositioning that had begun in the autumn of 1942. The end of nonbelligerence did not mean that Spain returned to full neutrality, first of all because, as has been seen, at no time had the Spanish regime been completely neutral. Beginning in October 1943 it started to move back into a quasi-neutrality still tilted toward Germany. Jordana was a genuine neutralist, but it was Franco who ultimately determined Spanish policy, and Jordana was able to move him only very slowly, step by step.

Spanish policy toward the Holocaust evolved in much the same way. Though Nazi-style racism was almost unknown in Spain, traditional prejudice against Jews was alive and well, and even tinged with a limited amount of modern anti-Semitism. Franco himself was, as European dictators of that era went, not especially interested in such matters, but Nazi anti-Semitic policy was viewed in Madrid with relative benevolence, an attitude that began to change only as the first reports about the Final Solution reached Spain in the spring of 1942. The Spanish regime by that point had already allowed thousands of Jewish refugees to pass through Spain with no special questions asked, and those who had somehow managed to enter without proper papers were not handed back, once they were fully inside Spanish territory.

The Final Solution first became an issue for Spanish policy with the beginning of the deportation of Jews from occupied France in 1943. Spanish representatives had already provided recognition and at least a certain amount of protection for Sephardic Jews who held Spanish citizenship, and, though the issue had first to be presented by the Germans themselves, the regime slowly and grudgingly took up the issue of repatriation, dragging its feet all the way. It expressed morbid fear that any substantial number of Sephardim might take up residence in Spain, despite the Spanish nationalist rhetoric to the effect that Sephardim lacked the disagreeable qualities of other Jews, having been raised to a higher level by Spanish culture. After much hemming and hawing, repatriation was permitted only in small batches, each new one to be preceded by the removal abroad of those who had arrived earlier, though finally 365 Spanish Jews were rescued directly from Bergen-Belsen. The Spanish consuls in Paris and Athens, as well as certain other Spanish diplomatic representatives elsewhere, had shown much greater humanitarian initiative, but Madrid was slow and reluctant to respond, so that altogether not very many more than a thousand Sephardim with citizenship were repatriated directly to Spain, though in varying degrees and for varying periods many more were protected in German-occupied territory.

The only broader initiative to rescue Jews took place in Budapest during the second half of 1944. By this time German policy had become an enormous international scandal, and there was a more concerted effort by several of the neutrals, particularly Sweden and Switzerland, to intervene in the last great battleground of the deportation of Jews. The Spanish government participated in this effort, though somewhat belatedly, so that much depended on the personal initiative of Sanz Briz in Budapest. The final irony in the long, uncertain record of Spain's dealing with the Holocaust was that the greatest hero of all, in regard to independent initiative and the risks to his own safety that he was willing to run, was not a Spaniard but the Italian Fascist purchasing agent Giorgio Perlasca, who functioned on his own as de facto chargé d'affaires in Budapest during December 1944–January 1945.

Franco's policy toward Germany was also increasingly influenced by internal conditions, not merely the disastrous economic situation but also the severe political divisions. The attitude of his military leaders was cooling considerably by the close of 1940, and not merely because of British bribery, though that presumably played some role. The revival of support for the monarchy in 1942 made Franco increasingly cautious and further inhibited his willingness to run risks abroad. Though the external opposition had been crushed, the internal discord within the Spanish regime was greater during World War II than at any time before or after. Franco always seemed imperturbably complacent, but this was not in fact the case; he faced greater challenges in his efforts to hold his regime together during the World War than during the Civil War.

The significance of Spain for Hitler was strategic and economic, and the latter aspect lasted longer than the former. He pressed the idea of Spain's entry into the war for little more than six months, though it apparently entered his mind from time to time later on. Economic concerns proved more enduring, and later a third factor entered as well, the political or psychological significance of having a friend, however militarily weak, in southwestern Europe. The Abwehr had an interest in Spain as a forward listening post and so did the German navy, which viewed Spain as a possible shelter for an eastern Atlantic base, but these were secondary concerns.

Hitler's interest in Spain's participation developed in August 1940, for two reasons. One was Britain's refusal to make peace and the resultant need to place greater strategic pressure on Britain, the other a related but not identical concern to seal the Mediterranean, northwest Africa, and the east Atlantic from the United States, which he thought might either use them to come to Britain's aid, take some of them for itself, or both. In 1940 Hitler did not as yet seek any quarrel with the United States, something he preferred to postpone. There were Nazi weapon plans for the future struggle for world power, with such designs as the Amerikabomber and the naval Z-Plan, both of which briefly went back on schedule in mid-1940, but these plans would require years to develop. Hitler saw correctly, however, that the Roosevelt administration would prepare itself to take action against Germany as rapidly as circumstances permitted. It was not exactly that Hitler was getting ahead of himself in his strategic plans so much as that his involvement in war with Britain had created a complex strategic situation that he had not planned and had to struggle with, as it turned out unsuccessfully.

Neither the Germans nor the Spanish lied to each other, but they nonetheless misled each other, each overemphasizing the other's positive words and gestures. The Spanish were determined to evaluate any sign of German support in a potentially grand manner, while the Germans, perhaps not altogether surprisingly, understood the effusive Spanish statements of support and identity with the German cause and eagerness to enter the war as indications of a Spanish disposition that could easily be activated.

When Franco, Serrano, and many others assured the Germans that they were wholeheartedly on the German side, they were sincere. Franco did not mean, however, a willingness to intervene à la Mussolini, which was how Hitler interpreted it. Hitler, for his part, could for a period have induced Franco to enter the war by sending supplies and providing an ambiguous pledge about Morocco, but he refused to deceive Franco in that way. At first he did not think it necessary, and later did not think it worth the potential trouble, as his attention shifted more and more toward the east. Southern Europe was never a primary concern, but a region into which Hitler moved only after his only significant ally had gotten into major trouble.

Mussolini's attitude toward Franco was rather more benevolent, even though after the end of the Civil War it amounted to little in the way of policy convergence. Italy did not have such extensive economic goals in Spain as did Germany, nor was it in a position to propose joint military action, while in Algeria the expansionist aims of Mussolini and Franco tended to collide. The Italian government did not make a major effort to bring Spain into the war, taking up the matter halfheartedly only at Hitler's request in February 1941, then proposing it as a desperation gesture two years later when even Hitler realized that it was not realistic. Ironically, the main influence of Italy on Spain during the war was that exercised by the collapse of the Fascists in July 1943, which soon prompted Spain to begin to lean away from fascism. The much greater political similarity between the Italian and Spanish systems and the relatively cordial personal feelings between their leaders, quite different in kind from those between the Germans and the Spanish, did not produce the same potential for direct military collaboration.

Even after Spain's flirtation with fascism began to wane, during the first months of 1944 the regime tried to cling to its special relationship with Germany, hoping to remain the "last friend" whose faithfulness would be rewarded by special recognition from a postwar Germany, which, even if technically defeated, would somehow manage to preserve its Great Power status. That such an attitude persisted for most of the first half of 1944 is one indication of the extent of the miscalculation, for by that time Franco had drawn Hitler's contempt. As long as there was any chance for Nazi survival, Franco did not want to have to trust the future of his regime to a Western Europe dominated by the Allies.

Ultimately, the main concern of both sides in the war regarding the Iberian peninsula was preemptive and negative—the goal of maintaining enough influence, suasion, or military pressure not so much to occupy it for themselves as to make certain that it was denied to the other side. The danger of an invasion of Spain by either side was not nonexistent, for each had contingency plans to move into the peninsula, but in each case the concern was defensive and preemptive, to be triggered only by aggressive action by the enemy. On the one hand, foreign invasion was a threat to be taken seriously, but on the other, at no time was it a likely or overwhelming danger, to the extent of dominating Spanish policy considerations. The tilt toward the Allies that finally began to develop in mid-1944 was a consequence simply of the mounting strategic and economic predominance of the Anglo-Americans.

Rather than reflecting prudence, Franco's policy managed to earn the condemnation of most other governments, ranging from the Germans to the British to the Americans to the French and even the Portuguese, who had reason to fear a possible Spanish invasion in conjunction with the Axis during 1940–41. Only the Italians and some Latin American politicians were more positive in their evaluation.

Franco's greatest achievement during the war was to have solidified his regime internally, for his economic policy was disastrous and his foreign policy often imprudent, ingenuous, and at times megalomaniacal. He was for long convinced that the survival of his regime depended on a German victory, but his future might have been more bleak had Hitler won. Franco eventually won Hitler's contempt, and if an astounding change of fortune had given Germany victory, the Führer might well have made good his threat to have Franco overthrown.[6] Conversely, the heavy-handed pressure of the economic warfare that the United States and Great Britain waged against Franco's regime in 1944, though stubbornly resisted for months, pushed him into changes that would make it possible for him to survive, as he would slowly shed his fascistic policies and, however slowly and grudgingly, adopt more moderate and pragmatic characteristics that enabled his regime to survive and eventually for a time even to prosper. The armed insurgency mounted first by the Communists in October 1944 and then by the anarchists actually proved a boon to the regime, for it raised the specter of reopening the Civil War and replacing a rightist dictatorship with a revolutionary regime, which encouraged moderate and conservative opinion to rally behind Franco. Numerous historiographic attempts to glamorize the insurgency of the maquis should not be allowed to obscure this reality.

All the other neutrals, even Portugal, pursued more productive economic strategies during the war, so that at its end, Spain remained economically almost prostrate and internationally nearly isolated. It was by far the worst economic and political performance of any of the neutrals,[7] and after the war would take longer to rectify. For much of the 1940s, health indices for the general population would remain distinctly lower than before the Civil War, while the economy continued to suffer from grave structural problems, poor social integration, and highly defective state policies.[8] Even Turkey, the only other country whose policy was almost as sinuous, came out of the war in better shape. The 1940s were to a large extent a lost decade for Spain, and the heritage of civil war and revolution was only partly to blame; disastrously flawed policies were more important. The initial policies of the regime had nearly led to disaster, though the new political formula devised by the very end of the war would enable it to survive, something that, paradoxically, only Hitler's defeat may have made possible.

José Varela Ortega has emphasized that, quite ironically, though Franco thought that his survival depended on Hitler, it more nearly depended on Stalin. What Hitler perceived as the Soviet threat drew him away from the Mediterranean, where he would otherwise have coerced and dominated Spain—undoubtedly to its perdition, one way or the other—and toward a massive commitment to the eastern front. The capacity of the Soviet regime to resist and to prosecute the war meant that, fortunately for Franco and for Spain, the Mediterranean would remain a secondary front. Then, once the war was over, Stalin's fixation on Soviet expansionism guaranteed the onset of the Cold War, which then made possible the rehabilitation of the regime and its relative stability and even long-term prosperity.[9]

In one sense, Franco was correct in believing that the victory of the Allies in the west would be fatal for his regime, but only in the very long run. If the restoration of democracy in the west were fully successful, as indeed it proved to be, Spain would also have to come to terms with democracy, but since the restoration and expansion of democracy was a long-term development that was accompanied by long-lasting hostility between the two surviving superpowers, the Cold War would give the regime a breathing space that would last as long as Franco's life, though not beyond it.

Notes

Chapter 1. The Spanish Civil War

1. Alexis de Tocqueville observed this process very clearly in the case of pre-revolutionary France: "Thus it was precisely in those parts of France where there had been the most improvement that popular discontent ran highest. This may seem illogical—but history is full of paradoxes. For it is not always when things are going from bad to worse that a revolution breaks out. . . . Thus the social order overthrown by a revolution is almost always better than the one preceding it": *The Old Regime and the French Revolution* (Garden City, N.Y., 1955), 176. (My thanks to Juan Linz for this reference.)

2. The political convulsions of the Republic have generated an extensive literature. Abundant references may be found in two of my works, *Spain's First Democracy: The Second Republic, 1931–1936* (Madison, 1993) and *The Collapse of the Spanish Republic, 1933–1936: Origins of the Civil War* (New Haven, 2006).

3. B. Bolloten called the disguise a "grand camouflage": *The Grand Camouflage* (New York, 1961).

4. C. M. Rama, *La crisis española del siglo XX* (Mexico City, 1960).

5. On the West European democracies and the Spanish war, see M. Alpert, *A New International History of the Spanish Civil War* (London, 1997); E. Moradiellos, *La perfidia de Albión: El gobierno británico y la guerra civil española* (Madrid, 1996) and *El reñidero de Europa: Las dimensiones internacionales de la guerra civil española* (Barcelona, 2001); J. Avilés Farré, *Pasión y farsa: Franceses y británicos ante la guerra civil española* (Madrid, 1994); S. Balfour and P. Preston, eds., *Spain and the Great Powers in the Twentieth Century* (London, 1999); T. Buchanan, *Britain and the Spanish Civil War* (Cambridge, 1997); M. Casanova, *La diplomacia española durante la Guerra Civil* (Madrid, 1996); C. Leitz and D. J. Dunthorn, eds., *Spain in an International Context, 1936–1959* (New York, 1999); W. L. Kleine-Ahlbrandt, *The Policy of Simmering: A Study of British Policy during the Spanish Civil War, 1936–1939* (The Hague, 1962); J. Martínez Parrilla, *Las fuerzas armadas francesas ante la guerra civil española (1936–1939)* (Madrid, 1987); M. Thomas, *Britain, France and Ap-*

peasement: Anglo-French Relations in the Popular Front Era (Oxford, 1996); and J. Tusell et al., eds., *La política exterior de España en el siglo XX* (Madrid, 2000).

6. Soviet intervention and Communist policy remain the most controversial political problem of the Civil War. See R. Radosh, M. Habeck, and G. Sevostianov, eds., *Spain Betrayed: The Soviet Union in the Spanish Civil War* (New Haven, 2001); A. Elorza and M. Bizcarrondo, *Queridos camaradas: La Internacional Comunista y España, 1919–1939* (Barcelona, 1999); D. Kowalsky, *La Unión Soviética y la guerra civil española: Una revisión crítica* (Barcelona, 2003); S. G. Payne, *The Spanish Civil War, the Soviet Union, and Communism* (New Haven, 2004); and F. Schauff, *Der verspielte Krieg: Sowjetunion, Kommunistische Internationale und spanischer Bürgerkrieg, 1936–1939* (Frankfurt am Mein, 2004).

7. Cf. J. Babiano Mora, "España, 1936–1939: La segunda guerra de la independencia," *Historia 16* 17:190 (February 1992), 25–34.

8. Manuel Azaña, diary entry for 13 Aug. 1931, in his *Obras completas* (Mexico City, 1964), 2:121.

9. Of the many biographies of Franco, the best is P. Preston, *Franco: A Biography* (London, 1993); the best pro-Franco account is R. de la Cierva, *Franco: La historia* (Madrid, 2000).

10. Quoted in J. Palacios, *La España totalitaria: Las raíces del franquismo, 1934–1946* (Barcelona, 1999), 17–19, 41, 71. The proclamation was first published in Las Palmas (Gran Canaria) on 21 July 1936 and has been subsequently much reproduced, usually cited incorrectly as being delivered in Tetuán, the headquarters in Morocco.

11. First published in Spanish in *Ideario del Generalísimo*, ed. J. García Mercadal (Zaragoza, 1937), 42–43.

12. Maistre himself did not favor such an extreme form of counterrevolution, but preferred to return to the Old Regime as nearly as possible. Cf. R. A. Lebrun, ed., *Joseph de Maistre's Life, Thought, and Influence: Selected Studies* (Montreal, 2001).

13. The best treatment of Franco and the origins of the regime during the Civil War is J. Tusell, *Franco en la guerra civil* (Barcelona, 1992). See also Preston, *Franco*, 120–322; S. G. Payne, *The Franco Regime, 1936–1975* (Madison, 1987), 87–228; I. Saz Campos, *Fascismo y franquismo* (Valencia, 2004), 79–150; and J. Tusell et al., eds., *El régimen de Franco (1936–1975)*, 2 vols. (Madrid, 1993).

On the FET, J. M. Thomàs, *Lo que fue la Falange* (Barcelona, 1999) and *La Falange de Franco: Fascismo y fascistización en el régimen de Franco, 1937–1945* (Barcelona, 2001), 15–167; J. L. Rodríguez Jiménez, *Historia de Falange Española de las JONS* (Madrid, 2000), 229–333; and S. G. Payne, *Fascism in Spain, 1923–1977* (Madison, 1999), 239–309. J. L. Orella, *La formación del Estado nacional durante la Guerra Civil española* (Madrid, 2001), correctly emphasizes the rightist and neotraditionalist aspects of the new state. The entire gigantic bibliography dealing with Falangism may be found in J. Díaz Nieva and E. Uribe Lacalle, eds., *El yugo y las letras: Bibliografía de, desde y sobre el nacionalsindicalismo* (Madrid, 2005).

14. The role of Catholicism is studied in J. M. Sánchez, *The Spanish Civil War as a Religious Tragedy* (Notre Dame, 1987); A. Alvarez Bolado, *Para ganar la guerra, para ganar la paz: Iglesia y guerra civil, 1936–1939* (Madrid, 1995); G. Redondo, *La Guerra Civil (1936–1939)*, vol. 2 of his *Historia de la Iglesia en España, 1931–1939* (Madrid, 1993); H. Raguer, *La pólvora y el incienso: La Iglesia y la guerra civil española;* J. A. Tello, *Ideología política: La Iglesia católica española, 1936–1959* (Zaragoza, 1984); and M. L. Rodríguez Aisa, *El cardenal Gomá y la guerra de España* (Madrid, 1981). On the conflict within the regime, see A. Ferrari, *El franquismo: Minorías políticas y conflictos ideológicos, 1936–1956* (Pamplona, 1993); J. Andrés-Gallego, *¿Fascismo o Estado católico? Ideología, religión y censura en la España de Franco, 1937–1941* (Madrid, 1997); J. Andrés-Gallego, A. M. Pazos, and L. de

Llera, *Los españoles entre la religión y la política: El franquismo y la democracia* (Madrid, 1996), 17–73; and G. Redondo, *Política, cultura y sociedad en la España de Franco (1939–1947)* (Pamplona, 1999).

15. R. Chueca, *El fascismo en los comienzos del régimen de Franco: Un estudio sobre FET-JONS* (Madrid, 1983), 311, and J. J. Linz, "From Falange to Movimiento-Organización," in *Authoritarian Politics in Modern Society*, ed. S. P. Huntington and C. H. Moore (New Haven, 1970), 167.

16. On the construction of the syndical system, see M. A. Aparicio, *El sindicalismo vertical y la formación del Estado franquista* (Barcelona, 1980).

17. There is a very great literature in Spanish on the Franco regime. Nearly all the multivolume histories of Spain devote considerable space to it, the most extensive being R. Carr, ed., *La época de Franco (1939–1975)*, vol. 41 of *Historia de España*, ed. R. Menéndez Pidal and J. M. Jover (Madrid, 1996). Individual one-volume accounts include my *The Franco Regime, 1936–1975* (Madrid, 1987); R. Moreno Fonseret and F. Sevillano Calero, eds., *El franquismo: Visiones y balances* (Alicante, 1999); and J. Zafra Valverde, *El sistema político en las décadas Franco* (Madrid, 2004), among others. A. Cazorla Sánchez, *Las políticas de la victoria: La consolidación del Nuevo Estado franquista (1938–1953)* (Madrid, 2000), treats the consolidation of the regime in its relation to society. In addition, many specialized volumes deal with *el primer franquismo*, as the first general phase of the regime is usually termed, particularly in the form of regional, provincial, and sometimes even municipal studies, far too numerous to be cited here. The theories of Falangism are treated in J. A. López García, *Estado y derecho en el franquismo: El nacionalsindicalismo: F. J. Conde y Luis Legaz Lacambra* (Madrid, 1996), and I. Saz Campos, *España contra España: Los nacionalismos franquistas* (Madrid, 2003).

18. The economic history of the Civil War has been much less studied than other aspects. A good introduction may be found in J. A. Sánchez Asiaín, *Economía y finanzas en la Guerra Civil española (1936–1939)* (Madrid, 1999), though P. Martín Aceña and E. Martínez Ruiz, eds., *La economía de la guerra civil* (Madrid, 2006), provides broader coverage.

19. The public expression of aspects of this new style is treated in G. di Febo, *Ritos de guerra y de victoria en la España franquista* (Bilbao, 2002).

20. J. Marías, *Ser español: Ideas y creencias en el mundo hispánico* (Barcelona, 2000), 264. Marías adds: "*The justly defeated; the unjustly victorious.* This formula, which I enunciated many years later, sums up in six words my final opinion about the Civil War. It might, I believe, express the feelings of those who had supported the Republic." In this regard, it should be remembered that Marías himself was briefly imprisoned by the regime after the end of the Civil War and endured persecution for many years, as he recounts in chap. 17 of his *Una vida presente: Memorias*, vol. 1 (Madrid, 1988).

21. There are no definitive general studies of the repressions during the Civil War, but see R. Salas Larrazábal, *Pérdidas de la guerra* (Barcelona, 1977); S. Juliá, ed., *Víctimas de la guerra civil* (Madrid, 1999); and A. D. Martín Rubio, *Los mitos de la represión en la guerra civil* (Madrid, 2005).

22. The most reliable studies are those of J. Ruiz, "A Spanish Genocide? Reflections on the Francoist Repression after the Spanish Civil War," *Contemporary European History* 14: 2 (2005), 171–91, and *Franco's Justice: Repression in Madrid after the Spanish Civil War* (Oxford, 2005). Ruiz argues for a higher total of executions but provides no convincing data to support it.

23. From around 2000 there began to appear a large volume of new studies and writings concerning Francoist repression, especially after the close of the Civil War, accompanied by a lesser volume of new writings about the Republican repression. Some of the more notable of the former include "La represión bajo el franquismo," *Ayer* 43 (2001), and

"Los campos de concentración franquistas en el contexto europeo," *Ayer* 57 (2005); M. Armengou and R. Belis, *Las fosas del silencio: ¿Hay un Holocausto español?* (Barcelona, 2004); J. Casanova et al., *Morir, matar, sobrevivir: La violencia en la dictadura de Franco* (Barcelona, 2002); I. Lafuente, *Esclavos por la patria: La explotación de los presos bajo el franquismo* (Madrid, 2001); M. Núñez Díaz-Balart, *Los años del terror: La estrategia de dominio y represión del general Franco* (Madrid, 2004); M. Núñez Díaz-Balart and A. Rojas Friend, *Consejos de guerra: Los fusilamientos en el Madrid de la postguerra (1939–1945)* (Madrid, 1997); J. Rodrigo, *Los campos de concentración franquistas* (Madrid, 2003); F. Sevillano Calero, *Exterminio: El terror con Franco* (Madrid, 2004); E. Silva and S. Macías, *Las fosas de Franco* (Madrid, 2003); and E. Silva et al., eds., *La memoria de los olvidados: Un debate sobre el silencio de la represión franquista* (Valladolid, 2004).

24. On the policy of repression see M. Richards, *A Time of Silence: Civil War and the Culture of Repression in Franco's Spain, 1936–1945* (Cambridge, 1998). On censorship and the purging of personnel see J. Sinova, *La censura de prensa durante el franquismo* (Madrid, 1989); F. Morente Valero, *La depuración del Magisterio Nacional (1936–1943)* (Madrid, 2000); A. Mayordomo and J. M. Fernández Soria, *Vencer y convencer: Educación y política: España, 1936–1945* (Valencia, 1993); R. Navarro Sandalinas, *La enseñanza primaria durante el franquismo (1936–1975)* (Barcelona, 1990); and M. Lanero Táboas, *Una milicia de la justicia: La política judicial del franquismo (1936–1945)* (Madrid, 1996).

25. R. Tamames, *La República: La era de Franco* (Madrid, 1973), 498.

26. M. Jerez Mir, *Elites políticas y centros de extracción en España, 1938–1957* (Madrid, 1982), 230. See also C. Viver Pi-Sunyer, *El personal político de Franco (1936–1945)* (Barcelona, 1978), and, on the intermediate level of officials, G. Sánchez Recio, *Los cuadros políticos intermedios del régimen franquista, 1936–1959* (Valencia, 1996).

27. On the military under Franco, see G. Cardona, *El gigante descalzo: El ejército de Franco* (Madrid, 2003); M. A. Baquer, *Franco y sus generales* (Madrid, 2005); and J. C. Losada Malvárez, *Ideología del ejército franquista, 1939–1959* (Madrid, 1990).

Chapter 2. Hitler's Strategy in the Civil War

1. *Hitler's Table Talk, 1941–1944: His Private Conversations* (New York, 2000), 33, 46, 667.

2. For the broader historical background of German-Spanish relations, see C. Kent, T. K. Wolber, and C. M. K. Hewitt, eds., *The Lion and the Eagle: Interdisciplinary Essays on German-Spanish Relations over the Centuries* (New York, 2000).

3. A. Viñas, *Franco, Hitler y el estallido de la Guerra Civil: Antecedentes y consecuencias* (Madrid, 2001), 85–112, provides full references.

4. I. Schulze Schneider, "La propaganda alemana en la Segunda República española," *Historia y Comunicación Social* 4 (1999), 183–97.

5. See Viñas, *Franco, Hitler,* 113–267, and also C. Vidal, *Intrépidos y sucios: Los españoles vistos por Hitler* (Barcelona, 1996), 29–52.

6. G. Palomares Lerma, *Mussolini y Primo de Rivera: Política exterior de dos dictadores* (Madrid, 1989); J. Tusell and I. Saz, "Mussolini y Primo de Rivera: Las relaciones políticas y diplomáticas de dos dictaduras mediterráneas," *Boletín de la Real Academia de la Historia* 179 (1982), 413–83; and also S. Sueiro Seoane, *España en el Mediterráneo: Primo de Rivera y la "cuestión marroquí," 1923–1930* (Madrid, 1992).

7. V. Peña Sánchez, *Intelectuales y fascismo: La cultura italiana del "ventennio fascista" y su repercusión en España* (Granada, 1995).

8. On the relations between Fascist Italy and the radical right in Spain, see I. Saz

Campos, *Mussolini contra la II República: Hostilidad, conspiraciones, intervención (1931–1936)* (Valencia, 1986).

9. On the long but sometimes troubled relationship between Hitler and Mussolini prior to 1936, see R. De Felice, *Hitler e Mussolini: I rapporti segreti (1922–1933)* (Florence, 1983); K.-P. Hoepke, *Die deutsche Rechte und der italienische Faschismus* (Düsseldorf, 1968); G. Bortolotto, *Fascismo e nazionalsocialismo* (Bologna, 1933); E. Schrewe, *Faschismus und Nazionalsozialismus* (Hamburg, 1934); M. T. Florinsky, *Fascism and National Socialism* (New York, 1936); and R. Quartararo, *Roma tra Londra e Berlino: La politica estera fascista dal 1930 al 1940* (Rome, 1980). The Italian Fascist polemic against Nazism in 1934 and the effort to create a non-Nazi Italian Fascist international association of movements are treated in D. M. Smith, *Mussolini's Roman Empire* (New York, 1976), 44–58; M. A. Ledeen, *Universal Fascism* (New York, 1972); and M. Cuzzi, *L'internazionale delle camicie nere: I CAUR, Comitati d'azione per l'universalità di Roma, 1933–1939* (Milan, 2005).

10. H. de la Torre Gómez, *A relação peninsular na antecâmara da guerra civil de Espanha (1931–1936)* (Lisbon, 1998), 93–94.

11. This is the convincing conclusion of Viñas, *Franco, Hitler,* 269–334, the definitive study of Hitler's decision to intervene in Spain.

12. Detailed discussions of German policy will be found in the principal studies: in addition to Viñas, R. H. Whealey, *Hitler and Spain: The Nazi Role in the Spanish Civil War* (Lexington, Ky., 1989); M. Merkes, *Die deutsche Politik gegenüber dem spanischen Bürgerkrieg, 1936–1939,* 2nd ed. (Bonn, 1969); and H.-H. Abendroth, *Hitler in der spanischen Arena: Die deutsch-spanischen Beziehungen im Spannungsfeld der europäischeinteressen Politik vom Ausbruch des Bürgerkrieges bis zum Ausbruch des Weltkrieges, 1936–1939* (Paderborn, 1973).

13. The classic studies of Mussolini in this period are R. De Felice, *Mussolini il duce,* 2 vols. (Turin, 1974–81), 1:323–808 and 2:3–466. The best account of his foreign policy in these years is R. Mallett, *Mussolini and the Origins of the Second World War, 1933–1940* (London, 2003).

14. On the decision to intervene, see P. Preston, "Mussolini's Spanish Adventure from Limited Risk to War," in P. Preston and A. L. Mackenzie, *The Republic Besieged: Civil War in Spain, 1936–1939* (Edinburgh, 1996), 1–51. The principal study of the Italian intervention is J. F. Coverdale, *Italian Intervention in the Spanish Civil War* (Princeton, 1975). See also G. Di Febo and R. Moro, eds., *Fascismo e franchismo: Relazioni, immagini, rappresentazioni* (Catanzaro, 2005); the collective work *Italia y la guerra civil española* (Madrid, 1986); and I. Saz Campos and J. Tusell, *Fascistas en España: La intervención italiana en la guerra civil a través de los telegramas de la "Missione Militare in Spagna"* (Madrid, 1981).

15. F. W. Deakin's term: *The Brutal Friendship* (London, 1962).

16. The principal study of these efforts will be found in M. Heiberg, *Emperadores del Mediterráneo: Franco, Mussolini y la guerra civil española* (Barcelona, 2003), 149–67.

17. Quoted in A. Viñas, *La Alemania nazi y el 18 de julio* (Madrid, 1977), 363.

18. Quoted in Whealey, *Hitler and Spain,* 54–55.

19. Ibid., 60.

20. Both quotations are from Merkes, *Die deutsche Politik,* 112–13.

21. On economic relations between the two states during the Civil War, see particularly C. Leitz, *Economic Relations between Nazi Germany and Franco's Spain, 1936–1945* (Oxford, 1996), 8–90, and also G. T. Harper, *German Economic Policy in Spain during the Spanish Civil War, 1936–1939* (The Hague, 1967), and R. García Pérez, *Franquismo y Tercer Reich: Las relaciones económicas hispano-alemanas durante la Segunda Guerra Mundial* (Madrid, 1994), 43–89.

22. *Documents on German Foreign Policy* (Washington, D.C., 1950), D, 3:884–86.

Chapter 3. Military and International Significance of the Civil War

1. The military aspects of the German intervention are treated in R. H. Whealey, *Hitler and Spain: The Nazi Role in the Spanish Civil War* (Lexington, Ky., 1989); R. Aria Ramos, *El apoyo militar alemán a Franco: La Legión Cóndor en la Guerra Civil* (Madrid, 2003); R. Hidalgo Salazar, *La ayuda alemana a España, 1936–1939* (Madrid, 1975); L. Molina Franco, *El legado de Sigfrido: La ayuda militar alemana al Ejército y a la Marina Nacional en la Guerra Civil Española (1936–1939)* (Valladolid, 2005), *El legendario cañón antiaéreo de 88 mm* (Valladolid, 1991), and, with J. M. Manrique García, *Las armas de la Guerra Civil* (Madrid, 2006), *Los hombres de von Thoma: El Ejército alemán en la Guerra de España (1936–39)* (Valladolid, 2005), and *Legión Cóndor. La historia olvidada* (Valladolid, 2000); A. Mortera Pérez and J. L. Infiesta Pérez, *La artillería en la Guerra Civil: Material de origen alemán importado por el bando nacional* (Valladolid, 1996); and R. P. Proctor, *Hitler's Luftwaffe in the Spanish Civil War* (Westport, Conn., 1983).

2. The Italian military intervention is treated in E. Chiappa, *Il Corpo di Truppe Volontarie italiano durante la Guerra Civile spagnola, 1936–1939* (Milan, 1999); W. C. Frank Jr., "Naval Operations in the Spanish Civil War, 1936–1939," *Naval War College Review* 37:1 (January–February 1984), 24–55; J. L. de Mesa, *El regreso de las Legiones (La ayuda militar italiana a la España Nacional, 1936–1939)* (Granada, 1994); F. Pedriali, *Guerra di Spagna e aviazione italiana* (Rome, 1992); G. Rochat, *Le guerre italiane, 1935–1943: Dall'impero d'Etiopia alla disfatta* (Turin, 2005), 98–141; B. Sullivan, "Fascist Italy's Military Involvement in the Spanish Civil War," *Journal of Military History* 59 (October 1995), 697–727; and especially A. Rovighi and F. Stefani, *La partecipazione italiana alla guerra civile spagnola (1936–1939)*, 2 vols. (Rome, 1993).

3. For the role of the Italian navy, see F. Bargoni, *L'impegno navale italiano durante la guerra civile spagnola (1936–1939)* (Rome, 1992), and, more broadly, R. Mallett, *The Italian Navy and Fascist Expansionism, 1935–1940* (London, 1998).

4. Soviet military intervention is treated in G. Howson, *Arms for Spain: The Untold Story of the Spanish Civil War* (London, 1998); D. Kowalsky, *La Unión Soviética y la guerra civil española: Una revisión crítica* (Barcelona, 2003); S. G. Payne, *The Spanish Civil War, the Soviet Union, and Communism* (New Haven, 2004); R. Radosh, M. R. Habeck, and G. Sevostianov, eds., *Spain Betrayed: The Soviet Union in the Spanish Civil War* (New Haven, 2001); and J. Salas Larrazábal, *Intervención extranjera en la guerra de España* (Madrid, 1974).

5. This is perhaps best brought out in John Mosier's revisionist *The Myth of the Great War: A New Military History of World War I* (New York, 2002). For one major aspect of this development, see M. R. Habeck, *Storm of Steel: The Development of Armor Doctrine in Germany and the Soviet Union, 1919–1939* (Ithaca, 2003).

6. The Jefatura del Aire's pamphlet *Cooperación de la aviación con el ejército* (Salamanca, 1937) was rudimentary, but the Nationalists learned to improve with practice.

7. Habeck, *Storm of Steel*, 344, 345, and "Dress Rehearsals, 1937–1941," in *The Military History of the Soviet Union*, ed. R. Higham and F. W. Kagan (London, 2000), 93–108.

8. The Soviets' thoroughness in this regard has been studied by the Russian artillery officer and military historian Yurii Rybalkin, *Operatsiia "Kh": Sovetskaiia voennaiia pomoshch respublikanskoi Ispanii (1936–1939)* (Moscow, 2000), 82–89, 104–28.

9. Though this was not the conclusion of the principal published French study of the war, General Maurice Duval's *Les leçons de la guerre d'Espagne* (Paris, 1938), translated by Michael Chapman as *Lessons of the War in Spain* (Reading, Mass., 2006).

10. For a further catalog, see Whealey, *Hitler and Spain*, 101–8.

11. P. Renouvin, *Histoire des relations internationales* (Paris, 1965), 8:112.

12. These three citations have been taken from the excellent discussion by W. C. Frank Jr., "The Spanish Civil War and the Coming of the Second World War," *International History Review* 9:3 (August 1987), 367–409.

13. A more distant parallel might be found in the French revolution of 1848, which also broke out under a liberal (though not democratic) regime and was to some extent fueled by a revolution of rising expectations stemming from the accelerated development of France during the 1840s.

14. Frank, "Spanish Civil War."

15. For further discussion, see, in addition to Frank's "Spanish Civil War," M. Habeck, "The Spanish Civil War and the Origins of the Second World War," in *The Origins of the Second World War Reconsidered*, ed. G. Martel, 2nd ed. (London, 1999), 204–24.

Chapter 4. A Tilted Neutrality

1. E. González Calleja and F. Limón Nevado, *La Hispanidad como instrumento de combate: Raza e imperio en la prensa franquista durante la guerra civil española* (Madrid, 1988).

2. Nationalism and pragmatism were stressed in C. Barcia Trelles, *Puntos cardinales de la política exterior de España*, published in Madrid during the summer of 1939. Brief overviews of the regime's foreign policy may be found in J. M. Armero, *La política exterior de Franco* (Barcelona, 1978), and in J. Tusell et al., eds., *La política exterior de España en el siglo XX* (Madrid, 2000), chaps. 10–14. C. Almira Picazo, *¡Viva España! El nacionalismo fundacional del régimen de Franco, 1939–1943* (Granada, 1998), seeks to define the nationalism of these years.

3. Serrano's speeches in Italy are collected in his *De la victoria y la postguerra (discursos)* (Madrid, 1941), and he has commented on this trip in H. Saña, *El franquismo sin mitos: Conversaciones con Serrano Suñer* (Barcelona, 1982), 135–39.

4. *Documents secrets du Ministère des Affaires Etrangères d'Allemagne* (Brussels, 1946), 3:23, 66–68; *Daily Express* (London), 19 June 1939; *Diário de Norte* (Porto), 24 June 1939. There is extensive treatment in R. H. Whealey, "German-Spanish Relations, January–August 1939" (Ph.D. diss., University of Michigan, 1963), 177–92.

5. This document has disappeared, but it was summarized in a report by Ambassador Eberhard von Stohrer, 2 July 1939, in *Documents on German Foreign Policy* (Washington, D.C., 1950), D, 6:605 (hereafter cited as *DGFP*).

6. These contacts and speculations are detailed in R. H. Whealey, *Hitler and Spain: The Nazi Role in the Spanish Civil War* (Lexington, Ky., 1989), 114–34.

7. This schedule would be met in full in increasingly inflated currency, the final modest installment being completed exactly on schedule on 30 June 1967.

8. Quoted in L. Suárez Fernández, *Francisco Franco y su tiempo* (Madrid, 1984), 3:53.

9. R. García Pérez, *Franquismo y Tercer Reich: Las relaciones económicas hispano-alemanas durante la Segunda Guerra Mundial* (Madrid, 1994), 100–104, and C. Leitz, *Economic Relations between Nazi Germany and Franco's Spain, 1936–1945* (Oxford, 1996), 108–11.

10. The only studies are C. R. Halstead, "A 'Somewhat Machiavellian' Face: Colonel Juan Beigbeder as High Commissioner in Spanish Morocco, 1937–1939," *Historian* 37:1 (1974), and "Un 'Africain' Méconnu: Le Colonel Juan Beigbeder," *Revue d'Histoire de la Deuxième Guerre Mondiale* 83 (July 1971), 31–60; and J. Tusell, "Los cuatro ministros de asuntos exteriores de Franco durante la Segunda Guerra Mundial," in *Espacio, Tiempo y Forma*, ser. 5, Historia Contemporánea, vol. 7: 311–56.

11. Complaints on this score were still being received in Madrid as late as the spring of 1940, as in the letter of the military attaché Colonel Antonio Barroso to Colonel Francisco Salgado Araujo, head of Franco's Casa Militar, 16 April 1940, in archives of the Fundación Nacional Francisco Franco (hereafter cited as FNFF), file 103, doc. 4469.

12. Quoted in J. Tusell, *Franco, España y la II Guerra Mundial: Entre el Eje y la neutralidad* (Madrid, 1995), 46. This key work remains the fundamental study of Spanish diplomacy in World War II. The principal defense of Franco's wartime policy may be found in L. Suárez, *España, Franco y la Segunda Guerra Mundial: Desde 1939 hasta 1945* (Madrid, 1997). W. Bowen, *Spain during World War II* (Columbia, Mo., 2006), provides the only general account of Spain during the war years, beyond those in multivolume general histories.

13. J. Tusell and G. García Queipo de Llano, *Franco y Mussolini* (Barcelona, 1985), 46–49.

14. Generally speaking, in Poland the left and right split in the standard way over the Spanish war, but the right held power. See M. J. Chodakiewicz and J. Radzilowski, *Spanish Carlism and Polish Nationalism: The Borderlands of Europe in the 19th and 20th Centuries* (Charlottesville, 2003), 51–117.

15. A. Dallin and F. I. Firsov, eds., *Dimitrov and Stalin, 1934–1943: Letters from the Archives* (New Haven, 2000), 151–65.

16. *Arriba* (Madrid), 2 October 1939.

17. FNFF, file 103, docs. 4492, 4493, 4489.

18. J. L. de Mesa, *Voluntarios extranjeros desconocidos en el Bando Nacional durante la Guerra Civil (1936–1939)* (Madrid, 1998), 186–87.

19. On the creation of the AEM, see M. Heiberg and M. Ros Agudo, *La trama oculta de la guerra civil: Los servicios secretos de Franco, 1936–1945* (Barcelona, 2006), 213–19.

20. This key meeting has been brought to light in the major study by M. Ros Agudo, *La guerra secreta de Franco (1939–1945)* (Barcelona, 2002), xxiii–xxv, 44–49.

21. Ibid., 45–55.

22. M. Heiberg, *Emperadores del Mediterráneo: Franco, Mussolini y la guerra civil española* (Barcelona, 2004), 196–98.

23. Yagüe detailed these problems in his report of 12 April 1939, in FNFF, file 15, doc. 658.

24. Preamble to the new "Bases Orgánicas del Ejército del Aire," presented to Franco in April 1939, in FNFF, file 105, doc. 4590.

25. He proposed to pay for a very small part of this by selling off a motley assortment of 130 obsolescent planes in the existing arsenal: reports of 3 and 4 October 1939, in FNFF, file 67, docs. 2673, 2675.

26. In proposals of February and March 1940, ibid., docs. 2659, 2681, 2698.

27. Ros Agudo, *La guerra secreta*, 55–58.

28. On the Spanish army during these years, see G. Cardona, *El gigante descalzo: El ejército de Franco* (Madrid, 2003); and P. Preston, "El Ejército," in *La Epoca de Franco (1939–1975)*, ed. R. Carr, vol. 41 of *Historia de España*, ed. R. Menéndez Pidal and J. M. Jover (Madrid, 1996), 301–82.

29. FNFF, file 34, doc. 1279; file 38, doc. 1399; file 67, doc. 2700.

30. R. de la Cierva, *Historia del franquismo* (Barcelona, 1976), 1:328–32.

31. Tusell, *Franco, España*, 650.

32. Quoted in Diario 16, *Historia del franquismo* (Madrid, 1982), 164. On the political activity of the army leaders during World War II, see M. A. Baquer, *Franco y sus generales* (Madrid, 2005), 76–197.

33. See D. M. McKale, *The Swastika Outside Germany* (Kent, Ohio, 1977).

34. Interviews with Patricio González de Canales and Luis de Caralt (the latter a member of the clandestine committee seeking to carry out the project) in Madrid and

Barcelona, January to April 1959. See A. Romero Cuesta, *Objetivo: Matar a Franco* (Madrid, 1976), which seems to consist primarily of the recollections of González de Canales.

35. An earlier report on Yagüe emphasized his internal political dissidence much more than his German contacts: Suárez Fernández, *Francisco Franco y su tiempo*, 3:146–47.

36. Junta Política de la FET, "Proyecto de Acuerdo de la Junta Política en materia económica," in FNFF, file 37, doc. 1369.

37. L. Caruana de las Cagigas, "Las implicaciones políticas de las relaciones entre España y Gran Bretaña durante la Segunda Guerra Mundial: Comentarios al Acuerdo de 18 de marzo de 1940," *Hispania* 51:179 (1991), 1043–73, and M. Alpert, "Las relaciones hispano-británicas en el primer año de la posguerra: Los acuerdos comerciales y financieros de marzo de 1940," *Revista de Política Internacional*, September–October 1976, 1329.

38. Quoted in Tusell, *Franco, España*, 56.

39. The principal study is C. B. Burdick, "*Moro:* The Resupply of German Submarines in Spain, 1939–1942," *Central European History* 3:3 (September 1970), 256–84; further details are added in Ros Agudo, *La guerra secreta*, 72–117.

Chapter 5. Franco's Temptation

1. R. De Felice, *Mussolini il Duce: Lo stato totalitario, 1936–1940*, 2 vols. (Turin, 1974–81); J. Tusell and G. García Queipo de Llano, *Franco y Mussolini* (Barcelona, 1985), 63–70.

2. J. Tusell, *Franco, España y la II Guerra Mundial: Entre el Eje y la neutralidad* (Madrid, 1995), 59–61.

3. Ibid., 61–62. As early as 16 April Beigbeder had told Stohrer that if Italy entered the war, Spain would "automatically" do so, but the foreign minister talked loosely and contradictorily to a number of foreign representatives; see *Documents on German Foreign Policy* (Washington, D.C., 1950), D, 192 (hereafter cited as *DGFP*).

4. Quoted in M. S. Gómez de las Heras Hernández, "España y Portugal ante la segunda guerra mundial desde 1939 a 1942," *Espacio, Tiempo y Forma*, ser. 5, Historia Contemporánea, vol. 7 (1994): 153–67.

5. Tusell, *Franco, España*, 65–69.

6. This rumor appeared in the *Daily Telegraph* (London), 3 June 1940, in *Le Temps* (Paris), 4 June 1940, and elsewhere as well.

7. *Documenti diplomatici italiani* (Rome, 1960), ser. 9, vol. 4: 920–30.

8. Tusell, *Franco, España*, 75–77.

9. Tusell and Queipo de Llano, *Franco y Mussolini*, 74–78.

10. The first scholarly study of the nonbelligerence policy was V. Morales Lezcano, *Historia de la no-beligerancia española durante la Segunda Guerra Mundial* (Las Palmas, 1980); the lengthiest secondary account is R. Garriga, *La España de Franco* (Madrid, 1976), 2 vols. The regime's two principal memoir-apologias are R. Serrano Suñer, *Entre Hendaya y Gibraltar* (Mexico City, 1947), and J. M. Doussinague, *España tenía razón (1939–1945)* (Madrid, 1950).

11. Tusell, *Franco, España*, 81.

12. The FET's official pamphlet of 1938, *El imperio de España*, affirmed that "our imperialism will not be an imperialism of oil or of rubber." Its task would be to restore and direct pan-Hispanic unity, in order to achieve a "new catholicity. . . . Spain aspires to be able to exercise in an effective manner rights of defense and of tutelage, . . . rights not of a protectorate . . . but of the defense of Spanish civilization in the world."

13. According to Hoare's memoir, published under his postwar title of Viscount Templewood, *Ambassador on Special Mission* (London, 1946), 47.

14. C. R. Halstead and C. J. Halstead, "Aborted Imperialism: Spain's Occupation of Tangier, 1940–1945," *Iberian Studies* 7:2 (Autumn 1978), 53–71.

15. Archives of the Fundación Nacional Francisco Franco (hereafter cited as FNFF), file 41, doc. 14790; M. Hernando de Larramendi, "Tánger durante la ocupación española, 1940–1945," in *Actas del Congreso Internacional sobre el Estrecho de Gibraltar* (Madrid, 1987), 3:571–82; S. Sueiro, "España en Tánger durante la Segunda Guerra Mundial: La consumación de un viejo anhelo," *Espacio, Tiempo y Forma*, ser. 5, Historia Contemporánea, vol. 7 (1994): 123–51.

16. Quoted in Tusell, *Franco, España,* 115. Beigbeder was so fixated on some sort of Spanish dominion in Morocco that even in a late phase of the war, when Germany's defeat was apparent, he still hoped to promote a rebellion led by the caliph of the Spanish zone, who was to proclaim himself sultan and, with Spanish assistance, invade the French zone to establish a new united Morocco under Spanish protection, a project even more fanciful than that of 1940 (ibid., 118–19).

17. FNFF, file 103, docs. 4467, 4474.

18. Quoted in N. Goda, *Tomorrow the World: Hitler, Northwest Africa, and the Path toward America* (College Station, Tex., 1998), 59.

19. The main study of the Moroccan obsession is G. Nerín and A. Bosch, *El imperio que nunca existió: La aventura colonial discutida en Hendaya* (Barcelona, 2001). For a penetrating overview of Spanish policy in the protectorate, see G. Jensen, "The Peculiarities of 'Spanish Morocco': Imperial Ideology and Economic Development," *Mediterranean Historical Review* 20:1 (June 2005), 81–102.

20. F. Piétri, *Mes années en Espagne, 1940–1948* (Paris, 1954); M. Séguéla, *Franco-Pétain: Los secretos de una alianza* (Barcelona, 1994); and M. Catala, *Les relations franco-espagnols pendant la Deuxième Guerre Mondiale: Rapprochement nécessaire, réconciliation imposible, 1939–1944* (Paris, 1997).

21. Tusell, *Franco, España,* 122–23.

22. Churchill to Juan Negrín (then Republican finance minister), 22 Feb. 1937, in FNFF, file 33, doc. 57, and quoted in D. Reynolds, *In Command of History: Churchill Fighting and Writing the Second World War* (London, 2004), 102.

23. The key study of Anglo-Spanish relations during the most crucial period remains D. Smyth, *Diplomacy and Strategy of Survival: British Policy and Franco's Spain, 1940–41* (Cambridge, 1986). E. Moradiellos, *Franco frente a Churchill* (Barcelona, 2005), and R. Hogg, *Churchill y Franco: La política británica de apaciguamiento y la supervivencia del régimen, 1940–1946* (Barcelona, 2005), are broader treatments.

24. Regrettably the memoirs of Mrs. R. Powell Fox, *The Grass and the Asphalt* (Cadiz, 1997), contain numerous errors and reveal little.

25. The first research on this scheme was published by D. Smyth, "Les chevaliers de Saint-George: La Grande Bretagne et la corruption des généraux espagnols," *Guerres Mondiales* 162 (1991), 29–54, which was then taken up in broader, possibly exaggerated, form by D. Stafford, *Roosevelt and Churchill: Men of Secrets* (London, 1999), 78–110.

26. Ros Agudo, *La guerra secreta,* 152.

27. Quoted in Tusell, *Franco, España,* 84.

28. T. Lüdke, *Jihad Made in Germany: Ottoman and German Propaganda and Intelligence Operations in the First World War* (New Brunswick, N.J., 2006); P. Hopkirk, *Like Hidden Fire: The Plot to Bring Down the British Empire* (London, 1994); R. W. Melka, "The Axis and the Arab Middle East, 1930–1945" (Ph.D. diss., University of Minnesota, 1966); C. Caballero Jurado, *La espada del Islam: Voluntarios árabes en la Wehrmacht* (Granada,

1999); R. De Felice, *Il fascismo e l'Oriente* (Bologna, 1988); E. Galoppini, *Il fascismo e l'Islam* (Parma, 2001); and M. Hauner, *India in Axis Strategy during World War II* (London, 1985).

29. It might also be noted that a relative Germanophilia, or at least a very positive evaluation of German abilities, has been seen in Spain since the late nineteenth century. Alfonso Alvarez Villar's "Notas sobre la germanofilia en España," *Revista de Psicología General y Aplicada*, 1963, 1147–53, reported results of an opinion survey that revealed highly positive attitudes toward the Germans after the war. Qualities attributed disproportionately to Germans included unusual intelligence, extraordinary industriousness, a spirit of discipline, great patriotism and military efficiency, and the most outstanding capacity among all peoples for scientific investigation and philosophy; most of these attributes were considered the opposite of salient Spanish characteristics.

30. The full text may be found in J. Palacios, *Las cartas de Franco* (Madrid, 2005), 114–15. Cf. D. S. Detwiler, *Hitler, Franco und Gibraltar: Die Frage des spanischen Eintritts in den Zweiten Weltkrieg* (Wiesbaden, 1962), 22–23, and also M. Ruiz Holst, *Neutralität oder Kriegsbeteiligung? Die deutsch-spanischen Verhandlungen im Jahre 1940* (Pfaffenweiler, 1986).

31. *DGFP*, D, 9:585–88.

32. Ibid., 605–6, 620–21. On these exchanges, see Tusell, *Franco, España*, 84–89.

33. Goda, *Tomorrow the World*, 61.

34. J. Lukacs, *The Duel: Hitler vs. Churchill, 10 May–31 July 1940* (New Haven, 1992); J. Costello, *Ten Days to Destiny* (New York, 1991); and C. Ponting, *1940: Myth and Reality* (Chicago, 1991). Cf. W. Churchill, *The History of the Second World War* (New York, 1950), 2:199.

35. M. Bloch, *Operation "Willi": The Plot to Kidnap the Duke of Windsor, July 1940* (London, 1984), presents a thorough study.

36. *Arriba*, 19 July 1940. This highly imprudent speech was later excised from the official 1943 edition of *Palabras del Caudillo*, by which time it had become highly embarrassing.

37. P. T. Pereira, *Memorias* (Lisbon, 1973), 2:213–32, and C. R. Halstead, "Consistent and Total Peril from Every Side: Portugal and Its 1940 Protocol with Spain," *Iberian Studies* 3:1 (Spring 1974), 15–28. There is a lucid summary in Tusell, *Franco, España*, 123–31. On an earlier proposal to bring Portugal under Spanish control, see H. de la Torre Gómez, *El imperio del Rey: Alfonso XIII, Portugal y los ingleses, 1907–1916* (Mérida, 2002). The background of Hispano-Portuguese relations is treated in three works by H. de la Torre Gómez and A. J. Telo: *La mirada del otro: Percepciones luso-españolas desde la historia* (Mérida, 2001); *Portugal e Espanha nos sistemas internacionais contemporâneos* (Lisbon, 2000); and *Portugal, España y Europa: Cien años de desafío (1890–1990)* (Mérida, 1991); and in H. de la Torre, ed., *Portugal, España y África en los últimos cien años* (Mérida, 1992).

For Portugal's role as staunch supporter of Franco during the Civil War, see I. Delgado, *Portugal e a Guerra Civil de Espanha* (Lisbon, n.d.); C. Oliveira, *Salazar e a Guerra Civil de Espanha* (Lisbon, 1987); A. Pena Rodríguez, *El gran aliado de Franco: Portugal y la guerra civil española: Prensa, radio, cine y propaganda* (La Coruña, 1998); F. Rosas, ed., *Portugal e a Guerra Civil de Espanha* (Lisbon, 1998); and A. Raya-Rivas, "An Iberian Alliance: Portuguese Intervention in the Spanish Civil War (1936–1939," *Portuguese Studies Review* 8:1 (Fall–Winter 1999–2000), 109–25.

The policy and politics of Portugal during World War II are treated in F. Rosas, *Portugal entre a paz e a guerra (1939–1945)* (Lisbon, 1990), and more extensively in A. Telo, *Portugal na segunda guerra*, 2 vols. (Lisbon, 1987–91). Conversely, the highly tendentious work of M. Loff, *Salazarismo e Franquismo na época de Hitler (1936–1942): Convergencia política, preconceito ideológico e oportunidade histórica na redefinição internacional de Portugal e Espanha* (Porto, 1996), should be used only with care.

38. K.-D. Bracher, *Zeitgeschichtliche Kontroversen um Faschismus Totalitarismus Demokratie* (Munich, 1976), 60–78.

39. The American historian Norman J. W. Goda has marshaled considerable evidence regarding these latter aspects of Hitler's thinking and planning in his quite original study, *Tomorrow the World*, cited in note 18. I follow a modified version of Goda's thesis in the pages that follow.

40. On Hitler's strategic alternatives, see H. Magenheimer, *Hitler's War: German Military Strategy, 1940–1945* (London, 1998), 19–33.

41. J. P. Duffy, *Target: America: Hitler's Plan to Attack the United States* (New York, 2004).

42. In the general European economic plan drawn up by Walther Funk, the German minister of economics, in July 1940, Spain played no role of any significance, being relegated to the outer southern zone, along with Portugal and Turkey, though the importation of minerals and foodstuffs from Spain was included. See J. Freymond, *Le IIIᵉ Reich et la réorganisation économique de l'Europe, 1940–1942* (Geneva, 1974), 110–14.

43. For a critique of the limited relevance of the Gibraltar operation alone, see B. Alexander, *How Hitler Could Have Won World War II: The Fatal Errors That Led to Nazi Defeat* (New York, 2000), 45–48.

44. There has been more speculation about the exact role of Canaris in German and Spanish affairs than about those of any of the other personalities in this story other than Hitler and Franco themselves. Canaris became a crypto-opponent of the Hitler regime, later passing information to the Allies, and is often credited with doing the same for Franco to discourage Spain's entry into the war. Yet little direct information has survived, and the several books about Canaris deal in large measure with rumor and speculation. R. Bassett, *Hitler's Spy Chief* (London, 2005), is totally unreliable. The best account of his dealings with Spain is still L. Papeleux, *L'Amiral Canaris entre Franco et Hitler: Le rôle de Canaris dans les rélations germano-espagnoles (1915–1944)* (Brussels, 1977). For a major biography, see H. Höhne, *Canaris* (New York, 1979). As a naval commander, Canaris was in fact always enthusiastic about the Gibraltar operation, but also skeptical about Spain's entry into the war, since he knew at firsthand the desperate conditions in the country, as well as the weakness of the Spanish armed forces.

45. The initial German calculations regarding an assault on Gibraltar are treated in C. B. Burdick, *Germany's Military Strategy and Spain in World War II* (Syracuse, 1968), 24–43.

46. García Pérez, *Franquismo y Tercer Reich*, 173–74.

47. Palacios, *Cartas de Franco*, 118–19.

48. *Documenti diplomatici italiani*, ser. 9, vol. 3: 478–79, 521–23; Tusell and García Queipo de Llano, *Franco y Mussolini*, 95–96.

49. Tusell, *Franco, España*, 102–3.

50. The most thorough study of Hitler's strategic concerns between the fall of France and the invasion of the Soviet Union is A. Hillgruber, *Hitlers Strategie, Politik und Kriegführung, 1940–1941*, 2nd ed. (Munich, 1982).

51. See the exposition in Alexander, *How Hitler Could Have Won*, 48–52.

52. "Most-high brother-in-law," a play on Franco's title of *generalísimo*.

53. There are two memoirs by Serrano: *Entre Hendaya y Gibraltar* (Mexico City, 1947) and *La historia como fue: Memorias* (Barcelona, 1977), followed by the marathon lecture, *Política de España, 1936–1975* (Madrid, 1995). Other semi-fictionalized accounts include H. Saña, *El franquismo sin mito: Conversaciones con Ramón Serrano Suñer* (Barcelona, 1982); R. García Lahiguera, *Ramón Serrano Suñer: Un documento para la historia* (Barcelona, 1983; and the absurd book by I. Merino, *Serrano Suñer: Historia de una conducta* (Barcelona, 1996).

54. Anyone wishing to understand the historical role of Serrano would do well to begin

with A. Gómez Molina and J. M. Thomàs, *Ramón Serrano Suñer* (Barcelona, 2003), and not to neglect its introduction, titled "El personaje real y el personaje inventado."

55. *DGFP*, D, 11:85–86.

56. Ibid., 81–91, 93–102.

57. Goda, *Tomorrow the World*, 77–78.

58. The texts are in the appendices to Serrano Suñer, *La historia como fue*, 342–48.

59. *DGFP*, D, 11:153–55.

60. The reasonably extensive German records of these final discussions may be found ibid., 166–74, 182–83. Spanish records were apparently expunged in 1945. On the Berlin discussions, see the account in Tusell, *Franco, España*, 131–43, as well as the memoirs of D. Ridruejo, *Casi unas memorias* (Barcelona, 1976), 215–23. Other extensive treatments include R. Garriga, *Las relaciones secretas entre Franco y Hitler* (Buenos Aires, 1965), 141–66, and *La España de Franco* (Madrid, 1976), 1:195–225.

61. *DGFP*, D, 11:199–200.

62. See the discussion in Goda, *Tomorrow the World*, 91–93.

Chapter 6. The Meeting at Hendaye and Its Aftermath

1. *Mundo*, 27 Oct. 1940.

2. Department of State, *Foreign Relations of the United States* (Washington, D.C., 1957), 2:820–26; J. Tusell, *Franco, España, y la II Guerra Mundial: Entre el Eje y la neutralidad* (Madrid, 1995), 147–49.

3. Tusell, *Franco, España*, 153.

4. Quoted in D. Detwiler, *Hitler, Franco und Gibraltar: Die Frage des spanischen Eintritts in den Zweiten Weltkrieg* (Wiesbaden, 1962).

5. Hitler's seemingly confused plans have been reconstructed best in N. J. W. Goda, *Tomorrow the World: Hitler, Northwest Africa, and the Path toward America* (College Station, Tex., 1998), 94–100.

6. *Documents on German Foreign Policy* (Washington, D.C., 1950), D, 11:216 (hereafter cited as *DGFP*).

7. Ibid., 283.

8. Quoted in D. Smyth, *Diplomacy and Strategy of Survival: British Policy and Franco's Spain, 1940–41* (Cambridge, 1986), 97–99; P. Preston, *Franco: A Biography* (London, 1993), 388–89.

9. The most scholarly presentations of this view will be found in R. de la Cierva, *Hendaya: Punto final* (Barcelona, 1981), and L. Suárez Fernández, *España, Franco y la Segunda Guerra Mundial: Desde 1939 hasta 1945* (Madrid, 1997), 249–56.

10. Fundación Nacional Francisco Franco, *Documentos inéditos para la historia del Generalísimo Franco* (Madrid, 1992), 2:1, 380–81.

11. Tusell, *Franco, España*, 160.

12. *DGFP*, D, 11:371–76.

13. Count G. Ciano, *Ciano's Diplomatic Papers* (London, 1948), 402.

14. This report, "Los derechos de España en el Africa Ecuatorial," was imprudent in the extreme, claiming the right to expand Spanish possessions from 28,000 square kilometers to 1,628,900 square kilometers, including all the former German colony of Cameroon, which it was known that Hitler intended to regain. See G. Nerín and A. Bosch, *El imperio que nunca existió* (Barcelona, 2002), 177–79.

15. *DGFP*, D, 11:376–79.

16. Cf. R. Serrano Suñer, *La historia como fue: Memorias* (Barcelona, 1977), 299–301.

17. *DGFP,* D, 11:380.

18. Ibid., 66–67.

19. Ibid., 78–79.

20. The main German transcript of the meeting has been lost and Spanish papers have been either destroyed or sequestered. Principal sources are ibid., 371–80; Serrano's two accounts, *La historia como fue,* 283–324, and *Entre Hendaya y Gibraltar* (Mexico City, 1947), 199–232; and that of the German translator, Paul Schmidt, *Europa entre bastidores* (Barcelona, 1952), 467–72. See the accounts in Detwiler, *Hitler, Franco und Gibraltar,* 51–66, and Tusell, *Franco, España,* 158–64. The independence of Franco's position is emphasized and perhaps somewhat exaggerated in the unpublished eight-page memorandum drawn up two days later by the Barón de las Torres, a diplomat in the Spanish delegation, and the brief recollection years later by the government overseer of the press, Enrique Giménez-Arnau (who accompanied Serrano), "La entrevista de Hendaya," *Razón española* 88 (March–April 1998), 133–42. The subsequently altered and finalized protocol was published in *DGFP,* D, 11:466–67.

21. M. Ros Agudo, *La guerra secreta de Franco (1939–1945)* (Barcelona, 2002), 58–62.

22. Ibid., 62–63. The most detailed discussion of Spanish thinking and policy on Gibraltar is J. J. Téllez, *Gibraltar en el tiempo de los espías* (Seville, 2005).

23. Archives of the Fundación Nacional Francisco Franco, file 27, doc. 15007.

24. Ibid., file 68, doc. 2803.

25. The "Estudio" listed the Spanish air force as of December 1940 as consisting of 81 "antiquated" fighters, 18 modern fighters, 9 less good fighters, 56 air-to-ground attack aircraft, 36 adequate bombers, 36 antiquated bombers, and 39 other planes. How these planes would hold off the British was not explained.

26. Quoted in C. B. Burdick, *Germany's Military Strategy and Spain in World War II* (Syracuse, 1968), 52.

27. J. Goebbels, *The Goebbels Diaries, 1939–1941,* trans. Fred Taylor (New York, 1983), 103.

28. *DGFP,* D, 11:452. Serrano published the original text, dispatched by Franco on 30 October, in his *Historia como fue,* 301–5.

29. Quoted in Goda, *Tomorrow the World,* 110.

30. Burdick, *Germany's Military Strategy,* 55–62.

31. See the analysis in M. Van Creveld, *Strategy, 1940–1941: The Balkan Clue* (London, 1973), 52–85.

32. Ibid., 64–70.

33. Quoted in R. García Pérez, *Franquismo y Tercer Reich: Las relaciones económicas hispano-alemanas durante la Segunda Guerra Mundial* (Madrid, 1994), 195.

34. Tusell, *Franco, España,* 165–66.

35. *DGFP,* D, 11:598–606, 619–23.

36. Espinosa de los Monteros to Franco, 25 Jan. 1941, in J. Palacios, *Las cartas de Franco: La correspondencia desconocida que marcó el destino de España* (Madrid, 2005), 151. Serrano presents his account in his *Historia como fue,* 305–8.

37. *DGFP,* D, 11:705–6, 725, 739–41, 787–88; Tusell, *Franco, España,* 167–69.

38. Tusell, *Franco, España,* 184–85.

39. Burdick, *Germany's Military Strategy,* 96–101.

40. *DGFP,* D, 11:852–58.

41. Burdick, *Germany's Military Strategy,* 103–4.

42. L. Papeleux, *L'Admiral Canaris entre Franco et Hitler: Le rôle de Canaris dans les rélations germano-espagnoles, 1915–1944* (Tournai, 1977), 134–59.

43. Serrano Suñer, *Historia como fue,* 286.

44. A. Cazorla-Sánchez, "Beyond 'They Shall Not Pass': How the Experience of Violence Reshaped Political Values in Franco's Spain," *Journal of Contemporary History* 40:3 (July 2005), 503–20.

45. The principal study is P. Sánchez-Gijón, *La planificación militar británica y España (1940–1942)* (Madrid, 1984).

46. The key study of American relations is the excellent account of J. M. Thomàs, *Roosevelt y Franco durante la Segunda Guerra Mundial: De la Guerra Civil a Pearl Harbor* (Barcelona, 2007).

47. Palacios, *Cartas de Franco,* 146–47.

48. Espinosa de los Monteros to Franco, 25 January 1941, ibid., 147–52.

49. *DGFP,* D, 11:967–69.

50. Burdick, *Germany's Military Strategy,* 114–17.

51. *DGFP,* D, 11:1056.

52. Ibid., 1069–70.

53. Ibid., 1140–43.

54. Ibid., 1157–58.

55. Ibid., 1173–75.

56. Ibid., 1188–91, 1208–10, 1217–18, 1222–23.

57. Burdick, *Germany's Military Strategy,* 119.

58. *DGFP,* D, 12:36–37.

59. Palacios, *Cartas de Franco,* 152–58.

60. *DGFP,* D, 12:58, 78–79; Tusell, *Franco, España,* 190–92; Detwiler, *Hitler, Franco und Gibraltar,* 80–94.

61. *DGFP,* D, 11:990–95, 1127–62.

62. J. Tusell and G. García Queipo de Llano, *Franco y Mussolini* (Barcelona, 1985), 119–22. Years later, during his notorious *cacerías,* Franco liked to pretend that he had boldly spoken the truth to Mussolini, claiming that he had told him: "Duce, Duce, if you could get out of the war, wouldn't you get out?" and, after Mussolini glumly nodded his head yes, the Caudillo supposedly said, "That's why I'm not getting in." This made an amusing story, but of course Franco made it up out of whole cloth. (This anecdote was provided by Fabián Estapé, interview in Barcelona, June 1974.)

63. Mussolini expressed his conviction that the Spanish regime was truly committed to the Axis, but not in a position at present to enter the war: *DGFP,* D, 12:96–98.

64. Ibid., 131–32.

65. Quoted in Tusell, *Franco, España,* 200.

Chapter 7. The Zenith of Collaboration

1. M. Ros Agudo, *La guerra secreta de Franco (1939–1945)* (Barcelona, 2002), 210–18.

2. W. Schellenberg, *Aufzeichnungen: Die Memoiren des letzten Geheimdienstchefs unter Hitler* (Wiesbaden, 1979), 112.

3. Ros Agudo, *La guerra secreta,* 218–28.

4. Ibid., 154–55.

5. J. Juárez Camacho, *Madrid Londres Berlín: Espías de Franco al servicio de Hitler* (Madrid, 2005).

6. See F. Rodao, *Franco y el imperio japonés* (Barcelona, 2002), 332–39, and R. K. Wilcox, *Japan's Secret War* (New York, 1995), passim.

7. Perhaps the best summaries of these operations will be found in T. Holt, *The*

Deceivers: Allied Military Deception in the Second World War (New York, 2004), 369–78 and passim. Regarding British intelligence and counterintelligence activities in Spain, see the mini-memoir by K. Benton, "The ISOS Years: Madrid 1941–3," *Journal of Contemporary History* 30 (1995), 359–410.

8. The fullest account is J. Juárez, *Juan Pujol: El espía que derrotó a Hitler* (Madrid, 2004).

9. Ros Agudo, *La guerra secreta*, 213, 231–34.

10. R. Sanz Hevia, "La inmóvil guerra de un buque encallado," *Historia 16* 24:295 (2000), 102–5.

11. Ros Agudo, *La guerra secreta*, 239–48.

12. Further details on some of these operations may be found in A. Escuadra, *A la sombra de la roca: La Segunda Guerra Mundial desde el campo de Gibraltar* (Córdoba, 1997), and J. Ramírez Copeiro del Villar, *Espías y neutrales: Huelva en la II Guerra Mundial* (Huelva, 1996).

13. Ros Agudo, *La guerra secreta*, 248–51.

14. Ibid., 120–21, 129–30; C. Leitz, *Economic Relations between Nazi Germany and Franco's Spain, 1936–1945* (Oxford, 1996), 144–45.

15. Ros Agudo, *La guerra secreta*, 121–22.

16. Ibid., 122–29.

17. R. Belis and M. Armengou, *El convoy de los 927* (Barcelona, 2006).

18. Here I follow the detailed outline in Ros Agudo, *La guerra secreta*, 291–93, and also I. Schulze Schneider, "La propaganda alemana en España 1942–1944," in *Espacio, Tiempo y Forma*, ser. 5, Historia Contemporánea, vol. 7 (1994): 337–51.

19. Ros Agudo, *La guerra secreta*, 293–98.

20. R. Garriga, *La España de Franco* (Madrid, 1976), 1:422.

21. Ros Agudo, *La guerra secreta*, 271–77; C. Velasco Murviedro, "Propaganda y publicidad nazis en España durante la segunda guerra mundial," in *Espacio, Tiempo y Forma*, ser. 5, Historia Contemporánea, vol. 7 (1994): 85–96.

22. Opinion in the Spanish press during World War II is treated in C. García Alix, *La prensa española ante la Segunda Guerra Mundial* (Madrid, 1974). For the kind of war coverage provided by Spanish newsreels, see S. Rodríguez, *El NO-DO, catequismo social de una época* (Madrid, 1999), and J. Martínez, "Información y desinformación: La II guerra mundial a través del NO-DO," in *Espacio, Tiempo y Forma*, ser. 5, Historia Contemporánea, vol. 7 (1994): 283–300, and "La guerra en el cine y la propaganda: NO-DO, 1943–45," in *España y la Segunda Guerra Mundial*, ed. S. G. Payne and D. Contreras (Madrid, 1996), 145–55. The Germans returned the favor in their portrayal of Spain in German newsreels: R. Van de Winkel, "Nazi Newsreels and Foreign Propaganda: How Occupied Europe Saw Franco's Spain through German eyes" (unpublished MS).

23. R. Garriga, *Las relaciones secretas entre Franco y Hitler* (Buenos Aires, 1965), 209–14.

24. Ros Agudo, *La guerra secreta*, 302–4.

25. R. Pardo Sanz, *¡Con Franco hacia el Imperio! La política exterior española en América Latina, 1939–1945* (Madrid, 1994), and "La política exterior española en América Latina durante la II Guerra Mundial," in *Espacio, Tiempo y Forma*, ser. 5, Historia Contemporánea, vol. 7 (1994): 193–218; L. Delgado Gómez-Escalonilla, *Diplomacia franquista y política cultural hacia Iberoamérica, 1939–1953* (Madrid, 1988), and *Imperio de papel: Acción cultural y política exterior durante el primer franquismo* (Madrid, 1992); R. Pérez Montfort, *Hispanismo y Falange* (Mexico City, 1992); T. M. Leonard and J. F. Bratzel, eds., *Latin America during World War II* (Lanham, Md., 2006); two special numbers on "América Latina y la Segunda Guerra Mundial," *Estudios interdisciplinarios de América Latina y el Caribe* 6:1–2 (1995); and M. Quijada, "España y Argentina durante la Segunda Guerra

Mundial," *Espacio, Tiempo y Forma*, 219–45. The Consejo de la Hispanidad, designed as an agency of cultural imperialism and in existence from 1940 to 1945, is treated in M. A. Escudero, *El Instituto de Cultura Hispánica* (Madrid, 1994), 41–106. On reaction in Latin America to the Civil War and the emergence of the Franco regime, see M. Falcoff and F. B. Pike, eds., *The Spanish Civil War, 1936–1939: American Hemispheric Perspectives* (Lincoln, Nebr., 1982).

26. P. Boschetti, *Les suisses et les Nazis: Le rapport Bergier pour tous* (Paris, 2004).

27. R. García Pérez, *Franquismo y Tercer Reich: Las relaciones económicas hispano-alemanas durante la Segunda Guerra Mundial* (Madrid, 1994), 125–44; Leitz, *Economic Relations*, 114–16.

28. García Pérez, *Franquismo y Tercer Reich*, 230–32.

29. Ibid., 95–114; Leitz, *Economic Relations*, 116–19

30. Leitz, *Economic Relations*, 119–24.

31. Ibid., 125–31; García Pérez, *Franquismo y Tercer Reich*, 144–55.

32. García Pérez, *Franquismo y Tercer Reich*, 209–27.

33. J. Tusell, *Franco, España, y la II Guerra Mundial: Entre el Eje y la neutralidad* (Madrid, 1995), 244.

34. According to the computations of García Pérez, in Leitz, *Economic Relations*, 137.

35. Ibid., 150–51.

Chapter 8. Temptation Continues

1. J. M. de Areilza and F. M. Castiella, *Reivindicaciones de España* (Madrid, 1941), 141; J. M. Cordero Torres, *Aspectos de la misión universal de España* (Madrid, 1942), iii; A. Aranda Mata, *Presente y porvenir de Marruecos* (Madrid, 1941), 11.

2. M. Roldán, *Marrueco: Geografía política y económica de la zona española de Marruecos* (Barcelona, 1942), 1; T. García Figueras, *Reivindicaciones de España en el norte de Africa* (Madrid, 1942), 7; and R. Gil Benumeya, *Marruecos andaluz* (Madrid, 1942), 11; all quoted in G. Nerín and A. Bosch, *El imperio que nunca existió* (Barcelona, 2001), 52.

3. Archives of the Fundación Nacional Francisco Franco (hereafter cited as FNFF), file 101, doc. 4448.

4. Quoted in Nerín and Bosch, *El imperio*, 141.

5. C. J. Hayes, *Wartime Mission in Spain, 1942–1945* (New York, 1946), 135.

6. D. Smyth, *Diplomacy and Strategy of Survival: British Policy and Franco's Spain, 1940–41* (Cambridge, 1986), 178–83.

7. Department of State, *Foreign Relations of the United States* (Washington, D.C., 1941), 2:895–97 (hereafter cited as *FRUS*).

8. C. R. Halstead, "Diligent Diplomat: Alexander W. Weddell as American Ambassador to Spain, 1939–1942," *Virginia Magazine of History and Biography* 82:1 (1974), 3–38.

9. C. B. Burdick, *Germany's Military Strategy and Spain in World War II* (Syracuse, 1968), 122–25.

10. N. J. W. Goda, *Tomorrow the World: Hitler, Northwest Africa, and the Path toward America* (College Station, Tex., 1998), 165–75.

11. *Documents on German Foreign Policy* (Washington, D.C., 1950), D, 12:176–78 (hereafter cited as *DGFP*).

12. Ibid., 569–70.

13. F. Torres García, *¿Por qué Juan Carlos? Franco y la restauración de la Monarquía* (Madrid, 1999), 299.

14. *DGFP*, D, 12:611–15.

15. *Documenti Diplomatici Italiani*, ser. 9, vol. 6: 896–97; J. Tusell and G. García Queipo de Llano, *Franco y Mussolini* (Barcelona, 1985), 126.

16. R. García Pérez, *Franquismo y Tercer Reich: Las relaciones económicas hispano-alemanas durante la Segunda Guerra Mundial* (Madrid, 1994), 249.

17. J. Tusell, *Franco, España, y la II Guerra Mundial: Entre el Eje y la neutralidad* (Madrid, 1995), 208.

18. M. Ros Agudo, *La guerra secreta de Franco (1939–1945)* (Barcelona, 2002), 119; A. Marquina Barrio, "La neutralidad o la pérdida de la neutralidad en la Segunda Guerra Mundial: Cuestiones pendientes de un debate todavía inconcluso," in *Espacio, Tiempo y Forma*, ser. 5, Historia Contemporánea, vol. 7 (1994): 301–10.

19. L. Pascual Sánchez-Gijón, *La planificación militar británica y España (1940–1942)* (Madrid, 1984), treats the full range of British military planning regarding Spain during these years.

20. *DGFP,* D, 12:664–66, 711.

21. Ibid., 774, 795–96.

22. Perhaps the best discussion of this crisis and its consequences is found in X. Moreno Juliá, *La División Azul: Sangre española en Rusia, 1941–1945* (Barcelona, 2004), 32–44.

23. *DGFP,* D, 12:928–30.

24. E. Moradiellos, *Franco frente a Churchill: España y Gran Bretaña en la Segunda Guerra Mundial (1939–1945)* (Barcelona, 2005), 227–28; R. Wigg, *Churchill y Franco: La política británica de apaciguamiento y la supervivencia del régimen, 1940–1945* (Barcelona, 2005), 65–68.

25. García Pérez, *Franquismo y Tercer Reich,* 247.

26. The best discussion can be found in Tusell, *Franco, España,* 222–25.

27. See the discussion in Moreno Juliá, *División Azul,* 64–66.

28. *DGFP,* D, 13:16–17, 38–39.

29. Quoted in Moreno Juliá, *División Azul,* 75. As Moreno notes, Serrano would later clarify in a book-length interview that he was referring to the extermination of the Soviet regime and not of the Russian people. See H. Saña, *El franquismo sin mitos: Conversaciones con Serrano Suñer* (Barcelona, 1981), 250.

30. Moreno Juliá, *División Azul,* 75–77.

31. W. L. Beaulac, *Franco: Silent Ally in World War II* (Carbondale, Ill., 1986), 24.

32. Smyth, *Diplomacy and Strategy,* 179–98.

33. *Arriba,* 18 July 1941.

34. *DGFP,* D, 13:222–24.

35. Ibid., 360.

36. J. L. Rodríguez Jiménez, *Los esclavos españoles de Hitler* (Barcelona, 2002), presents a slightly sensationalized account. See R. García Pérez, "El envío de trabajadores españoles a Alemania durante la Segunda Guerra Mundial," *Hispania* 170 (1988), 1031–65. By November 1941, German authorities were complaining of the government's dilatoriness, no workers yet having left: *DGFP,* D, 13:748–49.

37. The Dirección General de Seguridad reported on 11 July 1941 that 18,000 Spanish Republican workers were already employed in Germany: *Boletín* 158 in FNFF, file 62, doc. 24235; *Hitler's Table Talk, 1941–1944: His Private Conversations,* trans. Norman Cameron and R. H. Stevens (New York, 2000), 568.

38. Smyth, *Diplomacy and Strategy,* 202–5.

39. *DGFP,* D, 13:628–30, 647–48.

40. Tusell, *Franco, España,* 271.

41. *DGFP,* D, 13:441–43.

42. K.-J. Ruhl, *Franco, Falange y III Reich* (Madrid, 1986), 67–69.

43. Tusell, *Franco, España,* 271–72.

44. *DGFP,* D, 13:630–32. On the political machinations of Aranda, see A. Marquina Barrio, "Conspiración contra Franco: El ejército y la injerencia extranjera en España: El papel de Aranda, 1939–1945," *Historia 16* 32 (December 1978), 11–18.

45. *FRUS,* 2:911–13.

46. *DGFP,* D, 13:444–46, 459–60. Weddell was finally received by Franco early in October: *FRUS,* 2:924–29.

47. *DGFP,* D, 13: 22, 498–99, 774, 900–903.

48. Ibid., 904–6.

Chapter 9. The Blue Division

1. The early bibliography is listed in W. Haupt, "Die 'Blaue Division' in der Literatur," *Wehrwissenschaftliche Rundschau* 4 (April 1959); more extensive references are in C. Caballero and R. Ibáñez, *Escritores en las trincheras: La División Azul en sus libros, publicaciones periódicas y filmografía (1941–1988)* (Madrid, 1989). A good deal more has been published since 1989, though much of the publication is anecdotal and some re-creations are semi-fictional. G. R. Kleinfeld and L. A. Tambs, *Hitler's Spanish Legion: The Blue Division in Russia* (Carbondale, Ill., 1979), remains the best one-volume military narrative, while X. Moreno Juliá, *La División Azul: Sangre española en Rusia, 1941–1945* (Barcelona, 2004), provides the fullest perspective, treating political, military, and diplomatic aspects. The best brief synopsis is that of R. Ibáñez Hernández, "Españoles en las trincheras: La División Azul," in *España y la Segunda Guerra Mundial,* ed. S. G. Payne and D. Contreras (Madrid, 1996), 55–87.

2. Ibáñez Hernández, "Españoles en las trincheras." See further D. Smyth, "The Dispatch of the Spanish Blue Division to the Eastern Front: Reasons and Repercussions," *European History Quarterly* 24 (1994), 537–53.

3. Moreno Juliá, *La División Azul,* 395.

4. Erich Rose symbolized the tragic fate of hundreds of thousands of German men of mixed German-Jewish background and was apparently killed in the desperate Spanish counterattack at Krasny Bor in 1943. For his dramatic saga, see C. Caballero Jurado, "Erich Rose: El trágico destino de un oficial 'judío' de la División Azul," *Revista Española de Historia Militar* 54 (December 2004), 306–34.

5. The best account of the formation and background of volunteers may be found in Moreno Juliá, *La División Azul,* 94–101.

6. The basic history is J. Fernández-Coppel, *La Escuadrilla Azul* (Madrid, 2006). See also S. Guillén and C. Caballero, *Escuadrillas azules en Rusia: Historia y uniformes* (Madrid, 1999). Altogether, five squadrons were formed, each of the last four in relief of the previous one, on into 1944; some veteran pilots served in more than one. The Escuadrillas Azules were credited with downing 164 Soviet planes. Altogether, somewhere between 300 and 400 men served with the Escuadrilla Azul.

7. The only biography, F. Vadillo, *Muñoz Grandes, el general de la División Azul* (Madrid, 1999), is semi-fictional reportage. H. Berg, *Generalleutnant Agustín Muñoz-Grandes: Spaniens "Blaue Division" an der Ostfront* (Rastatt, 1963), deals only with his command in Russia.

8. The best accounts of the assembling of the legion will be found in Moreno Juliá, *La División Azul,* 111–43, and Kleinfeld and Tambs, *Hitler's Spanish Legion,* 25–76.

9. Kleinfeld and Tambs, *Hitler's Spanish Legion,* 77–153.

10. *Hitler's Table Talk, 1941–1944: His Private Conversations*, trans. Norman Cameron and R. H. Stevens (New York, 2000), 179–80.

11. Kleinfeld and Tambs, *Hitler's Spanish Legion*, 156–67; E. Barrachina Juan, *La batalla del lago Ilmen* (Barcelona, 1990).

12. Kleinfeld and Tambs, *Hitler's Spanish Legion*, 162–237; Moreno Juliá, *La División Azul*, 170–83.

13. There is a sizable literature on Krasny Bor in Spanish. For good brief accounts, see C. Caballero Jurado, *La División Azul en la batalla de Krasny Bor* (Valladolid, 2003), and Kleinfeld and Tambs, *Hitler's Spanish Legion*, 238–304.

14. A useful corrective will be found in X. M. Núñez Seixas, "Los vencedores vencidos: La peculiar memoria de la División Azul, 1945–2005," *Pasado y memoria: Revista de Historia Contemporánea* 4 (2005), 83–113.

15. Moreno Juliá, *La División Azul*, 196–204.

16. Ibid., Appendix 7, 410–13. By 1943 the Blue Division had become an embarrassment; it began to receive attention only after 1953, with the partial international rehabilitation of the Franco regime during the Cold War. It then enjoyed increasing treatment both in Spanish movies and in a long list of publications. The latter continue at a very brisk pace in the twenty-first century, though the film treatment came to an end after a few years. See S. Alegre, *El cine cambia la historia: Las imágenes de la División Azul* (Barcelona, 1994), and R. Ibáñez Hernández, "La cruzada antibolchevique en las pantallas: La División Azul en el cine y la televisión," *Aportes* 46:2 (2001), 36–53.

17. This is the estimate in W. Bowen, *Spaniards and Nazi Germany: Collaboration in the New Order* (Columbia, Mo., 2000), 198–201. Moreno Juliá, *La División Azul*, 207, finds evidence that 150 volunteers crossed the Pyrenees between 8 June and 20 July, as the battle of Normandy raged. After mid-August, German retreat made such passage impossible.

18. Ezquerra was not at first permitted to publish his rather rousing (if unverifiable) memoir in Spain, and it first appeared instead in Portuguese, *Lutei até o fim* (Lisbon, 1946), eventually to be published in Spanish as *Berlín, a vida o muerte* (Barcelona, 1975; Granada, 1994).

19. The most thorough treatment of casualties and the aftermath is to be found in Moreno Juliá, *La División Azul*, 310–69.

20. Ibid., 368.

21. The casualties of the Spaniards in the Red Army were proportionately much higher, in line with the gigantic casualties usually suffered by the Soviets, as approximately a quarter of the 800 died. See D. Arasa, *Los españoles de Stalin: La historia de los que sirvieron al comunismo durante la Segunda Guerra Mundial* (Barcelona, 2005). The political dimension is treated in D. Pike, *In the Service of Stalin: The Spanish Communists in Exile, 1939–1945* (Oxford, 1993).

22. Moreno Juliá, *La División Azul*, 385.

Chapter 10. Temptation Abates

1. G. Weinberg, "Hitler's Image of the United States," *American Historical Review* 69:3 (July 1964), 1006–21.

2. T. Fleming, *The New Dealers' War: F. D. R. and the War within World War II* (New York, 2001), emphasizes this aspect, perhaps overmuch.

3. For further discussion see G. Weinberg, "Germany's Declaration of War on the United States: A New Look," in *Germany and America: Essays on Problems of International Relations and Immigration*, ed. H. L. Trefousse (Brooklyn, 1980), 54–70, and "Die deutsche

Politik gegenüber den Vereinigten Staaten im Jahre 1941," in *Kriegswende Dezember 1941,* ed. J. Rohwer et al. (Koblenz, 1984), 73–80.

4. *Akten zur deutschen Auswärtigen Politik, 1918–1945* (Göttingen, 1969), E, 1:11 (hereafter cited as *ADAP*).

5. J. Tusell, *Franco, España, y la II Guerra Mundial: Entre el Eje y la neutralidad* (Madrid, 1995), 284–85.

6. J. Tusell and G. García Queipo de Llano, *Carrero: La eminencia gris del régimen de Franco* (Madrid, 1993), 61–64.

7. G. Kleinfeld and L. Tambs, *Hitler's Spanish Legion: The Blue Division in Russia* (Carbondale, Ill., 1979), 157.

8. *ADAP,* E, 1:199–200, 2:104–5.

9. Kleinfeld and Tambs, *Hitler's Spanish Legion,* 169–70.

10. *ADAP,* E, 1:502–3.

11. Ibid., 285–86, 216–17.

12. C. Teixeira da Motta, *O caso do Timor na II Guerra Mundial* (Lisbon, 1999).

13. F. Rosas, "Portuguese Neutrality in the Second World War," in *European Neutrals and Non-Belligerents during the Second World War,* ed. N. Wylie (Cambridge, 2002), 267–82.

14. In addition to Rosas, "Portuguese Neutrality," see A. J. Telo, "La estrategia de Portugal y sus relaciones con España," in *España y la Segunda Guerra Mundial,* ed. S. G. Payne and D. Contreras (Madrid, 1996), 131–44; C. Leitz, *Sympathy for the Devil: Neutral Europe and Nazi Germany in World War II* (New York, 2001), 144–74; and M. S. Gómez de las Heras Hernández, "España y Portugal ante la Segunda Guerra Mundial desde 1939 a 1942," in *Espacio, Tiempo y Forma,* ser. 5, Historia Contemporánea, vol. 7 (1994): 153–67.

15. Tusell, *Franco, España,* 305–7.

16. *ADAP,* E, 1:251, 232–33, 482–87.

17. *Palabras del Caudillo* (Madrid, 1943), 204.

18. Quoted in K.-J. Ruhl, *Franco, Falange y III Reich: España durante la Segunda Guerra Mundial* (Madrid, 1986), 136–37.

19. *ADAP,* E, 2:140–43.

20. Ibid., 1:265–67.

21. C. B. Burdick, *Germany's Military Strategy and Spain in World War II* (Syracuse, 1968), 125–65.

22. *ADAP,* E, 2:231–32.

23. Hayes's memoir of his ambassadorship is *Wartime Mission in Spain, 1942–1945* (New York, 1945). For brief evaluations of his role, see C. R. Halstead, "Historians in Politics: Carlton J. H. Hayes as American Ambassador to Spain, 1942–45," *Journal of Contemporary History* 10:3 (July 1975), 383–405, and J. W. Cortada, "La carrera diplomática de Carlton J. H. Hayes, 1942–1945," in *Relaciones España–USA, 1942–1945* (Barcelona, 1973), 145–87.

24. According to P. Martín Aceña, *El oro de Moscú y el oro de Berlín* (Madrid, 2001), 273–74.

25. K.-J. Ruhl, *Franco, Falange,* 38.

26. For the history and development of this institution, see E. San Román, *Ejército e industria: El nacimiento de INI* (Barcelona, 1999); P. Schwartz and M. J. González, *Una historia del Instituto Nacional de Industria* (Madrid, 1978); and *Empresa pública e industrialización en España,* ed. P. Martín Aceña and F. Comín (Madrid, 1990).

27. Quoted in Ruhl, *Franco, Falange,* 86.

28. *ADAP,* E, 1:294–96.

29. Ibid., 365–68.

30. Ibid., 2: 186–87, 369–70.

31. Ibid., 475–76, 3:16–18, 73–75.

32. Ibid., 2:186–88, 90–94.

33. Ibid., 1: 308–9.

34. *Documents on German Foreign Policy* (Washington, D.C., 1950), E, 13:903.

35. J. Palacios, *Las cartas de Franco* (Madrid, 2005) 187–89.

36. Ruhl, *Franco, Falange,* 106.

37. *ADAP,* E, 2:487–88, 513

38. Tusell, *Franco, España,* 316–19; *ADAP,* E, 3:63–65.

39. *ADAP,* E, 2:487–88, 3:100.

40. *Hitler's Table Talk, 1941–1944: His Private Conversations,* trans. Norman Cameron and R. H. Stevens (New York, 2000), 288, 320, 515, 689.

41. Ibid., 607–8.

42. Ibid., 516, 520.

43. Ibid., 568–69.

44. Ibid., 694, 691, 605.

45. Tusell, *Franco, España,* 314. Varela responded with a temporizing letter.

46. *ADAP,* E, 2:511–12.

47. Kleinfeld and Tambs, *Hitler's Spanish Legion,* 194–96.

48. Ibid., 193, 196; *ADAP,* E, 3:43.

49. *Hitler's Table Talk,* 569–70.

50. Kleinfeld and Tambs, *Hitler's Spanish Legion,* 196–97; *ADAP,* E, 3:140–41; Tusell, *Franco, España,* 314.

51. Cf. Tusell, *Franco, España,* 315–16.

52. *ADAP,* E, 174–80, 183–85.

53. R. Garriga, *La España de Franco* (Puebla., Mex., 1970), 1:234; Tusell and García Queipo de Llano, *Franco y Mussolini,* 165.

54. A. Marquina Barrio, "El atentado de Begoña," *Historia 16* 4 (April 1980), 11–19. A transcript of the conversation between Franco and Varela may be found in L. López Rodó, *La larga marcha hacia la Monarquía* (Barcelona, 1978), 503–7.

55. According to the version that Carrero gave years later to López Rodó, in the latter's *La larga marcha,* 29–30. See also Tusell and García Queipo de Llano, *Carrero,* 77–78.

56. H. Saña, *El franquismo sin mitos: Conversaciones con Serrano Suñer* (Barcelona, 1982), 271–74.

57. In the intensely partisan climate of the war years, the anti-German Varela bitterly resented his ouster and lobbied among his fellow lieutenant generals to dissuade any of them from replacing him, probably alleging that the honor of the military hierarchy was at stake. Franco therefore had to turn to a major general (*general de división*), Asensio. In the face of the latter's initial reluctance, according to Serrano, Franco railed in exasperation, "What is it you want? For me to be carried out of here someday feet first?" (ibid., 267).

58. One anonymous military pamphlet soon afterward urged direct action to eliminate the FET altogether, likening the beneficial effects of such a move to Ion Antonescu's suppression of the Iron Guard in Romania, which had been approved in advance by Hitler: "A military action by the Army in Spain would have the same benefit for Germany as did that of the Army in Romania when it faced up to the gang of crazies in the party" (Tusell and García Queipo de Llano, *Franco y Mussolini,* 170).

59. F. Gómez-Jordana Souza, *Milicia y diplomacia: Los Diarios del Conde de Jordana, 1936–1944* (Burgos, 2002), 130–76.

60. Quoted ibid., 176.

61. *ADAP,* E, 3:457–59, 313–14, 461.

62. Kleinfeld and Tambs, *Hitler's Spanish Legion,* 206–8.

63. *ADAP*, E, 3:451–54.

64. Ruhl, *Franco, Falange*, 175–76.

65. *ADAP*, E, 4:221–22.

66. Ruhl, *Franco, Falange*, 177–82.

Chapter 11. Temptation Ends

1. F. Gómez-Jordana Souza, *Milicia y diplomacia: Los Diarios del Conde de Jordana, 1936–1944* (Burgos, 2002), 130–31. See the brief introductory biography of Jordana by Carlos Seco Serrano, 9–43, and also 45–57, as well as the sketch in J. Tusell, *Franco, España, y la II Guerra Mundial: Entre el Eje y la neutralidad* (Madrid, 1995), 331–34, and in Tusell's "Los cuatro ministros de asuntos exteriores de Franco durante la Segunda Guerra Mundial," in *Espacio, Tiempo y Forma*, ser. 5, Historia Contemporánea, vol. 7 (1994): 311–36.

2. F. Rodao, *Franco y el imperio japonés* (Barcelona, 2002), 311–13.

3. C. J. H. Hayes, *Wartime Mission in Spain, 1942–45* (New York, 1945), 71; Tusell, *Franco, España*, 341.

4. *Akten zur deutschen Auswärtigen Politik, 1918–1945* (Göttingen, 1969), E, 3:566 (hereafter cited as *ADAP*); Tusell, *Franco, España*, 345–46.

5. J. M. Doussinague, *España tenía razón (1939–1945)* (Madrid, 1950), 82–84.

6. Hayes, *Wartime Mission in Spain*, 87–88.

7. *ADAP*, E, 3:526–29.

8. Doussinague, *España tenía razón*, 102–3.

9. *ADAP*, E, 4:260–62.

10. Ibid., 297–98.

11. According to an Abwehr report of 23 November, cited by G. R. Kleinfeld and L. A. Tambs, *Hitler's Spanish Legion: The Blue Division in Russia* (Carbondale, Ill., 1979), 228, 388.

12. *ADAP*, E, 4:282–83, 297–98, 318–22, 336–37, 345–46.

13. Quoted in Tusell, *Franco, España*, 363.

14. K.-J. Ruhl, *Franco, Falange y III Reich: España durante la Segunda Guerra Mundial* (Madrid, 1986), 182.

15. J. Tusell and G. García Queipo de Llano, *Carrero: La eminencia gris del régimen de Franco* (Madrid, 1993), 83–87.

16. Ibid., 87–90.

17. *Palabras del Caudillo* (Madrid, 1943), 523–27. The phrase concerning the Spanish formula "or by any other of the fascist peoples" has sometimes been misquoted in secondary works as "Spain and any other of the fascist peoples."

18. *Informaciones* (Madrid), 19 Dec. 1942.

19. A. Escuadra, *Bajo las banderas de la Kriegsmarine: Marinos españoles en la armada alemana (1942–1943)* (Madrid, 1998).

20. According to the research of M. Ros Agudo, *La guerra secreta de Franco (1939–1945)* (Barcelona, 2002), 228, 238–39.

21. Ilona had been renamed in September 1942, when it was feared that certain German planning documents might have been compromised.

22. *ADAP*, E, 4:325–26, 381–82, 384–86, 441–42.

23. A. Brissaud, *Canaris: La guerra española y la II Guerra Mundial* (Barcelona, 1972), 412–14; K. H. Abshagen, *Canaris* (London, 1956), 214–15.

24. *ADAP*, E, 4:442–43, 453–54.

25. Kleinfeld and Tambs, *Hitler's Spanish Legion*, 231–32.

26. Ibid., 232–33.

27. *ADAP,* E, 5:1, 29–31, 41–42, 94–95, 125–28.

28. C. B. Burdick, *Germany's Military Strategy and Spain in World War II* (Syracuse, 1968), 168–81.

29. R. Moreno Izquierdo, "Segunda Guerra Mundial: Los planes aliados para invadir España," *Historia 16* 22:268 (August 1998), 6–12.

30. *ADAP,* E, 4:574–75.

31. See the discussion in Tusell, *Franco, España,* 368–75.

32. *ADAP,* E, 5:135–36.

33. Ibid., 136–38.

34. Ruhl, *Franco, Falange,* 206–7.

35. Doussinague, *España tenía razón,* 130–37. The most thorough account of the political intrigues by the SS and Nazi Party and diplomatic officials will be found in Ruhl, *Franco, Falange,* 60–74, 94–121, 167–211.

36. Fundación Nacional Francisco Franco, *Documentos inéditos para la historia del Generalísimo Franco* (Madrid, 1994), 4:95–99.

37. Tusell, *Franco, España,* 381.

38. Ibid., 379–81.

39. Ibid.

40. Ros Agudo, *La guerra secreta,* 234–36.

41. *ADAP,* E, 5:311–13, 620–21.

42. Ibid., 6:4–6, 42–44.

43. C. Leitz, *Economic Relations between Nazi Germany and Franco's Spain, 1936–1945* (Oxford, 1996), 156–57.

44. *ADAP,* E, 4:519–21.

45. Leitz, *Economic Relations,* 159–60, and, for the entire range of negotiations, R. García Pérez, *Franquismo y Tercer Reich: Las relaciones económicas hispano-alemanas durante la Segunda Guerra Mundial* (Madrid, 1994), 328–46.

46. *ADAP,* E, 5:194.

47. García Pérez, *Franquismo y Tercer Reich,* 369–403; Leitz, *Economic Relations,* 160–62.

48. Leitz, *Economic Relations,* 162–64; A. Viñas et al., *Política comercial exterior en España, 1931–1975* (Madrid, 1975), 1:401–7.

49. García Pérez, *Franquismo y Tercer Reich,* 369–437; Leitz, *Economic Relations,* 167; Ruhl, *Franco, Falange,* 158–66, 219–36.

50. See the conclusions in Leitz, *Economic Relations,* 167–69.

51. On Plan D, see Tusell, *Franco, España,* 393–96, and A. Marquina Barrio, *La diplomacia vaticana y la España de Franco* (Madrid, 1982), 341–44; for Doussinague's own version, see his *España tenía razón,* 150–79.

52. *ADAP,* E, 5:361–62, 519–21, 678–81.

53. Ibid., 6:50.

54. Ibid., 44–45.

55. Tusell, *Franco, España,* 410.

56. *ADAP,* E, 6:179–81.

57. L. Suárez Fernández, *Francisco Franco y su tiempo* (Madrid, 1984), 3:375–76.

58. Tusell, *Franco, España,* 409–12; Gómez-Jordana Souza, *Milicia y diplomacia,* 204.

59. A good account of Operation Mincemeat may be found in T. Holt, *The Deceivers: Allied Military Deception in the Second World War* (New York, 2004), 369–78.

60. *ADAP,* E, 6:58.

61. Burdick, *Germany's Military Strategy,* 181–88.

62. *ADAP,* E, 6:354–55.

63. Dirección General de Seguridad, *Boletín* 158 (11 July 1941), in archives of the Fundación Nacional Francisco Franco (hereafter cited as FNFF), file 24, doc. 235.

64. Tusell, *Franco, España,* 389–90; R. De Felice, *Mussolini l'alleato, 1940–1945* (Turin, 1990), 2:1291–1305.

65. Tusell, *Franco, España,* 390–91; De Felice, *Mussolini l'alleato,* 2:1306–7.

66. *ADAP,* E, 6:248–49.

67. Fundación Nacional Francisco Franco, *Documentos inéditos,* 4:366–70.

68. Ibid., 4:41.

69. Tusell, *Franco, España,* 421.

70. Suárez Fernández, *Francisco Franco,* 3:379.

71. *ADAP,* E, 6:447–48.

72. Ibid., 526–27.

73. Tusell, *Franco, España,* 423–26.

74. This was the burden of an undated eleven-page letter by Asensio to Franco near the time that Asensio presented the petition of the lieutenant generals. Asensio charged that some of his fellow ministers had behaved with "frivolity" in two recent long and contentious recent cabinet meetings. He lamented that Spain was losing its independence of action and falling into the orbit of the United Nations (Roosevelt's new international organizational project for the states at war with the Axis), which was fundamentally opposed to the interests of Spain: FNFF, file 41, doc. 1448.

75. Tusell, *Franco, España,* 429.

76. J. L. de Arrese, *Escritos y discursos* (Madrid, 1943), 19.

77. *ADAP,* E, 6:554–55.

Chapter 12. Spanish Diplomacy and the Holocaust (I)

1. The Spanish name Sefarad stems from Obadiah 20, where Shepharad refers to the location of one group of exiled Jews. By the early Middle Ages the tendency among Jews was to identify the term with the extreme west of the Mediterranean world, primarily Spain. Spanish Jews and their descendants came thus to refer themselves as Sephardim and in Spanish as *sefardíes.* For a brief introduction to Sephardic history and culture, see P. Díaz-Mas, *Los sefardíes: Historia, lengua y cultura* (Barcelona 1986), published in English as *Sephardim: The Jews from Spain,* trans. George K. Zucker (Chicago, 1992).

2. An account of this process and of the Sephardic diaspora is J. Pérez, *Los judíos en España* (Madrid, 2005).

3. Traditionally, the forms of discriminatory toleration for Jews were generally rather more favorable in Muslim society than in the Christian West, with certain exceptions such as Spain and Venice. Persecution of Jews in the Islamic world, however, increased notably in the eighteenth century, at the very time of the beginning of broader tolerance in the West. The Jews of Morocco were by no means exclusively Sephardic, the first Jewish communities there dating from Roman times. By the twentieth century, however, there was a tendency to refer to all Jews in Morocco as Sephardim.

4. See the brief summary in B. Rother, *Franco y el Holocausto* (Madrid, 2005), 32–34.

5. E. Martín Corrales, *La imagen del magrebí en España: Una perspectiva histórica, siglos xvi–xx* (Barcelona, 2002).

6. G. Alvarez Chillida, *El antisemitismo en España: La imagen del judío (1812–2002)* (Madrid, 2002), 60–122, 137–67.

7. A. Bachoud, *Los españoles ante las campañas de Marruecos* (Madrid, 1988).

8. A. Marquina Barrio and G. I. Ospina, *España y los judíos en el siglo XX: La acción exterior* (Madrid, 1987), 19–25.

9. See the account in Rother, *Franco y el Holocausto*, 46–49, and, for further details, Marquina Barrio and Ospina, *España y los judíos*, 46–65.

10. I. González, *Los judíos y la Segunda República* (Madrid, 2005), and, on the outburst of enthusiasm in 1931, his article "Los judíos y la Segunda República," *Historia 16* 25:299 (March 2001), 78–87. See also Marquina Barrio and Ospina, *España y los judíos*, 81–130.

11. J. Goode, "The Racial Alloy: The Science, Politics, and Culture of Race in Spain, 1875–1923" (Ph.D. diss., UCLA, 1999). Italian concepts of race are treated in G. Israel and P. Nastasi, *Scienza e razza nell'Italia fascista* (Bologna, 1998); A. Burgio, ed., *Nel nome della razza: Il razzismo nella storia d'Italia, 1870–1945* (Bologna, 1999); R. Maiocchi, *Scienza italiana e razzismo fascista* (Florence, 1999); and A. Gillette, *Racial Theories in Fascist Italy* (New York, 2002).

12. For examples of philo- and anti-Semitism in Spain during the late nineteenth and early twentieth centuries, see Alvarez Chillida, *El antisemitismo en España*, 176–350, and his article "El mito antisemita en la crisis española del siglo XX," *Hispania* 56:3, 194 (1996), 1037–70.

13. The most comprehensive account is M. Sarfatti, *The Jews in Mussolini's Italy: From Equality to Persecution* (Madison, 2006). See also M. Michaelis, *Mussolini and the Jews* (Oxford, 1978); R. De Felice, *Storia degli ebrei italiani sotto il fascismo* (Turin, 1988); and L. Preti, *Impero fascista, africani ed ebrei* (Milan, 1968); and, for short-lived Italian Fascist denunciations of Nazi racism, D. M. Smith, *Mussolini's Roman Empire* (New York, 1976), 44–58.

14. On anti-Semitic propaganda in Spain during these years, see M. Böcker, *Antisemitismus ohne Juden: Die Zweite Republik, die anti-republikanistische Rechte und die Juden: Spanien, 1931 bis 1936* (Frankfurt, 2000), and E. Norling, "Los protocolos de los sabios de Sión," *Historia 16* 25:299 (March 2001), 67–77.

15. Franco's "Jewish support" seems to have been an argument used by Basque nationalists to try to persuade the Vatican not to recognize his regime.

16. Most specifically in *La Gaceta de Melilla*, 31 Aug. 1936, according to Rother, *Franco y el Holocausto*, 56.

17. Reprinted in F. Franco, *Papeles de la guerra de Marruecos* (Madrid, 1986), 189–95.

18. *Palabras del Caudillo* (Madrid, 1943), 102.

19. Alvarez Chillida, *El antisemitismo en España*, 401–3.

20. M. Ramírez Jiménez et al., *Las fuentes ideológicas de un régimen (España, 1936–1939)* (Zaragoza, 1978).

21. Alvarez Chillida, *El antisemitismo en España*, 404–5.

22. Rother, *Franco y el Holocausto*, 75–76.

23. Ibid., 57–67.

24. Ibid., 131.

25. Ibid., 132–37; Marquina Barrio and Ospina, *España y los judíos*, 164–68.

26. D. Wheeler, "And Who Is My Neighbor? A World War II Hero of Conscience for Portugal," *Luso-Brazilian Review* 26:1 (Summer 1989), 119–39, and R. Afonso, *Injustiça: O caso Sousa Mendes* (Lisbon, 1990).

27. Rother, *Franco y el Holocausto*, 136–42; H. Avni, *Spain, the Jews, and Franco* (Philadelphia, 1982), 72–79.

28. Rother, *Franco y el Holocausto*, 143.

29. Ibid., 144–46; Avni, *Spain, the Jews*, 94–127.

30. Rother, *Franco y el Holocausto*, 146–48; Marquina Barrio and Ospina, *España y los judíos*, 173–91.

31. F. Ysart, *España y los judíos en la segunda guerra mundial* (Barcelona, 1973); C. Lipschitz, *Franco, Spain, the Jews, and the Holocaust* (New York, 1984); P. von Zur Mühlen, *Fluchtweg Spanien-Portugal: Die deutsche Emigration und der Exodus aus Europa, 1933–1945* (Bonn, 1992).

32. Avni, *Spain, the Jews*, 90–93.

33. E. Eychenne, *Les Pyrénées de la liberté: Evasions par l'Espagne, 1939–1945* (Paris, 1983), 323–28.

34. Rother, *Franco y el Holocausto*, 157–58.

Chapter 13. Spanish Diplomacy and the Holocaust (II)

1. Fundación Nacional Francisco Franco, *Documentos inéditos para la historia del Generalísimo Franco* (Madrid, 1993), 3:346.

2. A. Marquina Barrio and G. Ospina, *España y los judíos en el siglo XX* (Madrid, 1987), 147.

3. B. Rother, "Spanish Attempts to Rescue Jews from the Holocaust: Lost Opportunities," *Mediterranean Historical Review* 17:2 (December 2002), 47–68.

4. Ibid.

5. Ibid.

6. B. Rother, *Franco y el Holocausto* (Madrid, 2005), 185–93.

7. Marquina Barrio and Ospina, *España y los judíos*, 179, 195–201.

8. Ibid., 180–83; Rother, *Franco y el Holocausto*, 201–5; H. Avni, *Spain, the Jews, and Franco* (Philadelphia, 1982), 136–37.

9. Rother, *Franco y el Holocausto*, 207–47; Marquina Barrio and Ospina, *España y los judíos*, 183–91.

10. On Italian Fascist resistance to the Holocaust, see J. Steinberg, *All or Nothing: The Axis and the Holocaust, 1941–1943* (London, 1990).

11. Rother, *Franco y el Holocausto*, 263.

12. Ibid., 268–70

13. Quoted in Marquina Barrio and Ospina, *España y los judíos*, 194–95.

14. Rother, *Franco y el Holocausto*, 270–77.

15. Avni, *Spain, the Jews*, 142–43.

16. This figure is from Rother, *Franco y el Holocausto*, 291.

17. Ibid., 298–305; Avni, *Spain, the Jews*, 147–56; Marquina Barrio and Ospina, *España y los judíos*, 197–200.

18. Rother, *Franco y el Holocausto*, 324–37; Marquina Barrio and Ospina, *España y los judíos*, 200–205; Avni, *Spain, the Jews*, 156–61.

19. Rother, *Franco y el Holocausto*, 306–24, 351–58; Marquina Barrio and Ospina, *España y los judíos*, 206–11; Avni, *Spain, the Jews*, 164–68.

20. When the Germans occupied Hungary and forced the appointment of a new ministry that would do their bidding, the incumbent Hungarian ambassador in Madrid, loyal to an independent Hungary, at first refused to give up the embassy, and Franco did not initially require him to do so. The Spanish government did not regard the military occupation of an ally by Germany as a positive act. For the general context of Spanish policy toward east-central Europe, see M. Eiroa, *Las relaciones de Franco con Europa centro-oriental (1939–1955)* (Barcelona, 2001).

21. The lengthiest publication is D. Carcedo, *Un español frente al Holocausto: Así salvó Angel Sanz Briz a 5.000 judíos* (Madrid, 2000). This well-written book is part historical novel, part journalism.

22. He then reported participation in further efforts of the nuncio. Sanz Briz to Lequerica, 14 Nov. 1944, in archives of the Fundación Nacional Francisco Franco, file 202, doc. 15510.

23. Rother, *Franco y el Holocausto*, 362–70.

24. Here again I follow the statistical conclusions found ibid., 375–76, which are the most carefully researched that we have. See also Marquina Barrio and Ospina, *España y los judíos*, 211–22, and Avni, *Spain, the Jews*, 168–77.

25. E. Deaglio, *La banalidad del bien: Historia de Giorgio Perlasca* (Barcelona, 1997).

26. Bedoya's chief writing in this regard was "El sentido de la libertad en la doctrina falangista," *Revista de Estudios Políticos* 10 (1943), 313–34.

27. The difficult relations between Israel and the Spanish regime after World War II are treated in R. Rein, *In the Shadow of the Holocaust and the Inquisition: Israel's Relations with Francoist Spain* (London, 1997).

28. The best succinct study of the legend is B. Rother, "Franco als Retter der Juden? Zur Entstehung einer Legende," *Zeitschrift für Geschichtswissenschaft* 45:2 (1997), 120–46. See also Avni, *Spain, the Jews*, 179–99, and Marquina Barrio and Ospina, *España y los judíos*, 222–25. The legend also eventually gave rise to speculation about the supposed Jewish ancestry of Franco, for which there is no direct evidence whatsoever. The principal conjecture in this vein is H. S. May, *Francisco Franco: The Jewish Connection* (Washington, D.C., 1978).

29. W. Bowen, "'A Great Moral Victory': Spanish Protection of Jews on the Eastern Front, 1941–1944," in *Resisting the Holocaust*, ed. R. Rohrlich (Oxford, 1998), 195–211.

30. Rother, *Franco y el Holocausto*, 405–10.

Chapter 14. Neutrality by Compulsion

1. *Akten zur deutschen Auswärtigen Politik, 1918–1945* (Göttingen, 1969), E, 7:250–54 (hereafter cited as *ADAP*).

2. J. Tusell, *Franco, España, y la II Guerra Mundial: Entre el Eje y la neutralidad* (Madrid, 1995), 463.

3. *ADAP*, E, 7:381–82. The Third International had been officially dissolved in 1943, but Soviet contacts with ordinary Spanish Communists during the main part of the war were very limited.

4. M. Ros Agudo, *La guerra secreta de Franco (1939–1945)* (Barcelona, 2002), 238.

5. Tusell, *Franco, España*, 464.

6. M. Heiberg and M. Ros Agudo, *La trama oculta de la Guerra Civil: Los servicios secretos de Franco, 1936–1945* (Barcelona, 2006), 251–52.

7. On wolfram production in Portugal, see D. Wheeler, "The Price of Neutrality: Portugal, the Wolfram Question, and World War II," pts. 1 and 2, *Luso-Brazilian Review* 23:1–2 (1986), 107–27, 97–108. For Spain, C. Leitz, *Economic Relations between Nazi Germany and Franco's Spain, 1936–1945* (Oxford, 1996), 170–99; R. García Pérez, *Franquismo y Tercer Reich: Las relaciones económicas hispano-alemanas durante la Segunda Guerra Mundial* (Madrid, 1994), 438–92; L. Caruana and H. Rockoff, "A Wolfram in Sheep's Clothing: Economic Warfare in Spain, 1940–44," *Journal of Economic History* 63:1 (March 2003), 65–99; and J. W. Cortada, *United States–Spanish Relations: Wolfram and World War II* (Barcelona, 1971).

8. Caruana and Rockoff, "Wolfram in Sheep's Clothing."

9. Leitz, *Economic Relations*, 170, 180–82.

10. Caruana and Rockoff, "Wolfram in Sheep's Clothing."

11. García Pérez, *Franquismo y Tercer Reich*, 445.

12. Cortada, *United States–Spanish Relations*, 177.

13. Dirección de Seguridad report to Franco, 29 Jan. 1944, in archives of the Fundación Nacional Francisco Franco, file 31, doc. 2554; file 64, doc. 2568.

14. *ADAP*, E, 7:374–77.

15. Ibid., 392–93

16. Ibid., 394–95, 415–16.

17. Tusell, *Franco, España*, 499–500.

18. *ADAP*, E, 8:25–26. The Sicherheitsdienst passed on the text to the embassy three months later, on 10 May 1944.

19. Ibid., 7:422–23.

20. Ibid., 429–31.

21. Ibid., 343–44.

22. García Pérez, *Franquismo y Tercer Reich*, 453–54.

23. Ros Agudo, *La guerra secreta*, 239.

24. C. J. H. Hayes, *Wartime Mission in Spain, 1942–45* (New York, 1945), 218–19; Cortada, *United States–Spanish Relations*, 79–83; García Pérez, *Franquismo y Tercer Reich*, 449–50.

25. García Pérez, *Franquismo y Tercer Reich*, 455–56.

26. Tusell, *Franco, España*, 473–76.

27. García Pérez, *Franquismo y Tercer Reich*, 466–72.

28. Ibid., 459.

29. Ibid., 478–79.

30. *ADAP*, E, 7:485–86.

31. Ibid., 491–93; Tusell, *Franco, España*, 503–4.

32. García Pérez, *Franquismo y Tercer Reich*, 460.

33. *ADAP*, E, 7:654–56; García Pérez, *Franquismo y Tercer Reich*, 460–62; L. Suárez Fernández, *Francisco Franco y su tiempo* (Madrid, 1984), 4:488.

34. This is the figure cited in Leitz, *Economic Relations*, 192.

35. García Pérez, *Franquismo y Tercer Reich*, 464.

36. Quoted in Tusell, *Franco, España*, 511.

37. García Pérez, *Franquismo y Tercer Reich*, 487–91. W. N. Medlicott, *The Economic Blockade* (London, 1959), 2:581, claims that German stocks in Spain by the spring of 1944 amounted to more than a thousand tons, possibly an exaggeration.

38. García Pérez, *Franquismo y Tercer Reich*, 476.

39. Dieckhoff suggested closing the Spanish consulate in Paris and requesting Japan to close the consulate in Manila: *ADAP*, E, 8:22–23.

40. Ibid., 26–27.

41. García Pérez, *Franquismo y Tercer Reich*, 479–80.

42. Ibid., 482–83.

43. Ibid., 483–84.

44. Carlos Seco Serrano, introduction to F. Gómez-Jordana Souza, *Milicia y diplomacia: Los diarios del conde de Jordana, 1936–1944* (Burgos, 2002), 37–38.

Chapter 15. The End of the Relationship

1. Tusell, *Franco, España, y la II Guerra Mundial: Entre el Eje y la neutralidad* (Madrid, 1995), 525–26.

2. R. Serrano Suñer, *La historia como fue: Memorias* (Barceona, 1977), 204.

3. There is a vivid sketch of Lequerica in G. Morán, *Los españoles que dejaron de serlo* (Barcelona, 1982), 110–20. The only extensive study, M. J. Cava Mesa, *Los diplomáticos de Franco: J. F. de Lequerica: Temple y tenacidad (1890–1963)* (Bilbao, 1989), is not a critical account and adds little.

4. Viscount Templewood, *Ambassador on Special Mission* (London, 1946); C. J. H. Hayes, *Wartime Mission in Spain, 1942–45* (New York, 1945).

5. An undated sheet of instructions for Spanish diplomats stressed the importance of reaching Catholic opinion abroad, to carry out the task "of enabling *the world to assimilate our political doctrine,* so that we can carry out the providential historical destiny of Spain, Teacher to Peoples and Apostle of the New Christian-Social Era that is approaching" (underlined in the original), in archives of the Fundación Nacional Francisco Franco (hereafter cited as FNFF), file 64, doc. 2571.

6. Lequerica to Duke of Alba, 17 Oct. 1944, ibid., file 202, doc. 15237.

7. Lequerica to Cárdenas, 28 Oct. 1944, ibid., doc. 15328.

8. Lequerica to Cárdenas and Cárdenas to Lequerica, 17 Nov. 1944, ibid., docs. 15504, 15466

9. *Boletín de Información Nacional y Extranjera,* no. 22, 10 Oct. 1944, ibid., file 101, doc. 4440.

10. R. García Pérez, *Franquismo y Tercer Reich: Las relaciones económicas hispano-alemanas durante la Segunda Guerra Mundial* (Madrid, 1994), 497–99.

11. M. Ros Agudo, *La guerra secreta de Franco (1939–1945)* (Barcelona, 2002), 132–34.

12. W. H. Bowen, *Spaniards and Nazi Germany: Collaboration in the New Order* (Columbia, Mo., 2000), 205. At that point *Enlace* was edited by the defrocked Basque priest Martín Arrizubieta, who promoted a mixture of Nazism and Basque separatism, combining the original racism of Basque nationalists with anti-Francoism, attempts to recruit more Spanish workers, and efforts to gain German support for the partition of Spain (this last a fundamental goal of Basque nationalists throughout the war and the immediate postwar period). A former chaplain in the Basque army during the Civil War, he escaped Germany with Basque assistance, and in later years in Spain worked for a time for the Catholic Church before moving on to the Communists. See ibid., 215, and X. M. Núñez Seixas, "¿Un nazismo colaboracionista español? Martín Arrizubieta, Wilhelm Faupel y los últimos de Berlín (1944–45)" (unpublished MS).

13. Bowen, *Spaniards and Nazi Germany,* 206–20.

14. Ibid., 219.

15. As quoted in C. Vidal, *Intrépidos y sucios: Los españoles vistos por Hitler* (Barcelona, 1996), 213–15.

16. R. Rhodes James, ed., *Winston S. Churchill: His Complete Speeches, 1897–1963* (London, 1974), 6:6935–36.

17. J. M. Doussinague, *España tenía razón (1939–1945)* (Madrid, 1950), 338.

18. Quoted in F. Díaz Plaja, *La España política del siglo veinte* (Barcelona, 1972), 4:149–52.

19. Quoted in D. Smyth, *Diplomacy and Strategy of Survival: British Policy and Franco's Spain, 1940–41* (Cambridge, 1986), 247–48, and D. Reynolds, *In Command of History: Churchill Fighting and Writing the Second World War* (London, 2004), 463.

20. F. Rodao, *Franco y el imperio japonés* (Barcelona, 2002), 479–500.

21. FNFF, file 41, doc. 1447. Franco's interview with the United Press the preceding November had prompted a clandestine sheet by the oppositionist sector of the Falange titled *Otra vez: La traición consumada.* It claimed that Franco's remarks "have fallen on our nation like a bomb," consummating the treason begun in 1937, and now "even the claim that Spain is a democracy cannot surprise us": ibid., doc. 1446. According to a Dirección

General de Seguridad report to Franco of 31 Aug. 1945 (ibid., file 25, doc. 854), the feeling of "resentment" still had not subsided among Falangists nearly four months after the fall of the Reich.

22. Similarly, the philologist Antonio Tovar, former FET press director and diplomatic translator for Franco and Serrano, evoked by contrast the strong mood of hope and enthusiasm that accompanied the inauguration of the Reich, as he had witnessed it as a student in Germany: "A great sensation of purity, revolution and the disappearance of filth was felt in the Berlin of those times!": *Pueblo*, 2 May 1945, quoted in Bowen, *Spaniards and Nazi Germany*, 227.

23. A. J. Lleonart et al., eds., *España y ONU (1945–1946): La "cuestión española": Documentación básica, sistematizada y anotada* (Madrid, 1978), 1:42–45.

24. R. P. Huff, "The Spanish Question before the United Nations" (Ph.D. diss., Stanford University, 1966), 2–22; Lleonart et al., *España y ONU*, 1:30–33; and R. E. Sanders, *Spain and the United Nations, 1945–1950* (New York, 1966).

25. The regime's diplomacy of survival has been studied in F. Portero, *Franco aislado: La cuestión española (1945–1950)* (Madrid, 1989).

26. Postwar British policy toward Spain is treated in Q. Ahmad, *Britain, Franco Spain and the Cold War, 1945–1950* (New York, 1992), and J. Edwards, *Anglo-American Relations and the Franco Question, 1945–1955* (Oxford, 1999).

27. The Soviet interpretation of Spanish policy during the later phases of the war is presented in S. Pozharskaia, *Tainaia diplomatiia Madrida* (Moscow, 1978), 189–241. For an overview of Soviet policy toward Spain, see J. Fisac Seco, "Franco, peón en la estrategia de Stalin," *Historia 16* 26:316 (August 2002), 60–78. The Dirección General de Seguridad report to Franco of 31 Aug. 1945 in FNFF, file 25, doc. 854, indicated that the clandestine Communist Party apparatus was trying to form small police and military cadres because the Communists thought they would be taking over, or at least participating in taking over, very soon.

28. The data in this section are drawn from García Pérez, *Franquismo y Tercer Reich*, 560–69, and from C. Collado Seidel, *Angst vor dem "Vierten Reich": Die Alliierten und die Ausschaltung des deutschen Einflusses in Spanien, 1944–1958* (Paderborn, 2001), 151–379, and *España refugio nazi* (Madrid, 2005), 141–316.

29. Vlasov sent a letter of friendly greetings in French, thanking the Generalissimo for his staunch anticommunism, but there is no indication of any follow-up: Vlasov to Franco, 27 March 1945, in FNFF, file 64, doc. 2558.

30. The fullest study is in Collado Seidel, *Angst vor dem "Vierten Reich"* and *España refugio nazi*, especially 24–140. See also his article "Zufluchtsstätte für Nationalsozialisten? Spanien, die Alliierten und die Behandlung deutscher Agenten, 1944–1947," *Vierteljahrhefte für Zeitgeschichte* 43:1 (1995), 131–57, and J. M. Irujo, *La lista negra: Los espías Nazis protegidos por Franco y la Iglesia* (Madrid, 2003). The evolution of postwar relations between Spain and West Germany is examined in P. M. Weber, *Spanische Deutschlandspolitik, 1945–1958: Entsorgung der Vergangenheit* (Saarbrücken, 1992), and B. Aschmann, *Treue Freunde . . . ? Westdeutschland und Spanien, 1945–1963* (Stuttgart, 1999).

31. P. Martín Aceña, *El oro de Moscú y el oro de Berlín* (Madrid, 2001), 257–302.

32. Ibid., 302–10.

33. Ibid., 259–60, 310–55.

Conclusion

1. J. Tusell, *Franco, España, y la II Guerra Mundial: Entre el Eje y la neutralidad* (Madrid, 1995), 647–48.

2. Ibid., 647.

3. Ibid., 649.

4. This is somewhat the argument of D. S. Detwiler, "Spain and the Axis during World War II," *Review of Politics* 33:1 (January 1971), 36–53.

5. I have discussed this proposition briefly in my article "Soviet Anti-Fascism: Theory and Practice, 1921–1945," *Totalitarian Movements and Political Religions* 4:2 (Autumn 2003), 1–62.

6. A. Speer, *Spandau: The Secret Diaries* (New York, 1976), 183–84.

7. See especially J. Catalán, *La economía española y la segunda guerra mundial* (Barcelona, 1995).

8. The subdirector of the Servicio de Estudios of the Banco de España, Germán Bernácer (a key analyst and theoretician sometimes called the Spanish Keynes), presented a searching "Informe sobre la situación económica española" in February 1946. In *El oro de Moscú y el oro de Berlín* (Madrid, 2001), 358, P. Martín Aceña has summarized its conclusions as pointing to "antiquated infrastructures, obsolete installations, high manufacturing costs, insufficient production to supply internal demand, speculation out of control, lack of incentive to save, shortage of capital and the progressive disarticulation of markets." It called for extension of foreign credit, an end to the policy of autarky, and the opening of the Spanish economy.

9. J. Varela Ortega, *Una paradoja histórica: Hitler, Stalin, Roosevelt y algunas consecuencias para España de la Segunda Guerra Mundial* (Madrid, 2004).

Index

monarchism (*continued*)
264. *See also* Carlists; Don Juan; Juan
Carlos
Mongolia, 8
Monroe Doctrine, 100–101
MONTANA (German holding corpora-
tion), 30
Moreno Fernández, Salvador, 95, 245
Moreno Juliá, Xavier, 153
Morocco (French), 77, 79, 86; Allied inva-
sion of, 179, 182–83; German interest
in, 132; in the interwar years, 47; Jews
in, 211; Spanish plans regarding, in
World War II, 51, 64–68, 72, 79, 86, 92,
94, 95, 107, 164, 172, 257, 268, 269, 274;
U.S. thoughts on, 174; in World War I,
21, 66
Morocco (Spanish), 21, 66, 82, 83, 180;
British plans for, 104, 141; as cultural
extension of Spain, 129–31; fears of
Allied invasion of, 72, 140, 158, 170, 183,
188, 190; Franco on, 91, 101, 214;
Franco's forces in, 22, 65, 90, 97, 107,
149, 183, 186; Franco's military experience in, 9, 10, 28, 65; German interest
in, 81, 82, 84–86, 89–90, 99, 101, 103,
106–7, 131, 132, 135, 144; in the interwar years, 47; Jews in, 209–11, 213–14,
216, 222, 229–30, 301n3; Nazis in, 54,
115; poison gas used in, 21; Spain's communications with, 98; Spanish prejudice
against people from, 211; troops from,
in Spain, 50; volunteers from, in Blue
Division, 148. *See also* Sahara (Spanish)
Múgica, Enrique, 264
Mundo (Spanish news magazine), 130,
216
Munich conference (1938), 41, 42, 48
Muñoz Grandes, Agustín: as Blue Division
leader, 149, 154, 161, 172–74, 178, 179,
188–89; as Falangist general, 54; and
Franco, 189–90, 200, 202; as increasingly neutral, 199; meets with Hitler and
other German leaders, 173–74, 189, 192;
on Spain's entry into World War II, 178,
189; in Spain's Gibralter plan, 94
Mussolini, Benito (the Duce), 81, 231;
bribery of Greek generals by, 70; and
Franco, 48–49, 63, 78–79, 107, 111,
112–13, 132, 274; and Hitler, 25–26, 48,
86, 89, 90, 95, 99, 100, 107, 112; Italian
Social Republic of, 204, 244; on Italy's
"nonbelligerent" status, 49–50, 63;
and Jews, 213, 214, 216, 225, 226;
letters between Franco and, 78–79;

Mediterranean-centered foreign policy
of, 21–22, 26, 31, 46, 61, 64, 72, 81, 89,
95, 113, 202; and outbreak of World War
II, 49–50, 268, 274; overthrow of, 202–3;
"parallel war" of, 61, 64, 81, 89, 95; relations of, with Spain during World War
II, 61, 83, 85, 112–13; reorganization of
cabinet by, 202; Serrano Suñer and, 137,
170, 201–2; and Spanish Civil War, 7, 10,
22, 24–27, 30, 31, 34, 42–43, 45, 46, 109;
and Spanish Civil War debt, 34–35, 46,
125, 267; on Spanish monarchy's restoration, 170. *See also* Italy
Mussolini, Edda, 204

Nacionales (Nationalists) (Spanish Civil
War), 8, 9, 149; British support for, 29,
68; Catholicism of, 13–14; economic situation of, 16; German support for, 25,
33, 243, 258, 266; Jewish support for,
213–14, 223; military training schools
for, 28, 33, 34; opponents of, 217; recognition of, as legitimate government, 26;
Spanish Civil War role of, as a Crusade,
13–14, 39, 74, 138; as Spanish Civil War
victors, 65; Spanish support for, 16–17;
as a term, 12. *See also* Franco Bahamonde, Francisco; Republicans
napalm bombs, 39
Napoleon, 75, 96
nationalism: discourse of, in Spanish Civil
War, 8, 12, 39, 40; Franco's belief in, 11,
12, 30, 44, 45, 108, 166, 266; nineteenth-
century Spanish, 211
nationalization (of industry), 8. *See also*
corporatism
Navarre (Spain), 148
Naviera Ibérica, 119
navy (American), 156, 157, 238
navy (British): in North Africa, 85–86,
118; shipping routes of, 270; in Spain's
Gibralter plan, 94, 95; Spanish-German
sabotage of, 117, 123, 187, 194, 237–38,
243–45, 248; strength of, in Atlantic,
103, 112
navy (German), 76, 80–81, 168, 196, 237,
273; Moroccan bases for, 79; Spanish
refueling of destroyers in, 102; training
of Spanish troops by, 187. *See also* submarines (German)
navy (Japanese), 157
navy (Spanish), 51–53, 56, 95, 98, 101,
117–19, 123, 134, 256, 260
Nazis: Beigbeder's contacts with, 47;
Falangists' admiration for, 142, 144,